D0177696

Bristol Libraries

1805951440

LOVE, PAUL GAMBACCINI

LOVE, PAUL GAMBACCINI

MY YEAR UNDER THE YEWTREE

Biteback Publishing

First published in Great Britain in 2015 by
Biteback Publishing Ltd
Westminster Tower
3 Albert Embankment
London SE1 7SP
Copyright © Paul Gambaccini 2015

Photograph on page 397 © Christopher Sherwood

Lyrics from 'What's A Matter, Baby (Is It Hurting You)' © Clyde Otis and
Joy Byers, reprinted with kind permission of The Clyde Otis Music Group

Every reasonable effort has been made to trace copyright holders of material
reproduced in this book, but if any have been inadvertently overlooked the
publishers would be glad to hear from them.

ISBN 978-1-84954-911-0

10 9 8 7 6 5 4 3 2 1

A CIP catalogue record for this book is available from the British Library.

Set in Adobe Garamond Pro

Printed and bound in Great Britain by
CPI Group (UK) Ltd, Croydon CR0 4YY

MIX
Paper from
responsible sources
FSC® C020471

This book is dedicated to Christopher Sherwood, whose love saved my life

Contents

Observant readers of this book will notice that some details of Paul Gambaccini's year-long search for information about his two false accusers are expressed in generalities rather than specifics. His original text has been slightly modified for legal reasons. English law protects the identities of false accusers, as quoted below.

Sexual Offences (Amendment) Act 1976 (as amended)

S. 4 Anonymity of complainants in rape etc. cases.

(1) Except as authorised by a direction given in pursuance of this section—

(a) after an allegation that a woman or man has been the victim of a rape offence has been made by the woman or man or by any other person, neither the name nor the address of the woman or man nor a still or moving picture of her or him shall during that person's lifetime—

(i) be published in England and Wales in a written publication available to the public; or

(ii) be included in a relevant programme for reception in England and Wales, if that is likely to lead members of the public to identify that person as an alleged victim of such an offence; and

(b) after a person is accused of a rape offence, no matter likely to lead members of the public to identify a woman or man as the complainant in relation to that accusation shall during that person's lifetime—

(i) be published in England and Wales in a written publication available to the public; or

(ii) be included in a relevant programme for reception in England and Wales; but nothing in this subsection prohibits the publication or inclusion in a relevant programme of matter consisting only of a report of criminal proceedings other than proceedings at, or intended to lead to, or on an appeal arising out of, a trial at which the accused is charged with the offence.

...

(5) If any matter is published or included in a relevant programme in contranvention [sic] of subsection (1) of this section, the following persons, namely—

(a) in the case of a publication in a newspaper or periodical, any proprietor, any editor and any publisher of the newspaper or periodical;

(b) in the case of any other publication, the person who publishes it; and

(c) in the case of matter included in a relevant programme, any body corporate which is engaged in providing the service in which the programme is included and any person having functions in relation to the programme corresponding to those of an editor of a newspaper,

shall be guilty of an offence and liable on summary conviction to a fine not exceeding level 5 on the standard scale.*

*i.e.: an unlimited fine in England & Wales

Introduction

My mother went into labour in the early hours of 2 April 1949. My father, awakened from deep sleep, drove her to hospital on the wrong side of a dual carriageway. They were intercepted by a policeman, who redirected them to the correct side of the road and escorted them to hospital. It was the last time police would take me anywhere for sixty-four years.

I was born in Westchester Square Hospital at 10.19 a.m. For the first two weeks of my life, I could not keep food down. Doctors feared I might have been born with an inverted stomach. Just as worst-case scenarios were being written, my tumultuous tummy settled. I was set for a lifetime of Italian food and dark chocolate.

Had I been born a girl, I would have been named Nancy. This may explain my subsequent collection of original *Nancy* comic strips by Ernie Bushmiller.

In my first year of life, my parents and I lived in a furnished room in the

Bronx. This arrangement became unsustainable the moment my mother became pregnant with my brother Peter, who followed me from mother's womb to doctor's hands fourteen months after I made the journey. We briefly moved to Yonkers, scene of Neil Simon's 1991 Pulitzer Prize-winning play *Lost in Yonkers*, but scampered back to the Bronx in time for the birth of the third and final Gambaccini brother, Philip, in 1952. It is Sedgwick Avenue, where we lived from when I was three to when I was nearly six years old, that is the site of my earliest memories. Although we moved to Westport, Connecticut, in 1955, I was always proud when our old street played a part in popular culture, as when local DJ Kool Herc invented hip hop at his parties in the early 1970s and when Robert De Niro's character drove the Sedgwick Avenue bus route in the 1993 film *A Bronx Tale*.

The first number one record I remember was 'You You You' by the Ames Brothers, a 1953 hit. The repetitive lyrics were incredibly easy for a four-year-old to remember.

'You, you, you,' Ed Ames and his brothers crooned, 'I'm in love with you, you, you / I could be so true, true, true / To someone like you, you, you.'

As easy as the words of the song by Robert Mellin and Lotar Olias were to memorise – 'Do, do, do / What you oughta do, do, do' – my first favourite tune was not from the hit parade. It was the children's song 'The Little White Duck' by Burl Ives. All I need is to hear the words 'There's a little white duck, sitting in the water / A little white duck, doing what he oughter' and I'm back in the Bronx, sitting in front of our phonograph. It was concealed in a cabinet so no one would think we were so crass as to have a record player in the living room.

My name and photograph first appeared in a newspaper in the 22 March 1954 edition of the *New York Daily News*. My dear mother and I were walking down Kingsbridge Avenue when two men took her aside. They offered her ten dollars if they could borrow me for a photo shoot in the Kingsbridge Armory publicising the Institute of Radio Engineers show. The next day, there I was on page ten: 'Paul Gambaccini (above), 5, of the Bronx, eyes glued on model plane circling over miniature countryside, operating control switch…' The headline read 'He's Just Plane Fascinated'. For the rest of my life, my brother Peter has occasionally joked that I am 'plane fascinated'. It was the first time I was the subject of inaccurate reporting: I was still four years old. A couple of years later, I realised that ten dollars was a lot of money, which it was for a child in the 1950s, and I asked my mother if she would go halves. She was not amused.

One day in late 1954, my parents took us to the town of Westport, Connecticut to look at our next home. Westport was an artists' colony fifty miles to the north-east of New York, close enough for my father to commute. A dead-end dirt road named Elizabeth Drive was having several houses built on it. Never before had I seen nature in the raw. Sedgwick Avenue bordered on the Jerome Park Reservoir, but that was a man-made body of water. Elizabeth Drive had a pond, with green bits floating on it and ducks swimming in it. A tree at the beginning of the street was in the fullest fall foliage I had ever seen, with leaves various shades of green, red, yellow and brown. I thought I even saw blue. For a boy from the Bronx, this was paradise.

Our move to the suburbs in 1955 was replicated across America by young families seeking larger homes and good educations. The Westport high school, Staples, had been named one of the top ten in the country. That was enough to convince my parents it was where we belonged. My father Mario's parents, Guido and Eugenia, had been immigrants from Italy, and he was a firm believer in the American dream: through education, future generations of Gambaccinis would rise.

The first full year we were in Westport, 1956, Elvis Presley exploded nationally with 'Heartbreak Hotel', 'Don't Be Cruel', 'Hound Dog' and 'Love Me Tender'. Although I missed his first network television appearance on the 28 January edition of *The Dorsey Brothers Stage Show*, I did see his performances on *The Milton Berle Show*, *The Steve Allen Show* and *The Ed Sullivan Show*. They were my introduction to rock 'n' roll.

In early 1957, my father finished breakfast before I did and left his favourite station on. What he did not realise was that this channel played the current American hits beginning at 9 a.m. every Saturday morning. When he left the kitchen, easy listening music was being broadcast. A few minutes later, in his bedroom upstairs, he heard 'Teddy Bear' by Elvis, unaware that I had not changed the station.

He thumped downstairs to the threshold of the kitchen.

'How can you listen to such damn music?' he boomed, making a balletic leap across the room and turning off the radio in a single graceful move that would have made Nureyev proud. It was the first time I had ever heard my father swear. If this music has this much power, I thought, there must be something to it. I became a regular listener to all the leading New York DJs, who could be heard in Westport, fifty miles outside the city.

When I told this story to Art Garfunkel years later, he was not impressed.

'You missed a couple of important years,' he said regretfully. He was right. I had missed the New York doo-wop movement, but at least I caught up with it in time.

I became a rock 'n' roll kid, listening to Top 40 radio three hours a day, but I never adopted rock 'n' roll fashions. This set the pattern for my life, in which I became what I call a 'lifestyle tourist'. I was as anti-war and pro-civil rights as any college student of the late '60s, but I never became a hippie, and though identifying with gay people in the '70s, I did not have sex with a man until the '80s.

I ceased listening to popular music radio during 1960. Most of the giants of rock 'n' roll were off the scene. Elvis was in the army, Little Richard had found God, and Jerry Lee Lewis had been disgraced by marrying his thirteen-year-old cousin.

I did not return to listening until 1961, when two events piqued my curiosity. My class went on a field trip to the Metropolitan Opera House on 39th Street in New York City. Getting off the bus, Chuck Whalen started singing a tune that sounded good.

'What's that?' I asked.

'That's "Runaway" by Del Shannon,' he said.

Later that year, Linda Muskus walked into the Greens Farms School gymnasium warbling something that sounded half-yodel, half-banshee wail, punctuated by the word 'Wimoweh'.

'What is that?' I inquired in disbelief.

'The Lion Sleeps Tonight', she replied, as if I should know. I went home, turned on the radio, loved the song and, figuratively speaking, never turned the radio off again.

One afternoon at around 1.40 in the last week of December 1963 – yes, Four Seasons fans, late December back in '63 – I was on the porch of our Westport house listening to WINS disc jockey Stan Z. Burns. He read a dedication to the British cruise line workers at the Hudson River docks. They wanted to hear the record that was number one in their country, 'I Want to Hold Your Hand' by a group I had never heard before, the Beatles.

My life changed in two and a half minutes. I, and millions of young Americans, had been waiting for deliverance. We had been in deep mourning for the past month for the slain President John Kennedy. The Singing Nun had gone to number one. We needed happiness. We needed hope. The Beatles gave it to us. Within a month, 'I Want to Hold Your Hand' was number one, on 9 February they performed on *The Ed Sullivan Show* to the largest television audience to date, seventy-three million, and by the first week of April they had the top five singles on the *Billboard* Hot 100. No one has dominated popular culture as quickly and utterly as the Beatles did in 1964.

For young musicians like Billy Joel and Tom Petty, watching *The Ed Sullivan Show* gave them their vocations. The Beatles also gave me a professional purpose. The popular music revolution they spearheaded was the most important cultural movement of my youth. If I was going to be alive in my time, I had to be involved.

A parallel example was my interest in comic books. My mother's mother, who lived across the street from us in the Bronx, had helped me learn to read by taking me through the Donald Duck ten-pagers by Carl Barks in *Walt Disney's Comics and Stories*, the bestselling comic book of the 1950s and, indeed, of all time. In 1960, I was shown a copy of the *Giant Superman Annual 1*. I was so thrilled I went to Westfair Smokeshop the next day and bought all the current DC comics, except for *Wonder Woman*. I loved them so much that the next day I went back and bought *Wonder Woman*.

So began my glorious ride through the Silver Age of Comics, which gained steam when Marvel launched *The Fantastic Four* in November 1961 and within two years began *The Amazing Spider Man*, *The Incredible Hulk*, *The X-Men* and *The Avengers*. I became one of the three most published 'letterhacks' in early Silver Age comics, and succeeded the visionary Jerry Bails, a hopeless task, as Executive Secretary of the Academy of Comic Book Fans and Collectors. The editor of *The Flash*, Julius Schwartz, named a character after me. The tailor, Paul Gambi, appears in DC Comics to this day. I have become reconciled to the likelihood that he will survive me.

I first learned I had a knack for public speaking in 1965. Our junior class president was expected to win the election to be the following year's Staples Student Organization president, the school's leading government position. Because he was considered a certain winner, no one wanted to run against him. A few of my friends begged me to run in the interests of democracy. At least there should be two candidates!

Losing has never been an attractive proposition, but I agreed that someone should run. I sighed and said yes, vowing to myself that if I won I would go home and play 'Dancing in the Street' by Martha and the Vandellas, one of my favourite acts from my favourite record company, Motown.

In the primary that preceded the election assembly, my rival won easily, as anticipated. I gave my speech feeling no pressure whatsoever, knowing I had no chance. On the other hand, the favourite did feel stress. He was nervous and awkward. On election day, I won in a landslide. I went home and played 'Dancing in the Street'.

The new junior class president, my friend Dick Sandhaus, asked me if the Staples Student Organization would like to co-sponsor a fundraising concert. I agreed. We visited three leading New York agencies, William Morris, General Artists and Frank Barsalona's new Premier Talent. At GAC we were present when an agent rushed in to tell his colleague some shocking news.

'The Rolling Stones want $12,000 a show or they'll leave!' he gasped.

Our host replied without missing a beat.

'Tell them they'll never get it.'

Sandhaus and I wound up promoting the Beau Brummels, who had just enjoyed two consecutive major hit singles, 'Laugh Laugh' and 'Just a Little'. The evening was a sell-out, beginning a string of 1960s concerts at Staples that are the subject of a book by Mark Smollin called *The Real Rock 'n' Roll High School*.

My grades were good enough, and my position as SSO president sufficiently impressive, for me to get accepted at Harvard, Yale, Princeton and Dartmouth. I assumed at first that I would choose Harvard, but was horrified when I visited its town of Cambridge, Massachusetts. I noticed a dead fish floating on the Charles River, which may not have shocked city dwellers but stunned someone like me who had grown up in a small town with clean water.

I dined in the Commons of one of the colleges at the invitation of my predecessor as SSO president, Tom Dublin. I sat at a table next to someone eating alone. I asked him if he was glad he had come to Harvard.

'Absolutely,' he replied. 'This is the one place where I can go down to the banks of the River Charles, read a book and not need another person in the world.'

Being a more sociable person than this young man, I was put off Harvard and travelled to Hanover, New Hampshire, to check out Dartmouth. As a snow lover, I was thrilled that there were still traces of the white stuff on the ground as late as mid-April. As a music lover, I was awed that the college radio station, WDCR, was playing the new singles 'I Am a Rock' by

Simon and Garfunkel and 'Did You Ever Have to Make Up Your Mind?' by the Lovin' Spoonful before they hit New York airwaves. I heard them as I was taking a walk on Route 120, the road to the nearby town of Lebanon, listening to DJ Scott McQueen on the show *Sounds for the Tri-Town*.

WDCR was the largest commercial station in the country run by students, a 1,000-watt AM facility. The Federal Communications Commission, feeling that northern New England had been ill-served by radio, had granted the trustees of Dartmouth College a licence. I felt that I had to attend Dartmouth if only for the radio station. I didn't want to be on it, I just wanted to be near it.

Inevitably, I was on it. During Freshman Week at the beginning of my first year, the college held an Activities Night, on which all organisations held open house for the new students. I checked out WDCR and was invited to take a voice test in front of programme director Bob Buck and chief announcer Scott McQueen. I passed.

My four years at WDCR while a Dartmouth student were so rewarding that two decades later I wrote a memoir about them, *Radio Boy*. Virtually everything I did in my adult career I learned to do in that tiny town of a few thousand people.

Towards the end of 1969, it was time to apply to graduate schools. Only one person at Dartmouth, my friend John Ritchie, suggested I seek a career in radio.

'You can do this,' he said.

But I fell under the spell of what was then established thinking. We were told that the future leaders of America would be lawyers. As Watergate would soon demonstrate, the future criminals of America would be lawyers, but that scandal was still a couple of years away. I applied to and was accepted by Harvard and Yale Law Schools. Being located in Connecticut, Yale was too close to home. I chose Harvard Law.

One morning, I was crossing the Dartmouth Green and ran into my classmate Bob Harrington.

'Have you applied to Oxford yet?' he asked, apropos of nothing.

'No, why?' I replied.

'It's a two-year paid vacation,' he said.

What a concept! I could have a two-year paid vacation and escape the last two years of the term of President Richard Nixon and Vice-President Spiro Agnew, both of whom I loathed. I could not understand why the American people did not see through them. Eventually they did, and both Nixon and Agnew resigned in disgrace, but by then I was gone.

I was accepted at University College, Oxford, and then applied for and won two scholarships. I sailed to England along with the rest of the year's American intake on the *Queen Elizabeth 2*, arriving in early October 1970.

I was still a virgin. I had been brought up a strict Catholic, taught that sexual intercourse was reserved for marriage. I only lasted half a year at my Dartmouth fraternity because I could not stand the constant pressure to leave the GAU (the Grand Army of the Unlaid). I finally succumbed in the spring of 1971, when a young woman who had been the girlfriend of one of my radio station colleagues stopped off in London en route to the Continent.

On one night of our three-day affair we stayed at the Regent's Park home of one of my Oxford friends. Not long afterwards, the daughter of the family was raped and murdered in Washington, DC, at the age of twenty-one. A suspect was tried, but because DNA profiling did not then exist he could not be convicted. Knowing that if he stayed in Washington he would kill the man he was certain had murdered his daughter, the father left government service and moved to New York. This was my introduction to the reality of sexual violence. I have never taken the subject less than completely seriously.

During the 1970s, my sex life was limited to women, but my identification was with gay men. It was not until the '80s that I first fully made love to a man. It takes time to shed religious and family pressures.

I suffered an emotional crisis at the end of my first year at Oxford, realising that I had unintentionally changed countries and was basically unemployed at the age of twenty-one. I missed broadcasting terribly, and BBC Radio Oxford would not even give me an audition because I was an American who would take the job of a British person. The depression and anxiety that resulted from my change of life were so severe that I had to take a year out from University College before returning in the autumn of 1972.

While at Univ., I spent half my days in London working for the still-young *Rolling Stone* magazine. I got to know John Walters, the producer of Radio 1's leading alternative DJ, John Peel. We would frequently meet at concerts and music business showcases. In 1973, after I had done a *Rolling Stone* cover story on Elton John, his publicist took me out to lunch to thank me. She was Helen Walters, John's wife. She brought her husband along.

'I'm starting a rock magazine programme in the autumn,' the producer mentioned during the meal at a Charlotte Street restaurant. 'I'm looking for a ten-minute American look at the scene. Would you like to do it?'

Would I like to do it? Would I like to fly to the moon under my own power? Having been turned down by Radio Oxford, I was now invited onto Radio 1! I could cope with my weekly talk because of my WDCR training. The ten minutes quickly became fifteen. Walters then trusted me with interviews of major artists. Even when, after graduating from Oxford, I spent a half-year in Boston, Massachusetts, as executive producer of WBZ, he allowed me to send tapes to Radio 1 via the BBC New York office.

WBZ, at 50,000 watts one of the most powerful radio stations in America, was part of the Westinghouse Broadcasting Company. If promoted, I would work my way up the Group W stations in various American cities. I had to make a career choice between being talent or management. I accepted an offer from Radio 1 to return to England to host a weekly show of American hits. This time, my work permit problem was solved because I would officially be the US representative of *Rolling Stone* in London. I wasn't the editor – Andrew Bailey held that position – but I was the resident American on an American publication. That was enough to make me legal.

A blessed career followed. I was the only person to ever have regular programmes on BBC Radio 1, 2, 3 and 4, not to mention the commercial channels Classic FM and Capital Radio. Since Radio 1 was at its peak a natural source of television presenters, I found myself also being a regular at one point or another on BBC One, BBC Two, ITV and, when they began broadcasting, Channel 4 and Sky TV. These clean sweeps were made possible because I had a wider range of interests than most presenters and because I was not so famous for one thing that I wasn't allowed to do something else as well.

What would be my ultimate calling card became apparent to me in the third-floor corridor of Radio 1 in 1976. I was appalled because Tony Blackburn had not known a particular pop fact. I then realised that none of the other DJs knew it, either. In fact, I was the only one who knew it. I was the freak!

The following year, brothers Jo and Tim Rice, Mike Read and myself published the first edition of *The Guinness Book of British Hit Singles*. We had slaved on it for four years because we wanted it as a reference book for our own research purposes. Ten months after its publication, I was stunned to see it listed as number six in the *Sunday Times* bestseller list. No one had told me it was selling! The next week we were number four. At this point, Guinness got back in touch and requested a second edition. We wound up doing ten editions, one every two years for two decades, with related titles in the off-years.

Throughout my life I have been nicknamed 'Gambo' wherever I have gone. The first person to use this name was Denis O'Neill, who was the leader of our 'gang' in fifth grade at Greens Farms School. This was no urban 'gang'. It simply was a group of friends who met on the playground every morning during recess. As leader, O'Neill had the right to assign our code names. He called me 'Gambo'. This nickname has lasted all my life. I hope his hasn't. He called himself 'Frenchie'.

In the same way, I received a professional nickname without seeking one. In the 1990s, BBC Two and Channel 4 started producing numerous documentaries on popular music history. Inevitably, a couple of guests appeared regularly as talking heads. I was one. To my amazement, the two channels independently started captioning me 'Professor of Pop'. Even more incredibly, I really did become a 'Professor of Pop' in 2009 when I served as News International Visiting Professor of Broadcast Media at Oxford University.

Throughout the mid-1980s to late noughties, I had a series of relationships with men that each lasted a couple of years. My partners always 'moved on', two marrying women, one moving to California in an attempt to become a film star, and one joining the United States Army without telling me. It amused me to see a photo of him sitting on Saddam Hussein's throne, but the Iraq War was out of my loop. I had lost him to Uncle Sam.

I was always comforted in periods of romantic loss by the lesson of Gene Kelly. I had once read in *The International Herald Tribune* that the great dancer and film star had gone three years between his first and second marriages. My first thought was: 'How did he cope for those three years?' My second was: 'If he could handle it, I have to.' I always remained an optimist, hoping against hope that I would one day find a permanent partner.

In February 2010, I received a friendship request on Facebook from a fellow graduate of Oxford University, Christopher Sherwood. I was losing my interest in Facebook and in fact remained on it for less than a year, because I was receiving a disturbing number of friendship requests from people around the world wanting to know what Freddie Mercury had really been like. This was my own fault, since one of my photos was an old favourite of the two of us in animated conversation, me wearing a tuxedo and Freddie in a Flash Gordon T-shirt.

Chris Sherwood got his request in during the last months of my Facebook site. His photo showed him holding a bottle of wine by the neck, which did not appeal to the teetotaller in me. But he had two things in his favour. First, he had been to my old university. I am as guilty as anyone of thinking that people who went to my school are less likely to be crazy than people who went anywhere else, a misconception proved wrong daily around the world, yet one that universities rely on in their fundraising. Second, Chris had been captain of the Oxford University Gymnastics Club, which meant that he was probably still fit and that he had a sense of self-discipline, a trait required both to stay in shape and to do a regular Saturday radio programme for four decades.

I noticed that two of Sherwood's photo albums concerned his recent trip to New Zealand. At this moment a notification popped up on my iMac screen. It named my friend Stacy Rowe, who lived in New Zealand. Oh, I thought, I get it, Chris met Stacy on vacation and Rowe is vouching for him.

In fact, nothing of the sort had occurred. Stacy's name popped up simply because he had gone online at that moment. The timing was a coincidence, pure and simple, but it was one that led me to accept Christopher's friendship request.

I soon received a message from Chris suggesting that we meet. I replied that I had two tickets for the following Tuesday's performance at the Hampstead Theatre of the Royal Shakespeare Company's production of *Dunsinane*, David Greig's sequel to *Macbeth*. If we got on, great. If we didn't, there was still the play.

We got on.

On 23 June 2012 we held our civil partnership at Le Manoir aux Quat'Saisons in Great Milton, Oxfordshire, chosen for its proximity to our common university. For our honeymoon we went to New York City and got married. Britain did not offer same-sex marriage at the time, although civil partnership bestowed all the important rights of marriage and getting wed in New York simply meant that we could file joint state income tax returns, an unlikely prospect. Chris and I married in the New York Botanical Garden. The beautiful site, undervisited because it is in the Bronx rather than Manhattan, is within walking distance of both the hospital in which I was born and our 1950s Sedgwick Avenue apartment.

Our celebrant was my childhood friend Steve Emmett, who in addition to being an expert on dietary disorders is an ordained Unitarian minister. When Steve and I were in choir in high school we stood next to each other in concerts. On the other side of me would stand Jon Gailmor. When Chris and I invited him to the wedding, Jon, a professional vocalist, asked if he could sing a song. I told him he could, provided it was 'The End' by Earl Grant, a 1958 Top 10 hit we played on CD in our English wedding. He replied that he did not know it, but would look it up. Within hours he emailed: 'I have to sing this song.' He did, so beautifully that Chris cried.

We planned our civil partnership and wedding for a year. Bearing in mind that the events comprised a ceremony and lunch at Le Manoir, an evening party at the Royal Festival Hall in London and our wedding in the New York Botanical Garden, it's a good thing we started a year early. After a few months we had still not decided what we were going to recite for vows. One evening, working at the computer, it suddenly hit me.

'All the Way!' I blurted.

Chris looked at me quizzically. I played him the Frank Sinatra classic, which had been a hit when I was eight years old. We studied the lyrics. It was as if Sammy Cahn had written them for us. Come the day – or, in our case, the days – we recited them together, trading off verses. We were emotional basket cases in two countries. Try it. Even if you have to marry someone to experience it, it's worth it.

'All the Way', written by Sammy Cahn and Jimmy Van Heusen, won the Academy Award for Best New Song of 1957. It originally appeared in the Sinatra film *The Joker is Wild*. The lyrics of the song, published by Maraville Music Corp., include the lines 'When somebody loves you / It's no good unless he loves you, all the way', 'Through the good or lean years / And for all the in-between years, come what may' and 'Who knows where the road will lead us / Only a fool would say / But if you let me love you / It's for sure I'm gonna love you all the way, all the way'.

The following year, our vows were tested. I was arrested by officers of

the Metropolitan Police at 4.38 a.m. on the morning of 29 October 2013.
I was kept on police bail until 10 October 2014.

Arrest a journalist, and he will keep a journal. While sitting in a cell at
Charing Cross Police Station for four hours waiting for a solicitor, I made
myself three promises.

First, I would lose weight.

Second, I would become a better piano player.

Third, I would write a book.

I wrote every day, naively thinking that the case would end after my
first bail period. How could it last longer, since I never even knew the two
persons I was told had accused me? Yet the Crown Prosecution Service
rebailed me persistently until, in my twelfth month, the case was finally
dismissed. I never dreamed that the ordeal, and thus the book, would be
so long. When my literary agent's editor finally printed off the first draft,
it was 873 pages.

During the Christmas period of 2014, I performed what I called my
'hatchet job' edit, cutting approximately half the text. This was easier than it
sounds. I was furious every day. The anger was redundant and easy to edit.

My literary agent's editor also executed his 'hatchet job'. When I read
his, I was delighted that he had only suggested taking out a couple of
points that I really wanted to keep. He acceded to me on these few passages with a shrug and a friendly 'It's your book.'

Then came the 'fine-tooth comb' edit, which I wound up doing twice,
and finally my publisher's edit and the lawyer's legal read. I had to make
sure I did not unintentionally say anything libellous about anyone.

From here on in, until the Epilogue, everything is as I wrote it on the
day it happened or the morning afterward.

Perhaps you should start reading this as I lived it. Set your alarm for
4.38 a.m. and go to sleep. Sweet dreams.

2013

My name is Kafka. Franz Kafka.

Well, OK, it isn't, but it certainly feels like it today. I have recently been wondering what my next book should be about. The answer comes ringing at my doorbell at 4.38 this morning. I am awakened from a deep sleep by the second half of my two-tone bell ring.

'Did I dream that?' I think. I decide to ignore it. If there really is someone there, they will ring again.

There really is someone there. They do ring again. This time I hear both halves of the ring.

My initial reaction is that the Chinese students next door are probably having another late-night party and a guest has come to the wrong door. I look through the peephole. This is no Asian. As a matter of fact, this is no single person. I instantly know what is happening. I open the door and am informed by Officer One that he is from Operation Yewtree and I am under arrest for blahblahblah buggery. My husband Christopher emerges from the bedroom in time to hear 'You are under arrest'. I look at Officer One and ask, 'Is this what you wanted to do when you grew up?'

I invite the group in. Officer One is not alone. He is accompanied by a posse, most notably Officer Two.

I am to accompany One and Two to Charing Cross Police Station. Some of the others are to remain for up to eight hours, searching my home for possibly incriminating material. I am asked if I have diaries and reply that I have thirty-eight years of them. They are all taken.

Both Mr One and Mr Two are polite. Not only do they allow me to have my normal breakfast of orange juice and croissant – they even let me take three minutes to squeeze the juice – they actually suggest I eat something before I go.

'I would not recommend the food in the canteen,' one of them says, a sentiment confirmed by murmurs of assent from the posse.

There is no time to shave, but I am allowed to defecate. I count my lucky stars I do relieve myself before going to Charing Cross, because I will be kept for four hours in a cell with no toilet paper. My captors would undoubtedly give me some loo roll if I request it, but there are some favours one does not want to ask of a stranger. Besides, the cell will have neither a basin nor soap, and at least at home I can wash my hands.

I put on a blue suit and wear my wedding shirt. I kiss my husband goodbye.

'Make them like you,' he says. 'I love you.'

'I love you,' I reply, and enter the underworld.

I have considered a visit from Operation Yewtree likely ever since I read on the BBC website that the Metropolitan Police, having failed to stop the serial offender Jimmy Savile in his lifetime, set up a dedicated phone line and website and encouraged members of the public to accuse celebrities of sexual offences. This was as if, after failing to catch Jack the Ripper, who, since he made careful incisions in the bodies of his victims, may have been a surgeon, the Met had started arresting members of the British Medical Association. You don't catch Jack the Ripper by arresting my GP, and you don't catch Jimmy Savile by arresting me.

'I've had it,' I thought at the time. I had been the first publicly known person to speak out about my former Radio 1 colleague, appearing on ITV's *Daybreak* programme with Lorraine Kelly several days before a documentary exposed him. As a result, my photo had appeared next to his in all British tabloid and middle-market newspapers on two different days, and I knew that, in a nation where tens of millions of people knew my name, all it would need was a couple of fragile individuals to take up the Met's invitation, add two and two, and get five.

For several months I was plagued by periods of darkness. If I were to be accused, and under the ludicrous circumstances I thought it a better than 50 per cent probability I would be, who would point the finger? I wasted hours of energy thinking back over my life. Who could accuse me? Everyone has had a bad date or two in their life. Could one of mine have been frustrated or disappointed? Was there someone carrying a grudge against me?

It turned out all these hours of gloom were wasted, because when the fickle finger of fate pointed at me, it came not from someone I remembered, but from someone I did not know. Yet the internal questioning took its toll: I developed an irrational phobia of walking across bridges, because once free of the shore my mind would start to drift into various scenarios of accusation. I would react emotively to these and experience inappropriate bouts of anger, which would lead to attacks of dread and fear while suspended over the Thames. I started taking buses to cross the river. Thank heavens I got my Freedom Pass earlier this year.

I warned Christopher and my personal assistant that they should not be surprised if one morning we had an early-morning knock at the door. I had read that Yewtree made its arrests at this time of the day, the better to make sure the suspect was at home and, a cynical lawyer later told me, to make the accused individual tired by the time he appeared in the interview room. I went to my solicitor David Gentle, who had prepared mortgages and wills for me for four decades, and warned him that he should be prepared for a false arrest. He looked at me as if I was speaking from another galaxy.

The only way to ensure one can survive a potential challenge is to entertain every possible outcome, from the best case to the worst. The best case, of course, was that I would never be accused. The worst was that I would be tried and convicted, serve a prison sentence of short-to-medium duration and be released back into society, utterly unemployable and unable to resume my career. As hideous as this prospect was, I could survive it. I would still have my devoted Christopher, a husband from heaven. I would have my friends, who were equally loyal. I would have my home and my interests, and I could live, albeit modestly, off my financial body fat and the years of recorded entertainment we accumulate but never actually consume.

I am ready for whatever inaccuracies the Metropolitan Police might throw at me. I am not afraid. When I step into the cell in Charing Cross Police Station this morning, I have been there in my mind before. I have walked through the whole thing. Now the day is here.

I arrive shortly after 6 a.m. and go through booking-in procedures. Everyone in the station house is polite and professional. A couple are even fans, which makes the occasion even more surreal. A friendly male nurse takes my blood pressure, measures my blood sugar levels and conducts a couple of other tests. A female officer to whom I will always be grateful keeps me topped up with cups of water all day.

One built-in problem with the early-morning arrest procedure is that the accused is unlikely to receive an immediate visit from his solicitor. In my case, we wait until 7.15 to ring David Gentle. Naturally, when the officer does call him, he goes through to answerphone. I am ushered to a cell, where I sit for about four hours. When David Gentle is contacted, he has to get in touch with a colleague of his who handles criminal cases. No mortgage or will is going to get me out of this one.

When arrested at home, I had made sure to take enough material, no matter how modest, to keep me busy for hours. I cut a pair of acrostic puzzles out of a book by Thomas Middleton, the master of the genre. I knew these would keep me busy for at least forty-five minutes each. I inserted them into a copy of the week's *Economist* magazine, which I had not yet started to read and which I put inside today's *Financial Times*. Thank heaven for my subscription to this newspaper, which has early-morning delivery service. With the acrostics, *The Economist* and the *Financial Times*, I am ready to sit in solitude for hours.

Of course, I am not going to be just reading and puzzling. I have to figure out my coping strategy. I know I will be expected to make a statement in which I will proclaim my innocence. But I am Yewtree 15. I am personally tired of reading statements of the 'Not me, guv' variety. I have to say something that is obviously by me and not a battery of lawyers. It comes to me instantly, because it is the truth.

'On Monday night, the 28th of October, I attended an excellent production of the Kander and Ebb musical *The Scottsboro Boys* at the Young Vic Theatre. It concerned a group of black men in Alabama in the 1930s who were falsely accused of sexual offences. Within hours, I was arrested by Operation Yewtree. Nothing had changed, except this time there was no music.'

I love this statement. I love it because it has come to me instinctively and in one piece, as John Lennon claimed the name of the Fab Four had come to him. 'It came in a vision,' he told *Mersey Beat* in 1961. 'A man appeared on a flaming pie and said unto them, "From this day on you are Beatles with an 'A'."'

I also love the statement because it is true on several levels. Anyone intrigued enough to research the story of *The Scottsboro Boys* would know that a lynch mob gathered outside their cell. This was parallel to the witch-hunt mentality that has gripped Britain in the wake of the Savile story. And, as Christopher later points out to me, there is another parallel: the

Scottsboro Boys were falsely accused by two friends, in their case white girls, whom they had never met. I am being falsely accused by two friends, both white men, whom I do not recall meeting.

That knowledge will come later. For the moment, I am sitting in a cell for four hours, working on an acrostic. I am grateful that it is difficult and taking me forever to solve. Every hour or so I recline for a rest. I notice the text on the ceiling: 'Crime Stoppers 0800 555 111. Anonymous information about crime could earn a cash reward.'

This is not what I needed to see right now.

'Are you sick and tired of feeling sick and tired?' reads another message on the ceiling. 'Ask to speak to a drugs worker now.'

This is not my idea of interior decor. If you're going to stencil something on the walls, give me Banksy any day.

My solicitor finally arrives. He is Zahir Ahmed, a colleague of David Gentle. I have never met him before, but then this is a day of firsts. Zahir has a few moments to speak to me before we go into the interview room. He has been given what is called a 'disclosure sheet' and reads me the accusations. They are contained in what is called a 'pre-interview briefing'. In this document, and throughout this book, I shall refer to the person who went to the police to accuse me as 'Primary', and his mate from the late 1970s, who the Met say corroborated his story, as 'Secondary'.

> Mr Paul Gambaccini was arrested by officers from Operation Yewtree this morning for a series of three historical sexual offences. Operation Yewtree is the overarching investigation that was set up with a witness appeal following the exposure of a television programme in 2012 into the late Jimmy Savile.
>
> Following this appeal many people came forward to police reporting abuse by Jimmy Savile and/or others. Two people have made allegations against Paul Gambaccini. These allegations do NOT involve Jimmy Savile.

Paul Gambaccini was arrested at 05.35 hours by Officer Two at his home address for the following three offences:

1) Indecency with or towards a child – Sec 1 Indecency With a Child Act 1960
2) Indecent Assault – Sec 15 (1) Sexual Offences Act 1956
3) Buggery – Sec 12 (1) Sexual Offences Act

Mr Gambaccini arrived at Charing Cross Police Station at 06.38 hours and was booked into the custody suite under custody number 01CX/9429/13.

FIRST VICTIM

A man by the name of Secondary alleges that he was introduced to Paul Gambaccini by a male who lived in the same block as Mr Gambaccini that was located in Hyde Park Square, London.

Secondary states that on numerous occasions Paul Gambaccini has performed oral sex on him, touched and inserted fingers into his anus and has anally penetrated him with his penis. All of these offences happened at various times over a period of approximately 1980–1984 (aged fourteen to seventeen) and they happened at a flat belonging to the neighbour of Mr Gambaccini.

Secondary also alleges that one accession [*sic*] he visited Paul Gambaccini's flat and whilst there Paul Gambaccini has penetrated his anus with his penis.

SECOND VICTIM

A man by the name of Primary also alleges that he was introduced to Paul Gambaccini by a male who lived in the same block as him.

Primary states that on two separate occasions whilst at the neighbour's flat Paul Gambaccini has anally penetrated him with his penis. He also states that whilst at the neighbours [sic] flat he performed oral

7

sex on Paul Gambaccini. He also states that over the period of time between 1978–1982 (aged fourteen to seventeen) Paul Gambaccini has anally penetrated him and performed oral sex on Primary. [In the margin, someone has written 'unsure of precise dates'.]

It is proposed to ask Mr Gambaccini questions regarding the above allegations.

I do not recognise myself in this text. I grew up within one mile of the Fairfield County Hunt Club, yet I've never seen so much horse manure in all my life. How could the police be so dumb as to fall for this?

'I try to wonder why people would make false accusations,' I tell Mr Ahmed. 'I can think of three reasons. First, money – they want to sell a story to the press. Secondly, their lives have reached middle age, they are unhappy, and they want to blame somebody. And third, they are fantasists – they actually believe it.'

'There is a fourth,' Zahir interjects. 'The acts may have happened, but with someone else, and they have put your head on his body.'

There is not much time to discuss our theories. I have to write out a statement to hand to the police before we enter the interview room. My solicitor explains to me which points have to be addressed, and I write.

Statement of Paul Gambaccini

I, Paul Gambaccini, was arrested today for three alleged offences, namely

1) Indecency with or towards a child
2) Indecent Assault
3) Buggery

These offences are alleged to have taken place between 1978 and 1984 at a flat in Hyde Park Square, London. I lived there between the years 1975 and 1983. I took over the lease from a generous elderly American who was returning to the United States. There were eight years remaining on the lease. During that time, I never had sex in that building outside my own flat. The only time I ever performed buggery in the flat was with a consenting adult male friend between 1982 and 1983. I never performed oral sex on anyone in that building. The first time I performed oral sex on anyone was well after I left Hyde Park Square.

I have been told by my solicitor through some limited disclosure that the alleged victims are Secondary and Primary. It is possible that I may have met them while I lived in Hyde Park Square, but I do not recall them.

I vehemently deny all the accusations. I understand you will have questions to ask during the course of the interview. I will be exercising my right to remain silent.

At the behest of Zahir Ahmed, I write a squiggly line, like an extended Zorro signature, over the remainder of page two of my statement, to ensure that no one adds an incriminating footnote. I personally do not fear the police would do that, but I do recall that years ago I had a $13 breakfast at the Waldorf Astoria Hotel in New York that appeared on my American Express credit card statement as $113. Someone had written in an additional '1' in the amount, presumably hoping to profit by $100. I'm pleased to say American Express removed the extra charge from my statement at that time. I have carefully monitored my credit card statements ever since.

Solicitor Ahmed suggests I answer each question with 'No comment'. Officer One and Officer Two welcome me into the interview room. They sit on one side, Ahmed and I on the other. We go through a ceremony of explanations as Two, as I am beginning to think of my case officer, opens a sealed cassette and inserts it into a tape recorder.

'Two?' one might think. The guy's trying to ruin my life, and I'm thinking of him as a friendly acquaintance? The fact is, I can't help it. Both he and One ... there I go again ... are civil throughout the six-hour-or-so interview, including a sandwich break, that follows. They allow me to step out of the room for toilet breaks whenever necessary. Since I am talking a lot, I am drinking a lot of water and therefore urinating a lot.

The questioning begins. The answering doesn't. I keep to my solicitor's advice and say 'No comment' to everything. It becomes apparent within ninety seconds that uncommunicativeness is not my style. Twice we break for a client–counsel conference, in which I protest the tactic. My decision to actually reject the advice is made after Officer Two asks, 'Who owned your flat before you?' I think it insane to answer 'No comment' to that and have a third and final conference on the tactic of silence. I give the name of Mr Hodnett, my benefactor, and we are away on a six-hour combination of solemnity and silliness.

I explain to the officers that I had initially been willing to use the 'No Comment' technique because of what I learned in the early 1980s dealing with tabloid newspapers. These were the dark days when celebrities feared exposure or invention in the British popular press. I had learned from watching friends of mine, beginning with the actress Debbie Arnold, suffer from the tactics of Fleet Street reporters. One's natural response to an absurd accusation – denial – was in fact a story in itself, along the lines of 'Abraham Lincoln Denies Beating His Wife'. Therefore, instead of confirmation or denial, I would have to make lateral statements if I were ever cornered by the popular press.

My opportunity to do so came in early 1984. A reporter from the *News of the World* called me at Radio 1.

'It is in your interest to talk to me,' he announced.

'When?' I replied.

'Now.'

'Where?'

'You choose.'

I selected Patisserie Valerie in Old Compton Street. In those days, that was the place to go if you wanted a good cake. I figured at least I'd get a decent snack out of this.

And so the foes met, cakes drawn in mid-afternoon. My opponent fired first with his whopper of an allegation.

'We have been told that you had sex with [a number one chart artist] on the floor of your kitchen at your birthday party watched by your guests, who included Boy George.'

This was the tallest of tales. The only true thing about it was that my kitchen did indeed have a floor.

'My lawyer will be very interested in that story,' I replied in my best lateral-speak.

'Someone who knows you has recorded a telephone conversation with you. His boyfriend is acting as his agent and has presented the tape to us to prove he knows you. He has then told us about your party.'

So much for gay solidarity, I thought.

'I've always wanted a good pension,' I responded.

After a while, it became evident to even the thickest of Murdochian skulls that his line of questioning was going nowhere.

'Well, Paul, at least tell me, you are gay, aren't you?'

No luck. I wasn't giving you that story, either.

Clark Kent and I finished our cakes and walked out into Old Compton Street. Before we parted, I spoke.

'May I ask you one question?'

'Sure,' the reporter answered.

'When you were a little boy, is this what you wanted to be when you grew up?'

'Paul!' he cried, as if he were the wronged one. And that was the origin of my first comment to Officer One this morning.

Back in 2013, the conversation ranges from the banal to the titillating. At some points I have to stop myself as I become aware I am telling anecdotes that, while interesting, are not to the point.

I tell my interviewers I had paid my Hyde Park Square rent cheques to a company called Hallia Financial Investments. They seem interested even in that. They're going to be checking up on a lot of people, I think.

I tell the police how I came to acquire the eight-year lease to the flat. I was a regular player on the Regent's Park Softball Club, which convened for open games on Sundays at noon between April and October. One of the other regulars was a Canadian named Jerry Rush, who lived in Stanhope Place, W2. His mother used a laundromat on Connaught Street, where she met an elderly American woman who lived in Hyde Park Square with another female and a male. The American told the Canadian that she was about to return to the United States because the man of the family, Edwin (or is it Edward?) Hodnett, was ageing and wanted to spend his final days in the country of his birth. Mr Hodnett was looking for another American who loved London to take the remaining eight years of his lease.

Consider, for a moment, his generosity. Nowadays an eight-year lease on a Hyde Park flat would be gold dust, and he could make a fantastic profit. In 1975, the lease was a means to be generous to a young man making his start in life. I can't even remember if I paid Mr Hodnett a nominal sum, but if I did it was truly meagre. I was living in Shepherd's Bush at the time, on BBC contributor's fees, which were not sufficient to support a Hyde Park lifestyle.

The police ask me to describe the layout of the floor of the building I lived in. I tell them it was simple and draw a schematic diagram, apologising for my atrocious draughtsmanship. There was a birdcage lift at one end of the floor. If you turned one way on exiting the lift, you came to a flat owned by a nice old woman named Pat.

I hesitate for a moment. I haven't thought about her in years. Pat is almost certainly now dead. Out of respect I give her a few seconds of silence.

I said it was curious, but I couldn't remember if there was a flat beyond hers in that direction. If there was, I had not had regular purpose to go there.

Turning the other way out of the lift would take someone past another flat. After that came my home.

'Tell us about the other flat,' one of the detectives requests.

I amuse the police with a terrific story involving a rock star friend of mine. I move on.

Everyone continues to be polite.

After a couple of hours we have a sandwich break. I am allowed out of the interview room to phone Christopher.

Chris is still at home. It is like a hit of oxygen talking to him. It transpires he had watched over the police officers as they took away sackloads of stuff. He tells me that the BBC website is reporting that two men have been arrested that morning, a 64-year-old and a 74-year-old. I am Yewtree 15 and he is Yewtree 16. From this point on I will refer to him as 'Sixteen'.

I return to the interview room and am hit with a further accusation, one not on the disclosure sheet. One of my accusers has claimed that I engaged in a threesome with him and Sixteen, me anally penetrating him while my neighbour performed oral sex on him.

I react spontaneously.

'Not only have I never had a threesome, if I did it would not involve Sixteen. If he were to be introduced into a sexual situation, I would turn into Mr Floppy.'

The new accusation is the prelude to unexpected pieces of information. Sixteen has also been arrested and is currently being interviewed upstairs. A neighbour of mine in the late '70s and early '80s, he is not a celebrity. He supposedly met Primary and Secondary while they were taking horse-riding lessons in Hyde Park and he was walking his dog. I also learned that Secondary was at a famous public school at the time, although why I am told this or whether it's true I have no idea.

I tell the police about everyone who lived in my flat during the years I was the leaseholder. The first lodger was the girlfriend of my softball teammate Jerry Rush. He had thought it would be a splendid arrangement if he could lodge his inamorata within walking distance of his flat, in which he housed his mother, sister and nephew. This had been a factor in Jerry's interest in my taking the property. It infuriates me that I cannot remember the surname of Jerry's partner Dale. As soon as I get to 'Dale', I think of my fellow broadcaster Dale Winton, and I can't get beyond that. It is terribly frustrating. What's most bizarre about this is that Dale was living in my apartment, sleeping in the bedroom next door, for at least three and possibly four years, and yet I can't remember her last name.

The second and only other long-term resident was male. If the police intend to interview him, can they be sensitive?

Yes, they promise.

Should I contact him first to warn him they will be coming? A policeman's knock on the door can be distressing.

No. They advise very strongly against me getting in touch with him. It might look as if I were trying to influence whatever he might tell them.

I bite my tongue and just hope that my former flatmate holds the same fond memory of me as I do of him, and resists any police attempt to have him badmouth me.

There were others who briefly lived in my flat. Brad Spurgeon, a Canadian who started his Hyde Park Square life in the kind of basement room only a young man would accept, was with me for a short time before he moved to a better place. Then a ventriloquist and now the world's leading journalist on Formula 1, he has long lived in Paris, writing for the *International Herald Tribune*. I saw the entire arc of his marriage, from courting his French girlfriend Nathalie, through their wedding, the birth of their two children and her early death from a brain tumour. I asked the officers to be sensitive to this tragedy if they interviewed him.

Another young man who briefly lived in my small third bedroom was a fellow Regent's Park softball player. Also named Paul, he was christened 'Moscow Paul' by the team to distinguish him from me. He was called this because he occasionally went to Moscow to visit a friend of his whose father was in the French diplomatic service. The team joked he was really on errands for the CIA.

On a couple of occasions, Paul took twenty-five of my surplus vinyl albums to exchange on the Russian black market for giant tins of the finest caviar. That is how desperate Russian youth were to access banned Western pop music in the late 1970s. I held caviar parties for the team in my apartment, with the full complement of blinis, chopped onion, egg, vodka and so forth. On one occasion I followed this spread with take-out from McDonald's, which my teammates devoured with equal enthusiasm.

Towards the end of his stay, Paul brought over from the United States an American female friend of his, Deborah. Our rapport was immediate. Our occasional but loving affair continued for three years, from 1978 to 1981. I know it began in 1978 because I recall us going to the premiere of the film *Grease*, with John Travolta and Olivia Newton-John in attendance. Artists and audience alike were stunned by the hysterical atmosphere in Leicester Square. I remember our romance tailed off in 1981 because of another unforgettable evening, but I don't bother to give the police these details. Deborah married and now lives in New York.

'I'll take that one,' Detective One jokes. I realise he's actually not joking and that someone is likely to fly to New York to see Debbie.

I explain that I do not know the present whereabouts of Moscow Paul. I have no idea if Yewtree are going to bother to search him out, but I spell his surname at their request.

As the session nears its end, I exasperatedly offer my theory, previously expressed to Zahir Ahmed, as to how someone can level false charges at someone.

First, money. That's the obvious motivation.

Secondly, their lives have reached middle age, they are unhappy, and they are looking for someone to blame.

Third, they may be fantasists. They may actually believe it. I know this seems hard to believe, but many people in public life have people who believe they have been lovers.

When I was on breakfast television, there was a man who would invite his female friend over, they would watch videos of me, he would find a frame he liked, freeze it and kiss the screen.

And last decade, I was walking on Shaftesbury Avenue when a man ran up to me and blurted out, 'You didn't say hello.'

'Hello,' I answered.

'No, you didn't say hello in the pub.'

'Hello.'

'You don't remember me, do you?'

'No.'

'We were lovers.'

'I don't remember you.'

'I was younger then, and better looking,' he cried, his face contorted in grief.

'I'm sorry, I don't remember you,' I said, hurrying towards Piccadilly Circus Station.

As I relate this story, the policemen's eyes light up. They look at each other and rummage through their statements.

'Secondary told us the exact same story,' Officer One says, 'except he said the conversation ended when you said, "Fuck off."'

'We have been talking for three hours, and I hope you will agree I don't use language like that,' I reply, miffed at the insinuation.

'Could it have been 2005?' he asks excitedly.

'I said it was last decade.'

'Yeah, he said he was in Waitrose in Finchley Road, saw you in the next aisle, and…'

'Waitrose in Finchley Road?' I interrupt. 'I've never been to Waitrose in Finchley Road in my life! Why would I go to Waitrose in Finchley Road? I live on the South Bank! If I really wanted to go to a Waitrose, I would go to the one in Holloway Road, it's closer.'

I tell the police that if I had actually known my accusers during 1978–84, their phone numbers would be in the diaries they have seized. Personal computers didn't exist in those years, and if you were going to contact someone you needed to have their phone number. If there are no numbers in the diaries, it is the best evidence that I did not know them. After sharing this tip, I fear that I might get my diaries back with my accusers mysteriously inked in by another hand. I also worry that the police will be able to discover on which evenings I would and would not have been free to meet my accusers, and wonder if they would be crass enough to alter the original unspecific disclosure sheet to include particular dates, as if Secondary and Primary had suddenly had a flash of memory thirty-five years later.

The interview ends shortly thereafter.

I emerge from the lengthy session to be informed that I was not charged with any offence at this time. I am released on bail and am to report back to Charing Cross Police Station on 8 January 2014. At that time, I will be charged, the case will be dropped, or they will request a further interview and a second bail period. Right now I should sign my bail conditions.

There are four, each matched with the reason 'why conditions appear necessary':

1) Live and sleep each night at your home address – Prevent disappearance

2) Not to contact the alleged victims Secondary and Primary – Prevent further offences; and to prevent witness interference

3) Not to contact the co-defendant Sixteen – Prevent further offences; and to prevent witness interference

4) Not to have unsupervised access to children under the age of eighteen – Prevent further offences; and to prevent witness interference

My eye was immediately drawn to the word 'co-defendant'. Am I actually part of a case with Sixteen?

'That should be "co-accused",' I am told, 'but we know what it means.'

I am now legally bound to Sixteen, something I had not considered until this moment. The very idea is preposterous and probably not good for me. The Met are playing hardball, and I am joining a game that is already in progress.

I sign the bail conditions and get ready to leave the police station. We first have to make sure that members of the press are not waiting outside.

Zahir Ahmed, who quietly took notes during the entire interview process, goes outside to see if the coast is clear. Lois Lane and Jimmy Olsen are elsewhere, so he gets his car to take me home. Officer Three attempts to reassure me by telling me that there are twenty officers on my case, and that although they are following the leads of my accusers, they will surely discover my innocence if I am not guilty. Somehow I do not feel reassured.

I get home around 6.30 p.m. I've been away over twelve hours. Christopher awaits. Nothing else matters.

Chris tells me he has received phone calls from Tom Morgan of *The Sun* and Danny Shaw of the BBC while I have been at the police station. They both said that a 64-year-old man had been arrested and wanted to check if it was me. Chris fobbed both of them off with diversions.

We go through what the police took away from the flat in the six or so hours they were here in my absence. Both of my computers are gone and so is Christopher's, on the grounds that since we are married we might be sharing. His cameras are gone. So are my US and UK passports. As I've said, thirty-eight years of my diaries have been taken. My iPhone is gone. This will be slim pickings for them, since I only use it when I'm out of London and it only has a few phone numbers on it. A number of my tapes have also been removed, which will provide boring viewing for any police person not interested in popular music. They will be looking for sexually explicit images, whereas in fact they are tapes of my old television programmes. I imagine an officer with his feet up on a desk watching me interview Mark Knopfler for three months.

While we can get away for a meal undisturbed, we go to Canteen in the Royal Festival Hall. I have chicken breast with salad and apple crumble with custard. We go to Costcutter on York Road so Chris can buy some milk.

We go home and hit the phones. Some people must be told as soon as possible.

During the day, Chris had called members of both our families. He had managed to head his sister Jennifer off at the pass before she reported that morning for duty as my personal assistant, at which she is excellent. At the age of twenty-three, she will now get to be part of our determined fightback. Chris had also tweeted an innocuous message on my account to suggest that business is as usual.

Now I call my brothers, Peter and Philip. Living abroad, they lack the context of the Jimmy Savile backstory and the subsequent Yewtree witch-hunt, so a little scene-setting is required. I fill them in on my experiences at Charing Cross Police Station. Fortunately, they know me better than the Metropolitan Police do and are with me 100 per cent.

I call Helen Boaden, head of BBC Radio, who oversees the two networks on which I currently serve, 2 and 4. Having been a minor player in the *Newsnight* Savile saga as head of news, she immediately understands the gravity of the situation. An old friend who was a guest at our wedding party, she intuitively knows the accusations are false.

Next up is Kevin Howlett, producer of my Radio 2 show *America's Greatest Hits*. This show is prepared and delivered via his independent company, Howlett Media Productions. The BBC lets us use the studio on Saturday evenings to broadcast the programme. My deal is with Kevin, not Radio 2. He has the contract with Radio 2.

Howlett is horrified, but not completely surprised. For the past year I have been warning him that I would not be surprised to receive an early-morning visit from the Sex Police, explaining that since my picture had appeared next to Savile's in the papers for two days after I publicly discussed his case, a couple of distressed individuals might make a connection between us. Kevin offers his complete sympathy and support. I know how deeply he is moved, and I appreciate his backing, but I also realise that I am now living in a parallel universe. I see my friends in their world, wave and blow them kisses, but their support will not be enough. I am going to need a heavyweight team to meet the Met.

I must call Tim Rice. I have known Tim since I was at Oxford. He gave the best-man speech at our London wedding. He has been a special friend, the kind with whom you share a private language … in our case, the arcane argot of the chart freak. (I call our kind 'chartologists', but that word has actually already been taken by people who make maps.) All I have to do is say that Bob Azzam is from Egypt and Tim and I are off down memory lane. (When we, Jo Rice and Mike Read were compiling the first edition of *The Guinness Book of British Hit Singles*, we had identified every chart artist's country of origin except Bob Azzam. When, after weeks of frustration, I told my Radio 1 producer Mike Hawkes we had unsuccessfully gone down every avenue to discover Azzam's birthplace, he replied, 'He's from Egypt. I have his EP.' Unrestrained glee ensued in four counties.)

Tim is appalled. He expresses his disgust at what his country has become. His sympathy and support, like Kevin's, are complete.

I call Sir Nick Partridge, whose retirement party I am due to host tomorrow evening. Nick has been chairman of the Terrence Higgins Trust for twenty-two years and is stepping down after three decades with the charity. He was its first paid employee. Nick and I lived through the darkest days of the Aids crisis side-by-side. It was for raising £300,000 for the THT to compensate for the loss of its government grant that the National Charity Fundraisers named me Philanthropist of the Year in 1995. Missing Nick's farewell will hurt, but he agrees that if I were to attend I would be the story and not him, and that would be a distortion of what is meant to be his evening.

My friend Chris Simpson, who lives in Holborn, comes down to the flat to lend his support. You always remember who shows up when most needed, no matter how unglamorous the circumstances. Turning up when you are facing the fuzz is an example of friendship above and beyond the call of duty.

My husband has made a pleasant discovery. No one took the iPad. I only bought the thing for travel purposes and have never used it myself, but it sure looks good now. Perhaps with its grey cover down, lying flat somewhere, it didn't look like a computer, and Mr and Mrs U-Haul didn't recognise it. Chris and I open my email.

Mark Jefferies of the *Daily Mirror* leads off the batting. Checking in at 19.04, he says, 'I was hoping you would be able to confirm that Paul is not involved in these arrests to clear up a rumour going around parts of the media today,' followed by a link to the BBC website. Next to write is Helen Boaden. She affectionately though tersely suggests I ring her reputational lawyer on a mobile. Helen knows from personal experience not to say too much in emails.

'Reputational' lawyer! When I considered going to law school in 1970, no such creature existed.

Next up on email at 8.36 p.m. is Sherlock Holmes from *The Sun*, writing under his earth name of Tom Morgan.

> Dear all, I am seeking an urgent statement please regarding the arrest of Paul Gambaccini today. He was seen by eyewitnesses leaving [his building] shortly after 5 a.m. Plain-clothed officers were then spotted leaving the building with evidence bags and Tupperware boxes. As it stands this story is running in tomorrow's paper. Please come back to me with clarifications. Many thanks for your time, Tom Morgan.

This is a most interesting communication. What eyewitnesses hang around anywhere at 5 a.m.? The only people in the foyer when I was taken away were the concierge Michael and members of the police. When I speak to Michael about this he confirms that he has never experienced a burning desire to phone *The Sun* about anything. Indeed, the concierges are highly professional and well-trained in saying nothing to the press, as I know from the years one of my neighbours, a lawyer, was involved in a long-running high-profile terrorism case.

Tom Morgan is the first reporter to use a bluff that the *Mirror*, *Mail* and *Guardian* would also use in the week ahead. The trick is to say that the paper is going to name me the next day and invite my comment. Of course, they cannot name me unless I do comment. This kind of invitation is a variation of the old *News of the World* tactic requesting a denial of an outrageous charge, which would then allow publication of the falsehood.

Curious eyewitnesses at 5 a.m. The weight of the state against me. *The Sun* at twenty paces. I am going to have an interesting year.

<hr>

30 & 31 OCTOBER 2013

I awake at 5.30 on 30 October, the day after my arrest. I used to wake up often at 5.30, in time to hear the first Radio 4 news block of the day, but this was before Christopher moved in. I altered my sleep cycle to accommodate his later nights and now greet the day between 7.00 and 7.30. This morning, however, there is no possibility I will get back to sleep. The brain mulls over information from the previous day while you sleep and wakes you, adrenalised, whenever it wants to. I am ready for action at 5.30.

I turn on the iPad to check my emails. My smugness at being a good boy getting up early is shattered. Helen Boaden has sent me an email timed 3.44 a.m.! She is passing on the BBC press office daily digest, which includes a leader from *The Sun*. The pearl in the Rupert Murdoch necklace wants to know why it cannot name the BBC star arrested for 'historic sexual offences' and suggests this demonstrates that the new Royal Charter is a bad idea. This is just what I need: to be the poster boy of the Wapping campaign against the Royal Charter. Of course, it is not lost on me that I was arrested by Operation Yewtree mere hours after the trial of Rebekah Brooks and Andy Coulson began. It would be wonderful for News International if some scandal could knock them off the front pages for a day or two. However, I do not personally know these two courtroom celebrities, and have no wish to get involved in their case when I will be more than busy enough with my own.

It only takes a couple of hours to realise that this arrest is one of the worst-kept secrets in police history. Jennifer makes it into work at 9 a.m. just before a cordon of journalists, photographers and TV cameramen surrounds the Whitehouse Apartments, where I have lived since 2000.

We are in for a siege. My friends Malcolm Jeffries and Chris Simpson arrange to take turns babysitting me whenever Christopher and Jennifer are away. We are not yet sure how this will affect me emotionally, so we can't take chances. I decide that, in the interests of my sanity, I will not look out the corridor window at the press, nor will I read any newspapers, visit any news websites or listen to news broadcasts.

I may need back-up against overzealous members of the press. Christopher is still home in the morning when a woman identifying herself as being from the *Evening Standard* tailgates her way into the building … that is, follows an occupant through the glass lobby doors before they shut and lock again. She persists in ringing our doorbell even though we do not answer. Chris sneaks a peek through the spyhole and sees Nancy Drew standing there with shopping bags, to make it appear as if she is not a journalist. We buzz the concierge downstairs to come and take her away. The intruder sees said concierge emerge from the lift, runs away and is found hiding in the basement.

I have to call David Munns, chairman of Nordoff Robbins and organiser of the annual Music Industry Trusts dinner, which benefits the music therapy charity and also the BRIT school. On Monday I am due to host the yearly MITS dinner for the fifteenth time. An honoree is chosen annually, with the evening themed around that person. The Men of the Year have ranged from Atlantic Records co-founder Ahmet Ertegun to the song-writing team of Elton John and Bernie Taupin. This time the prize is due to go to a Woman of the Year for only the second time, Kylie Minogue having been the first. Annie Lennox is the honoree, and I would love to pay her tribute. I first met Annie when she was a Tourist – a member of the group the Tourists, that is – and followed her through her years in Eurythmics with Dave Stewart, her solo career and her emergence as an important international philanthropist. We have done radio and television programmes together. Hosting her tribute dinner would be a thrill.

Alas, to quote B. B. King, the thrill is gone. I inform David Munns of my arrest. He howls in protest and says 'I hate this', referring to the witch-hunt. I express my fear that my presence on the evening would distract members of the press from focusing on Annie.

He understands and tells me he will discuss this at the production meeting the following morning, but I am experienced enough to know that the meeting is a mere formality. Because I have been accused of offending against teenagers, I cannot be associated with charities for young people until I am cleared. My string of MITS dinners ends at fourteen.

I put the phone down and speak to Jennifer, who was in the audience for *The Gambaccini Years*, the series of four programmes Radio 4 ran in August to celebrate my fortieth anniversary as a national broadcaster. I am about to metamorphose in record time from Mr Forty Years to Mr Who? I know what is happening, and I speak it aloud.

'So begins the unravelling.'

This sounds dramatic but is not overstated. I recall a Radio 2 colleague of mine temporarily taken off air while he was under a cloud of suspicion after a story originated by the *News of the World*. I know the zealotry of at least one former policeman I suspect of being Javert to my Valjean. I must be realistic if I am going to adjust to my new reality, no matter how unjust and preposterous it is.

I can forget about any sympathy from the press. Variations on Tom

Morgan's email informing me I am about to be named by a certain newspaper and inviting comment come from journals across the political spectrum. Mark Jefferies reappears in my incoming email tray with 'Hi, We understand Paul was arrested yesterday as part of Operation Yewtree and will be running this information in the paper tomorrow. If you or Paul have any comment, please come back to me asap.'

We receive ludicrous phone calls, which I hope embarrass at least some of the reporters who make them. We go to answerphone on the landline so we can audit all callers. We can phone out on Christopher's office iPhone.

And this is interesting: not a single paper calls his office. They are all obviously Googling him, seeing his website and assuming he is an actor and model, when in fact these are his sidelines. He works full time in advertising, but 'actor and model' (or even 'model and actor') are so much more titillating in a sex case that they stop their search there.

There are only four papers that do not harass us or our families over the next few days. The virtuous few are the *Express*, *Financial Times*, *Independent* and *Telegraph*. There is no pattern there, merely shared discretion.

It quickly becomes apparent that an international press dragnet is underway to get a quote about my arrest. All it takes is one sympathetic friend or relative who does not know how Wapping plays its game to say something to the effect of 'It's a shame Paul has been arrested' and BINGO! 'Paul has been arrested.'

A man identifying himself as the American head of the *Daily Mirror* sneaks into my brother Peter's apartment building in New York City, goes to his front door, knocks, claims to be my friend and attempts to engage him in conversation. Pete repeats variations of 'I don't know anything' until the man leaves. The *Daily Mail* calls Peter for a quote and a representative of a third newspaper tries to tailgate his way into his building.

'Don't let that man in!' Pete yells down to the tenant being followed through the front door. The woman whirls round and lets loose with a classic New York remark.

'Don't you dare come into this building!' The reprimanded intruder backs off, caught in the act.

My other brother Philip is called at his home in Switzerland by several reporters. Even my female cousins, who have different surnames and live in Connecticut, are emailed and phoned by UK journalists. Christopher's parents are visited in Norfolk. My former lodger Darren Cheek, who now lives in the north of England, is contacted.

I myself phone Jack Zoeller in Washington. Jack, my best friend from Oxford days, is the father of my godson Andrew and his brother Alec. Even Jack, famous for his stoicism, is audibly taken aback as I tell him my tale. Like most Americans, he has been unaware of Operation Yewtree.

'To give you an idea of how grim this is,' I tell him, 'a police officer went into our downstairs bathroom, looked at the photographs of your sons, and said, "Who are those boys?"'

It is obvious that I am settling in for the ultimate staycation, unable to leave the house unless I want to face a horde of journos. I sit on my bed and look out my window towards the North Downs. The police are spending a fortune on a case I know to be nothing. An international press dragnet is spending tons of money on what I know to be nothing. Meanwhile, actual crimes are being committed and real news stories are being ignored.

My neighbour Lee Evans, who lives across the hall, comes over to sympathise.

'You want me to get the boys to take care of them?' he asks in one of his comedic voices. I might have expected humour from Lee. I didn't expect him to stand in his twelfth-floor window and moon the press, which he does before they can photograph him.

At 11.09 Anthony Barnes of the Press Association sends the politest of the press emails.

> I can quite understand if you don't wish to respond or comment, but I
> am just dropping you a line on the off chance that you wished to issue a

statement. Rumours seem to be circulating that have linked your name to the two Operation Yewtree arrests earlier this week. We just want to check whether you wanted to either issue a denial that you were involved in the arrests or whether you wished to make your position clear in a statement. Obviously I can understand that any response to this email may be difficult, but at least you have my contact details if you would like PA to issue anything on your behalf.

Josh Halliday of *The Guardian* emails at 13.13:56:

Forgive the email out of the blue. I want to check rumours that you were arrested this week under Operation Yewtree on suspicion of sexual offences and, if correct, whether you are saying anything about that. Do you deny the allegations? Please feel free to give me a call on the numbers below. Again, just wanting to check the rumours.

Dominik Lemanski of the *Daily Star* chips in at 13.15:26: 'We hear you have been arrested as part of Operation Yewtree. Would you care to comment?' *The Guardian* and the *Daily Star* using the same tactics only ninety seconds apart!

I'm so bored with these identikit emails I don't even keep a similar request from Steven Wright, crime editor of the *Daily Mail*. At least he has a proper title. But I wonder: why is the *Mail* buying this nonsense, which so obviously serves the cause of its rival News International?

Whatever one thinks of the *Mail* generally, one has to admit that with its courageous work on the Stephen Lawrence case it has made the greatest contribution to journalism in the UK since Harold Evans of the *Sunday Times* exposed the full tragedy of the thalidomide scandal four decades ago. Having taken on the Metropolitan Police before, why can't they do so now, particularly since the smell of sulphur emanating from Yewtree is so strong?

Helen Boaden's libel lawyer Louis Charalambous arrives at 2.30 with the Alder Media representative Tim Toulmin. Tim is a 'reputational PR'. We politely but firmly discuss the statement that I will issue if it is revealed by the press that I have been arrested. I insist on my Scottsboro Boys statement. Louis and Tim feel it is too poetic to stand alone and must be accompanied by a firm denial of the accusations. I point out that my statement does include the phrase 'falsely accused'. They feel not all the papers will print my Scottsboro Boys in full and a simple denial will be better for my purpose. We agree to disagree in the sense that I will issue my statement and they will issue an accompanying statement of the standard variety.

Tim asks, 'Do you dread the press?'

'I don't dread the press,' I reply. 'The press are shit and I expect them to be shit. What I do dread is the bandwagon effect.'

Both Tim and Louis know what I'm talking about. Everyone who has been accused in the recent witch-hunt has experienced a 'bandwagon effect' of other persons alleging molestation after their name has been publicised. The initial accusation serves as a kite the police send into the air to attract lightning strikes.

Still, I don't have the time to worry about what other fragile individuals might be attracted to my kite. My attention is focused on performing my Saturday-night Radio 2 show. The BBC makes it clear in our very first phone calls that I will continue on air until I am named or charged and will then return when I am cleared. That means the Saturday show will go ahead unless the press names me.

I am in email correspondence with Radio 2's head of talent Lewis Carnie. Privately appalled at Yewtree and frequently expressing statements of solidarity, he nonetheless has to do a bit of BBC dirty work. The corporation wants to cover its backside against possible accusations of employing a person suspected of sexual offences. I am in sympathy, knowing News International is manipulating the post-Savile scandal for the purposes of anti-BBC propaganda. The BBC is the world's greatest broadcaster. News

International is not. Indeed, were I in the United States wanting to catch up with what's going on, I would turn on the Sci Fi Channel before Fox News. It's more believable.

And so I go through the charade of a 'statement' that will be ready for release in the event of my being charged or named by the press. Management chooses words it believes serve both itself and me:

> Paul Gambaccini has decided that, in light of recent media speculation/
> reports about him, he would rather not be on air at the present time.
> We respect his decision and, therefore, Paul will not be presenting on
> BBC Radio in coming weeks. Replacement programmes for the period
> will be announced soon.

Forever acting as the editor I briefly was at *Rolling Stone* in the 1970s, I email back minor suggested revisions: 'Almost there. May I suggest replacing the clunky phrase SPECULATION/REPORTS with ATTENTION. I suggest a full stop after the word DECISION, followed by PAUL WILL NOT BE PRESENTING ON BBC RADIO IN COMING WEEKS and the rest.'

The revisions are accepted at the BBC end and the statement is ready for any emergency.

Why on earth would I agree to a misleading statement like this? Because, if read carefully, it is in my favour. It merely says I will not be presenting 'in coming weeks', suggesting I will be returning relatively soon. It also uses the phrase 'replacement programmes', code for 'repeats of documentaries', rather than 'new presenters'. Radio 2 is not looking for anyone to replace me, and that is enough for me.

This leaves the problem of doing Saturday's show. How can I get out of the Whitehouse Apartments without going through the cordon of press?

Christopher comes up with an ingenious scheme. He knows the press would love a photo of him leaving the house, but he has managed to sneak by them on his way to and from work. He takes the underground passage into the car park, dons his bicycle helmet and protective glasses, and rides right past the photographers. They don't give him a second glance.

And so we devise Operation Howlett, named after producer Kevin Howlett. At 9.15 on Thursday evening, Kevin drives into the car park and descends to the lowest level. Informed of his arrival, I take the side lift to its lowest level. I cross over to the car park. Kevin and Chris are waiting at the door connecting the pedestrian passage with the parking lot. I climb into the back seat and put a blanket over my body. Kevin drives past the photographers unnoticed. We make it to Radio 2 undetected!

This is going to be a historic programme. For the first time since I began the American hits show in 1975, I am not going to play the number one. It is 'Rap God' by Eminem, an extended foul-mouthed rant in which Marshall Mathers's genuine talent is completely obscured by homophobia and anti-social violence. I have already tweeted that I believe any radio station airing this song should be prosecuted for broadcasting hate speech, but I don't expect the industry to take my view seriously. As a DJ on WABC used to say when I was young, 'Money talks, nobody walks.' Whatever that means, I think of it whenever I hear some record or radio executive rationalise selling and spreading murder music. Anyway, I am going to stick to the sentiment of my tweet. I will announce 'Rap God' as America's number one, say that it is 'explicit' and easily available on the internet, and will close the show with the number two, the former champ 'Royals' by Lorde.

One of our finest veteran technical operators has volunteered to engineer the programme. The recording goes without a hitch, but I am slightly concerned to meet Alex Lester's producer James Walsh, a gentleman who has moved to the BBC from commercial radio whom I have not seen in several years. I am aware that in his enthusiasm for our reunion, he might tell Janice Long, who is doing the midnight-to-two slot. What if she were to tell the nation that I was 'in the house' at what is for me an unusual time? That would really invite the photographers over to the Radio 2 building! My fears are groundless. Kevin and I escape Western House without detection and drive away, me once again under the blanket in the back.

After the time it should have taken to get home, I pop my head up to see how close we are. We are nowhere near the South Bank! We are in the City! I have forgotten that Kevin lives near Cheltenham in Gloucestershire and has no idea of how to navigate central London. We have to improvise our escape from the back roads of the City – 'Look for Bishopsgate!' I keep saying from the back seat – and Kevin even puts on his GPS. We have moved from heroics to farce, me in the back seat occasionally popping my head out from underneath a blanket and Kevin trying to follow a disembodied voice's direction. We finally make it back to the Waterloo roundabout and I get down for the duration. We sneak past the photographers again! I am deposited in the lower level of the car park and return home. We have done it! Operation Howlett has outfoxed the press! They can stay out there as long as they want.

---

1 NOVEMBER 2013

I don't rise until after 9 a.m., late for me, because Chris and I had not gone to bed until after three. Jennifer reports that the press cordon is still in full effect. Although it has been a dry autumn in London, there have been several showers since I have been arrested, a few heavy. We cheer whenever it rains, revelling in the number of press people who must be getting wet.

Sean O'Neill, crime editor of *The Times*, pipes in on email at 11.29. I am impressed that *The Times* has a crime editor. 'I wondered if you were able to make any comment or provide us with a statement in connection with widespread speculation that you were interviewed by police officers from Operation Yewtree this week?' As with all the others, I don't reply. And here come 'the others': at 15.45, Tom Morgan of *The Sun* is back again, claiming, 'Dear all, We are identifying Mr Gambaccini as a suspect in the

Operation Yewtree inquiry today. Please call urgently if you wish to make any clarification or statement.'

This time he is not faking. The *Sun* website names me later in the afternoon. A *Sun* tweet invites readers to go to the website for the scoop, but of course most of the people who do follow the link can't get through because of the newspaper's paywall. I envision these people all moving on to the BBC website, to the fury of News International.

The BBC goes with the story of my identification on its 6 p.m. newscasts. I know this not because I'm listening but because my friends inform me. I am sticking to my plan of not auditing the press. I know the accusations are false and do not wish to be reminded of them.

An ocean of supportive emails inundates my inbox. Friends with whom I am regularly in touch and some whom I have not seen in years send in their support. There is one last gasp from the tabloids, Mark Jefferies of the *Mirror* emailing at 18.10: 'Hi, Paul has now been named by the BBC as having been arrested as part of Operation Yewtree, please come back to me if you have any comment. Best regards, Mark Jefferies.' Well, hi to you too, Mark, and I don't. Best regards, Paul.

After the Jefferies email, no one from Grub Street bothers any more. The police have leaked my name to whomever they've leaked it to, *The Sun* has run it, the BBC has broadcast it, and there's nothing more to say until the next wave, should that ever roll in. The BBC issues its statement; my Scottsboro Boys statement and my lawyer's accompanying denial of accusations are released; and there is nothing more to say.

Tim Toulmin, the reputational PR from Alder Media, writes at 23.10:

> Just a little update about what has been going on in the media.
>
> In general, the statement has served its purpose. Almost all outlets have picked up either the thoughtful 'Scottsboro' statement or the more straightforward 'spokesman' statement. For example, Mail Online has printed your quote, while the BBC has opted for the drearier 'spokesman'

one, both online and in its 10 p.m. TV bulletin. The *Daily Mirror* is among those which published both statements. The bottom line is that your denial is everywhere.

There is a large amount of incredulity on social media that you could be accused of such things.

I have been in touch with managing editors, editors and heads of legal departments to let them have the statement personally, and particularly to draw attention to the bit that asks journalists to stop approaching you. This is to lay down a marker – if you are still being doorstepped in twenty-four hours we will have good grounds to circulate a more formal notice, after which point the problem should diminish.

Incidentally, this process has revealed a considerable degree of private sympathy for you. There is a lot of respect for you out there.

I have had a late conversation with *The Sun*. They are putting it on the front page but their focus is the BBC, which it accuses of a 'cover-up'. I will give you further insight, if you like, on the phone tomorrow. Best wishes,

Tim

Toulmin has obviously done his job to a T, or, as the original phrase went, 'to a tittle'. I can go to sleep knowing the Wapping worst is over.

---

2 NOVEMBER 2013

It appears that the BBC has played this one well. It has run the story early and prominently on what seems to be all networks, so it can never be accused of a cover-up, and then let it drop down the bulletins quickly. It is obvious they really do believe Yewtree are on to a loser with this one.

Christopher's parents arrive early in the morning on a pre-arranged visit from Norfolk. Rather than cancel because of the hostile circumstances, they show up to experience them first-hand. It is the first time they have ever walked a press gauntlet. Amusingly, the sentinels seem to have changed. The daily papers have had their bite, and the Sundays are now doing the stalking.

Chris's father Bill volunteers to cross the road to Waterloo Station to buy the papers. The rags have gone all out. I haven't had this many front pages since, er, I discussed Jimmy Savile on Radio 5 Live. But I am told this; I don't see them. I have decided that for the sake of my sanity I will not look at any British newspapers for the duration outside of the *Financial Times*. On Monday morning, Jennifer will act as my clipping service and put all relevant articles on the top shelf of my tallest closet, ensuring that I never see them, even by accident, until the case is over.

Tim Toulmin writes about 'a little update about where we are today'. He reports:

> A Sunday red-top editor called me last night at about midnight. He said he could tell from the way you had handled the matter that you were innocent. He very much liked your personal statement, which he contrasted favourably with people who make furious denunciations to TV cameras (who usually turn out to be guilty, he said). He predicted it would be a 24-hour wonder and that there wouldn't be too much in tomorrow's papers. He also had an insight into how the media got hold of your identity so quickly – and it wasn't from the police. I'll give you more detail when we speak next.
>
> Finally, the editor of *The Sun* has asked me to say that they would be delighted to interview you. I think I know what the answer will be, but I just thought I'd pass it on...

Good for Tim. Polite as well as perceptive.

The Sherwood family lunches at our place. The parents are joined by daughter Jennifer, oldest son Andrew and Christopher. Chris has not only been totally supportive, unquestioningly loyal and completely loving, he has been proactive on my behalf. He has researched solicitors who might represent me and run them past a QC friend of his, who sends him an email in praise of Kate Goold of Bindmans.

The barrister adds:

> Also if it gets to the stage where he needs Counsel (and I sincerely hope it does not), then I would suggest Mark Dennis QC, who was formerly Senior Treasury Counsel at the Old Bailey. I have known him since Bar School and he is one of the top criminal silks in the country.

The expression 'taking silk' is one that induces hilarity among Americans, who have no idea what it means in the British legal system. 'Taking silk' sounds like indulging in some sort of polite drug. However, if I have to go to court, I will be sure to be represented by someone who has taken silk.

---

3 NOVEMBER 2013

The visit from Christopher's parents concludes. It has brought the family together in an utterly unexpected way. It had initially taken his mother some time to come to terms with our relationship, but she is now completely behind us. She writes a beautiful note of support.

While Chris goes to the gym, my friend Christopher Simpson buys all the relevant Sundays. Jennifer will clip them tomorrow. Simpson is replaced around lunchtime by Malcolm Jeffries. They both know of my determination not to see the papers. Unfortunately, when I enter the dining room after a mid-afternoon nap, Malcolm has the *Sunday Times* open to a full-page story with the screaming headline 'BURN THE PAEDO!' He is reading about someone up north falsely accused of paedophilia who was killed by a lynch mob. This sends me over the edge for a few minutes. I take refuge by pounding the piano, but I can't disguise my anger. Malcolm has been my most constant friend and companion through the crisis, and I love him dearly, but everyone goofs up sometime, and this is his sometime. It takes about half an hour for me to calm down.

---

4 NOVEMBER 2013

And then there were none. Jennifer comes in for work and reports that all the reporters are gone. The dailies and Sundays have run everything they legally can and are off to harass somebody else.

I receive an email from Brad Spurgeon, the Canadian who stayed in my Hyde Park Square flat in the late 1970s.

Brad was an extraordinary young man, someone who had ambition and knew no fear. He had come from Canada to London to make a living even though the only two objects of quality he owned were a coffee machine and his ventriloquist's dummy, Peter. He had brought him over from Canada to do gigs in small clubs. Brad had no money and no guaranteed career, but he knew what he wanted to do and set about doing it. Today he has won the unofficial competition for the weirdest way of hearing of my problems.

'I hope all is OK,' he writes. 'I read the news of your situation while sitting in the business class of an Emirates flight back from Dubai today – paid for with my miles – in a bloody newspaper from New Zealand that I had picked up in the lounge!'

It occurs to me that Brad would be a perfect 'witness of fact' should my case go to trial. He was a teenager (or thereabouts) who actually lived with me while I was supposedly the worst pervert west of the Pecos. Bless him, he was so uncorrupted that he thought nothing of parading around the flat in his underwear. If I didn't react to an attractive male teenager who was actually in my apartment, I was hardly likely to go roaming next door looking for one.

Someone who wishes me well but fails to reassure me is a Dartmouth College radio colleague. Writing from his home in Pennsylvania, he says:

Recalling harsh words you spoke at your wedding celebration in New York (and relayed to me by Bill Aydelott), I instinctively sought out Murdoch's (remaining) London paper. I found the most glaring attempt to pillory someone – without actually committing libel – I had ever seen. I was immediately suspicious of the source ... A story from my realm reminds me just how dangerous this situation might be. Over a decade ago, the friend of a work associate (also in radio) identified a disadvantaged youngster from his neighborhood. Acting as an unofficial big brother, he occasionally invited the boy into his house to listen to music. He was later accused by the boy's mother of inappropriate conduct, and criminally charged. On the advice of his attorney, he pled guilty to minimise the risk of a long sentence. He wound up serving nine years in prison. I hope your circumstances allow you to immediately put this tale out of your mind! It is scary.

'Please let me know if there is anything I can do,' my old college friend concludes. Well, how about ... not telling me about people in similar situations going to jail?

---

5 NOVEMBER 2013

Christopher and I do something we never thought we would do in our lives. We audition solicitors.

We've taken recommendations from our friends and narrowed the selection down to two. The first arrives at 2.30. His is an extremely impressive mind, but he has three drawbacks for my personal case. First, he will be away on holiday for much of January and would not be able to report to Charing Cross Police Station with me on 8 January. Secondly, he is, no doubt justifiably, expensive. Finally, he is already representing another Yewtree suspect.

Kate Goold talks with Christopher and me for about an hour. The dynamic feels right. She is already representing David Miranda, the partner of journalist Glenn Greenwald, who was detained at Heathrow Airport for carrying documents related to the Edward Snowden revelations. This convinces me of Goold's bona fides.

It is pathetic that I have to consider finance, but I do. After all, my first visitor has estimated that if my case were to go all the way through a trial, the final bill might approach half a million pounds. Kate Goold is less expensive than him, which is to be expected of a younger woman. However, she is more talkative, so I suspect sheer word count might keep her meter running. Nonetheless, the dynamic is the key factor that makes me choose her. In a case which might euphemistically be called 'all-male', a female solicitor must be the way to go.

This evening I make my first outing since the siege began. Chris and I are having dinner with three friends from the 1970s, the actor Simon Jones and his wife Nancy, who as Nancy Lewis represented Monty Python in America, and Terry Gilliam. We opt for Mr Kong, my favourite Chinese restaurant, rather than go to a show-business hang-out with photographers loitering around the entrance.

Chris and I are greeted by Mr Kong staff as the regulars we are, with no hint they are aware I have just been smeared in all the papers. It is wonderful to be with old pals who do not need any convincing to be sure of my innocence. Nancy has always called Gilliam 'Terry G.', to distinguish him from fellow Python 'Terry J.', Terry Jones. Gilliam is both fascinated and incensed by everything we can offer him about the case. After all, this is a film director who so well depicted a dystopia in his classic *Brazil*.

'This is Kafka! This is Kafka!' he exclaims, and then explains. An iniquitous system demands that individuals be fed into it if it is to continue to exist. Once in, a person cannot escape until he has gone through it. I am going to have to endure months of mistreatment.

I tell him my case is straight out of the Soviet Union. He instinctively knows I am not exaggerating. In England in 2013, all that is required for a person to be denounced is to be denounced. Two people have denounced me, so I am denounced.

6–10 NOVEMBER 2013

This week is a blur. I spend almost all my time rebuilding my life in the aftermath of the Yewtree Technical Takeaway. I conclude that there is no point waiting for the return of my computer, which I have been told will take months. I have to buy a new one. Jennifer goes out and purchases a new iMac. We choose a new password for my email. I spend a good deal of time gathering important phone numbers and addresses, all lost to the police. I start loading a fresh iTunes selection from scratch.

I have long thought that society will have a temporary collapse when a major power outage shuts down all computers. Forget society, it has happened to me. The police have made me start my life all over.

Friends continue to nourish. My first friend in this country, my Oxford buddy Alastair MacGregor, invites me over to his London apartment. His wife, the actress Rosie Kerslake, cooks delicious food for Chris, myself and Mike and Joyce Smyth. It is not polite to gape with open mouths during a meal, but our dining mates cannot help their spontaneous reactions as we tell our tale of early-morning arrest and accusation.

I lunch with Malcolm Jeffries, I dine with Christopher Simpson. I eat with Andrew Fallaize on Saturday. On Sunday the 10th I have social visits from Darren Cheek, Keith, and Manchester friends Wes Butters and Letitia Cowan. That evening my husband and I go for a home-cooked meal at the house of Malcolm and his partner Coralie. We beat them at Scrabble. It is a perfect day: almost all of Team Gambo in twelve hours.

11 NOVEMBER 2013

Cycling in the gym, catching up on the weekend *Financial Times*, I read a column by Nigel Thomas, who quotes the British philosopher Peter Marshall: 'When we long for life without difficulties, remind ourselves that oaks grow strong in contrary winds and diamonds are made under pressure.' I silently promise to emerge from my ordeal as either the Hope Diamond or the Pontfadog Oak.

I have to cancel my attendance at an afternoon showcase of Nick Lloyd Webber's musical *The Little Prince* at the Savoy Theatre. This hurts, as I have known Nick since he was a nipper. Fortunately, he completely understands. Nick's show is one of many appointments I will have to miss because I am preparing my defence, should we ever go to trial. I spend hours every day mulling over and contacting possible relevant witnesses. I imagine strategies that would catch my accusers cold in court.

---

12 NOVEMBER 2013

Last week I experienced my first shun: being asked by a nearly hysterical host not to attend the launch of a book concerning *Top of the Pops*. I didn't mind not going, since I was only ever on the show three times as a presenter and on a couple of occasions as part of the full Radio 1 DJ team. I would have been on more often, but producer Michael Hurll, dividing the DJs into presenter pairs, teamed me with Mike Read, who cancelled our second appearance so he could keep a charity tennis commitment with Cliff Richard. A furious Hurll took us out of the rota.

The word 'surreal' is overused to describe events in one's life, but this one qualifies. Here I am, getting first an email from one host and then a communication from another begging me not to come to a party to which they have invited me. The tabloid press will be there, and photos of me might be taken that would damage the commercial potential of the book. Obviously these men have never heard Brendan Behan's observation: 'There's no such thing as bad publicity except your own obituary.'

Today, I am not only not uninvited – does that qualify as a triple negative? – but welcomed with open arms to a twenty-fifth anniversary gathering of Capital Gold DJs. I had been part of the original presenter team in 1988. Some of the warmest greetings are from former Radio 1 presenters who migrated to Gold when their days of presenting current material had passed. Paul Burnett is as witty as ever. Tony Blackburn and Andy Peebles are also supportive.

Tony Prince remembers our very first meeting when I came to Radio Luxembourg as a *Rolling Stone* reporter in 1971. Now, forty-two years later, he urges me to keep my strength.

What I don't expect is an approach from a DJ I don't know. Mike Osman breaks away from his former on-air team the Naughty Boys and wishes me well. He tells me that he was arrested by Operation Yewtree when they pulled in his pal Jim Davidson. Like the comedian, he eventually received word that 'no further action' would be taken against him.

'You will get the call when you don't expect it,' he explains. 'I got mine when I was on a beach in Spain on holiday with my wife. It will be the best day of your life.'

I'm embarrassed that, in all the publicity over Jim Davidson and his subsequent clearance, I missed the Mike Osman footnote. Here he is in front of me, and he is more than a footnote. He is a hero. He stood up to vilification for months and survived.

In the evening, Christopher and I go to the Wolseley for dinner with Derren Brown and Marc Hagan-Guirey. Derren has long been a renowned television and stage 'magician', if one can simplify his talents to one word, but Marc is also an artistic genius. He is the master, even if first in a field of one, of horrorgami, in which he takes a single sheet of paper and painstakingly constructs a famous building and set from a fright film. His show of spooky scenes sold out, my contribution being the purchase of his re-creation of Venice as depicted in *Don't Look Now*. Even the tiny woman is on set. Before going freelance, Marc worked at the advertising agency where Chris currently toils, so they have bound on that basis.

I tell Derren about the two men who claim to have been my lovers, even though I have never known them.

'Oh, I got that,' he relates.

There was a woman who thought we were married, to the point where she maintained a marital home. I never showed up and kept insisting we weren't married. She complained I was working too hard and never came home. One day she suddenly realised I wasn't her husband and she was really married to Antony Sher.

Those unfamiliar with the knighted actor Sher might be amused to know his spouse is actually the artistic director of the Royal Shakespeare Company, Gregory Doran. A less likely husband for Derren Brown's non-wife could scarcely be imagined.

So there's another possible witness: Derren Brown, living proof that fantasists follow celebrities.

---

13 NOVEMBER 2013

I am treated to lunch at the Delaunay by Elizabeth Dalkeith. This is more than just another of the social meetings we have been having for thirty-five years. It is a courageous show of support from Elizabeth, who as Liz Kerr worked for Radio 4 during the 1970s before marrying the Earl of Dalkeith (later the Duke of Buccleuch) in 1981. She is as willing as anyone to whom I have spoken to appear on my behalf as a 'witness of fact', should my case go to court.

As Julian Fellowes frequently reminds me, he and I both admired Liz in the late 1970s. I pursued my *Kaleidoscope* colleague romantically, a doomed chase since she was already psychologically committed to her future husband. Richard has always been quite friendly with me, although it isn't too difficult for a gentleman to be a gracious winner.

Like myself, Elizabeth, known for reasons I could never fathom as 'Bizzer' or 'Biz' to female friends, kept appointment diaries. Unlike myself, she still has hers, not having been victim to a police heist. She is willing to share her diary dates with my solicitor, proving that my romantic focus was indeed on her for a time, and to give a character reference.

Out of the blue, I receive a phone call from Nigel Evans. He has been given my number by the journalist Lesley-Ann Jones, who attended the Capital Gold reunion two days ago.

I met Nigel a couple of times in conjunction with the launch of the international gay rights charity the Kaleidoscope Trust. He is a different man today. He is as talkative as anyone I have ever known with the possible exception of Martin Scorsese. When I interviewed the outstanding film director, he had twice as much on his mind as he could physically say. It was frustrating watching a great artist speaking as rapidly as he could and yet still lagging behind his thought process.

Recently arrested and accused on several counts, forced to relinquish his position as Deputy Speaker of the House of Commons, Evans is manic. We have a twenty-minute conversation, during which I speak for two. He wants me to know what, based on his experience, lies in store for me.

'They will listen to every phone call you make,' he warns me. 'They will read every email. They will try to turn your Facebook friends against you.'

This sounds pretty extreme. He must be having a rough time. At least I got off Facebook months ago!

I go to Christopher's office in Soho to meet a blogger, John Ward. He formerly wrote for *The Guardian* but is now going to live in France as he writes for his blog The Slog. I give him the background on my case. He is not at all surprised that I don't know my accusers and don't even recognise their names. His overview of Operation Yewtree is pejorative. He knows and shares details about other cases that make me realise I'm not alone in feeling a victim of injustice.

In the evening, I go to the London Palladium for the opening night of Dame Edna Everage's farewell tour. Of course, it is Barry Humphries who is saying goodbye. He trots out a first half filled with characters from his decades of work. Some people only there to see Dame Edna are horrified by the grossness of Les Patterson, who has lived down to his usual standards. A few people are put off by an appearance of Sandy Stone, a 1950s creation of Humphries, who leads into the interval with serious as well as comic themes. I personally find his recollections of his deceased wife and daughter to be profoundly moving and horrifyingly honest: with Sandy preparing for death, Barry seems to be accepting his own inevitable, though hopefully not imminent, demise. When the curtain falls I feel I have witnessed Barry Humphries take comedy to the level of high art.

Michael Parkinson and his wife Mary, both of whom I worked with on TV-am in the 1980s, are present. Parky offers full support and inveighs against the current campaign against elderly entertainers. He had dinner with Jimmy Tarbuck last night and is horrified that he can't work in the current atmosphere.

---

18 NOVEMBER 2013

I call Amnesty International seeking to speak with its director. I could use a little moral support, and who better to turn to than Amnesty? After all, I have believed in and supported it for three decades, raising hundreds of thousands of pounds for it through organising two evenings at the London Palladium and two record albums. I also served on the committee that raised the funds for its current Shoreditch headquarters.

It was at one of the meetings of this committee that Harold Pinter gave me the most memorable image I have of this great playwright. Discussing fundraising possibilities, I mentioned that Elizabeth Taylor had generated substantial sums for Aids relief simply by attending dinner parties at which guests paid $10,000 each just to be in the same room with her.

'Who could have the same impact in Britain?' asked another committee member.

'The Spice Girls,' popped up a young supporter, dating this discussion as being circa 1998.

'I know one of the Spice Girls,' a helpful colleague joined in. 'I could ask.'

Harold, who had been listening to the conversation with a puzzled expression, finally spoke.

'Who are the Spice Girls?'

Today, the director of Amnesty is unavailable. An assistant promises to give her my message.

---

19 NOVEMBER 2013

I have my annual check-up with Dr Court. To my delight, I am given a clean bill of health. I have lost a kilo in the past year and have maintained low blood pressure.

'I don't know how you are coping with this,' he admits. 'If it gets too stressful, double your daily Seroxat,' which I currently take at the lowest possible dose.

I am offered an unexpected boost from Anna Ford. She takes me to lunch at a Japanese restaurant called Defune. I have known Anna since what must be the last half of the '70s, although she thinks it might have been 1980. My diaries will let me know if I ever get them back.

Anna recalls my telling her that I had gone celibate after my discovery of the New Disease, and is willing to testify to the same in court. This is potentially important, since I learned of what came to be known as HIV/Aids in mid-1983. I did not have sexual intercourse again until 1987, when we finally knew for certain how to avoid catching the deadly virus. Knowing what Anna is willing to testify would render Secondary's accusations of intercourse in late 1983 and 1984 manifestly false. Mind you, the police should know this by now anyway: I wrote all about this temporary sexual abstinence in my book *Love Letters*.

I lunch at the Wolseley as the guest of Jonathan Clyde of Apple Records. Jeremy King, co-owner of the venue, has not only given me his complete personal support, he has insisted I keep coming to the Rex group of restaurants rather than hole up at home.

Not a single person looks at me as if I am a pervert. I float the idea with Jonathan of asking Paul McCartney to supply a period character reference, since during the time frame in question Paul allowed me to be in the presence of his children, which this famous family man would never do if he suspected someone one iota. Jonathan thought that would be a reasonable request should matters ever go that far.

Melvyn Bragg comes over to lend his support. Perhaps I shouldn't call my decades-long friendly acquaintance 'Melvyn', perhaps I should say, as Wikipedia does, 'the Right Honourable the Lord Bragg FRS FBA FRSA FRSL FRTS'. Who in the 1970s would have guessed?

He suggests going public with an article in a broadsheet newspaper about the unfairness of being arrested without charge for a long period of time. Either *The Guardian* or the *Telegraph* would do. I am sorely tempted, but I am also aware that my solicitor feels I should stay out of the papers at a time when the bandwagon may still be rolling.

Melvyn assures me that support for me among those he knows is universal, but no one knows how to express this publicly or whether they should. I can't doubt them. I'm not sure yet, either.

I visit Chris at his office in Soho. I have been avoiding the British press, except for the *Financial Times*, but Chris feels I should see something. He draws my attention to an online story from the *Sun on Sunday*, repeating the weekend's print version. The rag has juxtaposed photographs of Max Clifford and me arriving at Barry Humphries's opening night at the London Palladium under the headline 'Here's to Yew'. The casual reader would assume Clifford and I know each other, which we do not.

The text relates to our arrests by Operation Yewtree:

> Operation Yewtree sex abuse suspects Max Clifford and Paul Gambac-
> cini arrive at the same star-studded bash.
>
> Showbiz guru Clifford, 70, and the BBC Radio 2 DJ, 64, were pay-
> ing tribute to funny man Barry Humphries in London's West End.
>
> Both were arrested by cops probing historical sex offences in the wake
> of the Jimmy Savile scandal. Humphries, 79 – best known as Dame
> Edna Everage – was launching his farewell tour.
>
> American Gambaccini was released on bail until January on suspi-
> cion of child sex offences.
>
> Clifford pleaded not guilty to eleven counts of indecent assault on
> seven alleged victims, 14 to 19.

I go through the roof. The Met has leaked again. On the day of my arrest
The Sun claimed to have heard of my arrest from 'eyewitnesses'. What
is their source this time? How would the *Sun on Sunday* have the confidence to report 'suspicion of child sex offences' unless the quote came
from the police or their recognised intermediary? The allegations against
me – that two men have accused me of overlapping four-year consensual
affairs when they were teenagers – have been reduced to as malevolent a
phrase as possible.

In the evening I attend the annual Radio 2 presenters' drinks party.
This used to be a yearly Christmas dinner until it got busted by the popular press for being an unnecessary licence fee payers' expense. Of course,
the money being wasted on my case by Operation Yewtree would pay for
more than a decade's worth of Radio 2 Christmas dinners, but why feed
us when you can arrest us?

The event was scheduled before I was arrested, but no one has suggested
I not attend. I walk in and feel the love. Only one person nods a hello
and slinks away and that is Terry Wogan. No wonder: he was the person most mentioned on the Twittersphere as being the '74-year-old man'
arrested with me. Actually, Wogan is seventy-five, but what's a year among

rumourmongers? Terry previously defended me most gallantly one year when Keith Allen told 'funny' sexual jokes about me at the Sony Awards, so I know his heart is true.

Graham Norton and Dermot O'Leary are the most supportive among the men and Clare Balding among the women, although everyone is kind.

'You've always been so open,' Graham says. I know what this is short-hand for. He means that because I was the only openly gay broadcaster of my generation, I would be the last person in the profession to have hidden secrets.

Johnnie Walker gets a point for honesty.

'Is there any truth to this at all?' he asks directly, showing both that he supports me and acknowledges that there might not be smoke without some fire. I assure him there isn't even a match. I tell him I don't know my accusers, and he believes me.

Tony Blackburn keeps saying, 'This is ridiculous … This is ridiculous.'

Chris Evans makes an unexpected, respectful and intelligent suggestion. He urges me not to accept any invitation to comment publicly on my situation.

'Don't give it heat,' he advises. 'Don't let this define the autumn of your life. I've been driving on Saturday evenings coming home from work, and I've been hearing the show. You're still the best, you're still the governor. Use this time to do something else and then come back. You've earned a break. Take it.'

His is the most articulate voice I have heard begging me to see this hiatus as an opportunity as well as a curse. I should do things I do not ordinarily have the time to do and trust that the future will somehow provide.

Anneka Rice is as loving as ever. I've known her so long this still-beautiful woman must have been five when we met. Whoops! I mustn't make jokes like that any more. Except, in this very dark time, black humour is the best kind. When you're falsely accused of forbidden behaviour, forbidden humour is the only kind that's equally absurd.

We then take the annual Radio 2 presenter photo. No one suggests I move aside, and Janice Long courageously stands next to me. As I am about to leave, Richard Allinson engages me. He is holding it together, but I can see he is devastated, shattered by shock that this could happen and that his country has fallen so low.

Richard and I are about to leave when controller Bob Shennan announces the live entertainment. It is The Feeling! I can't walk out on my old friend Dan Gillespie-Sells, nor his bandmate Richard. To my delight, they deliver an intelligent and first-rate twenty minutes. Afterwards Danny and I catch up, which is hard to do the first time you're talking to someone after you've been arrested. But he reveals only the slightest awkwardness, not over doubting my innocence but over the horror of the subject matter.

I leave saying my goodbyes, knowing they may actually be farewells. Whether or not this is the last time I attend a Radio 2 presenters' gathering is up to neither me nor the executives. It is up to the police and, pray we don't go this far, a jury.

Someone at the party has told me that Richard Littlejohn wrote a good piece about Jim Davidson in the *Daily Mail*. I haven't read any press about Yewtree since my arrest, but anything encouraging is worth seeing. I have often disagreed vehemently with Littlejohn's views, particularly on matters relating to homosexuals, but it turns out that this time he gets it. He believes Davidson has been falsely accused and isn't afraid to say so:

> Davidson was quizzed about an incident alleged to have taken place twenty-five years ago. He has always maintained his innocence, but has been on bail for eight months while the police attempted to build a case against him.
>
> His house in Hampshire, where he had lived for only a year, was searched from top to bottom, his computer confiscated and sacks of 'evidence' taken away.
>
> What the hell did they expect to find in relation to an alleged sexual

assault purported to have occurred a quarter of a century ago? This was just another fishing expedition.

The investigation even spread to the Falkland Islands, where Davidson entertained the troops in the '80s. That line of inquiry is apparently still active. This week, however, Davidson was told that he would face no further action over allegations that he sexually assaulted ten women.

Where did all these allegations come from? Davidson insists that he was initially interviewed about a single complaint, which he categorically denied.

From the moment detectives decided to widen the Jimmy Savile inquiry, I have been expressing concern that the entire operation was turning into a deranged witch hunt.

Littlejohn's courage is amazing. He has spoken truth to power and called Yewtree what it is.

One photo accompanying the article freezes me in my tracks. There, in the dark of night, carting off a brown bag of 'evidence' is one of my case officers. Is this man opening an Apple Store?

Before we go to bed, Christopher tells me he has discovered the meaning of the beautiful, loving cards recently sent to me by his sister's daughter, our niece Megan. It turns out that the six-year-old heard news reports of my arrest and started crying. Her mother explained to her that nasty men had been bad to me and were saying unkind things. Making the cards was her way of turning sorrow into beauty.

---

21 NOVEMBER 2013

I wake up angry. This is bad for my body. I occupy the morning with tasks unrelated to my case in a successful attempt to calm down.

I converse with Tasmin, the press expert at Bindmans. She feels the *Sun on Sunday* have used grossly unfair tactics but may be legally protected.

For now, she writes to them insisting on a couple of rephrases in the surviving online article. Calm down, she advises. This is not the time for further action.

I worry about Amnesty International. It has been four days and I have had no return call.

I have also not yet heard from Stonewall. It is Britain's leading gay rights group. I would have thought it would be keenly interested in my case.

I feel a particular connection to Stonewall since I helped arrange its initial funding in 1989. I was excited when Ian McKellen told me about the organisation, which he was founding with four other activists.

'Do you know how we could get some funding?' he asked.

'Have you asked Elton?' I instinctively replied, knowing my pop star friend to be the most generous man I have ever met and a keen supporter of charities close to his heart.

'No,' Ian replied. 'Can you arrange it?'

I called John Reid, then Elton's manager, to arrange a dinner at his house at which the two of them would meet McKellen and another Stonewall co-founder, Michael Cashman. After a pleasant meal, financial matters were dealt with quickly.

'Tell us about Stonewall,' Reid asked. McKellen and Cashman gave the details.

'How much do you need?' the host queried.

'£100,000,' Ian replied.

'I can give £50,000,' John Reid said.

'I can give the other £50,000,' Elton John said.

After dinner, when we were in Reid's long driveway, I never saw two happier men than Ian McKellen and Michael Cashman. Stonewall was up and running.

I can't expect younger men and women to be interested in this kind of history, but I personally feel attached to Stonewall. I have supported it through the years. I am disappointed it does not show me any support now.

Today, I learn that Richard Godfrey still works at MTV, but I cannot get a reply on his phone number. As I reach out in my mind to persons who might be able to offer relevant supportive testimony on my behalf, I think of Richard, who lived in my Hyde Park Square building while a teenager and met both Sixteen and myself. He would state that I was not predatory towards him, that he had not heard of me being a manipulator of persons his age, and had only been helpful to him with career advice. I'm pleased that Godfrey went on to become a leading producer of live music television events.

It is frustrating that I can't get in touch immediately with people who might be helpful in my fightback. The *New York Times* does offer some cheer, however. The Scottsboro Boys have received posthumous pardons!

———————————— 22 NOVEMBER 2013 ————————————

Today is the anniversary of President Kennedy's assassination. Everyone of my generation knows what they were doing when they heard the news.

I was in the first term of my years at Staples High School. We were in the Friday afternoon X period, the time of the week during which each homeroom performed administrative formalities. This week we were getting yearbook photographs taken in the gymnasium. One by one, the homerooms were called to the gym. My homeroom consisted of students with surnames beginning with 'G'.

At the beginning of the X period, Principal Stanley Lorenzen announced over the loudspeaker system that shots had been fired at the presidential motorcade in Dallas. Governor Connolly had been hit but the President had been spared. Minutes later, he amended his initial announcement to report that Kennedy had been injured after all.

In a few more moments, we heard the fatal news. Lorenzen announced that the President was dead.

'Why do they always kill the great ones?' Mary Ann Golden howled in anguish.

'Well,' said class conservative Bob Gerrity, 'only history will judge whether he was great.'

'Oh, Bob,' admonished Sue Gillen. 'Don't you know when to shut up?'

So began our week of national mourning. If I close my eyes, my mother is racing out of the house, calling me to the television set.

'They've shot Oswald!'

She and my father had witnessed the broadcast of Jack Ruby killing Lee Harvey Oswald, the first live murder in American television history. Now that I, too, was in front of the TV, CBS News, in what seemed a gesture of personal consideration to me, broadcast the first instant replay ever, spooling back to show the shooting again.

We watched, and watched, and saw hours of our fellow Americans being equally miserable. Even when school resumed the following week, our Spanish teacher was so broken up he was unable to present lessons, letting us have a study period instead.

This year, producer Kevin Howlett and I had prepared a Radio 4 programme of music recorded in reaction to the death of JFK. It will go unaired until I am cleared.

Someone who had not been born in 1963, the Coventry broadcaster Johnny Rickard, drops by and tells me that 'everybody knows' that Yewtree is part of the battle between Rupert Murdoch and the BBC. Why else would a large number of BBC stars be arrested with the Murdoch press urging the police on? I find myself thinking that if 'everybody knows' it, it would help if somebody wrote about it.

I feel quite relaxed after a gym session and then have dinner with a friend in Carluccio's. My sense of calm goes over the Waterloo Station balcony outside the restaurant when he tells me that his female friend working in child counselling says it's too bad for me, but Operation Yewtree will help abused persons come forward.

I am outraged at her ignorance and insensitivity. Even with my dear friend, I lose my temper and go into a tirade. Before the witch-hunt, the vast majority of persons claiming they had been abused were telling the truth. There was little motivation for someone to make a false accusation. Now money and publicity had been offered by the government and police and, human nature being what it is, some people were making accusations for money and publicity. Yewtree will set the cause of the abused back ten years, as the public comes to think that many accusers are chancers and fantasists.

This is a terrible moment. My friend and I love each other deeply, but at this moment we are ten miles apart.

─────────────── 24 NOVEMBER 2013 ───────────────

I watch the Joseph Welch moment again on YouTube. This is when the attorney dared defy the high-flying Senator Joseph McCarthy. I had seen it on television when I was five years old. I didn't recall they were at the same table, only feet apart. Nor did I remember that the congressional hearing burst into spontaneous applause at the end of Welch's remarks, live on national TV. It was the turning point in the Red Scare of the early '50s. I wait for our Joseph Welch moment in the fight against Operation Yewtree.

PR executive Gary Farrow, whom I have known for forty years, sends an email with a subject heading but no text. The heading is 'Nice piece bt Terry Gilliam in today's *Sunday Mirror*'. Does 'bt' mean 'by' or 'about'? Passing Holborn Station on our way to our weekly bowling at All Star Lanes, I glimpse the *Mirror*. The front page carries a story about how an encounter with a 'BBC star' led to suicide! I give the paper a pass. At least I enjoy a four-bagger (four consecutive strikes) during the bowling.

We have lunch with my old friend Keith. He has been approached by Officer Two from Yewtree and will be interviewed on Tuesday. The policeman asked if he was surprised by the call. Keith replied with words to the effect of, 'No, you've got thirty-eight years of Paul's diaries, and I'm in over half of them.' (Actually, we've known each other for nineteen years.) We have no idea what might have precipitated the interview request, since Keith was a lodger of mine for five years or so between the years 1997 to 2003, well outside the period of inquiry. My guess is that the police might suspect he knows one of my accusers from a pub, but I don't have any real idea.

Finally, a leading executive of Amnesty International returns my phone calls of last week.

'I don't expect you to take up my case,' I tell her, 'but I think you should know about it.'

I detail the fiasco I face. Several times I hear her say, 'Hmmm.' She does a lot of hmmm-ing.

'I'll check my diary and come back to you with dates for next week,' she promises.

In the evening, the television programme maker Rhys Thomas calls from New York City. He wants me to know he has just had a shouting match with a BBC executive. The Beeb wants to drop me from the forth-coming series *The Life of Rock with Brian Pern*, even though I have already filmed and been paid for my contribution. The BBC feels it needs not to be associated with me until I am cleared. Thomas is furious at this edito-rial interference, but can do nothing about it. He wants me to know he will continue to fight for me and will reinstate me in the programme if it is repeated later in 2014.

I have given the BBC forty years of service. If they distance themselves from me now, an obvious consequence will be that we are distant from each other. I may or may not return to radio, but I will never again feel as close to the BBC as I did for decades.

Although I am annoyed by my exclusion from *The Life of Rock with Brian Pern*, I am furious at my excision from the ITV show *The Nation's Favourite Elvis Song*. I have received an email from the production com-pany thanking me for my contribution and telling me that I will be pleased to hear that the programme will be transmitted soon. In keeping with my stated preference that I would rather not be on air at this time, I have been removed from the show.

I am staggered by the presumption and cowardice behind this decision. I phone Jimmy Tarbuck, realising that he actually met Elvis in his lifetime.

'Jimmy, you won't believe it,' I tell him. 'ITV have cut me out of a programme about Elvis.'

'I do believe it,' he replies. 'They've cut me out of the same programme.'

It's a good thing I'm lying down during this conversation or I would fall over. ITV have cut two men who have not been charged with anything out of the same show! I make a mental memo to award ITV the Tiny Testicles of 2013 prize when this is all over.

---

25 NOVEMBER 2013

Kid Jensen and I have lunch. He may be David Jensen to today's radio listeners, but he'll always be 'Kid' to me. Our meal at Mr Kong's is excellent, but his fond greeting is more important. My former Radio 1 colleague is intuitively sure of my innocence and offers to be a period character reference if necessary. Kid and his family spent time living in Hyde Park Square during the '70s, so he could be a relevant witness should we have to go to court.

---

26 NOVEMBER 2013

The doorbell rings at 8.45. I know what it probably is. John the concierge promised yesterday to bring in his copy of the 24 November *Sun on Sunday*, in which Terry Gilliam had spoken in my defence. It's probably John with the newspaper, which Gary Farrow had misidentified as the *Mirror*.

Chris, however, is unaware of this. His immediate thought is that it's probably the police again. He rushes upstairs, dreading another encounter with the fuzz. He asks for voice identification and is relieved when it is, in fact, John.

The concierge has come through, and so, bless him, has Terry. 'Cops'

Yewtree witch hunt is like something from Soviet era', is the headline, probably the truest header *The Sun* has ever run. Terry has laid into the police with his customary brio.

'This is not unlike life in the former Soviet Union,' he is quoted as saying, although his remarks have probably been simplified and edited to make them as punchy as possible. 'It's civilisation based on victimisation – and that makes everyone in the public eye a potential target.'

The interview is being run as part of a series called 'Stars of Monty Python', but Terry is clearly as interested in talking about other subjects as the reuniting group.

'Paul is a close friend of mine who I have known for years,' he reportedly states.

> In his case the police came at 4.30 a.m. They took everything. He's been
> suspended from the BBC – you're guilty until proven innocent.
>
> Now he's got a year ahead with no work or anything. His next year
> is going to be a living hell and it's going to cost him a lot of money.

Terry makes a point that is relevant for the entire society: 'I want to say outrageous things because nobody's making fun of this. There's a timidity out there because people are frightened.'

All these quotes are, of course, the copyright of the *Sun on Sunday*. I should tip my hat to the reporter Dan Wootton, who has captured Terry's spirit well.

Not everything turns out well today. A deputy editor of the *Panorama* programme comes to the flat for a two-hour conversation. The flagship BBC public affairs programme is considering doing a show on Yewtree, presented by the award-winning Chris Rogers. To do or not to do *Panorama*? I am favourably inclined going into the meeting and absolutely terrified coming out. In an attempt to do her due diligence, the deputy editor asks me if I 'fancied' seventeen-year-old Chris Rogers when I first met him in the TV-am building. 'I know you did not have sex, but did you fancy him?'

I am completely floored by this. I tell her that I did not go to the TV-am building to pick up, I went to the TV-am building to appear on TV-am. Besides, I always followed the informal US Army slogan I learned from my Oxford friend Jack Zoeller: 'Never within five miles of the fort.'

OK, perhaps not Chris, but could I ever have had sex with someone under the legal age of consent?

What is this inquisition? I thought the point of recording *Panorama* as my case went along was to support my case, not to be grilled as if in the dock.

Kate Goold calls and recommends against the *Panorama* project. The police, if they heard of the surreptitious recordings, might demand all footage. I could make an off-the-top-of-the-head factual error that could be used against me. I might unintentionally contradict something I had said in my police interview.

There is another sinister possibility. The broadcast of the *Panorama* show after my case had been dropped might raise the ire of the police, who might return with new allegations. It is also possible the programme might inspire a few unstable viewers to make fresh accusations.

What a difference a day makes! I began today thinking I was going to do episodic cinema verité for *Panorama*. I've ended the day preferring to walk on gilded splinters.

---

27 NOVEMBER 2013

Chris Rogers's associate Marshall calls concerning the *Panorama* programme, trying to talk me into it. I refer him to Kate, whose objections I consider convincing. I know that Chris and Marshall mean only well, but I can't put myself in a position where the police might use my activities against me. It is difficult trying to convey to even friends what it is like having the full weight of the state against you with their unlimited financial resources.

Chris is so fired up about his possible project it is hard for him to accept it might hurt me. Objectivity usually means presenting both sides of a story. The problem with this in my case is that there is no legitimate 'other side'. What I have to say is true. What my accusers and the police have to say is not. I can't give them 'the oxygen of publicity'.

––––––––––– 28 NOVEMBER 2013 –––––––––––

Liz Kershaw, a BBC Radio colleague, posts me the Ministry of Justice guidelines for questioning a mentally ill person. I still don't know whether my accusers are liars looking for a payday, fantasists who believe I was their long-term lover, or distressed individuals – although I'll never know why it hasn't occurred to them they would probably have been jealous of each other if I had been the partner of both of them simultaneously, as their accusations allege.

Kershaw was the first person to introduce me to the mutation of the British legal system Operation Yewtree represents. Two weeks before I was arrested, she rang me in disbelief to tell me that she had been phoned by the Metropolitan Police to ask if she would like to make an accusation against Dave Lee Travis.

'No,' she replied. 'Don't you need evidence?'

'No,' she quoted the officer. 'We only need people who agree.'

Later in the morning we have the first meeting of the Ivor Novello Awards committee since my arrest. I am deeply moved that I am surrounded by love and total support. Lily Allen is particularly shocked, since she had missed the news entirely. Tom Robinson is so furious he suggests I get David Hare to write a play about it. He points out that this is the kind of present-tense subject matter Hare has excelled in between his more conventional dramas.

When I get home, I have further reason to smile. *Who's Who 2014* has arrived and I'm still in it! It will be interesting to see how long that lasts.

After lunch with host John Miskelly at the Ivy, I announce I am going up to MTV to track down Richard Godfrey, formerly of Hyde Park Square. I tell Colin Bell, John's other guest, that I am assuming my alter ego of private investigator.

'It's cheaper that way,' Colin says.

Miskelly offers to introduce me to the human rights champion Helena Kennedy QC. We'll see if that happens.

I Google Helena and learn that she is also known as Baroness Kennedy of The Shaws. What in heck are The Shaws? British titles have always baffled me. Liz Dalkeith is one of my oldest friends, but I never know what her title is at any given time. She has been a lady, a marchioness and a duchess. Call back tomorrow to see what she is then.

I get onto the Northern Line to go to Camden Town. It has been a week since I left my first message for Richard Godfrey, now an executive with MTV, and I have been disappointed that he has not gotten back to me. The receptionist had told me his extension was broken, meaning he might not be getting his messages, so I decide the direct approach might be best.

I walk past Camden Market. It is to preserve this open-air bazaar that the local council decided not to accept the offer of London Transport to build a superstation at Camden Town, where the two branches of the Northern Line meet. I'm proud of how the arrival of TV-am boosted the area.

I enter our old building. MTV and its sister companies now occupy what had in the early 1980s been purpose-built breakfast television offices and studios. It was an architectural triumph, given an unorthodox seal of approval when I interviewed Grace Jones in what was then the sumptuous foyer. I had feared the assignment, given that she had recently thumped Russell Harty on BBC One, but she was all sweetness and light, loving everything about the building from the egg cups on the roof to the sweeping spaces inside.

This afternoon I get no further than the new reception area, because

Richard Godfrey is not in. At least I am given his mobile number and am allowed to leave a note for him. I return home to the South Bank and leave a message on his phone.

Within an hour he calls! It appears the police have not contacted him. He has been in Los Angeles, supervising the Video Music Awards, which explains why he has not returned my call.

Richard is horrified by news of my situation. He recalls the years in which he lived in Hyde Park Square, although it would be more strictly accurate to say that his parents lived there while he attended university. Nonetheless, he calculated that he was eighteen when the family moved in and confirms that I never approached him in any sexual way.

Richard has only fond memories of our association. More to the point, he agrees that, if I had been conducting years-long relationships with two underage boys, he or his family would have noticed it. Godfrey enthusiastically offers to appear as a witness on my behalf, should the matter ever go to trial, and asks me to let him know if there is anything else he can do.

After dinner it's back to Junior G-Man mode! I visit the long-term home of Jerry Rush, the Regent's Park Softball Club teammate who arranged for me to get the Hyde Park Square flat back in 1976. I have not seen him for years, and have only confirmed by Googling business records that he still resides in his old apartment near Marble Arch. I don't have a past or present phone number for him – how could I, since the police took my thirty-eight years of diaries and all my address books? – so have to pilgrimage in person. Will he still be living with his mother, his sister Maddy and nephew Lee? Will his mother still be living? I am about to find out.

Maybe not. There is no reply to the doorbell. I had been so preoccupied with what I would say to the Rush family upon reintroduction that it hadn't occurred to me that they might not be home – all, some or one of them. Just when I'm about to go away, a voice comes over the intercom. It is Maddy! I am admitted and climb the stairs to their apartment, just as I did over a quarter of a century ago.

Before she phones Jerry to let him know I am visiting, Maddy informs me that there has been a recent death in the family. It is not Mother, who is now ninety years old and still going on her long walks. Maddy's son Lee has died from brain cancer that spread to the spine. He was only forty.

I am horrified. Lee had been an unofficial mascot on our softball team when he was about eight. He had become a leading lawyer on the Cayman Islands before passing away two years ago. Lee was the first person I knew who liked rap. I gave him my copy of Ice-T's 1988 album *Power*, and he loved it.

Now I am in the presence of a still-grieving mother, pouring out the story of her son's life and death and how the spirit survives, must survive, the passing of the body. Maddy tells how she received a signal from her son on the second anniversary of his death, and I let her relate the story in detail.

She finally calls Jerry. He is ten minutes away and will be home as soon as possible. It turns out that two representatives from Yewtree have been to see him. Maddy assures me, 'We told them how much we love you, how much we respect you!' and then goes into her own theory. Many people who make irresponsible accusations are mentally ill, she says, and I must engage a qualified expert who can judge how sick these two men are. She can get me in touch with a specialist if I wish.

Jerry returns. He is simply an older example of my teammate. I wouldn't be surprised if he could wear many of the same clothes. He is still a vigorous businessman, always promoting and devising new products, and is now enthused about a tracking device that would make sure parents never lose track of their children nor farmers their beasts.

We naturally start with the loss of Lee. Grief is thick in the air. The past is still alive and well – ninety-year-old Mother sleeps soundly upstairs – but the future of the family has been lost. The natural order has been inverted.

Rush explains that the police did interview him politely, assuring him that they were treating the case even-handedly. He informed them he had his reservations about that, but submitted to questioning. He remembered having obtained the Hyde Park Square flat for me. He also told them about Dale, his girlfriend, my lodger, now a woman living in Melbourne. Her surname is Witton, not Winton! No wonder I was confused.

Jerry and I part in the street as I head for Marble Arch Tube Station and he goes to his car. I express once again my love for Lee. Jerry and I vow to meet again, but we have lost all of our innocence. The carefree days of 1970s softball are history.

---

30 NOVEMBER 2013

My Saturday routine has been altered by the fact that I no longer have an evening radio show, but I still get up to the *New York Times* crossword puzzle. Famously, Saturday is the most difficult day of the week. Monday is the easiest, then things get harder until New Yorkers tear out measurable amounts of their hair on Saturday.

I go to dinner with Tony King, Charlie Lycett and his wife Niki de Metz. I show them my 'disclosure statement'. They are appalled. They are beyond appalled. I was present at Charlie's baptism. He has known me all his life. He cannot believe anyone would try to smear me in such a fashion. Tony, the only person to work with the Beatles, the Rolling Stones and Elton John, is also horrified. He, however, shows that he could have been a solicitor if he had not gone into the music business.

First, he advises me to lay low until either I am charged or the case is dropped. He knows the 'bandwagon effect' is real, and feels it is best for my name to remain out of the news during a period when the police hope further accusers will come forward. If I were to speak out, it might bring more distressed persons out of their closets. This is precisely the advice I have received from my solicitor, who keeps calming me down when I want to take the public initiative.

Secondly, Tony makes a sage observation. He notes that both accusers limit their supposed acts of sex to when they were between fourteen and seventeen. What happened the day they turned eighteen? An outbreak of boredom? Did they fall out of love with me? Or has someone told them that in 2013 the police are not prosecuting men who had sex with persons between the ages of eighteen and twenty-one in the 1980s?

I award Tony King his honorary law degree and return home, realising that I really do have to work on anger management. Tonight, I am furious.

<hr />

1 DECEMBER 2013

My old friend the journalist Nick Wapshott writes in his *Newsweek* blog an article called 'Leonard Bernstein's False Confession to a Crime He Did Not Commit'. It concerns McCarthyism in America in the early 1950s, mentions that the all-time great artist Paul Robeson was forced into retirement, and concludes with a quotation from Voltaire's *Candide*: 'Even in those cities which seem to enjoy the blessings of peace, and where the arts flourish, the inhabitants are devoured by envy, cares and anxieties, which are greater plagues that any experienced in a town when it is under siege.' I send an email inviting Nick to get in touch.

Boy, does he get in touch. We have a 45-minute call, with his wife Louise Nicholson listening on the speakerphone. Nick twice refers to my situation as 'wretched' and is completely sympathetic, although we agree that neither he nor any other supporter should write an article for Reuters, *Newsweek* or anyone else until I have been charged or the case has been dropped.

Nick and Louise knew me in the full 1978–84 period. Yewtree have me reliving this era as thoroughly as any oldies radio station.

Deborah Gelston emails from Baltimore, where she has taken her son Andrew back to university. She reports that a Yewtree detective has been in contact to interview her in New York. I am vaguely amused that he will see Deborah before I will, bearing in mind that the Met still has my passports.

I send late-night emails to my old friendly acquaintance Brian Paddick and my solicitor Kate Goold. In Googling Brian's current activities, I am startled to discover he is now Baron Paddick. Is this some sort of Wikipedia prank by the kind of web writers who specialise in inserting shocking information into biographical entries? No, it turns out that on 1 August 2013, Brian was named 'the Lord Paddick, Baron Paddick of Brixton'.

───────── 2 DECEMBER 2013 ─────────

I write a handwritten letter to my University College friend Karl Marlantes. In the autumn of 1970, Karl was my first philosophy tutorial partner. We studied under John Mackie. Karl was a few years older than I, having served in Vietnam. Although we rarely talked about his experiences there, I learned enough to know that his life had been changed forever. He struggled for thirty years to write a novel based on his stint there.

Marlantes was no mere foot soldier. The website of the *Atlantic* magazine reports that Karl was awarded 'the Navy Cross, the Bronze Star, two Navy Commendation medals for valour, two Purple Hearts and ten Air Medals'. When he finally finished his novel, which he called *Matterhorn*, he became the oldest first-time author to make the top ten of the *New York Times* bestseller list.

Karl has sent me a clipping from *The Present Age* by Kierkegaard, addressing it to Danger Dog. (He has called me this ever since 1970, when we cracked up over one of those semi-literate headlines in *The Sun* where a noun is used as a qualifier in the way Americans only use adjectives.) Yes, there aren't many friends who send you excerpts from nineteenth-century Danish philosophers, but what's the point of studying PPE (Philosophy, Politics and Economics) together if you can't share the occasional burst of Kierkegaard?

The reading suggests that the toughest of challenges makes a man only tougher.

Karl writes:

> Danger Dog,
> Kierkegaard is always at odds with 'conventional wisdom', which would
> hold that no one in their right mind would want to go through what
> is happening to you. Still, I think he's right in this case – and send it to
> you as perhaps some solace. The dogs of the public have been unleashed
> on Danger Dog – but Danger Dog is the biggest dog in the fight and
> can only grow bigger because of it.

What a sympathetic soul Karl proves himself to be yet again! I write to
him: 'Who says PPE does not prepare one for life? Your letter concerning
Kierkegaard inspires me. I appreciate it so much.'

Just as I am filing Karl's correspondence in the Yewtree Support file, I
receive a welcome email from Kate Goold.

'Your Hyde Park Square flatmate called me this morning,' she writes.
'He wants to express his best wishes and support for you. I will fill you in
on Wednesday but I had a relatively brief conversation where he did all
the talking, but it was productive and informative.'

This means the world to me. Nigel Evans had warned me that the
police would try to turn old friends against me, but one of the best has
stayed steadfast.

My brother Philip tells me his entire side of our family will be having a reunion over Christmas in New York and Connecticut. New Yorker
brother Peter will be there as well. Phil encourages me to come over to
see his new granddaughter, my great-niece Emilia. I will have to petition
Yewtree to ease my bail conditions for the Christmas period to allow me
to attend the reunion, but I am certainly called to New York.

In the days before I bought my own New York apartment in 1997, I
often stayed at my old friend Deborah's place in New York. She, husband
Philip Gelston and children Laura and Andrew were usually at their New

Hampshire home during Christmas and summer holidays, when I was most likely to be in New York. I call, and she extends an invitation to stay again this time, although her family will be away at the time. And she gives me some news. A detective has indicated to her that he will be flying to America at some point between mid-December and mid-January to interview her in New York and Moscow Paul in Los Angeles. Indeed, Paul has already been tracked down and talked to on the phone.

I am floored by the efficiency and expense account of Yewtree. I had no idea where 'Moscow' now is, but they have found him. Now they will visit him in California, something I have never done. Mention of 'mid-January' is the killer tip-off that the 8th of the month will not be the end of my case. I really can expect to be in legal limbo for some time to come.

---

3 DECEMBER 2013

I delay breakfast until meeting Brian Paddick at 10 a.m. at Le Pain Quotidien next to the Royal Festival Hall. This gives me time for a long letter to Dermot O'Leary, who has inquired about my well-being, and a phone conversation with Malcolm Jeffries.

Brian and I order our breakfasts. I go for my Le Pain usual of orange juice, pain au chocolat and regular hot chocolate. He goes for a pain au chocolat and a coffee. I realise I am about to consume more calories than he is, and grimace.

Lord Paddick intuitively senses that I have been wronged. But he tells me that under the British legal system, the police are expected to arrest anyone accused of an offence by two different people. I lodge my by-now-familiar complaint that Secondary and Primary are not two different people in the way that someone from Hull and another person from Taunton would be. They are lifelong friends with intersecting minds, who have had three dozen years to come up with a story about me. Paddick understands, but repeats that the police were correct to arrest me.

What he does bemoan is that the public do not understand how little ignominy should be attached to the mere act of being arrested. There is no assumption of guilt and no charge. It is newspapers that blow up an arrest into a major legal event, and they who should be criticised. Perhaps the public should be educated into the intricacies of its own legal system.

Baron Paddick suspects that my entire case stems from my accusers' knowledge that I lived in the same building as my co-accused. We cannot guess whether Primary holds a grievance against Sixteen and is using me to get at him or whether he is claiming knowledge of Sixteen to get at me. Paddick concurs that it is particularly creepy that their accusations require that I enter the flat of another person and his partner and foul their nest by having sex in their bed with third parties. Neither Brian nor I are familiar with a sexual pathology in which a man walks into his neighbours' house and has sex in their bed with someone else.

I inform Brian of the grisly suggestion of a threesome with Secondary and Sixteen. He is repulsed by the accusation. Trying to imagine such a scenario, I mentally return to Kate Goold's recent question of whether I had any distinctive physical characteristics that would be noticed by any-one who saw me naked. If my accusers could not cite an obvious feature that I could display in a courtroom, a juror would probably conclude they had not been with me. Christopher and I have gone over my entire body and concluded that I have no such trait, which is, in this sense, a bit of a disappointment.

And then I see a mental Polaroid. I am on a golf course in 1980 mak-ing the difficult decision to shave off my beard.

OMG, as the social media generation would put it. There must be photographs from the late '70s in which I have my beard. If I can present some of those to a courtroom after Secondary and Primary have denied that I had a beard when they met me, it would be game, set and match.

The baron must fly. He has to catch a train to meet his siblings to discuss the estate of his mother, who has just passed away. What a generous man he has been, giving me his time while mourning the death of a parent.

I rush home and ask Jennifer to go through all my old photo albums to isolate pictures of me with a beard. It turns out there are tons of them. We also have a 1977 calendar showing me with a moustache and a 1980 version with a beard. We will have to track down the 1978 and 1979 versions, but there is enough to elate me. Can we get Secondary and Primary to swear that I was clean-shaven when I was in fact bearded? It is one of the several possible scenarios in which their case dissolves in seconds that keep me going.

Chris Rogers, my old friend from the TV-am building, calls, hoping to resuscitate my interest in doing a *Panorama* programme. He senses my indifference. In my situation, my focus is constantly moving, and *Panorama* is so last week.

---

4 DECEMBER 2013

Jennifer and I execute a £40,000 transfer from one bank account to another to cover legal fees already incurred and those expected in the near future. That's more than I've been paid for all the episodes of *Counterpoint* I've ever hosted put together.

To look forward rather than backward, I ask Kate Goold to contact the Metropolitan Police and ask if I can make a Christmas trip to New York. It is important I see the new baby in the family. I had an Italian great-uncle named Emilio. Coincidentally, this baby's parents have named her Emilia.

It seems so debasing that I have to ask the police permission to visit the city of my birth. In a separate conversation with Kevin Howlett, he asks helpfully if I should go abroad for a while to reduce my stress levels. When I tell him the police have both my passports, he is in shock.

I meet old friend Ivan Massow. I have known Ivan since he lived in a squat, since when he has been on a roller-coaster of financial and political triumphs and setbacks. He is still wondering whether he should run for Mayor of London as a Conservative. Today, however, he is thinking of something else. After treating me to lunch at Scott's, he urges me to spread a disinformation campaign about my penis on social media. My accusers or their representatives monitoring Facebook and Twitter will pick this up and, should my case go to trial, repeat it in a courtroom. I can then reveal that it is false, proving that they are unfamiliar with my body.

This is the kind of strategy I would have loved to see in an episode of *The Defenders* when I watched TV as a boy, but it is not one I wish to try in my own adulthood. Ivan tries his hardest to convince me, but I turn him down politely.

It is a day of fabulous food. In the evening, Christopher and I go to the Wolseley with Alice Arnold and Clare Balding. We tell my broadcasting buddies about the story Derren Brown had related in the very same restaurant only a few feet away, the one about the woman who was so convinced she had married the magician that she maintained a family home. Clare goes into an extended narration about her own troubles with an unwelcome admirer.

---

5 DECEMBER 2013

Jennifer and I are jolted into financial reality by an email invoice from Bindmans. It seems the media department bills separately from my solicitor, and I am being charged £1,225 plus VAT, a sum which is not going to be taken from the money I had given them on account. I write out the cheque and post it straight away, as I do all bills, rather than have it loom in my in-tray like a dark cloud. I email Chris with the news.

'Maybe you should send your own invoice to *The Sun* for that bill,' he responds. 'It was their fault, after all.'

What a concept! If we could only all bill *The Sun* for thirty years of slanted reporting!

I email Brad Spurgeon in Paris, realising that I should warn him that the police may contact him.

He replies almost at once, and puts things into perspective by referring to his late wife.

> What a terrible mess for you. But, you know, whenever in the last five years I have run into really trying periods or moments where I feel the world is falling apart – or could – I always think about how happy, how delighted Nathalie would be to be able to be in the same situation of disaster … i.e., alive, rather than losing so much of her 'promised' life. What doesn't destroy us makes us stronger, as they say.

Of course he's right. I may be experiencing a tour of Dante's lower circles of hell, but at least I'm alive. God bless the memory of beautiful Nathalie.

Brad informs me that the police have indeed contacted him and will visit him in Paris by mid-January.

> I told them that I had something to say about you and the period that I was living in your apartment, and that I would be delighted to speak to them about it. I told them it would only no doubt serve in your defence, since I had nothing negative to say. I feel that it would be best to not talk to you about any of it before I've spoken to the police, for the same reason you say. I really don't need to know anything, anyway. I did tell the police in one of the emails that I knew nothing at all about the case other than what I'd read in the initial reports of your arrest in the media. They then gave me what sound like the barest outlines of the situation, so I do have an idea – and one or two theories – of what might be going on. But again, I have absolutely no problem not knowing anything else, at least until I speak to the police. There can be nothing I say that can harm your case, of that I'm certain.

Within three hours I receive an email from someone who is less non-chalant about a visit from the police. My former lodger Keith has not been in touch for over a week after our last dinner together. The last time he had written, 22 November, he had signed off 'Any news? I have news. Is it safe to converse like this? Do they read and listen to EVERYTHING?'

Now he explains his silence.

> I am really sorry I've been invisible – a combination of my now being off work until January (!!!!) and having to tie up loads of loose ends and making sure that everyone has everything that they need, and not knowing what to say to you – I've been freaking out a little since my visit, and they actually asked that I don't contact you until my state-ment has been signed (which it hasn't yet) and with them having your number and email addresses and my numbers and my email addresses I wasn't sure if they were watching and listening. I feel terrible that I feel terrible about my experience given that it is only a fraction of what you are feeling.

He signs off simply 'K'.

I have to do serious anger management before I develop an ulcer or some other internal illness. I draw inspiration from my Dartmouth College gov-ernment professor Vince Starzinger. The first year I attended University College, Oxford, the Zinger was on sabbatical in London. A sabbatical seemed such a glamorous thing to be on!

I have unintentionally started my sabbatical year. I never knew I was going to have one, but I've got one now! When I was twenty-four, before I joined BBC Radio 1, I was a writer who played the piano a lot. After forty years of being in the public eye as a broadcaster, I am about to see how I would have fared if I had stayed my original course. I will spend the year writing and playing the piano a lot, as well as going to the gym more frequently. Memories of years twenty-five through sixty-four, for the time being, get stored in the attic.

Maybe I will also return to life as a voracious reader. I hardly ever read novels any more, and it's time to catch up. I remember John Cleese remarking he had better spend more time reading the great books, because he's running out of years. Not only are there many classics I have to read for the first time, there are some I should go back and revisit. I read like a crazy boy when I was between ten and fifteen, and some novels I read too soon. For every Doctor Dolittle book (and I did read the entire series), I also consumed a *Crime and Punishment* or a *Moby-Dick*. Surely I will get more out of them now than when I was twelve.

Chris and I are treated to dinner by Sir Nick Partridge. The venue is Green Man & French Horn on St Martin's Lane. To my shame, I must have walked past it a hundred times and paid it no attention because it looked like a pub. Although it is proud of its wine list, it satisfies even a teetotaller like myself. Radishes with butter and sea salt are delightful, the sharpness of the radishes cut by their green tops, and a skate is worthy of J. Sheekey or Scott's. We share three desserts, two of which, white chocolate mousse with griottes and warm rice pudding with winter fruits, are sublime. (A third, winemaker's tart, pleases the oenophiles at the table.)

If this book occasionally sounds like I am recording all my meals, I should point out that at one point in my young manhood I was unknowingly put on the shortlist to be the next editor of *The Good Food Guide*. Every year I was sending in extensive critiques of my London restaurant experiences, and the management thought I might make a good editor. The simple word that I was a teetotaller put paid to that.

Chris and I return home after dinner with Nick Partridge. I am temporarily, to quote Big Dee Irwin, happy being fat.

Then, just before going to bed, I look at the *New York Times* website. Nelson Mandela has died.

'It is a time for private thoughts.'

This is one of the most moving sentences I ever heard anyone say. It was said by David Frost, many years before I appeared with him on his television programmes *Breakfast with Frost* and *Through the Keyhole*.

I was watching the 24 November 1963 NBC repeat broadcast of the BBC *That Was the Week That Was* tribute to President John F. Kennedy. When David concluded the programme with the words, 'It is a time for private thoughts,' I was touched to the core. Every one of us mourning the young President had reason to reflect. And imagine what force this statement had to the latent broadcaster in me: here was a host announcing not speech, but a moment of silence!

Now, half a century later, it is once again a time for private thoughts. Nelson Mandela, the most impressive man I have ever met, has died.

Brother Peter is the first to email.

'The news upset me more than I imagined, considering it was not unexpected,' he writes.

> Your cousin Mary Ann called, just two minutes after I'd learned, and she heard me too choked up to talk, for the first time (I don't ever cry around her).
>
> Most of the true giants are people we read about in books. We haven't gotten to see many in our own lifetimes, at their most courageous and epochal moments. He was the exception. I don't see anyone of his stature left.

Joan Armatrading sends an email with a stunner of a story. She had attended the premiere of the Mandela film *Long Walk to Freedom*, which I had seen the week before in a press preview.

> Perhaps about ten to fifteen minutes from the end of the film I was told he had died. The rest of the audience did not know the news. When it

ended the stars of the film came on stage to tell the audience the news. There were gasps, tears and some wailing. It was a big and very collective shock. It was strange to leave such an evening with everyone in such a sombre mood. He really was a great man. God bless Nelson Mandela.

This Nobel Peace Prize winner had affected my life in many ways. My first visit to London was to take part in an anti-apartheid march ending in Trafalgar Square in 1970. I was one of the broadcasters of the Nelson Mandela seventieth birthday concert at Wembley Stadium in 1988, the programme that had the highest global television audience in history up to that point (basically Live Aid plus China). To use one of the most over-employed phrases in broadcasting, one that in this case happens to be literally true, I was humbled to host Mandela's ninetieth birthday dinner in London and his ninety-first birthday concert in Radio City Music Hall.

Each of those events holds myriad memories, but the most lasting was an exchange with Mandela himself.

'Thank you for everything you are doing,' he told me during the interval of his ninetieth birthday dinner.

Stunned at this reversal of who should be saying what, I blurted out, 'Thank YOU for everything YOU are doing.'

Without missing a beat, Mandela said, 'Without people like you, we could not do what we do.'

Nelson Mandela really was a man of humility, even though he had reason to be immodest.

This morning, even though I occasionally dwell on my own problems, I have private thoughts about Mandela.

7 DECEMBER 2013

I fruitlessly search the internet for a contact address for my old friendly acquaintance Cy Chadwick. A friend of my lodger's partner, he attended

my birthday parties for a few years in the 1990s. We might have socialised personally had he not lived in Leeds, where he worked as an actor on
Emmerdale. I have occasionally wondered what he has been doing ever
since his character in the show was sent to prison for manslaughter. Now
Cy is the latest celebrity to be charged with a historic sexual offence. The
twist is, he himself was only a teenager at the time.

It was only yesterday afternoon that I finally met with two representatives of Stonewall. I was jolted when the first thing one of them said
to me was, 'I hope you realise we cannot take your case.' However, they
became deeply concerned when they realised that my case suggests a re-
criminalisation of homosexual sex between the ages of sixteen and eighteen.
At a time when historical records are being modified to erase the convictions of gay men who had sex with persons in this range when the ages of
consent were different for same-sex and heterosexual intercourse, Yewtree
seems intent on punishing me for precisely these (in my case fictitious)
acts. This is a red flag to anyone committed to gay rights.

The deadline for our 2013 London Film Critics Circle nominations is
approaching. Each year, over three-quarters of the films with a serious
chance of winning awards are released in the United States in the last six
weeks of the year. Many of these movies will not be released commer-
cially in the UK until early 2014. This means that the first two weeks of
December are a mad season in which we desperately try to see screenings
of unreleased films arranged by frantic publicists, who try not to set their
showings in competition with each other. We are sometimes sent 'screen-
ers', promotional DVDs, so we can watch some films at home.

This evening I watch *Saving Mr Banks*, in which Emma Thompson
gives a highly praised performance that may win her an acting nomina-
tion. I remember being on her first television programme, when she and
university friends Stephen Fry, Hugh Laurie and Paul Shearer appeared
on a BBC Two show on which my co-authors and I were promoting
our latest Guinness book. Emma stunned me by flawlessly delivering a

ninety-second comedy monologue direct to camera on live television. The courage involved in this act would test even a veteran. It was obvious she was going to go places, although not obvious where.

The film takes me out of myself. For the first time since my arrest, there is a two-minute period of time when I am not conscious of my dilemma.

---

8 DECEMBER 2013

Malcolm Jeffries and I take some afternoon entertainment, if that can be the word, in the movie *Kill Your Darlings*. I travel to Regent Street to meet Malcolm, who is a devotee of the Beat poets. We are both unprepared for the riveting performance of Dane DeHaan. Dane DeWhat? We thought we were here for Daniel Radcliffe, or perhaps Michael C. Hall. This guy DeHaan steals every scene he's in. Rarely is a performer so convincing in a role that you can't believe he isn't that actual person. Dane DeHaan will be in my final list of Supporting Actor nominations.

This evening, Christopher and I are dinner guests of Jerry Rush and his current partner Roxane. Hospitality in someone else's home is an honour these days. It is a personal commitment in the face of the opposition of the state. I am greatly touched by their support and encouraged by Jerry's report that Dale Witton has been in touch from Australia to say she is 'incredulous'.

---

9 DECEMBER 2013

Kate has finally contacted Richard Godfrey. We have a statement from someone who lived in my Hyde Park Square building supporting my character.

It is funny how lyrics of songs jump out at you when they are personally appropriate. Before Chris and I chose 'All the Way' for our marriage vows, the most intense experience I ever had with this phenomenon was with 'Nothing Compares 2 U' by Sinead O'Connor, which was a number one in the aftermath of a romantic break-up. It seemed to have been written by Prince precisely for my predicament.

Today, a tacky tune from 1971 turns up on my iTunes and suddenly seems profound. It is 'Desiderata', the recitation by Les Crane of Max Ehrmann's 1927 poem, which went to the American Top 10 and turned up on millions of tea towels and wall hangings around the Western world. From 2.07 to 2.38, it seems to have been written for me: 'Take kindly the counsel of the years, gracefully surrendering the things of youth. Nurture strength of spirit to shield you in sudden misfortune. But do not distress yourself with imaginings. Many fears are born of fatigue and loneliness. Beyond a wholesome discipline, be gentle with yourself.'

<hr />

11 DECEMBER 2013

I have been shunned by the Labour Party.

Tonight it is holding its Thousand Club Christmas drinks at the Inter-Continental London Westminster. Before my arrest I was invited to this event and accepted. The invitation is on my desk at this moment.

> Charlie Falconer and Jan Royall warmly invite
> Mr Paul Gambaccini and Guest
> To join Ed Miliband and The Shadow Cabinet for the:
> Thousand Club Christmas Drinks 2013

Not so warmly now, I'm afraid. Two days ago Christopher received an email reminding him of the event. I did not. Chris emailed me from his office asking if I had received a similar email. No, I replied. Oh well, probably an oversight, he thought. No, probably a deliberate shun, I told him. I have not been contacted since my arrest by a single representative of Labour expressing sympathy for my plight, asking me what the matter is all about.

Yesterday Chris emailed the fundraising events marketing officer of the Labour Party. She preferred to speak rather than communicate in writing.

> Hi Chris,
> I hope you're well. Do you mind letting me know your mobile number so I can give you a call? Otherwise, please do call me on either of the numbers below.
> Donor Stewardship Officer

Chris was told there had been a meeting and it had been decided it would be best if I did not appear at the Christmas Drinks. Reporters and photographers would be there, 'and you know what the press are like'. Either the paparazzi will take photos of me instead of Ed or photos of me with Ed. Neither will be good for Ed.

Only a year ago I hosted a fundraiser for Ed Miliband in my flat. Leading dignitaries of the party from Iain McNicol to Chuka Umunna were in attendance alongside celebrities including Joan Armatrading, Ben Elton, Brian May and David Tennant, although Brian's main reason for attending was to ask Miliband his policy concerning the badger cull. One year later, I am persona non grata, simply because the police have arrested me on bogus allegations, and neither Ed nor anyone else from Labour have had the basic human decency to call to see how I am coping or even what this is about.

It has obviously not occurred to anyone in the Labour Party that something more than manners is at stake here. An injustice is occurring in its own house, yet it turns away from the victim for fear of taint. So much for the party that fought heroically for the rights of the poor, the black and the gay. It is now more afraid of a photo opportunity gone wrong than it is committed to social justice. The heroism of leaders from Clement Attlee to Neil Kinnock has yielded to cowardice.

Memories of my relationship with Labour flash through my mind like snapshots in a photo album.

I recall hosting an evening of entertainment in a theatre in the Strand for the benefit of Neil Kinnock's 1992 campaign. In one of the shrewdest business strokes of my lifetime, Leslie Hill had just picked off Central Television for £2,000 in Margaret Thatcher's television licence auction. I told the crowd, 'Just think. If we had each put in a fiver, we could own Central Television.'

Sitting backstage during another artist's performance, Steve Coogan and I were joined by the former Labour Prime Minister James Callaghan. Steve and I exchanged looks of disbelief as Callaghan rubbished the man who had been his contemporaneous American President, Jimmy Carter.

On the evening of 7 April 1992, two days before the general election, Neil held his last event before the voting. It was in the atrium of the Millbank building where both the BBC and Sky News have maintained their Westminster studios. Neil and Glenys were to appear before a cheering throng of supporters and take their place on stage at a table with four chairs.

FOUR chairs? There were only two Kinnocks! I ran over to Ben Elton and told him that we had to take the two extra seats or it would appear no one wanted to be associated with Neil. We took the places just in time for the arrival of the happy couple – except, we learned later, they were not so happy, as the latest polling taken after the Sheffield rally showed the Conservatives were almost certain to win. Nonetheless, Ben and I probably never got as much television time as we did that night, the mysterious right-hand men of a prime ministerial candidate.

The leadership of Labour changed after the 1992 defeat. I remember the evening of 11 May 1994, the night before John Smith died. A fundraising dinner was being held at the Park Lane Hotel in London. Before the meal, I told John that many people were concerned that he was working too hard.

'I can't stop,' he said. 'There's too much to do.'

I crossed the room to Barbara Follett, who was then the conduit from celebrities to the party. If a comedian had a good topical joke, they would phone it in to Barbara, who would pass it on.

'He's a great man,' Barbara said.

'Yes, he is,' I replied. 'It's a shame he'll never be Prime Minister.'

'What do you mean?' she asked, shocked.

'He can't win with the name of the party. "Labour" has too many negative connotations right now. The party has to do what a couple of the continental left-wing parties have done, which is to change the name. It has to be something like New Labour.'

Barbara got my point. I never made it again. John Smith died the next day. Tony Blair took over the leadership and changed the unofficial name of the party to New Labour. I often wondered if I was responsible for the rebranding or if someone closer to Blair had a similar idea. After all, if the point was obvious to a non-politician like me, it probably also was to someone who practised the dark arts for a career.

Now I ring the donor stewardship officer. Her phone goes to an answer mode that does not appear to take messages. I forget about talking to anyone from the current party and ring my old friend Michael Cashman MEP, who takes my call in Strasbourg. You can always vent to a fellow veteran of the political wars, and Michael performs the useful functions of sounding board and supporter.

I call Christopher and tell him that I have severed my relationship with the Labour Party. They are terrified of being associated with me now, but a year from now, after I have been cleared, everything will be diffcrent. With a general election looming, I will be a symbol of justice whose support would be useful to them.

Goodbye and good riddance. There is something more important to worry about. I go to Kate Goold's office, expecting a quick handover of my passports, which have been given to my solicitor by the police along with a couple of CDs containing tax-related documents from my computer. I am quite wrong. The meeting, which I expected to take fifteen minutes, lasts an hour and fifteen.

Kate Goold feels that the case must be going my way. The people the police have interviewed have all been supportive of me. Yewtree are spending considerable sums sending detectives to Los Angeles, New York and who knows where else, all to interview persons who will be useful in my defence.

The solicitor has noticed something else. The transcript of my police interview contains a moment where Officer Two relates that one of the accusers claimed that Sixteen ingratiated the duo with cigarettes and alcohol before doing whatever he is alleged to have done, the details of which are still unknown to me. In the transcript, Two asks me if I know what nickname Secondary and Primary had for Sixteen. I have no idea. It is 'Fag Daddy'.

For a second I think of the American use of the word 'fag', which is a derogatory expression for a gay man. Then I realise Two means it in the English sense of a cigarette. Oh, I get it. The adult who supposedly gave teenagers cigarettes was their 'Fag Daddy'.

There is no suggestion that I was in on this softening process, and if there were it would not fly. I have never had a cigarette in my mouth in Great Britain. This sounds a rather extreme position to take, but the fact is that when I was eight years old my father used to take us for family drives on weekends. President Eisenhower had introduced the Interstate Highway System, and families were going out for rides on the new invention, the motorway. On one occasion we rounded the S-shaped curve on Interstate 95 near the Stamford, Connecticut, railway station. A thick waft of stale smoke floated backwards into my face just as the car turned. I was nauseated. It was like receiving aversion therapy at the age of eight. I never had the desire to smoke a cigarette, and only tried one when I was twenty-two years old. It lasted ten seconds in my mouth and that was the end of my smoking career. If I had ever been in a room with Sixteen and two other persons, the introduction of lit cigarettes would have caused me to leave.

Kate Goold points out that my disclosure statement does not mention my involvement in 'grooming', which she believes on that short section of the transcript is part of the accusations against my co-defendant. If that is so, if the accusers are claiming that they were 'groomed' for sex, but not by me, that would remove the lower end of the time period in which I was alleged to have offended against Primary.

While preparing a cheese salad for my friend Andrew Fallaize, I receive a phone call from Iain McNicol, General Secretary of the Labour Party. He is in South Africa for the funeral of Nelson Mandela. We have played phone tag that morning.

Iain has been phoned by Michael Cashman. He is calling to express his personal regret for the attitude shown to me by the party, both in shunning me after my arrest and in uninviting me to the Thousand Club Christmas drinks.

McNicol understands my position. I apologise that, since he is the person calling me, he is the one getting a full earful of my feelings. He mentions, as no one else did, that he was a guest in my home for the fundraiser just a year ago. He does not attempt to change my feelings. I tell him I had a great ride. Although I left the Labour Party for the duration of the Iraq War, I did return. I have many good memories of some good people.

'I know,' he says, and those two words are enough for me.

---

12 DECEMBER 2013

Sean O'Neill, crime editor of *The Times*, sends an interesting email that is a little late.

> Mr Gambaccini,
>
> I wondered if you might speak with me about your recent experiences in dealing with the Metropolitan Police.
>
> I have been concerned for some time that the Met is particularly zealous and heavy-handed when it comes to investigating cases of what it calls 'reputational importance' for the police force and is a lot less eager when chasing cases that might cause it political difficulties (e.g., there

were no early-morning raids and only a small handful of cases looked at in the MPs' expenses affair).

There are, it seems, legitimate questions to be asked about the conduct of Operation Yewtree. I'm not pushing to find out specific details about the allegations that have been made against you, but rather seeking a broader opinion on how you think the police have gone about their business in this operation.

If you wish to contact me, my details are below. However, I fully understand if at this time you'd rather not speak about the situation.

I feel like screaming out to the NUJ for an honest reporter, any reporter, to notice what is under their collective nose, but I don't dare draw attention to myself now that we have reached the 'bandwagon effect' stage. Kate Goold confirms that I must not speak to O'Neill.

'Sean is a good one,' she says, 'but he should know better.' She promises to reply in the negative for me, but to thank him for his interest.

It has now been more than a fortnight since the executive from Amnesty International promised to phone me back within a week. OK, there's another one for the 'fair-weather friend' category, to be listed alphabetically before the Labour Party. There is a fundamental difference between organisations, which fear contamination and threats to their survival, and friends, who stay fast.

─────────── 13 DECEMBER 2013 ───────────

The Metropolitan Police, having released news of my arrest to the press in near-record time, have done themselves one better. They've informed the press that I've been rebailed without letting me know. Chris has emailed me at 12.12 p.m.: 'It seems to be in the news that you and the 74-year-old have been rebailed until March.' In other words, the date of my scheduled return to Charing Cross Police Station has been moved from 8 January to two months later.

Strange, I think: no one has told me. Jennifer runs into the room to tell me that I am on the BBC and ITN websites as having been rebailed.

I call Kate Goold. What is this all about? Wasn't I supposed to turn up at Charing Cross on 8 January? It turns out that she hasn't heard anything either. She is out of the office seeing clients and will phone the firm to see if the police have contacted her there.

Five minutes later, she calls back. Apparently the police sent her an email at 9.30 a.m., informing her that I had been rebailed until 26 March. Meanwhile, I have called the BBC website news desk and learned that the Press Association was informed of my rebail by the Metropolitan Police at 10.52 a.m. I tell the correspondent he knew about it before I did. He gasps.

Chris and I go to Aurora, a fine and unpretentious restaurant on Lexington Street, to have a Christmas meal with Christopher's theatre producer friend Andrew Harmer, a lawyer by profession. The poor man talks to Chris while I sit in a furious funk, only occasionally emerging to engage in the conversation. We tell him about Wednesday's contretemps with the Labour Party.

'They call this fundraising group the Thousand Club,' I tell him. A bell of recognition rings in my mind, and I look at Chris.

'It was based on my idea in the first place!' I am amazed that I have just remembered what should have been obvious. I explain to Andrew Harmer.

'When I was named Philanthropist of the Year for raising £300,000 for the Terrence Higgins Trust, getting 300 people to donate £1,000 each, the Labour Party borrowed the idea and called it the Thousand Club. Now they're shunning me!'

I ask Chris if I can borrow his phone to call Kate. I go outside and pace back and forth in front of the restaurant, venting my anger against the police for rebailing me without telling me.

'This is the least professional organisation I have dealt with in at least twenty-five years!' I shout. Motorists do double takes as they see a familiar face barking into a mobile phone turning various spectral shades of red. Finally Kate tells me she has talked to Officer One, who claims, 'We have not broken any of our rules', and affirms that Operation Yewtree has never leaked any detail of any case.

It is as obvious as the sun rising in the east that someone in the Met lets the press know everything about me short of my shoe size. It doesn't matter who does it, from the commissioner to the cleaner, the effect is the same on the suspect.

Kate promises to seek an official explanation of the incident, with the caveat that she will be attending her son's school concert at 3 p.m. Enjoy it, I tell her. It's OK, I've spoken my mind.

After lunch I return home for what I hope is an afternoon of decompression. Instead, I am invigorated by a phone call from Charlie Falconer.

Since we met in the 1990s, Charlie has become Baron Falconer of Thoroton. Now he is calling in his position as head of the Thousand Club, apologising for the way I was treated. I am touched by his concern. In my unusual current circumstances, a day is like a week, and the whole matter of the Labour Party is behind me now. To discuss it seems like time travel, but talk about it we do, for over an hour.

Falconer latches on to my point that in a situation such as mine, 'Friends stay fast but organisations flee from fear of taint.' This is a man with experience of organisations! But he is also a man with experience of the law, and he shows more interest in the details of my case than anyone outside of my husband and my solicitor. He confirms Brian Paddick's important point that two agreeing persons justify an arrest, and that the police had no alternative but to arrest me.

Charlie agrees that my situation is terrible but won't go so far as I do about 'darkness at the heart of the state'. He tells me he feels the state will not let me down. I can only hope he is right. He invites me to lunch in early January at the Delaunay. This is my favourite restaurant, so he gets bonus points.

14 DECEMBER 2013

I receive an email timed 8.15 a.m. from Kate Goold.

> Dear Paul,
>
> On the face of it, the police have not done anything in breach of their
> own rules or guidance and have certainly not done anything unlawful.
> I have copied Tasmin into this email to establish whether she has any
> views on any action that can be taken, but I am afraid that I think it
> is unlikely.
>
> Best wishes, Kate

Chris sends an email to Kate: 'What on earth are their rules and guidance?'

15 DECEMBER 2013

Being shunned by the BBC, the Labour Party and Amnesty International was bad enough. Today I learn I've been shunned by someone really important.

Chris and I go bowling this morning in our usual Sunday-morning match at All Star Lanes in Holborn. I manage two turkeys.

When it is all over, I return my personal bowling ball to storage and we change back into our civilian shoes. I note the glass cabinet that displays signed pins from celebrity bowlers.

My pin has been removed.

Stephen Fry, Johnny Vegas and Emma Watson are still represented. I am gone.

This hurts me where I live. I've been bowling for over half a century. To be a non-person in my local alley is the ultimate insult.

Perhaps my signature on the pin blurred with time and could no longer be read. Maybe I've simply been replaced by a more recent signatory.

Maybe. Maybe.

─────────────────── 16 DECEMBER 2013 ───────────────────

The BBC website reports that solicitor Henri Brandman has stated, 'My client, Jim Davidson, is delighted to have received news today that there will be no further action relating to an allegation of a historic sexual nature in the Falkland Islands. I will not be making any further comment on his behalf.'

Davidson was a Yewtree veteran who had spent eight months on bail before the Crown Prosecution Service decided in August that he would not face charges over alleged sexual offences in the UK. He then faced an accusation concerning the Falklands. This, too, is now history.

Jim, in this respect at least, may I follow in your footsteps?

─────────────────── 17 DECEMBER 2013 ───────────────────

Kate Goold confirms my new rebail date is 26 March. I tell her that this is a medium-term catastrophe for my career. This year's Academy Awards ceremony will be held on 2 March and I will not be available for Radio 4 work until at least three and a half weeks afterwards. That means the mini-series *And the Academy Award Goes To…* I had been working on before my arrest will either have to go on without me, if it is to be broadcast in time for the Oscars, or will have to be cancelled for 2014.

The next series of Radio 4's music quiz *Counterpoint* starts recording in April and must book a presenter before, not after, 26 March. I cannot be booked if my availability is uncertain.

Most damaging economically, the end of March is the conclusion of the Radio 2 programming year. A new year-long cycle begins the first week in April. My long-running series *America's Greatest Hits* cannot be recommissioned until I am able to present it. No one will know until the evening of 26 March if I will be available to work the following week, and the advance time required for commission ensures I will lose this slot. Considerations like contract signing and *Radio Times* listings dictate earlier resolution. I am having coffee this Friday with the network's head of talent, Lewis Carnie, but I can't see how we can get around this one.

I hear dismay in Kate's silence. She realises that this case, besides being a travesty of justice, is now also an economic calamity.

Rob Ketteridge, head of arts documentaries, or whatever they are calling his position nowadays, has called with an extraordinarily generous and considerate message. In light of my rebail and the impossibility of knowing when Yewtree will drop its case against me, *And the Academy Award Goes To…* has been suspended until I return. No one will replace me.

'It is your show,' he reminds me. Indeed, it was … the format was my idea, and I have presented all editions, but these days it is so rare that an organisation is kind that this simple statement is a breath of oxygen.

'It will be here when you come back.'

What a gentleman. Rob has taken sides. So has the producer of the programme, Sara Jane Hall. They have shown courage.

Chris remains on the ball. Today he has bowled a blinder. Last night he pointed out to me that two graduates of Secondary's school who shared his surname can be found on the internet. They are of the age range that they could be his brothers.

One is a researcher, writer and academic. The other is a journalist.

It would be amusing if Secondary were a brother of this unlikely duo. If, as my disclosure statement says, he was fourteen in 1980, he would have been born in 1966, quite possibly a sibling.

Then Chris sends me a link to an old story from the Mail Online. A video link reveals footage of one of Secondary's potential brothers. He is giving his views on homosexuals.

'You're an ignorant people,' he says. Why ignorant? 'Because you don't even understand what your bodies are for. How ignorant can you get? Even the animals know.'

The Mail Online reports the researcher has said to them that he has changed his views with time.

It doesn't really matter whether he has moved on or not. The old message is still being spread. It is for sale on iTunes, and to prove it I download his entire spoken word album, confident that my single purchase will not send it into the *Billboard* chart.

I have nothing against him personally, whatever he is currently calling himself. Indeed, he has recently met the programming standards of BBC Radio, being invited to speak on both BBC Radio 3 and Radio 4. The point is that if Secondary is indeed the brother of this man, he cannot help having been exposed to pernicious views about gay people. Could this view have shaped his attitudes, partly motivating his legal attack on me? (Bear in mind I was the first and only 'out' Radio 1 DJ when Secondary was at school.) Conversely, could his supposed homosexual tendencies be the cause of his older brother's aversion?

Of course, the brothers may not be related to Secondary after all, and I have wasted an evening and the cost of an iTunes album. But if they are brothers, this is at least of tangential interest.

Chris and I spend the time before bed trying to figure out how to learn whether Secondary, the researcher and the journalist are brothers. If the disclosure sheet is correct about Secondary's age, fellow pupils could remember him. We turn to the internet. How many contacts are we going to have to make?

---

19 DECEMBER 2013

John Miskelly sends me an invitation to be a guest at the Labour LGBT dinner on 12 March. I have to inform him of my shunning by the Party and the termination of my relationship with it. He is astonished and asks if attending might bring the subject of the shun into the room, but I grace-fully tell him that the time to think of the Labour Party is passed. I have greater concerns, like my freedom and my future, on my mind.

<hr />

20 DECEMBER 2013

Thinking about the witch-hunt makes me recall the first such moral panic of my lifetime, the McCarthyism of the early 1950s. I go to the hall closet to retrieve my copy of our *For One Night Only* programme about the Weavers' triumphant 1955 Carnegie Hall reunion concert.

I gasp. My Radio 4 programme box is not there. Neither is my Radio 2 programme box. These are the metal containers in which I have stored CD copies of the shows of which I am proudest. They are gone. When I was out of the house after having been taken to Charing Cross Police Station on 29 October, the police stole my career.

Lewis Carnie hosts me to tea in the hotel across the road from Broadcasting House. He affirms Radio 2 will have me back as soon as I am cleared. Next quarter, my time slot will be occupied by documentaries and a series devoted to the music of Laurel Canyon produced by Kevin Howlett and presented by Johnnie Walker. It is significant that the network has not sought a new DJ to fill my slot. This reassures me that Walker is, in addition to hosting his own programme, keeping my chair warm.

In the evening I discover that Gwyneth Williams, controller of Radio 4, has called. I ring back. Settling down with a tea, she sends love and says that the 2014 series of *Counterpoint* will be delayed until my return. I am almost speechless with gratitude.

<hr />

21 DECEMBER 2013

Today is the winter solstice. For the past fifteen years, my former lodger Keith and I have awaited its arrival with relief. It means that, though the days will continue to grow colder, they will also grow longer. The worst of the darkness is over. 21 December has become a personal holiday for Keith and me. We always celebrate it together.

Not this year, though. We are discouraged from seeing each other by the Metropolitan Police until Keith has signed his statement, which is awaiting formal preparation by Yewtree. Although he has long ago given his interview, he has still not signed the formal document. It looks as if we will not be able to celebrate the solstice until after Christmas. Keith acknowledges the dilemma in an email to Chris, but he cannot communicate with me personally. As Peter Gabriel said in the title of his song for the movie *City of Angels*, 'I grieve'.

───────────── 22 DECEMBER 2013 ─────────────

Christopher and I are treated to a long Christmas lunch with Jude Kelly and her partner Andrew Cracknell. We are joined by Jude's daughter and her partner. It is wonderful for life to be normal if only for a couple of hours. After the obligatory update on my case, we talk about other things, such as the exciting news of the upcoming wedding of the young couple.

───────────── 23 DECEMBER 2013 ─────────────

The Media Guardian this morning leads with 'Christopher Jefferies says ITV drama will show "destructive nature" of press. Peter Morgan will write the two-parter.' Jefferies was the retired teacher vilified in the press as the presumed murderer of his tenant, Joanna Yeates, when in fact the killer was his neighbour. He speaks to *The Guardian*:

> I suppose one of the things that I hope will emerge from the film is
> one of the things that emerged from the Leveson Inquiry, [which]
> was to make people realise the kind of press – at least certain sections

of it – that we have in this country and how destructive they are and how amoral they are.

It's about the damage that can be done. It happens to be about me but it's about the damage that can be done to somebody by certain elements of the media, who are not in the least bit concerned with the people whose reputations they trash.

He successfully sued several newspapers for libel and 'received an apology from Avon and Somerset police for distress he suffered during the murder investigation'. Respect!

24 DECEMBER 2013

Awakened in the middle of the night by the howling winds of a major storm, I see an email from Dame Helena Kennedy timed at 00.34. She has been informed of my situation by John Miskelly. Dame Helena is a QC and distinguished fighter for human rights.

'I am sorry you are going through such a hellish time,' she tells me. 'A madness has been let loose after Savile and it is completely out of control. We have created a craze for victimhood … Putting a contemporary lens on our lives in another era is so distorting. Let's talk.'

I call and we have a long conversation. She is very supportive and promises to speak at length on 3 January.

My breakfast is cheered by a *Financial Times* front-page headline: 'Father of modern computer science Turing is pardoned for being gay, sixty years after suicide'.

The story begins:

Almost sixty years after his suicide and sixty-two years after Britain had him chemically castrated, Alan Turing, the father of modern computer science and breaker of the Enigma code, will today be pardoned for his

1952 conviction for being gay. Turing – whose code-breaking work is said to have shortened the course of the Second World War by two years – has been granted a posthumous pardon under the Royal Prerogative of Mercy by the Queen, following a government U-turn.

Hailed as a genius by colleagues at Bletchley Park, the wartime code-breaking centre, he was prosecuted for 'homosexual activities' after reporting a burglary at his Manchester home. When police discovered he was gay, they arrested him using Victorian laws against homosexuality. An estimated 49,000 gay men, now dead, were criminalised under the Criminal Law Amendment Act of 1885, which has since been repealed.

'Everyone who taps at a keyboard, opening a spreadsheet or a word-processing program, is working on an incarnation of a Turing machine,' *Time* magazine wrote in 1999, after naming him one of the hundred most important people of the twentieth century.

Speaking of computers, Chris gets his back from the police! I'm so proud of him. He fought and fought and fought, and he's getting it returned just in time for our Christmas trip, on which he will be doing some coursework.

Officer Four asks him, 'How's Paul doing?' and when told I am doing 'surprisingly well' despite seizures of anger, she replies, 'Good.'

When Chris tells me this, I am stunned. It's one of the first hints of humanity in the Metropolitan Police we've encountered in two months. Dare I think that perhaps, as some of my well-intentioned friends tell me, Yewtree actually is more interested in justice than the number of celebrity scalps it hangs on the wall? Is it possible that reason will prevail in 2014?

2014

We missed it. Christopher and I missed the New Year. We were at JFK airport in New York, boarding our flight back to London, when I checked the clock. It was 7.04 p.m. New York time, 12.04 a.m. in London. We had missed the New Year countdown! We exchanged a kiss and boarded the aircraft.

'Happy New Year,' we told a stewardess in the upper deck.

'We had our champagne a few moments ago,' she replied conspiratorially. She was in this 12.04 a.m. business with us.

On the streets of New York during the last week of 2014, I breathed the air of freedom. During the holiday week I realised that, if things really went south for me in Britain, I could one day relocate to the city of my birth. The virus sweeping the UK has not reached the US. Everyone with whom I discuss my situation expresses incredulity at the witch-hunt.

My American friends expressed their support in ways that are deeply moving. I realise that my life, far from being unfortunate, is blessed. I have my health and my love. The ordeal that I am experiencing, even if it goes to the extent of a trial or unjust imprisonment, will end, and if need be I can then move to New York.

Christopher and I had brunch with Stephen Fry on New Year's Eve, our last day in New York. He is on Broadway in the Globe production of *Twelfth Night*. Stephen offered to blog on my behalf but realised that now is not the right time. We need to keep my name out of the press to avoid encouraging more distressed individuals to invent sex stories. He remembered our meeting on the occasion of his first television broadcast, but recalled a detail I had forgotten.

'You told me, "Stephen, enjoy your five years. They're going to be great." At the time, I thought, five years, that will make me happy.' He laughed. I shrank.

———————————— 2 JANUARY 2014 ————————————

I am slightly obsessed by the desire to find out something, anything, about my accuser Secondary. If he was fourteen in 1980, as claimed in my disclosure sheet, he would have been born in 1966. Noting that he went to the same school at the same time, I write to a senior Liberal Democrat politician of my acquaintance. I am certain he has never received correspondence like my handwritten letter. I tell him: 'I have been falsely accused of sexual offences by someone I do not know, but whom you may.' I invite him to get in touch with me. Will he be a braver man than anyone in the Labour Party?

I email James Stirling, head of programmes at BBC 6Music, to try to reach a couple of old boys whom I have identified as being born in 1968 or 1969. I am grateful when he replies within the hour, telling me he has forwarded my email address to both of them. One is in California, so I might not hear from him for a while, if ever, but the other responds quickly.

'I was at school from spring 1983–88,' he recalls. 'If Secondary was fourteen in 1980 he would have been in his final year when I arrived, so I would never really have come across him. I'll ask some school pals, discreetly, if they recall the names if that would help?'

<hr>

3 JANUARY 2014

The theoretical entity that is Secondary still needs fleshing out. I recall that many years ago I visited Secondary's school at the invitation of the son of one of my Oxford contemporaries. On Google, I am staggered to discover he is now working in private equity in London. I email him asking if there is an old members book, in the way there is at American universities.

Just after midday I have a fifty-minute phone conversation with Helena Kennedy. Once again she tells me she is horrified by developments. She advises me not to hire a private investigator at this point, although I'm dying to know something about my accusers. Since it would take about nine months from any charge to a trial, we can wait to hire a PI until we see if one is actually needed.

I thank Helena, who, though she cannot solve my case for me, provides plenty of food for thought and some much-needed support. It's good to know that a high-powered legal figure is on my side.

<hr>

4 JANUARY 2014

Ruth Rosenthal, a friend from the days either side of 1980 when I wrote a column for the *Radio Times*, sends an email with sad tidings.

> Have been meaning to be in touch for ages then this morning's news of Phil Everly's demise has me thinking of you and has spurred me on to write and wish you all the best for the new year...
>
> The Everlys were the top of my teenage loves for their somewhat triste music. Their great harmonies and tunes are as memorable and evocative as ever. Am sure you loved them, too … truly the end of an era.

Memories flood over me. I recall how 'Bye Bye Love' seemed to be in the charts for ever – twenty-seven weeks in the Top 100 is a long time when you're eight years old – and how 'Take a Message to Mary' was just about the saddest song in the world when I was ten. 'Oh Lord, this cell is cold,' it concludes. Never once did I think when I was emotional about this song that I would one day be wrongfully detained in a cell myself.

Learning about Phil Everly's demise from Ruth is the first time I have learned of a pop death from a friend in decades. In recent years the news has always come to me from media outlets seeking comment. Even some members of the public sense that this time is different. Chris offers me a selection of tweets:

> @RitchAmes: Where is pop coffin chaser Paul Gambaccini, Phil Everly has died…
>
> @DomUtton: Pop star deaths just aren't the same without Paul Gambaccini
>
> @MattISpures: Sad news about Phil Everly. Gambaccini must be gutted at the lost work at the moment

Matt, you're right. And God bless Phil Everly.

---

6 JANUARY 2014

Gary Osborne, chairman of the Ivor Novello Awards committee, sends me an email stating, 'I suspect you're not usually a reader of the *Sun on Sunday* … but Jim Davidson's article in yesterday's edition is worth reading if you haven't already.'

I click on the link, and it sure is. 'Jim Davidson: My sex arrest agony' is the headline, with the subheads 'Every minute I thought I would end up going to jail' and 'I feared cops were out to convict me but I was not going to be Savile's scapegoat'. Well, so far, so good. But wait! After the start of an article in which Jim refers to a 'year of absolute hell' in which he's 'been tortured by thoughts of being slammed in a prison cell' with 'sinister forces' against him, I run into the paywall.

'Join Sun+ to read the full exclusive interview', I am invited. It will cost £1 for a one-month trial. I can't do it! I can't pay my tormentor 1p, let alone £1! I write back to Gary Osborne, asking if he can download the article and send it to me. The tension is terrific ... but I have to learn to wait.

—— 7 JANUARY 2014 ——

I have managed to get hold of the award-winning journalist Patrick Strudwick via Sam Dick of Stonewall. My email address for Patrick had been wrong ... really wrong. I had him listed as '@express.co.uk', and he is less like an *Express* journo than anyone I know. He is not interested in weather catastrophes.

I need to talk to Patrick because last year he sent me a sympathetic email expressing his regret for the stress I must be under because of Operation Yewtree. Recently I have wondered if this means he had known about police investigations into my past before I did.

Years ago I was able to partially fund Strudwick's higher education. This year I have been paying 30 per cent of the fees for the outstanding jazz violinist John Garner, who is studying at the Guildhall School of Music & Drama, and the whole shebang for Peter Smith, the former head of the Hopkins Center for the Arts at Dartmouth, who, at the age of eighty, courageously undertook a PhD at York University. Now comes the news that Peter has decided the academic route is not the best for completing his long-anticipated biography of the actor Wilfrid Lawson and is simply getting on with writing the book. I will receive a partial refund of his tuition, which will be very useful after the turning of my financial worm.

I have a long phone conversation with Patrick. It turns out he knew nothing of Yewtree's investigation into me and was commenting on remarks in the Twittersphere about my appearance on *Panorama* discussing Jimmy Savile.

Strudwick makes several good points concerning my main query, which is why whatever we call the remnants of Fleet Street aren't pointing out what to me are the glaring defects of Operation Yewtree. The former clarinettist ... there's a fun fact for Strudwick fans ... tells me that the main reason there is no investigative journalism being done about Yewtree is that there is almost no investigative journalism being done these days, period. It is too expensive for newspapers with falling circulations and reduced advertising to even contemplate.

Secondly, the public is not crying out for it. The phone-hacking inquiry had a tough time getting any traction while the victims were only well-off celebrities. The moment the scandal reached Milly Dowler, however, it metastasised. Careers were ruined and the *News of the World* was closed. I should not be surprised there is no rush to expose Yewtree at this stage of its existence.

I go to lunch at the Delaunay as guest of Charlie Falconer and Margaret McDonagh. I am touched by their genuine faith in me, but I am also aware of something I bring up at lunch ... that their Labour Party's torch has been passed to a new generation that is more interested in photo ops than the fight for civil rights. The struggles of the past have already been fought. The young now seem more interested in presentation than content. I am certainly not encouraged by Ed Miliband himself, who never did phone me to find out what is happening, even when Jude Kelly told him before Christmas that I have been stitched up.

Oh well, there's always Matthias Goerne at the Wigmore Hall with Leif Ove Andsnes. I take Christopher for his first sighting of the great baritone, who is presenting an imaginative programme of Mahler and Shostakovich songs on the theme of death. I am tremendously impressed and think I am hearing the best baritone singing since I saw a Dietrich Fischer-Dieskau recital at the Royal Opera House. Andsnes, the fine Norwegian pianist who ordinarily appears in his own concerts, accompanies with sensitivity and is clearly deeply moved by being part of the double act. I marvel at how mellifluous Goerne's voice is and tell Chris I am awed by the singer's 'mellifluity, if that is a word, but it seems like it should be'. A dictionary check later confirms it isn't. Rats. I would love to be quoted praising 'Matthias Goerne's mellifluity'. 'Matthias Goerne's mellifluous voice' doesn't have the same impact.

The hunt for any details on the life of Secondary has not been a success. My Oxford friend sends a third email to report that he has found out Secondary's year of entry and his year of departure but nothing else. As they say in New York, that's all she wrote.

Moscow Paul calls from Los Angeles at around 10.20. This is the first time we have spoken this century. He has been visited today by two police officers. This is a surprise to me, as I thought only one was going to make a visit to the United States, but Paul explains that there have to be two policemen so they can witness each other's behaviour.

I am slightly surprised by news of my old lodger's latest employment. He is now head of a private equity fund. The last I knew, he was a lawyer. A lot can happen in a couple of decades!

Paul says he has been with the officers for seven hours. No wonder he needs to let off steam! We are on the phone for approximately an hour and a quarter. He has always loved to talk, and sometimes repeats himself as if we are trapped in a tape loop. I don't mind, because what he has to say is positive. He has told the police he was 'shocked' when informed of the accusations against me. He only knew me to have one romantic involvement in all the time he knew me.

'It was with a woman,' he explains. 'You were broke up about it, and we had the only heart-to-heart we ever had.' He is of course referring to Liz Kerr, later Dalkeith.

Inevitably, he has been asked if I ever tried it on with him. 'Absolutely not,' he says he replied, telling the officers there was 'no come-on' at any time. I was 'very polite', 'a gentleman' who was 'more asexual than anything'. 'I only found out Paul was gay when my friend Deborah told me years later.'

Then Paul surprises me. He still sees Sixteen and his partner, who are still together! Being blessed with a strong marriage myself, I am glad that their partnership has survived the years.

Of course, the police ask my old softball teammate questions about Sixteen as well as myself. Using legal language worthy of Bill Clinton, he says he told the police: 'I can neither implicate nor exculpate.'

Then comes what, for me, is the evening's blockbuster. The equity fund manager innocently asked the police why they had to reveal my identity to the press. An officer replied that they didn't, the BBC and I had supplied my name by issuing a statement.

I go off my nut. I can't understand why the Met insists on maintaining, let alone spreading, a falsehood. I am not accusing any agent of Yewtree of anything. It would be incredibly foolish of my case officers to talk about it with newspapers. I have never accused them of speaking with journalists. But why do they keep denying the obvious? The Met is a huge organisation, like the Pentagon, the CIA or, yes, the BBC. It only takes one person to leak. If no one in the police department is giving information to the press, then the nation's tabloid reporters have the gift of extrasensory perception. It is the only other possibility. The Met leaks, or Wapping has ESP. Which is it?

---

8 JANUARY 2014

Liza Tarbuck and I have a good old chinwag. After several false dawns, her family now hopes the case against Jimmy will be dismissed on the 25th of this month. I emphasise that he and I must stay healthy, fit and sane.

I get a card from Alan and Alison of Zager Associates, former producers of the Sony Awards, wishing me well on the 8th. I realise this is the 8th and quite a few people probably still thought today was my decision day. They haven't heard that I have been rebailed until 26 March. The thought of informing everyone of the change is overwhelming. I can't email everybody, so email nobody.

The post brings a hard copy of the Jim Davidson *Sun* story from a considerate Gary Osborne. I recognise many elements of my own experience. Among the lines that resonate the most are 'One woman said I drank champagne when I hate it and that I had a chauffeur with a hat when I never have. Another claimed she worked in an upstairs bar at another theatre. There IS no upstairs bar – there is not even an upstairs!' This is the level of intellectual rigour I have been subjected to in my case. Reading the article, Christopher asks an interesting question: if these accusers are telling falsehoods, why aren't they being prosecuted for wasting police time?

I send Jennifer to the lobby of the Amnesty International headquarters in Shoreditch to make sure my name is still on the foundation stone. She reports back that it is! The organisation may be blanking me today, but at least it acknowledges my role in its history.

This evening's sanity break consists of another pilgrimage to the Wigmore Hall, this time with Malcolm Jeffries.

Christian Zacharias plays two Mozart sonatas and Schubert's piano sonata in B flat D960. For the first three movements, I cannot contain my excitement. I could learn to play this! Then comes the fourth movement. Well, we can forget about that. Zacharias has captured the profundity of the piece – 'profundity', unlike 'mellifluity', is definitely a word – just as Alfred Brendel did on his farewell tour. The difference for me is that in my changed circumstances Schubert's final instrumental composition resonates more deeply.

After I get home I expect to hear from Deborah as I did Moscow Paul last night. After all, the Yewtree road show was due to be in New York today. But tonight's surprise is of a different and more disturbing nature.

Christopher calls from the toilet of the restaurant in which he is having dinner with a banker friend. The banker has sent a bottle of wine to Prime Minister David Cameron, who is at a nearby table, and explains he does this whenever they are in the same restaurant together. Chris tells me I should assume that all of my emails have been read by the police. When he gets home, he explains that his host had recently been summoned by the board of his employer, an international bank. They were enquiring about why they had been approached by the police to gain access to his emails after my arrest. It turns out that the email firewall put in place by the bank was so impenetrable the police had sought manual permission to access Christopher's message, sent on his, not my, account.

Chris had emailed the man the evening my arrest was announced in the press. He was merely cancelling a dinner engagement, but perhaps the Met assumed critical evidence could emerge in emails sent at this moment. They would have been quite disappointed to go to all that trouble and merely read of altered meal plans.

A tangential remark by Christopher's banker friend reveals that the Baroness Shackleton of Belgravia, the prominent solicitor Fiona Shackleton, sought him out shortly after my arrest to tell him everyone knew my case was of no substance. How she knew this and why she was interested may remain unknown.

The idea that Christopher's emails were being read by the police infuriates me. Not for nothing did I consider Edward Snowden the Man of the Year in 2013. Christopher Sherwood is my husband, he is not me, and he should not be persecuted because the police are pursuing a deranged case against me. I am furious at the way they are treating him. He had done his best to protect his emails, going into his office the day after my arrest and changing his password, and emailing from a different computer after the police took his, but it obviously hasn't been enough to stop a determined John Law. I am sick at heart to realise the police have probably attempted to read all my emails, too, which means that this book has been compromised. I have periodically sent copies of the work in progress to my assistant Jennifer and my former lodger Darren, but since I did so by email they may have been accessed by the police. I had thought I was protecting the book in case the police returned to my apartment and took my new computer, but it turns out that was not the threat this time around!

In his incisive and optimistic way, Christopher reminds me that each turn of events I have faced during this case has presented both an opportunity to become angry and reason to find comfort. My sense of invasion is overbearing at this moment, but there is the probability that if Yewtree are reading Christopher's emails they are probably subjecting my accusers to the same scrutiny.

I close this traumatic day by sending an email to solicitor Kate Goold. For the subject heading I put 'Hello Police'. I write

Dear Kate,

You should know that tonight Christopher received evidence that his emails have been intercepted and read by police. We should assume they are doing the same to me. Hello, big boys.

I will call you tomorrow from a secure phone, although obviously nothing is safe with these guys.

Best wishes,

Paul

<hr/>

<h3 style="text-align:center">9 JANUARY 2014</h3>

I have a lengthy telephone conversation with Kate in the afternoon. We discuss a couple of issues, including whether we should protest to the police about either their claim that the BBC and I revealed my arrest to the press or their monitoring of Christopher's email. I tell her we are beyond that now. I no longer look to the British police for any civility or decency. Besides, whether they are cruel or not, it is their way of doing business, not the business itself. It is time for us to cut to the chase by preparing for the worst possible scenario. Who should be my barrister if we must go to court to clear my name? I do not want to be caught unprepared by a sudden charge.

Kate has someone in mind who is supposedly excellent in sex cases. I must remind her, however, that this is not just a sex case, and is perhaps not even primarily a sex case. It may fundamentally be a case of false memory, which is another subject altogether. Anyway, we will convene when her current case in Clapham is concluded, most likely on the 22nd, by which time she, Christopher and I will have asked our contacts for their recommendations. I hope I never have to put on the armour, but I have to be prepared to go to battle.

10 JANUARY 2014

I've never listened to more Rolling Stones in my life. After the police took my computers with no promise of early return … and there's still no sign of them … I had to buy a new iMac and set up a new iTunes. I've had numerous loading sessions. Yesterday it was time for one of Brendel's recordings of the Schubert D960, which I saw Christian Zacharias perform the other night. I listened to it this morning and got so into my work that I didn't change the artist selection. The sonata went straight into Beethoven's piano concertos Nos 4 and 5 as conducted by Simon Rattle. Pure bliss!

My Top 10 most played songs since my arrest have been:

1) Brown Sugar / Rolling Stones
2) Ain't Too Proud to Beg / Temptations
3) Put a Little Love in Your Heart / Jackie DeShannon
4) I'm Doing Fine Now / New York City
5) Jumpin' Jack Flash / Rolling Stones
6) Street Fighting Man / Rolling Stones
7) Where Did Our Love Go / Supremes

8) Eleanor Rigby / Beatles
9) Palisades Park / Freddy Cannon
10) #9 Dream / John Lennon

Well, that list dates me! It's telling that two are New York City-related ('I'm Doing Fine Now' being by a group of that name and 'Palisades Park' concerning the amusement park that used to sit on the Palisades across the Hudson River from Manhattan). It's also revealing that the three Rolling Stones tunes are my 'anger' songs. I've been angry a lot in the last two and a half months! When I get through the rage I turn to 'Put a Little Love in Your Heart'. It's corny, but it's true.

The real winner in this list is saxophonist Bobby Keys. He supplied the immortal solos on 'Brown Sugar' and on two songs in the lower half of my post-arrest Top 20, 'Whatever Gets You thru the Night' by John Lennon and 'The Wanderer' by Dion.

---

11 JANUARY 2014

In the middle of a morning with Christopher, I have a very strange thought. What is the name of the operation the police are conducting against me? Yewtree? What does that have to do with anything? And what is it I am supposed to have done? Oh, yes … I remember now. Well, how stupid.

And that's it. Somehow, today, I feel very distant from the case.

---

12 JANUARY 2014

For the second day in a row, I feel less pessimistic about my chances. By now the police have gathered seven or eight statements, depending on whether they have seen Brad Spurgeon already or are planning to do so early this week. I assume all are favourable to me in some way.

If I were to be charged, it would mean the police do not believe these eight individuals have an accurate insight into me, despite having been flatmates and/or lovers. It would also mean they are willing to bring a case with international dimensions, involving persons from the United States, Canada (Brad's home country) and Australia (if they get around to interviewing Dale Witton). Are they willing to risk the reputation of the Metropolitan Police in Anglophone countries around the world on the unsubstantiated word of two fabulists?

---

13 JANUARY 2014

I finally speak to my friend and former lodger Keith. It is the first time we have communicated in weeks. He had been discouraged from doing so by the Metropolitan Police until he had signed his statement, which apparently took some time in being drafted. (The Christmas break may have been the reason for the delay.) Even though the reunion is of voice only, it is joyful.

Keith is not surprised to hear that Christopher's emails have been compromised. When he had received his statement he could not return it electronically. The police communication included the news that 'We are monitoring email to the full extent of the law'.

I am so angry I am reminded of the first line of the film *The End of the Affair*: 'This is a diary of hate.'

Keith and I agree to meet for dinner. There is one piece of news for which I cannot wait. I had assumed the delay in having his statement prepared and signed must have been caused by something substantial. Had he in fact known Secondary?

'No,' he tells me. 'I was never asked that question.'

I am treated to lunch at the Criterion by my neighbour of the early and mid-1990s, Jean-Paul Floru. When we were neighbours, JP, an immigrant from Belgium, was an aspiring artist. Now he is a Conservative serving as councillor for Hyde Park ward. I missed the join, but I enjoy the incongruity. Floru offers to be a character witness for me should I go to trial, even though he knows it would be risky for him as an aspiring parliamentary candidate.

'I thought about it for days,' he tells me, 'but I would want to do it.'

Well, bravo. Here is the first courageous politician I have met in my entire case, and he turns out to be a Tory. But, of course, he is not 'a Tory' – he is Jean-Paul Floru, and he is a decent man.

---

14 JANUARY 2014

Kate Goold has recommended several possible QCs should I go to trial, and I have to attempt to make sense of her list. Noting the name of Doughty Street Chambers, I Google the firm and am staggered to see it is the company co-founded by Geoffrey Robertson. Everyone who uses my downstairs bathroom is confronted by the large photograph of the 1970 University College, Oxford freshmen, in which Geoffrey and I are near each other in the back row. Thinking fate has brought us together again, I suggest him to Kate. She throws some cold water on the coals.

'Geoffrey has a great reputation,' she writes,

> but sadly I have never worked with him personally. Whenever I use your bathroom I always have a good look at the photos and try to spot people but I missed Geoffrey – how remiss of me! My understanding was that Geoffrey focused more on appellate, media and quasi-civil work now and did not have such a focus on jury trials. I may be wrong and can certainly check with his senior clerk. I will also clarify whether he deals with many sexual allegations as I think it does help if you conduct this type of work fairly regularly. There are numerous rules about cross-examining complainants of sexual offences and special measures and it can be a minefield.

Kate makes the interesting point of the recommendations that 'most QCs' profiles do not list sexual cases due to their sensitive nature and confidentiality so if you are looking at them please do not be put off by the lack of sexual cases listed'. She is particularly keen on two possible representatives. We will hold our QC summit next week.

—————————— 15 JANUARY 2014 ——————————

I have received kind emails from considerate friends who understand that the phalanx of celebrity sex stories dominating the popular press will be upsetting me. It is difficult to avoid them, though I try to, because even the BBC website is dominated by them.

A letter and signed photo sent by Bill Roache to a fan in 1965 is introduced as evidence against him in support of a complainant's accusation that, according to the *Telegraph*, 'Roache forced her to perform a sex act on him in the gents' toilets at Granada Studios in Manchester in the summer of 1965'.

Doesn't anyone realise that at least until the late 1980s it was considered obligatory for show-business celebrities to be polite? Everyone dedicated time to answering fan mail. Anyone with more than a handful of fans had photo cards printed up which they inevitably signed 'Love, [name]'. To write 'love' was considerate, not predatory. I cannot estimate the thousands of photos I have sent out in my life with my signed inscription 'Love, Paul Gambaccini'. I would hate for one of them to come back at me now.

I have lunch with Oliver Davies, a talented composer who makes the bulk of his earnings from television commissions, particularly in animation. A few years ago we wrote an unproduced musical, *TV 22*. Ollie shows me his new studios, which are, bizarrely, next door to the office of Christopher's old ad agency The Minimart, where he still does some freelance work.

Oliver is generous in deed and spirit, paying for lunch and demonstrating without having to say it that he is 100 per cent certain of my innocence. He had even predicted to his wife when Yewtree was set up that I would probably be arrested, having been successful in the 1970s, working for the BBC, and having spoken publicly about Jimmy Savile. One of Oliver's relatives had received a rough ride from the police years ago, so he is disposed to disbelieve the accusations against me.

After seeing an Australian film called *The Rocket*, I meet Keith at Mr Kong for dinner. It is a joyful reunion. To my astonishment, it turns out that shortly after my arrest was publicised, a man from Brighton phoned Operation Yewtree to say he had briefly dated Keith in the early 2000s and on one occasion my lodger had told him something salacious about my sexual preferences.

Keith was furious. He never said such a thing. He thought the entire approach was dubious anyway, since the man used a different surname contacting the police from the one he used when they were dating.

I am deeply moved to be able to resume my friendship with Keith. We schedule a piano recital by Paul Lewis at the Royal Festival Hall on 4 February.

---

16 JANUARY 2014

Chris leaves at 8.10, in time to make his personal trainer course. I am sorrier than usual to see him go, because I am feeling a bit low. Keith's news last night that another person I don't even know had phoned Yewtree to accuse me of bad habits depresses me. Person A calls the police to say that Person B had said something about Person C more than a decade earlier. If this isn't the Salem witch trials, I don't know what is.

At 3.30 in the afternoon I email Brad Spurgeon in Paris.

'Greetings from London,' I begin.

> I have observed what I think is the embargo on contacting you. I recall

your saying sometime in mid-December that you would be interviewed by the police by the 15th of January. Has this occurred? Can I contact you now, or are you still instructed to remain silent until you have signed a statement at some further point in the future?

I hope you are having a good 2014.

As always, Paul

God bless him, Brad replies almost immediately.

Hi Paul,

No, there was absolutely no embargo or instruction to me as to whether I should speak to you or not over the last month. I had myself thought that since you were under pressure from the police, and since the only things I would have to say to the police would be in your favour or defence, that there was really no point in us having to discuss your situation. Whatever the problem is that you've had – and the police only gave me the vaguest idea of what it was – I just thought it was probably best for you personally and for the case itself, if we did not talk. But I'd be happy to talk and learn anything about it.

What is very odd, though, is that after the police contacted me twice and I responded to them twice – without giving any of the details of my time at your apartment in 1977–78 – and they told me that they would like to come to Paris to speak to me between mid-December and mid-January, well, they never wrote back to me again. I had told them that my preference was for it to happen in December, since I had been planning to travel on a holiday with my girlfriend. They never responded after that! So I basically sat here waiting for a response, and kept wondering what was happening.

Having been puzzled as to why they never got back to me I decided at one point to do a search on the Nexis database to see if there had been any developments in the case, and I saw there had indeed been the development of your bail having been extended for a few months. So at that point I assumed that they might come back to me later. But it did not feel very professional that nothing was said in the meantime.

In any case, there never was any suggestion by the police that I not communicate with you in any way I want!

I hope you're keeping the 'morale' as the French say, and that you're working on your projects…

I'm knocked sideways. Los Angeles and New York were worth a trip, but Paris was not? I tell Kate Goold, who offers a possible interpretation.

'That's very interesting,' she responds. 'They must be realising that everyone they speak to will only be supportive.'

<hr>

17 JANUARY 2014

I phone my solicitor David Gentle. This time I am going to ask him to perform his biennial task of updating my will. I am taking Amnesty International out and reassigning its legacy to the friends who babysat me during the week my home was under siege from the media. I silently dedicate this alteration to the executive who stiffed me and will refer to it in future as 'the £50,000 shun'.

In the evening, Christopher and I attend his friend Sarah's leaving party. She is off for a year's legal work in Belize. Sarah, who used to be a criminal barrister, has been remarkably helpful and knowledgeable about my case. Tonight she points out that, if I were to be charged, not interviewing Brad Spurgeon in Paris could be a breach of regulations. Police are required to follow all lines of inquiry before a charge. If they didn't, merely because Brad had told them in advance that he would only be saying things in my defence, they would be lax in their legal duty.

Sarah's husband James, a Liberal Democrat activist, is not surprised when I tell him of my shunning by the Labour Party. He is a bit flummoxed, however, when I tell him that the powers that be have not replied to my letter after a couple of weeks. James notes that Ed Fordham, a Liberal Democrat friend, is due to see Christopher soon. Chris should stir Ed into action. If anyone has clout on this type of matter, it would be Fordham.

---

18 JANUARY 2014

I have a good talk with Liza Tarbuck. I keep her abreast of all the developments in my case. After all, she is uniquely placed in being both contiguous with me on Radio 2 and the daughter of another suspect. I tell her the two recent revelations – that Christopher's email has been monitored and that someone who dated Keith a few times more than a decade ago has called Yewtree to report on a remark he thinks my then lodger made about me, leading the police to interview my old pal. This level of police intrusion is like having a colonoscopy that never ends.

Whereas everyone else has been shocked by the reason for Keith's interview, Liza is not. When I tell her that he got the impression that the Met will drop my case on the next appointment date, 26 March, she says, 'Don't get your hopes up.'

Of course, she and her family have been led to believe numerous times that Jimmy's case will be terminated at the end of a certain month. She now is hoping that her dad will be officially cleared of all suspicion on 28 January.

The day's post brings a Liberal Democrat 'thank you but no thank you' letter.

> Dear Mr Gambaccini,
>
> Thank you for your letter … Your letter does not specify who the person is who has made the allegations against you but in any event as it is over twenty-five years since … [my colleague would have come across him, we] … do not feel it likely that we could shed any light that would be relevant to those allegations.

I am very sorry not to be able to provide a more helpful reply.

With best wishes,

Yours sincerely,

[Mr Lib Dem]

Move over, Ed Miliband. You have a fellow Profile in Cowardice. A noted Liberal Democrat. At the slightest whiff of scandal, without even knowing who the person I am referring to is, they run down the street waving their arms in the air, like old women fleeing Godzilla.

I phone Tim Rice, who is back in the country after a Christmas in Australia. He had the dubious pleasure of watching England get batted from 2013 into 2014 in the Ashes. I read Tim the Liberal Democrat letter.

Sir Tim reacts by saying, 'I don't like what this country is becoming,' and condemns the eagerness of one generation to judge its forebears from forty years previous using the morals of today. He thinks it quite understandable of me to consider moving to New York if I am unjustly convicted.

I have my usual Saturday afternoon back rub and return to an unusual Post-it from Christopher.

'Enjoy your emails. Lots of love, Sher (lock) xxx'

I turn on the computer and, son of a gun, my beloved husband has continued his trawl of the Twittersphere looking for conversation about me. He has come across a series of tweets from someone named Theodore Price. A couple have misspelled my name, but they are welcome. He is begging Operation Yewtree and the Mail Online to contact him, saying he knows Paul Gambaccini is innocent and has proof. One tweet directed to '@MrCelebUK' repeats the assertion that I am innocent and that the writer has proof 'nobullshit'.

Now I'm embarrassed. What is MrCelebUK? I Google and discover he is one of the Twitterati, with over 80,000 followers. Theodore Price knows his social media.

This means nothing to me, Vienna, even though I'm dying of curiosity.

Chris, too, knows better than to approach someone directly. He has informed my solicitor Kate Goold rather than contact Price himself, lest he be accused at a future date of interference in the case. Kate sends several tantalising emails saying that she has had a long and productive conversation with Theodore, whom she considers a potential witness. However, she is entering the theatre and will be out of contact for several hours. She will welcome my call in the morning.

---

19 JANUARY 2014

I phone Kate Goold. She is serving her children breakfast and will return my call in twenty minutes.

Oh, the tension! Rather than ulcerate, I might as well have some fun. 'Mashed Potato Time' by Dee Dee Sharp comes up on my iTunes, and I give Christopher a demonstration of the Mashed Potato and the Jerk. I could get a job on *Hullabaloo* if it were still running.

My solicitor calls back. She has had a long conversation with Theodore Price, who is outraged by the accusations against me and wants the world to know I am innocent. The only problem is he doesn't know what the accusations against me are. What he wants to do is to be a character reference of sorts.

Theodore has told Kate that in the early 1980s he met me in the nightclub Heaven. He has said that he was underage, although he was six feet tall at the time and looked eighteen. He was a troubled individual. He says that on one difficult night I offered to let him stay in my apartment. Price wants the world to know that I did not touch him or try to seduce him but instead tried to be helpful. He claims I gave him £20 for his immediate needs, asking him to return it when he could, and that he one day did, during a chance meeting on Oxford Street.

This is not the kind of story I had expected at all. The time period is over thirty years ago, and I don't remember the name of Theodore Price.

Besides, it's difficult to remember not having sex with someone. I have not had sex with over a million people.

But everything Price says to Kate rings true. He has accurately described where my flat was. Furthermore, I did sometimes let people stay for free, since the third bedroom was often unoccupied. I was a product of the hippie era and did believe in sharing with those in need. And there are two particular details that are on target. The first is the precise amount of £20. This was what Alan Price and Teddy Warrick each loaned me to start my life in London. In their honour, I would sometimes give someone with a tough-luck tale the same sum. I would ask the person to pay it back as a challenge to their self-respect and self-discipline. Most did not. One person once did, on Oxford Street … just where Theodore Price claimed he repaid his debt. Could he have been that person? Kate is convinced he might prove a good period character witness and arranges to interview him.

The phone is busy for a Sunday. The Great Unravelling continues. Is there any thread left on this spool? David Munns calls from Canada to inform me that he must wrap up the plans for this autumn's Music Industry Trusts dinner. Since I have not yet been cleared, they must plan for Jo Whiley to take my place as host again. A second year! The career damage is threatening to become permanent. That is no disrespect to the deserving Whiley, whom I would be happy to see as my successor … some day.

I call Elton John and ask if he and his husband David Furnish can contact a former classmate of Secondary to learn something about him. Elton promises to ask. As his late producer Gus Dudgeon used to say, 'What a bloke!'

I succumb further and ring newspaper radio critic Gillian Reynolds. She had previously indicated she would do anything in my support. This is 'anything'. I ask if she knows a particular journalist well enough to find out if he has a brother named Secondary. She says she will make discreet inquiries.

20 JANUARY 2014

I make someone happy today, but they don't know it yet. We have our final meeting of the Ivor Novello Awards committee, on which I sit as an advisor. The panel reach deadlock on an important category. No one seems right for the prize. I suggest a singer/songwriter whose recent work I have adored. After the group listens to a couple of his songs, he is embraced. I will watch with pride in May, unless the Metropolitan Police have other plans for me, when this person experiences what will be a highlight of his career. It is satisfying to know that, even operating in the shadows, I can make a difference.

As I listen to Martha Argerich play Tchaikovsky's piano concerto on my iTunes, I see a *New York Times* web headline that Claudio Abbado has died. I had seen Abbado conduct the Lucerne Festival Orchestra only recently at the Royal Festival Hall. This was a mature relationship, like Bernstein with the New York Philharmonic or Rattle with Berlin. But unlike those two, the Abbado–Lucerne pairing was unique, for this conductor had founded his orchestra. At the pinnacle of his career in 2000, he assembled the players he thought best for the purpose of interpreting the deepest classical works, using the Mahler Chamber Orchestra as its nucleus. He asked the musicians to listen to each other as they performed. They sounded as if they were one voice, even when performing complex passages.

I had been astonished, as had so many others, that Abbado conducted without scores. The *New York Times* reports he felt that if he hadn't memorised a piece, he didn't really know it.

After an early-evening recital introducing the restored Royal Festival Hall of patrons, I write to Jerry Rush asking if Dale Witton has received an invitation to be interviewed in her home city of Melbourne. I had thought that if the police were serious about interviewing the principals of my flat in the late '70s and early '80s they would certainly speak to Dale, who was there for about four years. In light of their decision not to chase up Brad Spurgeon in Paris, perhaps they had given up on interviewing persons they did not expect to dish dirt on me.

Jerry replies quickly. He does not know if the Met have contacted Dale in Australia. However, one of the officers did have Jerry sign his statement on Christmas Eve. He did not expect the police to give themselves away, but he got the impression that things were looking 'very positive' for me. It is a nice thought on which to go to bed.

---

21 JANUARY 2014

Tomorrow is the day Christopher and I will meet our two potential barristers. Today I read up on them. I can't make a decision until I've met them. They are both serious and highly recommended individuals. The one that will be right for me will feel right and will have a proven smooth working relationship with my solicitor Kate Goold. The choice must wait for tomorrow. Arrrgh!

At yesterday's Ivor Novello Awards meeting, songwriter Mick Leeson told me he realised it must be very hard for me not working, since I am ordinarily so active. It's so hard that even when I'm not presenting the charts, I'm keeping one. Here is how the Top 10 tunes on my iTunes has changed since the last time I looked on the 10th:

(1)   1)   Brown Sugar / Rolling Stones

(3)   2)   Put a Little Love in Your Heart / Jackie DeShannon

(10) 3)   #9 Dream / John Lennon

(–)   4)   Pretty Ballerina / Left Banke

(4)   5)   I'm Doin' Fine Now / New York City

(7)   6)   Where Did Our Love Go / Supremes

(–)   7)   I Heard It through the Grapevine / Gladys Knight & the Pips

(–)   8)   Whatever Gets You thru the Night / John Lennon

(5)   9)   Jumpin' Jack Flash / Rolling Stones

(8)   10) Eleanor Rigby / Beatles

My most played classics since my arrest have been:

1) Schubert: Piano Quintet in A Major, 'Trout' / Alban Berg Quartet & Elisabeth Leonskaja
2) Mozart: Clarinet Concerto in A Major, K622 / Alessandro Carbonare & Claudio Abbado
3) Beethoven: Piano Concerto No. 4 / Alfred Brendel & Simon Rattle
4) Beethoven: Piano Concerto No. 5 / Alfred Brendel & Simon Rattle
5) Barber: Adagio for Strings / Leonard Bernstein

This confirms what I have thought: I have been on a Brendel binge lately. However, Daniel Barenboim is moving up in the pianistic stakes with both Beethoven's 'Moonlight' Sonata and various 'Songs without Words' by Mendelssohn. Having whetted my appetite by talking about them, I will now go downstairs and play them.

22 JANUARY 2014

I awake to an item on the *Today* programme. Justin Webb is interviewing the parents of a former BBC journalist now working for Al Jazeera who was arrested in Egypt in December and has still not been charged with anything. Webb is incredulous that someone could be detained under such circumstances. I stare at the radio and send a mental message: what do you think is happening in your own country? Being in jail with neither charge nor arrest is undoubtedly worse, but don't the *Today* journalists realise that people in Britain are being falsely arrested and not charged for months? For heaven's sake, I have been on the *Today* programme countless times, interviewed by all the legendary presenters from Jack DeManio to John Humphrys. If they don't even notice what is happening to one of their own, they're looking in the wrong direction.

I have more pressing things to worry about. Christopher and I go to Kate Goold's office on Gray's Inn Road for our meeting with potential barristers.

One development requires urgent attention. After Christopher offered to make a statement, Officer Four has agreed to meet him. The Met had not asked him to speak because they believe that spouses often lie in defence of their partners. Is this an opportunity for my husband to make the ultimate character reference, or is it a manoeuvre in which the police hope he will be tripped up into inadvertently saying something incriminating?

Chris and I know he is in a position to say something that could potentially hit the Yewtree case below the waterline, but we don't know if he should at this point. This is the fact that in our entire four-year relationship I have never performed one of the alleged sex acts with him, nor have I with any of my earlier significant lovers, all of whom would be willing to say so in court. Yes, I have conferred with all of them. It has come to that. Engaging in this particular sex act with my accusers is one of the three main allegations against me. Chris and I are only too aware of the advice we have received from other suspects that anything said to the police pointing out flaws in accusations will only result in the allegations being modified, not dropped, in the hope of making the prosecution case more potent. Perhaps we should wait for a court case to drop bombs.

Officer Four has someone else to interview, too. Yewtree did indeed pick up on the tweets of Theodore Price. Four is going to meet him. I don't know what to make of this. His intentions seem the purest, and Kate Goold is convinced of his honesty. But introducing a man who claims to have been underage to a case that focuses on men who claim to have been underage seems like skating on thin ice. I just have to shrug my shoulders and believe in the kindness of strangers.

Both Kate and Christopher are convinced that Theodore Price is clearly heterosexual. A large percentage of his tweets seem to focus on attractive women and television shows such as *Celebrity Big Brother*.

'I found myself wondering what CBB is,' Goold explains early in today's meeting. 'Was it some sort of code? Was it another message to the police and the papers? Then I realised.'

Chris laughed. He also had to endure a running commentary on *Celebrity Big Brother* while scanning tweets.

Our first potential barrister arrives for his interview. This case is now old enough for Christopher and me to be having flashbacks. We recall the afternoon when we sat at home in our dining room talking to potential solicitors. Now we are in the office of our chosen solicitor meeting prospective barristers. When this is all over, I may take up the job of professional auditioner.

Our discussions end later in the day. Mark Dennis is our choice. Although both candidates are excellent, he is senior and has more experience, which can only be helpful, and in this situation the rave recommendations from people we trust are convincing. Christopher and I are legal neophytes, and we must take the advice of leading individuals we know and respect.

Much of what may lie ahead will involve judgement calls, not just obeying advice. On one pressing matter we agree with Mark Dennis: Chris should meet Officer Four on Saturday and be completely open.

---

24 JANUARY 2014

I sigh deeply. Today I must follow up on my promise to Kate Goold to approach old friends for 'period character references'. I have already written to former lodger Brad Spurgeon, so Kate can get in touch with him as soon as she wishes.

I send an email to Elton John. I title it 'The Yard Went On Forever'. I am rather proud of that subject heading. It was the title of a 1969 Richard Harris album written and produced by Jimmy Webb. It never made any sense to me until now. Scotland Yard is taking its sweet time. The solicitor John Harding was right when he once told me that there are two time zones in the world: Greenwich Mean Time and Metropolitan Police time.

I begin a letter to one of the world's most beloved actors, someone I knew in his days at the National Youth Theatre, requesting a character reference. I dream of an acknowledgement that within the National Youth Theatre in the time period at issue, there were no sinister reports about me, which there would have been had I overstepped any line with any teenager even once. I realise the actor might consider it risky to support someone he has not seen in years. Before I can conclude the letter, I get a response from Elton.

> Dear Paul,
>
> I have spoken with Kate. I am writing a handwritten letter praising and defending you. Especially the allegations of alcohol. It was a very easy letter to write as we have known each other for decades and I cannot recall any occasion where this issue of alcohol ever materialised. I told Kate that of all my friends you were the least excessive in anything you do except for your obsession with pop trivia!!!!!! The letter will be delivered to her on Monday as I am leaving for LA on Sunday.
>
> Any further assistance that you need please don't hesitate to email me. I am so angry that you are having to put up with this absolute nonsense. You will be vindicated. Love to you and Chris from us all. Exxxx

My hero! Elton has a heart big enough to accommodate a football stadium.

Writing to the actor is harder. I realise that if his agent does pass on my request, which is by no means guaranteed since I have become untouchable, I will have to bring the star up to speed and ask for a favour in the same breath. I give it a go.

I email the letter and the contact details of the actor's agent to Kate Goold, who will handle the approach. I suspect the agent might consider the matter too incendiary for a film star to approach and might not even forward the request, but when you are fighting the full weight of the state you have no pride.

To end the day with a laugh, I cross the street to the National Film Theatre to see the late-evening screening of Buster Keaton's *The General*. The more experience I have had as a film viewer and television performer, the more impressive Keaton's achievements have seemed. His most casual-looking stunts required incredible precision and courage. He also remembered to act while doing complicated physical business. His work has survived nine decades so far and will for many more.

I sleep well.

———— 25 JANUARY 2014 ————

Christopher spends two hours in the Royal Festival Hall giving Officer Four his statement.

In the evening, when he has collected his thoughts, he emails Kate Goold.

> This morning I met Four, who took a signed statement from me. So that you're aware, I was very open, honest and upfront with her. The basic content was as follows:
>
> My own sexual history with older men over a three-year period prior to meeting Paul. This appeared of particular interest to her and she implied this would be helpful in dismissing any ideas that perhaps Paul had 'groomed' me. I did get a sense that perhaps our relationship was indeed being viewed by the police as adding credibility to the accusations.
>
> The story of how we met – the fact that I had contacted him and approached him, the fact that we had a series of dates before there was any sexual contact.
>
> I briefly touched on our own sexual development as a couple. I also gave examples of how our activities are always taken back to the bedroom because Paul is uncomfortable with anything else. I didn't give any other detail beyond that on our shared sexual activities.
>
> I then made my observations about Paul's character – the way he

behaves in social settings, his dedication to his work including the no drink, drugs or smoking, and avoidance of air conditioning in restaurants.

I also told an anecdote about when he stumbled across a straight porn DVD in our lodger's drawer while he was in the process of moving out. Paul called me into the room in excitement to see the DVD. I laughed at this, but what was more striking to me was the presence of all the sex toys which Paul hadn't recognised as sex toys – I had to tell him what they were! It was another example of his sexual conservatism.

I stated that we had discussed threesomes and the fact that Paul had never had one, and had no intention of ever having one.

That pretty much sums it up, I believe.

The meeting was pleasant. Officer Four seemed keen to make the statement as favourable for Paul as possible. Let me know if you have any further questions.

Many thanks,

Chris

My husband's statement on my behalf was bolstered by his provision of the correspondence between us that took place on Facebook prior to our first meeting. He thus proved that he had made the first contact between us and had spoken of his preference for older men before we even met.

---

26 JANUARY 2014

I have to do something about this. Today when I open my iTunes menu, the name of Secondary's potential brother stares back at me with his homophobic downloads. To force the names of all other artists down my playlist, I have a massive ABBA download session.

It is a Sunday, but Kate Goold is still on the case. She writes to Christopher:

Many thanks for the very clear detail of your statement. How sad and depressing that the police appear to have viewed your relationship in the way they did. Clearly your ability to dispel any such suggestions can only be of help to Paul's case.

Enjoy the rest of your weekend.

Best wishes,

Kate

It is astonishing that after all their experience the Metropolitan Police still don't have a perspective on the reality of celebrity. Far more persons approach celebrities for sex than the other way round. There would not be the phenomenon of the 'groupie' were this not so.

Fame is the reaction of other people. It is not a quality that resides in genes. Famous persons, at least of my generation, became so as a reaction to something they did, which they did for its own sake. I never sought to be 'famous'. I sought what I called 'the successful completion of projects'. If I wrote a book, I wanted it published. If I constructed a radio or television programme, I wanted it broadcast. When these things happened, the project was complete and I could move on to the next one. The reaction of readers, listeners and viewers was their own business, not mine. More of them desired sex with me than I ever did with them. Can't the police grasp this simple truth about the nature of fame?

—————— 27 JANUARY 2014 ——————

I receive a phone call update from another recent sex suspect, Nigel Evans. His case as well as his profession is completely different from mine, so I listen with great attention, as he does to mine. Nigel is going to court on 10 March and my sympathies are with him.

Good news comes from seeing last night's Grammy Awards clip of 'Same Love' by Macklemore and Ryan Lewis, in which Madonna bizarrely joined featured vocalist Mary Lambert. Even odder, Queen Latifah, who is some-how qualified to do so, married thirty-three couples, mixed and same-sex, while the song was being performed. I am thrilled that CBS, an American television network, has aired same-sex marriage and allowed its advocacy. Christopher and I got there first, but not by much.

In the evening I call Jimmy Tarbuck to wish him well. Liza had told me that tomorrow is the date of his next court appearance. He still has no idea as to what will happen. During the course of our conversation, he reports that a friend of his has used an expression to describe what he is going through. It is the same expression that Nigel Evans said earlier today was used by one of his friends to describe his plight. It is one that sums up what all of us are going through in the Britain of 2014. It is 'a form of torture'.

---

28 JANUARY 2014

After I had prepared for bed last night, Moscow Paul called from Los Angeles. As he said, 'twice in thirty years isn't bad'. He is genuinely concerned that I have been falsely accused and tells me he is so upset that he called Yewtree when the officers who interviewed him returned to London. Paul told them that he thought I was completely innocent. One of them said, 'So do I.'

That would be progress. These days I grasp at anything that will keep me afloat. Yesterday, Nigel Evans thought it a good sign that my passports had been returned before Christmas. Today I am grateful that one police officer apparently thinks I should not be charged. This is how those of us in the maelstrom survive, hanging on to pieces of driftwood until we one day reach dry land.

I learn that Pete Seeger has died. I am heartbroken. He was one of the greatest of Americans, fighting all his ninety-four years for freedom, and triumphing over the McCarthy blacklist to make decades of important contributions to human rights. His hit songs that he wrote, co-wrote or arranged included 'We Shall Overcome', 'Turn! Turn! Turn!', 'If I Had a Hammer', 'Guantanamera' and 'Where Have All the Flowers Gone?' His group The Weavers were number one for thirteen weeks in 1950 with 'Goodnight Irene', reached number two with 'Tzena Tzena Tzena', scored Top 5 hits with 'On Top of Old Smokey' and Woody Guthrie's 'So Long (It's Been Good to Know Ya)' and first popularised 'Kisses Sweeter Than Wine'. Even though they were Decca's bestselling group, the company buckled before McCarthyism and deleted all their records. They returned to catalogue later.

I interviewed Seeger only last year. I write to my former Radio 2 producer Kevin Howlett:

Needless to say, I have not been asked to make a single comment. Sigh. This is one tribute I would like to have made.

And, of course, I see our situations as being very similar. Hopefully I will emerge from this singing, as he did.

We shall overcome,

Paul

---

29 JANUARY 2014

I get a call from Liza Tarbuck.

I had rung Liza earlier to find out what had happened to her father in his meeting with the police yesterday. I couldn't figure out why I couldn't find any reports of it via Google. It turns out that this was because the session was not decisive, as it had been hoped it would be. Instead of having his case dismissed, Jimmy Tarbuck, who has suffered nine months after arrest without charge, was hit with a new accusation.

A woman has alleged that in 1963 on *Top of the Pops*, Tarbuck told her he would get her a dancing job on the show if she performed fellatio on his road manager. I immediately spot two flaws in this: *Top of the Pops* was not on the air until 1964, and Jimmy Tarbuck was never on it.

The friends of Tarbuck and Nigel Evans are right. This is torture.

It is remarkable how police officers of the witch-hunt, fine people as individuals, do such harm as a unit. They drank the Kool Aid and believe they are performing a useful social function when in fact they are profoundly damaging the nation. They seem to think I should cheer up because they are looking at my case objectively and will not charge me if they believe I am innocent. They do not seem to realise that it is a moral outrage that a human being can be dragged out of society, publicly humiliated and indefinitely deprived of employment simply because someone else has lost their bearings.

---

30 JANUARY 2014

I have a confidential conversation on my allegedly safe phone with Kate Goold.

She has been told that 26 March will indeed be 'effective'. This does not mean that anything will be decided on that date, just that the meeting will go ahead. So much for the meaning of the word 'effective'.

---

31 JANUARY 2014

Gary Osborne emails to say that Jim Davidson is about to appear on the Matthew Wright show on Channel 5. I tell Gary I can't watch. I would get angry when he talks about Yewtree. However, I will read any relevant reports of revelations.

Upon reflection, however, I view Jim's victory on *Celebrity Big Brother* as potentially important for me. After all, he was voted the winner by the public, which suggests that the tide may have already turned against the witch-hunt and that getting convictions on innocent persons like myself may be difficult.

1 FEBRUARY 2014

My iTunes once again comes up with 'Pretty Ballerina' by the Left Banke. It's a beautiful record, but I ache to hear 'Walk Away Renee', their first hit and the original version of the classic song. This is one way in which I have new reason to resent the Metropolitan Police every day. They continue to negatively impact my daily existence by depriving me of items I would use regularly, such as my original iTunes collection and my 38-year accumulation of addresses and phone numbers. There is no getting around it. Three months is more than long enough for them to return objects and computer programs that have no possible bearing on my case. Do the Met not have a single photocopier?

It's down to the record wall to once again import selections from *Hard to Find 45s on CD, Volume 6: More Sixties Classics*, which must be in the Top 10 of the least sexy album titles of all time. I upload and listen for the first time in months to several songs from my adolescence, not just 'Walk Away Renee'. I hear 'Lightning Strikes' by Lou Christie and I am once again driving my first car. '(Just Like) Romeo and Juliet' by the Reflections comes on and I'm on my paper route in the Westport, Connecticut, trailer park. 'Guantanamera' by the Sandpipers plays and I think once again of the great Pete Seeger, who arranged this classic Cuban song. I visualise Pete leading half a million of us singing 'Give Peace a Chance' in Washington on 15 November 1969. The minute I think of Pete Seeger I am strengthened again in my determination to fight until my name is cleared.

2 FEBRUARY 2014

It's Groundhog Day, literally.

Ever since the 1993 Bill Murray movie *Groundhog Day* made the bizarre Pennsylvania ceremony internationally famous, crowds have been coming from far and wide to await the appearance of what today's *Chicago Tribune* calls 'the rotund rodent'. Nicknamed Punxsutawney Phil after the town in which he resides, the animal emerges from his burrow and either sees his shadow, which foretells six more weeks of winter, or does not, which guarantees an early spring. There have been several Punxsutawney Phils since the town began using groundhogs as weather forecasters in 1887. Phil is rather like Lassie, who the public did not seem to realise had to have been several dogs, given her lifespan. (Viewers also did not know that the collies playing Lassie were male, but that is another subject.) The current groundhog is not as well travelled as his 1986 predecessor, who went to Washington to meet President Ronald Reagan. He lets the world come to him, as tourists from countries as distant as Australia and Russia do.

Today Phil came out of his burrow and saw his shadow. That means the next six weeks are apparently going to be like the last six.

This is the last thing I need to read.

—————————————— 3 FEBRUARY 2014 ——————————————

I am named in a report on Mail Online headlined 'Beloved pop star "abused ten-year-old boy": alleged victim and witness have spoken to Savile police officers'. I am not going to be a horse's ass and comment on cases I know nothing about, but it takes me only two seconds to realise that the *Daily Mail* has once again conflated the different strands of Operation Yewtree. Legally, a newspaper is allowed to refer to Yewtree policemen as 'Savile police officers' because the Savile and 'others' cases fall under the same general investigation, but this is mischievous. It is like talking about Manchester United and Oxford United football clubs in the same breath. No matter how much I love Oxford, these two teams are never going to be in the same league.

To mislead the public further, the *Mail* accompanies the article with a huge picture of a very unattractive Savile. Towards the bottom of the piece it breathlessly reports that Yewtree 'has led to sixteen arrests, with four people charged and five suspects remaining on bail'. The list follows.

Only someone familiar with legal terminology would recognise that I have been arrested but not charged. But anyone with half a brain would notice that I am, after Davidson, the youngest of this group. I am waiting for someone to point out that I am not part of the Savile generation, being more than two decades younger than the knighted Yorkshireman, and never socialised with him. I am not even Oxford United to Manchester United; I am more Tooting & Mitcham.

Christopher points out a sentence in the report that cries out for further attention. 'The operation has cost £2.7 million so far, of which £490,000 has been paid out in overtime to the thirty-strong detective team.'

Could the fact that the *Daily Mail* is keeping track of Yewtree finances be an indication that they are preparing to pounce as soon as a couple of acquittals come in, charging a waste of taxpayer money? I'm delighted that officers have flown to Los Angeles and New York and will go to Melbourne to interview persons in my case who will only say supportive things about me, but the expense would not have been necessary if this case had not been launched in the first place.

---

4 FEBRUARY 2014

One of the hardest aspects of this ordeal is not knowing when blows will land. Just as I did not go to bed the evening of 28 October 2013 knowing that I would be awakened by police in the pre-dawn hours the following morning, I have no idea when the next disappointments will strike. Late yesterday I suffered a one–two–three combination that, though not severe, was enough to lower my spirits.

First, Kate Goold reported the latest on my mystery supporter.

> Theodore Price rang me after he was seen by Officer Four.
>
> He is still keen to see me even though he has made a statement to the police. The benefits of seeing him are that I can obtain a signed

statement from him so, if he disappears or changes his account in any way, I have a statement that is supportive (but the police should already have one as long as he has told me the correct position). The only disadvantage I can see is to your purse. It may well be an expense that is not necessary if the police already have a supportive signed statement. I have to meet him in Coventry and I imagine this will take up at least six hours of my time.

If you agree to me travelling to Coventry, please let me know and I will try and buy a cheaper ticket in advance.

Many thanks,

Kate

I grimace. A trip to Coventry would take at least six hours and cost me, shall we discreetly say, more than £1,000. This is all to take a statement from a person I can't visually remember, although he is saying at least some true things. This is a heck of a way to spend a four-figure sum.

Kate writes again in the early evening with another slight disappointment. I was infuriated on Day 1 that the police did not check to see if I lived at the Hyde Park Square address during the entire time period in question, which I had not. For a full quarter of the time I was at my new home in the borough of Islington. Now Goold tells me this isn't an easy thing to check:

I have been in touch with the Land Registry.

Unfortunately Land Registry advisors Dawn Ross advised me that the first freehold for flat nine was registered in 2004 when it became compulsory to register properties. The first leasehold was registered in 2006.

It was only compulsory to register them when they were sold so it's likely that the same owner had the freehold from the '50s all the way to 2006 and didn't register any of the leases.

Do you have any other information that may show when you left the property? A lease/tenancy agreement/Land Reg details for the Islington flat [you moved to] may assist.

I plan to see Theodore Price on Monday as I don't want to stress with the tube strike.

I will have to remind Kate that the Islington property was a house, not a flat. Fair comment on the Tube strike, though.

Then something hits me that I haven't thought of in ages. Aysgarth Road! While I was living in Hyde Park Square, I accumulated enough money to buy my first property. I purchased a terraced house in Dulwich Village and let two of my friends live in it at below market rent to allow them to raise a deposit on their own home. In 1983, I sold the house and added the proceeds to several more years of savings to buy my next home. There should be property records on both the Dulwich Village building and the Islington house. I ask Kate to check them both out. They would support the conviction that I moved in 1983, not 1984 or later.

It had to happen one day, but I didn't know it would be today. I receive my first email of congratulations for having my case dismissed. Billy Hynes, who used to work in Gosh! Comics and is a good friend of Keith, sends me his first communication since my arrest:

Hi there, Paul,

I hadn't written as I had no idea, and can't imagine, what you've been going through or your state of mind these last months.

I had spoken to Keith a couple of times.

Andrew from Gosh! just gave me the great news about the charges being dropped and I'm so happy for you.

I'm sure this isn't the end of difficult times but I just wanted to take the opportunity to wish you well and let you know my thoughts are with you.

Take care of yourself and, though I can't imagine what I could offer, you know where to find me.

All the best, your friend
Billy

My heart skips a beat when I read the words 'charges being dropped'. If I could learn about my rebail from other people, could I now be learning of my dismissal from someone else? After two seconds, I realise the email must be a well-intentioned mistake. The 'charges' can't be 'dropped' because there are no 'charges'. I haven't been charged with anything. Nonetheless, I Google myself to see if there is any news I haven't heard.

Billy Hynes has been misled. Rats.

For two seconds, I thought I was a free man.

---

6 FEBRUARY 2014

At 11.25 a.m., Christopher, who is working from home today, calls me into his office. An ITV correspondent has tweeted a news flash!

WILLIAM ROACHE NOT GUILTY ON ALL CHARGES!

I dance. I actually dance with joy.

I go out for lunch and get back ninety minutes later.

I dance again. Christopher joins me.

Is this the beginning of the fightback, or just a one-off? We will know more when the DLT jury reports, which is expected to be at the end of next week.

The *Daily Telegraph* runs an article timed 11.33 on its website. Credited to 'Gordon Rayner, Chief Reporter', it is headlined 'Roache not guilty: high-stakes gamble backfires for CPS'. Note the timing. Rayner could not have turned this around in eight minutes. This piece was waiting to run, and therefore reflected a viewpoint which was being entertained seriously at the *Telegraph* before the verdict was announced. (Of course, a very different kind of article was also probably ready to run in the event of conviction.)

Trying William Roache over allegations dating back fifty years was a high-stakes gamble for the Crown Prosecution Service which has backfired with potentially far-reaching consequences.

Accusations that the CPS has indulged in a 'celebrity witch-hunt' had already gathered strength following the acquittal last year of another *Coronation Street* star, Michael Le Vell, in a similarly high-profile trial on child sex abuse charges.

Its failure to convict Roache, 81, on rape and indecent assault charges will now have to be taken into account when the CPS makes charging decisions on other celebrities currently on bail … Freddie Starr, Paul Gambaccini and Jimmy Tarbuck are among those who remain on bail after being arrested last year under Operation Yewtree, the police investigation which followed Savile's posthumous exposure as a paedophile.

I am delighted that the nation's leading quality right-wing newspaper feels it is less likely today than it was yesterday that I will be charged.

Kate Goold brings me down to earth with an email concerning a film star from whom I had requested a character reference.

I am afraid that the actor is unwilling to assist.

His agent emailed that unfortunately he is unable to provide a reference as he only met you a few times.

I am sorry that this is the case. Remember, you have many many good friends who are standing by you.

I am not as disappointed as I have been with other shunnings. After all, as the actor says, I only met him a few times. I had thought that was enough to provide the specific information I required. He obviously feels uncomfortable being placed in this situation he did not seek, and I don't follow up.

Towards the end of the day, Rod Taylor, the director of my mid-1980s television show *The Other Side of the Tracks*, calls with supportive words. Rod is not involved in any of the recent and current cases, but simply because his career spanned decades he knows almost all the principals. He relates to me a sentence he has received in a letter from one of the celebrities. It chills.

'I have promised the family I will not self-harm, although the thought is always there.'

---

7 FEBRUARY 2014

Although I continue to avoid physical copies of British newspapers, I cannot resist reading the online broadsheet reports on the William Roache acquittal. I am praying for some sort of serious commentary on the sexual show trials sweeping the nation.

Jonathan Brown of *The Independent* reports: 'Although his arrest did not form part of Operation Yewtree, the Metropolitan Police-led inquiry launched in the wake of the Jimmy Savile paedophile scandal, the defence argued that the "spectre" of the DJ haunted proceedings throughout.'

The Independent notes: 'Mr Roache's *Coronation Street* co-star Michael Le Vell and former *Street* actor Andrew Lancel were both found not guilty following trials in the North West last year.'

Jennifer reports for work. She says there is a story on the front page of the *Daily Mail* titled 'How did it ever get to court?'

I quickly locate the story on Mail Online. Jennifer's comment turns out to have been a literal quotation.

'How did it ever get to court?' the long headline begins. 'As Roache is cleared of sex charges, a disturbing question'. [It really grates on my long-ago service at *Rolling Stone* that online newspaper sites are intentionally ungrammatical, but I have to quote them accurately!]

Reporters James Tozer, Paul Harris and Paul Bentley are blunt in their opening lines:

> Police and prosecutors were accused of serious errors of judgment last night after William Roache was cleared of sex abuse.
>
> After a jury took less than six hours to reject the allegations dating back almost half a century, there were furious claims the case had been brought as part of a 'celebrity witch-hunt'.

The *Mail* is definitely on to the truth:

> Barrister Neil Addison, a former Senior Crown Prosecutor, said: 'I do think that there is [a] witch hunt in the sense of the post-Savile era.'
>
> And a relative of the star said: 'There was never enough evidence. It should never have got this far. It all started with Jimmy Savile and now they're picking people out. It has all got out of hand.'

Reading Mail Online reminds me of something I meant to check long ago. My cousin Melanie Cecarelli told me over Christmas that the *Daily Mail* reporter who pestered her and her sister MaryAnn Meyer when I was arrested was a man named Daniel Bates. I Google him and, son of a gun, there he is with 1,877 bylines. I wonder how many other relatives of innocent people he's bothered.

---

9 FEBRUARY 2014

Joy of joys, I may yet attain one of my post-arrest goals. When I was hauled in, I weighed 14 stone 11 pounds, 207 in American. I decided that if I was ever going to appear in the dock, it would be at under 200. I wanted to look better under pressure than the public remembered me without it. This morning's weigh-in was 14 stone 4, an even 200! Now the pressure is really on to lose another pound!

I continue to be astonished at how, when you are under investigation for historic sexual offences, every other news story seems to be about sexual offences. The BBC website carries the headline 'Porn inquiry police face no criminal charges'. I check the date. It is not yet 1 April. Three Metropolitan Police officers 'quizzed over claims they exchanged porn on mobile phones will not face criminal charges, Scotland Yard says'. The story explains, 'The officers are from the Diplomatic Protection Group, which guards foreign embassies and controls access to New Scotland Yard and Downing Street', and continues, 'The officers, who are all male, allegedly sent each other picture messages using phones, and the Met said the images were "extreme" but did not involve children.'

One rule for you, one rule for me. Good grief, I'm quoting an After the Fire song from 1979! I go to YouTube to watch their *Top of the Pops* performance of 'One Rule for You'. To my pleasure, I still like the record. But what is it with the drummer, who changes headgear every few seconds and projects a self-assertive personality? A YouTube comment claims: 'The drummer was later a Chief Superintendent in Gloucestershire Police.' You can't get away from these guys.

---

10 FEBRUARY 2014

I write to Susan Fisher, head of friends and patrons of the Royal Opera House, to explain why I cannot renew my membership. This is one letter that will be unique in her lifetime.

I have cut back expenditure since my income became nil. Outside of a couple of visits to the Rex family of restaurants, we haven't dined out expensively at all. I've halted all patronage of the arts, philanthropy to charities and sponsorship of higher education. I haven't even pursued my hobby of collecting old comic books and comic art, and have indeed sold a couple of hundred items. It's an insane world when you survive by selling comic books, but this world I am forced to live in is insane.

11 FEBRUARY 2014

I am cheered by a text message from Dame Helena Kennedy. I am also baffled by it: it arrives as three successive emails with Vodafone listed as the
sender. Christopher has to reassure me that I can open the emails without fear of spamming my contacts list.

'I hope you feel a bit of reassurance after the Roache acquittal,' Dame
Helena texts. 'I think the CPS will be very concerned about any prosecution which will relate to 30/40 years ago.'

That was Text One.

Text Two:

'Juries don't like this stuff.'

And finally:

'Yours ever, Helena'.

Imagine if all communications were sent in instalments like this! Charles
Dickens might text:

'It was the best of times', which seems vaguely interesting.

Wait, there's a second one.

'It was the worst of times'.

Can't this guy make his mind up? Oh, wait:

'It was the age of wisdom'.

And then:

'It was the age of foolishness'.

And we give up before he even finishes his first sentence.

12 FEBRUARY 2014

I pay my dentist Dr Peter Lawrence a visit for the first time in two
years. Although I am a stickler for regular health check-ups, I have
been distracted lately. Dr Lawrence understands. He inveighs against
Operation Yewtree, even though he has an extremely senior Met man
as a patient. It is Peter who introduces the phrases 'McCarthyism!'

and 'Witch-hunt!' into the conversation. I resolve to visit the dentist more often.

Today is a day of long phone calls. Joan Armatrading clocks in at forty-three minutes, Radio 4 producer Marya Burgess at forty-one. I am horrified to learn that what I thought inevitable has come to pass: Marya is taking early retirement. The BBC's decision to bloat and overpay the executive class while starving radio programme makers of funds has burned out another great talent.

For One Night Only, the series devoted to concerts that became memorable live albums, was a highlight of my career. I attempt to assure Marya that she will make programmes for independent production companies. She expresses the hope that we will somehow work together again. I love an optimist.

Anna Ford calls and agrees to talk to my solicitor Kate Goold. Anna has a period recollection that would be useful if we go to trial.

I have a mid-afternoon crumble with Chris Simpson at Le Pain. I remind him how annoying it has been that the Metropolitan Police have never shown any interest in the context of my case. The accusations claim that I had sex with Secondary through 1984. In fact, it was in the late spring of 1983 that I discovered the New Disease while visiting New York. When I returned to London, I announced to my housemate: 'From now, anal sex is banned in this house.' I told him it would take a few years, but only a few years, for science to discover what it was that was happening to gay men in the United States, as well as to haemophiliacs and intravenous drug users.

I took what we now know as HIV/Aids completely seriously from the moment I learned of it. To deny, or not even acknowledge the possibility, that I changed my sexual behaviour instantly is to mock the memory of my lost loved ones. I will not allow that. I grow firmer in my tone as I discuss this. Simpson becomes visibly distressed. He was alive in 1983, but had not yet reached puberty. He never had to live with the possibility that one-third of his friends could die due to a new disease. Contemplating it now, he is near tears.

<hr>

13 FEBRUARY 2014

The day begins with a three-hour session with Kate Goold. My solicitor wants a definitive timeline of my sexual history so that she is not surprised if Yewtree throw new allegations at me on 26 March. I am not looking forward to this discussion at all, but realise I will be having this kind of intimate conversation for the duration of my case. The Metropolitan Police have dragged me to their own level.

I am treated to lunch at the Ivy Club by Harriett Brand, a friend for at least forty years. Having known me during the entire period of allegations, she dismisses them all as nonsense without having to hear the specifics. I point out, as I have on previous occasions, how odd it seems to me that everyone else in the restaurant is merrily consuming fine food and drink without having a thought of what is, for me, the most pressing issue in the nation. I think once again of the famous Martin Niemöller quote concerning Germany in the 1930s:

> First they came for the Socialists, and I did not speak out – because I was not a Socialist.
>
> Then they came for the Trade Unionists, and I did not speak out – because I was not a Trade Unionist.
>
> Then they came for the Jews, and I did not speak out – because I was not a Jew.
>
> Then they came for me – and there was no one left to speak for me.

If the sex police can get away with Yewtree and parallel prosecutions up north, there is no telling who they might impose their chilling powers on next. The people in the Ivy should be crying out for reform today, before it is too late, but they seem more concerned about whether a particular glass of wine is drinkable or not.

<hr>

14 FEBRUARY 2014

It's off to Paris on the 0755 Eurostar. Chris and I are celebrating the Valentine's Day weekend and the fourth anniversary of our meeting on 16 February 2010 with a three-day trip to the City of Love. There is nothing wrong with being a walking cliché if you're going to have fun doing it.

We have plenty to read on the train. Not only do I have my morning's subscription copy of the *Financial Times*, I buy the *International New York Times* at St Pancras. We buy some other papers, too. The reason is that they are full of reports and commentary on the acquittal of Dave Lee Travis on twelve of fourteen counts. The other two met a hung jury.

Paris co-operates with our arrival. The rain stops. We lunch at Angelina's, enjoying the world's finest hot chocolate, their chocolat africain, and have a good walk. We have dinner at a large restaurant on the border of Les Halles, Au Pied de Cochon. I have resisted this place for forty-four years on the grounds that I don't eat pig meat, but curiosity finally gets the better of me. After all, it does have a number of seafood dishes, of which I order the daily special of sea bass. Although large, it is a minnow compared to what our neighbour is eating. A very large woman is negotiating what appears to be the €99 Prestige platter, a plateau de fruits de mer to end them all (except for the €170 Royal). She is clearly a serious eater, downing not only headline items like oysters and crab but little creatures such as cockles and whelks that are often overlooked in luxury restaurants.

She is eating as we sit down. She is eating through our first course, through our main and through our dessert. She only finishes as we pay the bill.

Halfway through the meal, Chris and I lean across the table to confer. We have had the same thought at the same time. This is far too much food for one person to order for herself. Is it possible that on this Valentine's Day a widow has come to eat the plateau that she and her husband used to consume together? Romance and tragedy fill the air at the same time. If our interpretation is correct, she is honouring her deceased partner in the best way someone can: extremely personally. If we are wrong, she is simply a pig, likely to have her trotters served soon in Au Pied de Cochon's signature dish.

We walk off our dinner with a stroll through the Marais and the Place des Vosges and back along the Rue de Rivoli. We've done it. We've gone to a country where we breathe the air of freedom and had a life-affirming day. It will be good to remember in the months to come that civilisation and sanity are only two hours and nine minutes away.

───────────────── 15 FEBRUARY 2014 ─────────────────

The weather is with us, in the sense that it is not raining. We enjoy a private morning in our Rue de Pyramides Airbnb and then set off in the direction of the Madeleine.

Where to eat?

Chris makes the suggestion that we try Hodiard, the gourmet food store where his friend Gerry once worked. Saturday at noon is not rush hour for a first-floor restaurant in the Place de la Madeleine, and we have the place to ourselves. We eat a light meal at a leisurely pace with almost the entire floor of the building as our own. Chris takes a picture of me next to some Hodiard-branded merchandise to send to Gerry. I love the closing of this particular circle.

Oh, Gerry! There was a time at the very beginning of my case when I wondered if I had been arrested because of the 5 Live interview I gave Nicky Campbell in which I repeated your story of being at a wedding early in the 2000s at which a reporter for the *Scottish Sun* boasted that 'everyone [at the newspaper] knew the Savile necrophilia story'. I was trying to encourage a serious national discussion about Savile, maintaining that this was not just a scandal for the BBC but cause for conversation between all segments of society. This was when I rhetorically asked Nicky, 'Who vetted the knighthood, Koko the Clown?' and pointed out that Sir Jimmy was a guest at Chequers, the dispenser of romantic advice to royals, and the recipient of a papal knighthood. (Seeing a photo of Savile with Margaret Thatcher or a member of the royal family is now titillating, but seeing the Pope with his hand on Jimmy's shoulder is positively brain-bending.) I told Campbell the press knew about Savile for decades and revealed nothing, so was in no position to point fingers at the BBC, and that numerous policemen were aware of his assumed activities. A large number of his supposed offences occurred in public health facilities. How did he win access to these? In other words, I said more than once in an interview that is still available on YouTube, we have to include all segments of society if we want to have a serious conversation as to how this historic personality flourished despite his failings.

Fat chance of that. The next day, the papers were full of the story 'Gambaccini Accuses Savile of Necrophilia'. I hadn't. I had mentioned that a reporter from the *Scottish Sun* had boasted about knowing it. Not a single newspaper mentioned that publication or the quotation. All credited me with originating the accusation.

Equally as distressing, no newspaper, not even a broadsheet, seemed interested in conducting the serious conversation about Savile I had proposed. The entire interview with Campbell had been in vain. Now I have to wonder: did my accuser see my photo juxtaposed with that of Savile in one of those newspapers? Had he made a distorted association between the two pictures when the Metropolitan Police opened Operation Yewtree and invited the public to denounce celebrities? Or, if one is feeling paranoid, did the police and popular press want to silence me before I spoke more about their parts in the broader analysis of the DJ's role in British society? Should I never have tried to talk sense about Jimmy Savile?

Christopher and I walk to the Arc de Triomphe via Boulevard Hauss-mann. It is precisely because I don't feel any personal connection with either the wealthy shopping areas or economically deprived neighbour-hoods of Paris that I have never seriously considered living there. Certainly, walking back down the Champs-Élysées is no encouragement, either. This thoroughfare, which was the quintessence of taste and luxury when I first came to the French capital in 1970, has deteriorated in my lifetime beyond the power of prediction.

And then it hits me. Who cares? It doesn't matter if I don't love all parts of a big city. After all, neither Chelsea nor Hackney holds partic-ular charms for me, and I've been a Londoner for four decades. All that counts is the neighbourhood in which you live. Do you love it? In that case, the city is liveable.

I adore my Paris, even if it is not the entirety of Paris. My Paris is the area that includes the Palais Royal, the Louvre, the Tuileries, and, oh yes, Angelina. Let's throw in Le Souffle, where we have dinner. I've been eat-ing there for at least thirty-five years.

I could live here and be happy. If everything goes wrong for me in Eng-land, I will certainly spend more time here. Christopher confirms he could get jobs in advertising and as a personal trainer. I wonder if I could find a flat that would accommodate a piano.

---

16 FEBRUARY 2014

My day starts at the unearthly hour of 2.23 a.m. I am awakened by a ter-rible nightmare.

In my dream, a pop star friend of mine is about to be arrested by an agent of Operation Yewtree. To give him time to get away, I engage the unaccompanied police officer in battle. I kill him. Another officer enters. I kill him, too. Four officers in turn come into the premises. I kill them all.

I have never struck a single blow against another human being, except for boxing Denis O'Neill when we were in elementary school. For a non-violent person like myself, dispatching four police officers is a bit of a task. They meet their ends in highly unusual ways. I seize the left arm of the first officer and stick his hand in the gap of a half-full bookcase, slamming the books together on his wrist until his blood circulation stops. The remaining three officers also take ages to succumb in hand-to-hand combat.

I awake after the fourth policeman has met his maker. Even though the room is cool, my T-shirt is soaked through to the skin.

It takes me two and a half hours to get back to sleep. I toss, turn and fantasise about what living in Paris would be like. I've lived in London for forty years. Why not live in New York or Paris now? It's the police who have raised the issue. By denying me my present, they have unintentionally opened the door to possible different futures.

Christopher and I spend the afternoon in and out of the Louvre. We see some art in the Denon pavilion, have lunch and sunbathe at the Café Marly on the north side of the courtyard, walk to Notre Dame, have takeaway chocolat africain from Angelina, view more art in the Sully building, snack in the Carrousel du Louvre and return by Métro to the Gare du Nord. Lou Reed, we had a 'Perfect Day'. I'm glad I spent it with Chris.

―――――――――― 17 FEBRUARY 2014 ――――――――――

Freddie Starr, another Yewtree suspect arrested but not charged, has given an interview to the *Daily Mirror* that has been quoted over the weekend by the *Daily Mail*. He says, 'I've been tarred with the same brush as Savile and Gary Glitter. What's happened to me is unlawful. The cops and the Crown Prosecution Service are playing dirty.

'I will expose them and bring Operation Yewtree down on its knees.'

The comedian, whose work I am embarrassed to admit I've never seen, went to a police station on Wednesday the 12th expecting a charge-or-dismiss decision. Neither occurred. He was instead re-arrested. Now his lawyer has apparently filed 'for a judicial review into the conduct of the police and CPS'.

This is great, from my point of view. Someone wants to do something I want done without my having to do it. If I were a drinking man, I would buy Freddie Starr a drink. The problem is I don't drink. Perhaps one day I'll offer him a chocolate milkshake at Shake Shack.

I email Kate Goold to express my delight that Freddie is putting his head above the parapet for the rest of us. She agrees this is good. She knows I get angry, and is pleased that another suspect is willing to be publicly furious for the rest of us. The main consideration keeping me quiet is Solicitor Goold's point that any individual publicity at this stage might only attract more band-wagoners to make wild allegations. Given the police's demonstrated tendency to group multiple accusations against a single suspect, it is best not to attract any attention at all. Indeed, I am so far down most Yewtree reports that I still meet people who have had no idea I have been arrested. Just because this is the top story in my life, it doesn't mean everyone else knows the case even exists.

As I go to bed just before midnight, I am aware that Officer Four should be interviewing my long-term former lodger Dale Witton in Melbourne at this very moment, or soon afterward. I have not seen nor spoken to Dale in decades, but I know that what she says must defend me. I am buoyed by a sudden realisation. It isn't just that the police have gone on a world tour to collect statements in my defence. It's that they must realise that all of these people, whom they now know to be respectable professional adults, will turn up to testify for me in any trial. The Met must know that if they charge me, it isn't just my account of events that will defend me. All these likeable honest people will also appear. Knowing this, Yewtree would have to be incredibly misguided or malicious to proceed.

— 18 FEBRUARY 2014 —

'Home Again' by Carole King comes up on my iTunes. The first lines are:

'Sometimes I wonder if I'm ever gonna make it home again / It's so far and out of sight.'

When *Tapestry* was new in 1971, these lines had deep meaning for me. I had just suffered an emotional collapse upon realising that I had unintentionally changed countries, losing everything I had ever known in the United States without knowing what I would gain in Great Britain. Hearing 'Home Again' that summer, during which *Tapestry* played ceaselessly in public establishments as well as in private homes, I would dare to wonder if and when I would be restored to equilibrium. Peace of mind seemed 'so far and out of sight'.

Today the song plays and it means something equally profound but utterly different. Will I ever be restored to employment? Will my reputation, so unfairly smeared by police and press, recover? 'It's so far and out of sight.'

––––––––––––––– 20 FEBRUARY 2014 –––––––––––––––

Today is Jennifer Sherwood's birthday. Christopher and I treat her to lunch and then take her to the Menier Chocolate Factory's production of *Candide*.

When I count my lucky stars, I include Jennifer. One of her predecessors had to retire after becoming addicted to drink and drugs – both, I'm afraid to say, without my noticing. Indeed, my failure to pick up certain telltale signs is perhaps the ultimate proof that I could never 'groom' anyone! There is no telling how effective this previous PA would have been, or if he could hold it together, if he were on duty during this great test. Jennifer, on the other hand, has been both professional and hard-working. To my delighted amazement, she has been able to handle the demands of my case like dirty water off a duck's back. And she's still only twenty-four!

One year ago I could never have dreamed she would be part of my inner circle in this great campaign. Yet here she is, part of the Dream Team that includes her brother Christopher, Malcolm Jeffries and Christopher Simpson. I am blessed.

Candide turns out to be just about the best version of this show there can be. The stagecraft is imaginative and the cast sing and act beautifully. I know about half the players and hope none of them does a double take seeing me in the front row, but either they have forgotten my face or they are concentrating on their work. OK, maybe both.

In the evening, Jennifer goes off to dinner with friends while Chris and I go to the Two Brydges Club, probably the most misspelled restaurant of all time, where we are treated by my old *Guinness Book of British Hit Singles* assistant Tony Brown and his husband Richard Chaplin.

Within the first five minutes it becomes obvious that Richard and Tony know that Cliff Richard is, to use baseball parlance, 'on deck'. I don't literally throw my hands in the air, since I am holding a beverage, but I do so rhetorically. Here I am, complaining that my identity was revealed after my arrest. Cliff's identity has been widely revealed before his arrest!

---

21 FEBRUARY 2014

Chris sends a 'preview of the *Sunday Times*' with the first four paragraphs of a column by Camilla Cavendish headlined 'Chasing Savile's ghost threatens to leave today's victims behind'.

This is the kind of article I need. The left-wing papers have failed in their coverage and are weak. Pressure from the right is more likely to influence powerful persons in 2014 Britain, and the right is coming through.

Chris has also sent me a link to ITV's interview with Director of Public Prosecutions Alison Saunders. She continues to refer to all complainants as 'victims'. Not once does she use the words 'accuser' or 'litigant'. If anyone is contemplating sending this woman a Christmas present, they should send her a dictionary.

It's one small step for man, one giant leap for Paul Gambaccini. I stood on the scales this morning, afraid that yesterday's visit to Shake Shack might have affected my weight, and I saw a number I have not seen in over a decade. '14 stone 3 pounds', it glowed in its luminescent wonderfulness – 199, in American. My goal of reducing to under 200 has been achieved.

Primary, you are one helluva diet doctor.

Not satisfied with a dozen defeats, the Crown Prosecution Service is coming back at DLT on his two hung counts. 'Dave Lee Travis to face retrial on sex offence charges' is the number one most-read story on the BBC website this morning.

The outstanding Channel 4 reporter Michael Crick, an acclaimed veteran of *Newsnight*, comes over for a nearly two-hour-long briefing on my recent experiences. I have been appalled at how television news people have been passive pussycats during the witch-hunt. I emphasise that I am not seeking publicity of any kind and must lay low in case any unhinged individuals see or hear my name, but a telejournalist of his distinction should know what's going on.

In the early evening I see a preview of *The Grand Budapest Hotel*, my favourite Wes Anderson film since *Rushmore*. His previous movie, *Moonrise Kingdom*, was also excellent, but this had even broader scope and subject matter. It is touching that so many fine actors, whether Anderson veterans such as Jason Schwartzman and Bill Murray or first-timers like Ralph Fiennes and F. Murray Abraham, turn out to support his idiosyncratic projects. Fiennes has probably never spoken so much beautiful poetry nor so many foul epithets in his career.

In the last minutes of the movie, the dark armed forces that plunged Europe into World War Two take over the hotel, but a flash forward reveals the nation after its liberation. Coming out of the film, I experience an epiphany. I realise that I have succeeded in one of the goals I set myself after my arrest, one that is more important than reducing to under

200 pounds. I have written a book. It is the true story of a terrible episode in the history of British justice. I was for a long time worried that if I had a health catastrophe as a result of Yewtree-induced stress, this book would not be finished. It is now long enough to be published, albeit with heavy editing and a couple of passes through libel lawyers. Three of my friends have copies of the book and Christopher will ensure that it is published if something terrible happens to me. Whatever occurs from here on in, my story will be told.

25 FEBRUARY 2014

I have a coffee with Chris Rogers and his *Panorama* colleague Marshall Corwin. Just when I thought I couldn't be stunned any more, he tells me he knew I was going to be arrested four days before I was.

'Who told you?' I ask him, assuming it must have been a policeman.

'Someone from Absolute Radio,' he says. Absolute Radio? They're not even journalists!

Apparently someone who works there had been on the Twittersphere and had read a tweet that I was going to be arrested. How did that tweeter know? Easy, Rogers explains.

'Anyone can operate an account on Twitter using a false name,' he says. 'The police do it all the time to leak information.'

It's embarrassing that I never thought of that. Another shock awaits at home. Michael Crick has checked ancestry.co.uk. Secondary is not the brother of the researcher and the journalist. We're back to square one on him. We downloaded a homophobic iTunes album for nothing!

I have a wonderful three-hour dinner with Nancy and Simon Jones and Terry Gilliam. It was with this trio that I had my first post-siege outing at Mr Kong on 5 November 2013.

I suggest that we go to Le Caprice. We can pretend it is thirty years ago and we are all chic. In fact, in the '80s I did patronise the restaurant, even though

I was never chic. It was the first collaboration between the two maîtres d', Jeremy King of Joe Allen and Chris Corbin of Langan's Brasserie.

Having been a habitué of both Joe's and Langan's, at which I had many adventures, I was a first-generation regular of Le Caprice. We even filmed a segment of *The Other Side of the Tracks* there. The restaurant really became exclusive when local resident Diana, Princess of Wales, made a series of visits.

I followed Jeremy and Chris when they accepted a financial offer they could not refuse and began a new series of restaurants. Part of the joy of dining is eating in places where you feel comfortable. Their genius was to lend their physical presence as well as their personalities to their restaurants. Every one of their regulars felt like a member of a large family, as if we were all travelling through life and career together to some unknowable future destination. Until we got there, we might as well share 'our' restaurants.

My companions have not heard news of my experiences since early November, save for a couple I had told Nancy over the telephone.

The revelation that shocks Terry the most is that the Ministry of Justice has posted the 'Criminal Injuries Compensation Scheme 2012' on the internet. It is the shopping list for anyone who wishes to make an allegation against a celebrity, or anyone else, for that matter. A key line is clause nine: 'A person may be eligible for an award under this Scheme whether or not the incident giving rise to the criminal injury to which their application relates has resulted in the conviction of an assailant in any part of the United Kingdom or elsewhere.' In other words, fire away, and even if the accused is not convicted, you're in the money.

The 'Tariff of Injuries' is presented in Annex E. It lists the amount of money a complainant can claim for scores of various injuries. I cannot help but notice that, even on the limited information I have, my accusers stand to collect at least £22,000 each, considerably more if the Multiplier Table applies.

It was only last autumn that a Metropolitan Police deputy assistant commissioner encouraged members of the public to make sexual allegations and told them, 'You will be believed.' For no other crime, be it murder, armed robbery or stealing sweets, have potential accusers been told: 'You will be believed.' This is antithetical to the presumption of innocence that is at the cornerstone of British justice. They were also told by the government that they may receive compensation. This combination of incentives provided the mechanics for the witch-hunt that is now underway.

27 FEBRUARY 2014

I am rightfully disciplined by a wise Tony King. I phone this music-business veteran, whom I have known for over forty years, and ask if he has a contact number for Cliff Richard's office. I want to offer him whatever value my experience might give him. King knocks me back, not in an unfriendly way, but firmly.

> Don't you think Cliff has his own circle of supporters in place? Don't you think if he wanted to reach out, he would? And don't you feel that it would be bad for you if the police found you had been contacting him? They might suspect you of trying to interfere with their inquiries.

Tony is correct on all counts, and I thank him for his advice. He has inadvertently put his finger on a larger problem I didn't realise I have. I am too involved in this whole business. Because I am denied information on the progress and even the nature (beyond basics) of my own case, I am trying to learn from other cases. For example, it seems significant to me that *Panorama* learned about my forthcoming arrest from Absolute Radio, that Malcolm Jeffries heard about Max Clifford's imminent arrest from a friend who works at *The Sun*, and that several people have told me they heard of the pursuit of Cliff Richard from different sources. The only conclusion that can be drawn from this is that some police, even if only two or three, collude with the media.

Today marks the passing of four months since I was arrested. I still have not been charged or dismissed. This book is going on forever. I am thinking of calling it *War and Pizza*.

I have a bizarre experience at the Coliseum. Attending the premiere of the English National Opera staging of Handel's *Rodelinda*, I bump into Nigel Evans! It turns out that the husband and son of the soprano playing the title character, Rebecca Evans, are sitting in a box behind me. The unrelated Nigel, their family friend, is a guest at the two intervals. We talk during the breaks and again at the end of the show. We have both noted the personal relevance of some of the lyrics in the surtitles, particularly a reference to undeserved blows being 'seldom fatal'. My personal favourite comes in the final act, with the repeated proclamation that 'cruel persecution yields no reward'.

Rodelinda is three and a half hours long, but because I love Handel's style as well as substance, it all goes by quickly. The director Richard Jones seems to know exactly what elements of the antiquated and stiff plot to ever-so-slightly send up without mocking the piece itself, so there is humour as well as musicality in the production. I suspect I have witnessed a breakthrough role for Iestyn Davies as the deposed king Bertrarido. This production must be a new career high point for both him and Rebecca Evans. Whoa! Upon searching for the libretto of the opera on Google, I discover that Davies made his Metropolitan Opera debut in *Rodelinda* in the role of Unulfo. Obviously this work has been crucial in his career.

After the show, I delay my departure, and Nigel his visit to the aftershow party, to exchange further stories of our experiences. When there are only about a dozen people going through variations of what you are living through, you want to share all the details, even if each case has its own character and nobody really knows if there is a shred of truth in anybody else's allegations. I hear horror stories of Evans's case similar to what I heard earlier this week about Freddie Starr.

Nigel promises that, whatever happens in his case, friends in Parliament will ask appropriate questions about our experiences in the House. He focuses on the taxpayer-expense angle of my case, as I am likely to hold the record for most travel costs incurred.

'What hotels did they stay in?' he asks rhetorically. 'What did they eat? Where did they go at night?' I can see that I am not the only person in our group who is interested in every detail of everybody else's case.

'Before you go,' Nigel concludes, 'can we take a photo for the book?'

'Are you writing a book, too?' I ask, somewhat disappointed that he will inevitably steal my thunder but grateful that someone else is speaking out.

'Of course,' he says, 'and you?' When I let on that I am, he says, 'Then you can use this photo, too. This is the night we met at the opera. It was meant to be.'

He snaps the selfie.

1 MARCH 2014

I receive a beautiful postcard from Jeremy Vine. It is not the front image that is beautiful, although it is interesting: a 'collage of manipulated film stills' from *The Man Who Fell to Earth* by the movie's star, David Bowie. It is the handwritten text that uplifts:

> Dear Paul,
>
> I'm recording some quiz shows at BBC Glasgow at the moment and you've been in my mind. I HOPE you are getting to the end of this process. I know the strain it will have placed you under. I felt bad that we have only had a couple of snatched conversations about it, but please be assured of my support in this awful marathon … home soon, I hope.
>
> Warm wishes,
>
> Jeremy V.

Jeremy shows insight as well as compassion. He understands both my torment and the importance of his support. I am sure many of my other colleagues are on my side throughout this ordeal, but they are paralysed by the challenge of saying something useful about it. As a result, they do not correspond. With the exception of a few, I will never know that they were thinking of me.

---

3 MARCH 2014

Holly Johnson has sent a very kind email. I have known the former lead singer of Frankie Goes to Hollywood since early 1984, when he came in to Radio 1 the week 'Relax' entered the Top 40 and the band was due to go on *Top of the Pops*. On that occasion he told me he was nervous about the TV appearance.

'It doesn't matter,' I reassured him. 'Fear is an internal event. No one can see your fear, unless you actually wet your pants. What matters is what they can see, the external world of your performance.'

His considerate message says:

> I was in the audience at the EMI Party at Somerset House you compered a while back. I really loved what you said about the people talking not really loving music, which one is in no doubt that you do and always had.
>
> There are people out there who feel really positive about you still and your great contribution to music here in the UK.
>
> Thank you for being so friendly (thirty years ago) to a young man of twenty-three who came into Radio 1 in 1984 to do Newsbeat and talking about 'Walk On the Wild Side' by Lou Reed.

The last reference was to my explanation that the classic single was played on daytime Radio 1 because the playlist committee didn't understand the reference to 'giving head'. Many of the DJs knew, but were not going to tell.

It was a pleasure taking an observer's place on Frankie's historic ride. Before 'Relax' broke big, and it did take months, I saw them mime to it and the B-side 'Ferry Cross the Mersey' at the Camden Palace. The only problem was, the club disc jockey was unfamiliar with the group's version of the Gerry and the Pacemakers classic and played it at the wrong speed. Usually in these cases a DJ would play a 33 ⅓ rpm record at 45, but on this evening this record was played at a slower speed … maybe a 78 at 45. Perhaps realising no one in the audience knew what the disc actually sounded like, Frankie gamely mimed to the slowed-down single. It was like 'Ferry Cross the Mersey' on downers.

Nona Hendryx and her partner Vicki Wickham were house guests of mine in November 1983 and enthused about 'Relax' long before it became a hit. It was a sweet turnabout when Frankie were the toast of the town in 1984 and attended her London concert, visibly enthusiastic. Nona and Vicki are the kind of long-term friends you suddenly realise you've known for decades. Their mutual dedication has been a constant source of inspiration. It was also delightful to see Nona as the answer in a *New York Times* crossword earlier this year.

When it came time to record the winter 1985 season of *The Other Side of the Tracks* in late '84, it made sense to film Frankie Goes to Hollywood when they actually did go to Hollywood. We shot the sequence at the Sunset Marquis, a popular rock 'n' roll hotel.

Holly's supportive 2014 email is particularly meaningful coming from a man who has always kept his personal life private. I know he means what he says. Messages like his are oxygen to me.

This weekend I continued the cull of my record collection. I will be selling off about one quarter of it to help raise money for legal fees, although it will make only a small dent in the total costs. It will be heartbreaking for some true music fans to know that I have to break up one of the country's finest music libraries, but this is serious. There is no time for sentiment when you are fighting for your life.

I have even greater problems to worry about. Today, Solicitor Goold agreed with my prognosis that, given the aggressive position of Operation Yewtree and the Crown Prosecution Service in other cases, I must accept that there is a greater than 50 per cent chance that I will be charged.

We discuss my fear that the climate of persecution the British establishment has created may make it unsafe for me to ever live in this country again. Another distressed individual could pop up in a couple of years and be taken seriously by these zealots. I call my producer Kevin Howlett and ask if it would be possible to broadcast my Radio 2 show from New York. I tell Chris it looks as if there is a greater than 50 per cent chance that we will have to move back to my hometown, where there is no hysteria about 'historic sexual offences'.

I find myself wondering about decent men and women working in the police service. So far, 95 per cent of the officers on my case seem to be honest people interested in justice. What do they feel about this witch-hunt? Is it practical to hope they might revolt against the 'brand catastrophe' that is tarnishing their organisation's reputation?

---

4 MARCH 2014

Last night, Malcolm and I went to the BFI to see Antonioni's *L'Eclisse* (*The Eclipse*). This is the classic 1962 film in which Alain Delon and Monica Vitti manoeuvre or, to use a British word, faff for two hours trying to decide whether to have an affair or not. I had previously seen the famous last seven minutes of the movie, probably in the four-hour – when you're fascinated, you can sit through anything – *My Voyage to Italy*, Martin Scorsese's personal tour of Italian cinema. However, it is only when seeing the sequence in context that one feels its full force.

This is the moment when neither Delon nor Vitti, who have arranged to meet for a date, show up. For seven minutes the camera examines the cityscape, pedestrians and motor vehicles. There is no sign of either lover.

They have independently lost interest in each other. As the liner notes quote Ron Peck from *Sight & Sound*,

> This is an extraordinary sequence, acknowledging that it has lost both the original characters and the narrative. Other lives, which we know nothing about, cross the screen and disappear, leaving in the end just the city – functioning, automatically, part of a vast man-made machinery, within which individuals find temporary escape and pleasure in passing sensations of motion and contact.

I found the entire film, which might seem meandering to audiences accustomed to fast-paced editing, fascinating. At one point Vitti ends an embrace by expressing the wish that she loved Delon either more or not at all. Of course! We've all been there in our lives! We've all had periods when we date people whom we like but don't love, wondering if second-best is preferable to nothing. What shall it be, dinner and a drink with someone we merely get along with, or sitting at home with *Moby-Dick*?

---

5 MARCH 2014

Ian McKellen sends a supportive email from New York, where he continues to appear with Patrick Stewart in Sean Mathias's repertory production of *Waiting for Godot* and *No Man's Land*.

'I often wonder how u are coping and send love, if it helps!' he writes. It does.

'I do hope the charges are soon dropped, so that you can begin to return to normality,' Ian continues. 'Perhaps the Roache and Travis verdicts are encouraging: though why you should be linked to anyone else's supposed misdemeanours is part of what's unfair about it all.'

McKellen has got it in one with his linking of the show trials with the police's failure to stop Jimmy Savile in his lifetime, but he has made the understandable mistake of assuming I have been charged with something. I have to tell him I have not and that this is part of the unique iniquity the British police and Crown Prosecution Service have indulged in with their treatment of me, Jimmy Tarbuck and Freddie Starr. Long-term arrest without charge is a tactic that results in great stress, devastating financial losses and lasting character defamation.

I have a sudden desire to see the Joseph Welch moment again. In Googling it, I come up with an extract of Edward R. Murrow from his *See It Now* broadcast of 9 March 1954.

'No one familiar with the history of this country can deny that Congressional committees are useful,' he tells his CBS television audience.

It is necessary to investigate before legislating. But the line between investigating and persecuting is a very fine one, and the junior senator from Wisconsin has stepped over it repeatedly. His primary achievement has been in confusing the public mind as between the internal and the external threats of Communism. We must not confuse dissent with disloyalty. We must remember always that accusation is not proof and that conviction depends upon evidence and due process of law.

We will not walk in fear, one of another. We will not be driven by fear into an age of unreason if we dig deep in our history and our doctrine and remember that we are not descended from fearful men, not from men who feared to write, to speak, to associate and to defend the causes that were for the moment unpopular.

This is no time for the men who oppose Senator McCarthy's methods to remain silent, nor for those who approve. We can deny our heritage and our history, but we cannot escape responsibility for the result. There is no way for a citizen of a republic to abdicate his responsibilities. As a nation we have come into our full inheritance at a tender age. We proclaim ourselves, as indeed we are, the defenders of freedom wherever it continues to exist in the world. But we cannot defend freedom abroad by deserting it at home. The actions of the junior senator from Wisconsin have caused alarm and dismay amongst our allies abroad, and given considerable comfort to our enemies. And whose fault is that? Not really his. He didn't create this situation of fear, he merely exploited it, and rather successfully. Cassius was right. The fault, dear Brutus, is not in our stars, but in ourselves. Goodnight and good luck.

When I was a boy, I considered Edward R. Murrow the ultimate broadcaster. Today I have been reminded why.

It is Wednesday, new comics day, and several important hardcover editions of classic newspaper strips are due. I am particularly excited by the oversized *Gasoline Alley: The Complete Sundays* Volume One. Collecting the large-format work of Frank King from 1920 to 1922, it is a perfect example of an art form that no longer exists. During my lifetime, newspapers have discontinued their Sunday comic sections, and those strips that do appear are much reduced in size from their predecessors.

When I get home, I speak to Kate Goold about developments in the Max Clifford case. She must terminate our conversation for a meeting. The phone rings almost immediately afterwards. A friend of Dwina Gibb, Robin's widow, calls to interview me for her book about David Bowie. Before my arrest, she had requested and obtained my permission for such a conversation. Now, I cannot do it. I just can't do it. My mind is elsewhere. She understands.

---

6 MARCH 2014

'Policing stands damaged today' – Theresa May, Home Secretary.

How many times in my dreams have I seen that kind of news report? Today, it becomes reality, not as one of my revenge fantasies but in conjunction with a report to the House of Commons on the Stephen Lawrence case. The BBC website states:

> A judge-led public inquiry will be held into the work of undercover
> police following a review into the original Stephen Lawrence murder
> investigation. It found a Metropolitan Police 'spy' worked within the
> 'Lawrence camp' while a previous inquiry into matters arising from his
> death was under way. Home Secretary Theresa May described the find-
> ings as 'deeply troubling'.

But wait! Even Prime Minister David Cameron chips in on this one,
tweeting, 'Like the Home Secretary, I find the conclusions of the Stephen
Lawrence review profoundly shocking. It's important we have a full inquiry.'

And, apparently, not just a 'full inquiry'. According to the BBC, Mrs
May said that 'a new law was needed as it was untenable to rely on the
outdated common law offence of misconduct in public office to deal with
serious police corruption'. Furthermore, 'she would bring forward propos-
als to strengthen protections for police whistleblowers'.

Even I could not have written this story. This is better than my wild-
est dreams. The Metropolitan Police are being held responsible for one
of their runaway operations. Can it happen again? I am firmly convinced
that, although the wheels of justice sometimes turn slowly, they eventually do turn.

---

7 MARCH 2014

The report by Mark Ellison QC into the Metropolitan Police handling
of the Stephen Lawrence case dominates the news.

Neville Lawrence, father of the murdered teenager, says, 'I am very, very
wary of what's going to happen now. The Metropolitan Police seem to be
always trying to hide what they are and put a different face out there all
the time, and I now feel I will never be able to trust these people.'

BBC reporter Fiona Irving, standing in front of the rotating New Scotland Yard sign, says direct to camera, 'In the 1990s public inquiry, Sir

William Macpherson accused the police of institutional racism. This review raises the possibility of institutional corruption.'

It certainly does. The Ellison report states: 'We have very recently been informed that in 2003 there was "mass shredding" of the surviving hard-copy reports generated by Operation Othona' – a so-called 'top-secret anti-corruption intelligence initiative' set up by Commissioner Paul Condon in 1993. As the BBC reports, 'The "chaotic state" of Met Police records meant a public inquiry might have "limited" potential to find out more information.'

---

8 MARCH 2014

Nigel Evans and I exchange telephone messages. We are each out when the other calls. I urge him to stay strong on Monday, when, as I do not have to remind him, his trial begins.

---

10 MARCH 2014

Yesterday was the most beautiful day of the year. Not a single cloud appeared in the sky all day, and the temperature soared to 19 degrees Celsius (66 degrees Fahrenheit).

It was so warm so early in the day that, for the first time in the year, I went out without a jacket. Christopher even wore shorts.

Ribble Valley MP Nigel Evans appears today at Preston Crown Court, accused of sexual offences against seven men during the period 2002–13, two counts of indecent assault, six of sexual assault and one of rape. It is reported that Nigel has posted a Facebook thank-you to his supporters, saying, 'It has meant so much and given me strength. I will not be commenting on the events in Preston over the next few weeks for obvious reasons.'

My attention is drawn to his statement that he will continue to hold surgeries during the trial. At least Nigel has been able to work during his nightmare! I have been involuntarily retired from my profession.

I attend the first of three lessons at Urban Golf that Chris gave me as a birthday gift last year. The instructor gives me priceless advice within five minutes. I had played regularly as a teenager and again in my thirties but only occasionally since. As a result I lost my swing off the tee. The horizontal motion of batting in softball affected the arc of my golf swing. But the instructor notes something else: I am tense and constricted in addressing the ball, trying to control the result. I am concentrating on hitting the ball rather than swinging through. I have to let my hands drop, stand back from the ball rather than suffocate it, and move my body rather than confine my motion to my arms. Son of a gun, I immediately have fewer topped balls and start hitting for an average 140 yards with the seven iron, which is the club in use today.

There must be a lesson here for my case. I should stand back, let my hands relax, and breathe. One lesson I should definitely take is to stand back from the details of other persons' cases. There are so many elements in the current Clifford and Evans trials that letting them all impact me personally is a gateway to madness.

---

11 MARCH 2014

In the afternoon I am treated to tea in the House of Lords by Baroness Helena Kennedy. John Miskelly and Colin Bell are fellow guests. Helena is as generous as she is sharp. If I am charged, we will immediately contact a private investigator from America to force my accusers to go ten rounds with Wolverine. I ask Helena if she would be willing to testify about her intimate experience with the police during the 1970s, when she was constantly subjected to officers boasting about the number of gay men they had turned in during the Pretty Police campaign against homosexuals. She agrees without hesitation.

Baroness Kennedy then does something strategic. She takes me on a walking tour of some of the rooms of the House of Lords so that anyone aware of and interested in my case will see me standing loud and proud. We enter a room with a bar. The first person on the other side of the door is Baroness Mary Goudie. She stands, approaches and whispers in my ear, 'Stay strong.' It means as much as anything anyone outside Team Gambo has said so far.

12 MARCH 2014

I hope I can keep myself from getting knotted up following every detail of the Nigel Evans trial, but sometimes I can't help but 'peek'. An article from a service called Wales Online blows my mind. 'Nigel Evans trial: What we learned from the second day at Preston Crown Court' runs down developments in detail, and I cannot believe what I read. All three of the day's witnesses say they did not wish to bring charges but the police transformed their remarks into criminal charges.

'Not in a million years' did the first witness think his story of having Evans put his hand down his trousers in a gay pub would wind up in court. '"Abused" is rather strong,' he says. 'It was a liberty.'

The second person, who said the former Deputy Speaker put his hand down his trousers twice during the 2003 Conservative Party conference, said it was more the behaviour of a 'drunken lech'. The thought of complaining to the police at the time had never occurred to him. Last year when questioned by a detective, he said he did not wish to make a complaint and only gave a statement as a witness so that his account was 'on the record'.

> 'To be honest I didn't think there were any grounds to be charged,' he
> said. 'I would not have believed that six months on I would be standing in a witness box.'

He said he had not seen it as a police matter.

'It never entered my mind,' he said.

After further discussion of these two individuals, one of whom wrote in his police statement, 'I have absolutely no intention of making a complaint to the police and I am making this statement as a witness and not as a victim,' the article went on to 'the third alleged victim', who 'claimed Evans tried to kiss him in the Houses of Parliament'. About this person, cross-examination revealed that 'the witness agreed two years later in 2011 he travelled to Evans's home and stayed over there for a number of nights'. Crucially, this man wrote in his statement that 'I do not want to make a complaint against Nigel because I do not believe he has committed any offences'.

So here we have three people behind three of the charges against Nigel Evans, none of whom pressed charges themselves. How can there be crimes with no victims?

13 MARCH 2014

This is bad. Taking a steam bath last night, I found myself wondering what year it was. Without any deadline pressures, without typing the date on the top of every radio running order, I have been existing outside time as it is experienced by people who are still in employment or education. One day is very much like the last, hopefully with more minutes of sunshine and warmth, and I make the most of each … but whatever number it has been assigned is now pretty irrelevant to me. Is it 2013 or 2014? I couldn't remember until I recalled that my sixty-fifth birthday is coming up on 2 April. Since I was born in 1949, it must be 2014.

Lewis Carnie, head of talent at Radio 2, takes me to tea at the Langham to catch up on my case. He knows I am to report to police on the 26th, less than two weeks away. Lewis admits that when I was arrested he thought that the police would realise they had been misled and drop the case by my original rebail date of 8 January at the latest. Now he has seen the triviality of most of the accusations in cases both north and south, he realises he was an optimist. I go through the possibilities of the 26 March meeting:

1) Dismissal

2) Charges based on the original accusations

3) Charges based on the original accusations plus those of 'bandwagoners' who emerged after the police publicised my arrest

4) The original accusations dropped but new ones based on 'bandwagoners' put in their place

5) Re-arrest as a result of 'bandwagoners'

6) Some 'bandwagoners' might be women, since it has never been publicised that my accusers are male

7) Another rebail to a point later in the year

Lewis will have to decide, in concert with head of radio Helen Boaden and perhaps director general Tony Hall, whether I should be allowed back on air if Option 7 is the one the police choose … to punt me further down the year without either charge or dismissal. Keeping a person off air when they have been charged is one thing; denying them employment when they are being kept on a hook in the hope some fish will bite is another. Whatever the organisation's decision will be, Carnie expresses the personal opinion that my treatment by the police is 'unfair'.

---

14 MARCH 2014

The phone rings. Kate Goold informs me that the police have passed my file to the Crown Prosecution Service. This apparently happened some days ago, perhaps so my case officer could clear his plate for the Max Clifford case. It is now up to the CPS to decide whether I will be charged or dismissed. Goold expects a decision by the time I am due to turn up at Charing Cross on 26 March.

This is, so far as I can tell, neutral news, although I wish the police had thrown the allegations out before the case reached first base. But there is some good news, too: there are no bandwagoners! All the publicity failed to inspire a credible 'Me, too!' accusation. Even if the CPS gives the case a green light, it will only be me against the two original accusers, whose argument against me is 100 per cent bull doo doo. (One of my favourite all-time worst records is the 1974 single 'Bull Doo Doo' by Spiritual Concept.)

It is a tremendous relief not to have to worry about bandwagoners. It is stressful to realise my legal status for the next year will be determined within the next twelve days. The two reactions seem to cancel each other out.

Christopher and I have dinner with Vincent Zurzolo and Frank Cwiklik of Metropolis Collectibles. They have come from New York for the weekend's comic convention at ExCeL, the biggest gathering of UK fans this year. Chris and I always have dinner with Vinnie and his wife Josephine when we are in New York. Tonight, Frank sits in for Jo, who is working back home. I give them eleven comics that have been graded and encapsulated and three bound volumes of old issues to put in their next major auction. They already have quite a few items from me for this event.

The Gotham duo are impressed by Joe Simon's personal bound volume of *Black Magic* 1–6 from the early 1950s. *Black Magic* was one of the titles produced by Simon and his partner Jack Kirby, now the most famous artist in comics history. Frank demonstrates his knowledge when I flash three high-grade issues of *New Funnies* from the early 1940s, saying, 'Dell collectors require high-grade copies, so these will go.' Even a veteran who has seen everything, as Vinnie has in this hobby, pauses when he sees *The Comics* 5 from 1937.

'Nineteen thirty-seven,' Zurzolo emphasises. I point out this was probably one of the first hundred comic books printed.

'It was,' Cwiklik confirms.

I had collected this book for its baseball cover. The batter has turned to the catcher and, pointing to the pitcher, says, 'That guy can't put me out' just as a thrown ball is heading for his right temple. As a former boy pitcher, I always loved this cover. But my perspective on it has changed. I now associate this with the fatal beaning of Ray Chapman in 1920. I can't keep a comic that reminds me of death in my favourite sport.

15 MARCH 2014

This is, in weather terms, one of the dream weekends of the year. In the morning, I journey into Soho to buy some Italian comestibles from Camisa. My former Islington lodger Nick Fletcher and his husband Trond are coming over for dinner tomorrow night. Trond, a doctor, is the subject of one of my favourite coincidences. After Live Aid, many commentators in the British press suggested that Bob Geldof might be a worthy winner of the Nobel Peace Prize. I thought it would be odd if I knew the holder of what may be the world's greatest award. In the event, Geldof did not get the honour. It went to the United Nations peacekeeping forces. It happened that Trond was serving in the group at that time. No matter how tenuously, I had indeed known the winner of the Nobel Peace Prize ... it just wasn't the person I thought it might be.

After returning home and napping, I take the original art for the interior of *Brother Power the Geek 2* to ExCeL to give to Vincent and Frank from Metropolis Collectibles. Because Frank had mentioned the previous evening that old issues of *Felix the Cat* by Otto Messmer were inexplicably 'hot', I bring along a bonus page of art by the Good Cat Artist from number twenty-nine.

As Frank holds the fort, Vincent and I walk around the convention hall. ExCeL gets zero out of ten for aesthetics, but the space suits its purpose. There are rows upon rows of dealers. I say to Vinnie, 'This is bigger than the first one.'

'Yes,' he replies, 'they've grown.'

'No, I mean 1964. The first one.'

I am referring to what is recognised as the first convention of comic fans, held in a function room in New York in 1964. It has taken on mythic status in fandom. From that seed has grown a year-round calendar of conclaves around the world, climaxing in the San Diego Comic-Con that has become an important part of the annual Hollywood calendar. Every studio presents trailers for its upcoming fantasy and superhero films at San Diego.

When I mention 1964, Vincent smiles. He knows I have him. He couldn't have been there because he wasn't born yet. He can't believe that I was in the same room as, and got to nod a hello to, Steve Ditko, the original artist of *Spider-Man*, who became a virtual recluse when his co-creation became famous beyond his dreams. An appearance at Comic-Con by Ditko today would cause gridlock in San Diego.

17 MARCH 2014

With only nine days remaining, I still have no idea whether my case will proceed to charge or be dropped.

I take the second of Christopher's three birthday golf lessons from Urban Golf in Soho. The teaching continues to be helpful. I swing a driver without duffing for the first time in decades. At the twenty-minute mark, the instructor innocently asks if I am still on the radio. Internally sighing, I tell the tale of how I am one of the persons arrested by Yewtree. He did not know this, but commiserates, because he believes the entire operation is a witch-hunt.

Jonathan Clyde of the Beatles' Apple company treats me to tea at Bafta and passes on unusual support. He has met the editor of the *Mail on Sunday*, Geordie Greig, while visiting his daughter in India. Greig has offered me space whenever I would like to write about the British justice system. A few months ago, I might have bitten at this kind offer. Now I await a phone call that might come at any moment. Anything I write could be outdated by the time it hits the street or even the web.

<hr>

18 MARCH 2014

Starting an acrostic puzzle, I Google for the first line of William Ernest Henley's poem 'Invictus'. I am aware that this verse inspired Nelson Mandela in prison and other great persons in extremely difficult times. I am shocked to see that it perfectly captures my predicament:

Out of the night that covers me,
Black as the pit from pole to pole,
I thank whatever gods may be
For my unconquerable soul.
In the fell clutch of circumstance
I have not winced nor cried aloud.
Under the bludgeonings of chance
My head is bloody, but unbowed.
Beyond this place of wrath and tears
Looms but the horror of the shade,
And yet the menace of the years
Finds, and shall find, me unafraid.
It matters not how strait the gate,
How charged with punishments the scroll,
I am the master of my fate:
I am the captain of my soul.

Having ruminated on the profound insights in this great poem, I segue to music. Invictus was the name songwriter/producers Eddie Holland, Lamont Dozier and Brian Holland gave their label when they left Motown. I play their greatest Invictus hit, the record whose *Rolling Stone* review began my

professional career: 'Band of Gold' by Freda Payne. I follow with their contemporaneous smash 'Give Me Just a Little More Time' by Chairmen of
the Board. It is incredible that these two classics were simultaneous releases
from the same company.

Christopher and I go to Kate Goold's office for a meeting with Chris
and Marshall from *Panorama*. A third representative from the programme
is unable to attend because she is taking heat for an edition devoted to
North Korea … not, Chris and Marshall hasten to point out, an episode
they themselves made in the pariah state.

The Dynamic Duo now hope to make a programme about the police
when the Yewtree wind has blown itself out. They are wondering if I could
make a video diary to capture my reactions to my ordeal on a daily basis. I
nix this because I don't need another source of stress in my life. Besides, all
my energy in capturing this case is going into this book. Kate objects for
another reason. She fears publicity before, during and after any possible trial.
These days it takes very little to elicit an accusation against a celebrity and
she does not feel I will be safe even when my case is technically concluded.

Later in the day, I get an email from Christopher.

'Could you handle it?' is the subject heading.

The link takes me to an ad for the next production at the Old Vic, a
theatre which is visible from my bedroom window.

The play is *The Crucible*.

You couldn't make it up.

I've seen the Arthur Miller classic on stage (the 1984 RSC production at
Christ Church Spitalfields starring Alun Armstrong as John Proctor) and
on screen (Nicholas Hytner's 1996 film with Daniel Day-Lewis in the same
role). It is the quintessential work on the witch-hunt that spread through
Salem, Massachusetts, written in 1953 as an allegory on McCarthyism.

I pass. Chris has never seen it, so he should.

It is strange to think that *The Crucible* will be playing outside my window every night for three months.

Before going to bed, I phone my godson, Andrew. The funeral of his grandfather Sid Evans is tomorrow at the Islington Crematorium, which for some reason is in East Finchley. He confirms the start time of 11 a.m., but not before a little family drama on the telephone which involves a woman in tears and someone else raising their voice. Looking at the location of the crematorium on Google Maps, it seems about as far away from a Tube station as a location can be, but the forecast is for warm and dry weather, so at least I'll have a good walk.

19 MARCH 2014

A funny thing happens on the way to the funeral: it isn't there.

I start early, suspecting that it will take a long time to walk from the Tube station to the crematorium. Indeed, it is thirty-five minutes. I arrive for the 11 a.m. service with three minutes to spare. A large number of people have gathered. I marvel that Sid had so many friends. My only problem is that I don't know any of them. Where is the family? At least I can greet them. Seeing none of them, I go inside. Still seeing none of them, I get suspicious and check the poster listing the times of the day's services.

This isn't the funeral of Sidney Evans, it is the service of a Mr Newcombe! Sid isn't due until 12.30. I have unintentionally crashed the funeral of someone I didn't know!

Thinking a couple of kind thoughts about Sid and my godson, I walk the 35-minute return journey to East Finchley Tube.

I hear a phone ring. I look at several likely recipients of the call, but none answer. I then remember that I have brought my own 'safe' phone, the one the police theoretically don't know about, and it is ringing, for the first time ever outside of my home. It is godson Andrew, informing me that the funeral is going to be at 12.30 and that his family is waiting for transport. Will I be going?

'I've already been,' I tell him, explaining that I had been the first one there by ninety minutes, had thought good thoughts and left. He is flustered, but understands. His grandmother, who has understandably been in a tizzy, had given him the wrong time.

---

20 MARCH 2014

Late this afternoon, Christopher and I are going to make our first visit to the chambers of Mark Dennis, my prospective QC. Kate Goold will be in attendance at the meeting, which I am told could last up to two hours.

During the day I will be reading the set of statements Kate has gathered on my behalf from 'witnesses of fact' who are willing to appear on my behalf in court. A glimpse has revealed to me a couple of howling errors when potential deposers talk about matters outside their direct experience. One woman has referred to my former partner 'Angelo Apollo', when in fact Angelo is the brother of Apollo. Another has recalled a visit to her home by me and Chris Hamill, whom she assumed was my boyfriend. In fact, my companion was my then assistant, Nicholas Potts. A misidentification of Chris Hamill, who might be called as a witness in the case, would be a serious own goal. So it's a morning of reading kind words about myself … looking, not for praise, but errors.

I should have known I would not be allowed to bathe in my own wonderfulness. Shortly after typing the last paragraph, I receive a phone call from my solicitor. Although I had been told the Crown Prosecution Service would decide whether to charge or dismiss me by next Wednesday, 26 March, I have been rebailed until an undetermined day in early May. It seems the CPS is searching for information that is not mine to provide. Other than that, I know nothing. Bearing in mind that the entire case is a fantasy, this 'information' could be anything up to and including an account of alien abduction.

I drearily undertake a series of phone calls and emails, informing my dear ones that we have yet more time to wait.

Christopher and I spend two hours with barrister Mark Dennis and Kate Goold at the QC's chambers in the early evening. We discuss the implications of the latest rebail and our possible trial strategies.

I come away from the meeting with two strong impressions. First, my barrister will be a tremendous asset.

Secondly, I am convinced that I have been overly generous to my accusers. I have referred to them as 'liars or fantasists'. It has been pointed out to me that while it is common for an individual to have imagined a sexual relationship, it is very unlikely that two people would have the same fantasy. In other words, my accusers are probably chancers pure and simple.

Exhausted at the end of the two hours, Chris and I ask Mark if The India, next to his chambers' front door, is in fact an Indian restaurant. It is. Is it good? It is … or so he is told. We enter and find to our shock that there is no trace of a restaurant. There is no one to greet us in reception, and when we go down the stairs into the subterranean areas there is still no one in sight, although we can hear people laughing. Yesterday I went to a funeral that wasn't there. Tonight I am at a restaurant that isn't there. Spooked, we retreat back to Waterloo and have an Indian meal at the trusty Thames Tandoori.

---

22 MARCH 2014

I realise I have not updated my Top 10s in two months. Time does pass!

Here is the latest, based on the number of plays on the iTunes on the new iMac I had to buy when the police seized my other two:

(1) 1) Brown Sugar / Rolling Stones
(2) 2) Put a Little Love in Your Heart / Jackie DeShannon
(–) 3) Street Fighting Man / Rolling Stones
(5) 4) I'm Doing Fine Now / New York City

(6) 5) Where Did Our Love Go / Supremes

(3) 6) #9 Dream / John Lennon

(4) 7) Pretty Ballerina / Left Banke

(–) 8) Band of Gold / Freda Payne

(–) 9) My Feelings for You / Alex Miller

(RE) 10) Palisades Park / Freddy Cannon

This list reminds me of how taste is utterly personal. All the new entries make sense to my life and hardly anybody else's. 'Street Fighting Man' is there because it is my number one anger record.

'Band of Gold' is my first *Rolling Stone* review record, so that matters a great deal. 'My Feelings for You' is a demo that probably only a handful of other people have.

I have been listening to more and more classical music as I get deeper and deeper into whatever this case is going to turn into. Here are the changes since January:

(–) 1) Mendelssohn: Songs Without Words Opus 19 Nos. 1–4 / Daniel Barenboim

(–) 2) Sibelius: Finlandia / Leonard Bernstein

(1) 3) Schubert: 'Trout' Quintet / Alban Berg Quartet

(4) 4) Beethoven: Piano Concerto No. 5 / Alfred Brendel & Simon Rattle

(2) 5) Mozart: Clarinet Concerto / Alessandro Carbonare

(–) 6) Beethoven: Piano Sonata No. 8 / Daniel Barenboim

(–) 7) Beethoven: Piano Trio No. 5 'Ghost' / Emanuel Ax, Pamela Frank, Yo-Yo Ma

(–) 8) Handel: Selections from 'Messiah' / Eugene Ormandy

(–) 9) Mendelssohn: Violin Concerto / Isaac Stern

(3) 10) Beethoven: Piano Concerto No. 4 / Alfred Brendel & Simon Rattle

Why I am on a Mendelssohn binge I will leave to musical psychoanalysts, although I suspect that they will accuse me of favouring his sentimentality to the intellectual rigour of Bach. In the face of such a charge, I will plead guilty, and that is the only charge to which I will plead guilty this year.

—————————————— 24 MARCH 2014 ——————————————

Jerry Rush has sent an email that gives me some hope. Responding to my report on my latest rebail, he writes about Dale Witton's meeting with Officer Four in Australia. I have not personally contacted Dale this century.

'Dale met with Four and said her statement was seven pages long,' Jerry says.

> Much of it related to how and why she was in the UK, how she met me and how she met you. She said she heard about your arrest and said the charges [sic] were totally out of character and that she did not see anything even slightly untoward in your behaviour the whole time she lived in your flat.
>
> Dale went on to say that Sixteen and his partner were neighbours and she was often in their apartment. She said most of her statement dealt with Sixteen.
>
> She said if asked, she would be pleased to come to court and speak on your behalf.

It's very touching that someone I have not seen in decades is willing to travel halfway around the world to defend me. The other point that intrigues me is that over half of her statement dealt with Sixteen, not me. Could it be that the Met now realise they have no case against me, but do not find it tactically easy to dismiss the allegations? The police cannot easily acknowledge that my accusers have lied without entertaining the possibility that they have falsely accused him, too.

Christopher and I have dinner with Keith at Brasserie Blanc. In two days it will be his fortieth birthday. His party will be on Saturday night, but we want to celebrate personally before then.

We return home and an email firestorm has started. Jimmy Tarbuck has been released! We dance. Literally.

And then, we stop. After an hour, the euphoria wears off. As I Google from news site to news site, I become aware that the Crown Prosecution Service and North Yorkshire Police remain unrepentant. They do not apologise for subjecting one of this country's most accomplished men, a great philanthropist who has brought happiness to millions, to a year of undeserved emotional torture. He has been on 332 days of bail over nothing. They do not proclaim him innocent. A CPS spokesman merely repeats the tired line: 'We have determined there is insufficient evidence for a realistic prospect of conviction and have advised the police that no further action be taken.' In other words, the Crown Prosecution Service does not care that a blameless man is sentenced to life under a cloud of suspicion. He has been released from his hell not because he is innocent but because there is 'insufficient evidence for a realistic prospect of conviction'. North Yorkshire Police, instead of apologising, reassure the public that they 'take all allegations of sexual offences extremely seriously and will conduct thorough investigations'.

I exchange emails with Liza. Jimmy sends me thanks for offering him support.

---

25 MARCH 2014

I have a slight pain on the left side of my chest. Occasionally, referred pain twinges the fleshy part of my left palm.

'Don't let me have a stroke at four in the morning,' I beg the heavens. 'Don't don't don't.' I have to live to see off the Metropolitan Police.

To be honest, I don't know if the pains on my left side are the result of yesterday's golf lesson or of stress. What is true is that Tarbuck's release has plunged me back into the pit of my predicament. With Jim out of the witch-hunt, I am now bound to receive a bit more personal publicity.

I spend nearly two hours of the afternoon with Christopher Hird of Dartmouth Films. He is a friend of Anna Ford and a colleague of Louis Theroux.

Christopher and Louis are thinking of making a film about Operation Yewtree when 'this' is all over, although no one is quite sure how to define 'this'. Hird tells me, 'You might be surprised at how everyone thinks your case is completely ridiculous.' Since each person's version of 'everyone' is different, I am always glad to hear that another population of 'everyone' is on my side. I fill Christopher in on some of what I have experienced. He tells me that in the event of his making a documentary about Yewtree he would not expect any of the accused to appear on screen. In return, I tell him I would be happy to give him background briefings on my experiences.

While I am speaking to Christopher I get a phone call from Lewis Carnie at Radio 2 telling me that he has arranged tickets for me to see *Stephen Ward* this evening. Curtain is three hours away! I must see this because it is the latest collaboration between my old friends Andrew Lloyd Webber and Don Black.

As anticipated, I grimace every time crooked police or politicians appear on stage. The title character was the victim of one of the worst frame-ups in British history, as chronicled by Geoffrey Robertson in his 2013 book *Stephen Ward Was Innocent, OK*. The hardest moment for me comes when Ward commits suicide by sleeping pills. This I don't need.

26 MARCH 2014

I wake up at 6 a.m., do the *New York Times* crossword online, and return to bed.

At 7.54, the doorbell rings. I am awakened from sleep and instinctively think the dread words, 'Is it Yewtree again?' Christopher's heart races from adrenalin. He is thinking the same thought.

It is not the Metropolitan Police. It is the concierge John, hand-delivering an article from *The Sun* by Jane Moore along with this week's Abel & Cole fresh fruit and vegetables.

Jane's piece is thrilling. 'False allegations taint innocent stars forever' is the headline of an article in which she uses the occasion of the Jimmy Tarbuck release to analyse Operation Yewtree and related cases.

'Despite *fourteen* police officers raiding his home and taking away diaries, videos and his, er, wife's computer, nothing incriminating was found,' Moore writes, 'except, as Jimmy quips, "I like golf and football."' She compares Tarbuck's experience to that of the similarly arrested-without-charge Jim Davidson, noting that the younger comedian 'says he helped to clear his own name through him and his lawyers systematically amassing evidence to disprove each claim'.

> But, much like Tarbuck, not before he had no doubt suffered months and months of sleepless nights and lack of work.
>
> Laughably, they are the lucky ones.
>
> Their fellow comedian Freddie Starr, 71, has been arrested for the fourth time over similar claims that he refutes and is bailed until next month. And Radio 2's Paul Gambaccini is still in limbo after being arrested for historic abuses which he also categorically denies. Meanwhile, their accusers are protected by their cloak of anonymity.

Moore is a real professional. She manages to acknowledge the other side of the story while still making her case.

> No one is blaming the police. As the Stuart Hall case proves, all such serious claims must be investigated in the name of justice.

But in many of the arrests under the banner of Operation Yewtree, there seems to be a policy of 'collar now, then wait for the ensuing publicity to provide evidence'. If any.

Then Moore strikes home.

> Yes, there are all too many genuine victims of sexual abuse.
>
> But by the law of averages, there are also some liars who are out to make a fast buck.
>
> As it stands, over-the-top arrests are being made on the assumption that all accusers are telling the truth until proven otherwise.
>
> And when, as in some cases, their story just doesn't stand up, they simply carry on with their lives as if nothing ever happened.
>
> Sadly, the same cannot be said for those they accuse who, as Tarbuck says, will always suffer a taint from the 'no smoke without fire' brigade.

As I have said before, not only no fire, not even a match.

Opening my email, I see Jane's husband Gary Farrow has sent me a screen grab of her article. I reply, 'Love to Jane for accuracy and advocacy. She has it 100 per cent.'

And with that, Christopher and I have breakfast.

---

28 MARCH 2014

Why is it that almost every time I try to type 'police' on this computer, predictive text prints 'polio'?

My new rebail date has been set for 7 May at 5.30 p.m. Kate Goold has assured me that there is nothing sinister in the late-afternoon time. My case officer expects to be busy in court that day.

I have bounced back from my low mood of two days ago. I have even dared to hope. It has occurred to me that the Crown Prosecution Service rationalisation for delay seems tenuous. Surely the choice to charge or dismiss cannot rest on a single piece of 'information'. The Metropolitan Police must have made a recommendation, and the CPS must have an opinion of it.

There are only two possibilities: charge or dismiss. But if they have decided to charge, they would have by now. No single piece of 'information', especially one that I cannot provide, could change their mind. There would be no reason to delay. I would be charged by now.

On the other hand, if they have decided not to charge, there is reason to delay. The CPS dropped the Jimmy Tarbuck case and would not want to stop two high-profile cases in the same week for fear of looking, as Oscar Wilde might say, 'careless'.

In the evening, Christopher and I attend the media night for the transfer of *Jersey Boys* from the Prince Edward Theatre to the Piccadilly. I have seen the musical before but wish to catch the performance of John Lloyd Young, the Tony-winning original Broadway Frankie Valli. He does not disappoint. Although there are a few awkward timings in dialogue, the show is still strong.

I remind Chris at the interval how exciting it was to be young at a time when a group could make its breakthrough with three number ones in half a year, as the Four Seasons did with 'Sherry', 'Big Girls Don't Cry' and 'Walk Like a Man' in late 1962 and early 1963, the Beatles and Supremes did the following year, and the Jackson Five did in 1970. Today's new artists release records at wider intervals, ensuring they do not achieve the sense of excitement those four predecessors did.

29 MARCH 2014

Yesterday, the *Coventry Telegraph* headlined, 'Lawyers for comic Freddie Starr hit out at police'. The story reads:

Lawyers for comedian Freddie Starr have accused Scotland Yard of a 'flagrant breach' of his human rights by leaving him on bail as part of a 'policy' decision.

Dean Dunham, who represents the 71-year-old, claimed the Met had decided to push back his bail until May while PR guru Max Clifford's trial over unconnected allegations continues.

Mr Dunham said: 'Freddie Starr was due to answer police bail on 1 April 2014. This would have been the ninth rebail date during what has so far been an eighteen-month period of being on police bail.

Two weeks ago, officers confirmed that they had concluded all lines of inquiries and investigations and that the matter now sat with the Crown Prosecution Service for a charging decision.

However, last night officers from Operation Yewtree contacted this firm and explained that Freddie was to be rebailed again, this time to 6 May.

Remarkably, they then confirmed that the reason for the decision to rebail was nothing to do with any ongoing investigation but rather based on the fact that they did not want to publicise the decision in relation to Freddie whilst the Max Clifford trial continues to be heard.

This is purely a 'policy' decision that is not based on anything directly to do with the allegations made against Freddie. To rebail Freddie in these circumstances is frankly wrong and is a flagrant breach of his human rights.

As I have said before, I am delighted that Freddie Starr, or his representative Dean Dunham, are saying all the things that those of us who are wrongly accused would love to say but don't dare. But there is a good reason we don't dare. A person who is under the gun should not insult the shooter. There are three stages of cases like ours. The first is a police investigation. The second is a Crown Prosecution Service decision. The third is a jury verdict. There is no point in playing to a gallery consisting of the press and general public when it has zero influence over your fate. During the police phase, only the police determine what happens to you. During the Crown Prosecution Service phase, it is the CPS. If it gets to a jury, it is all down to them. There is no point antagonising the people who are in charge of your legal life, yet Freddie, through Dean Dunham, has publicly criticised the police when they were in control of the investigation and the CPS when it is about to decide his future. This is a tactic that will be looked back on as either courageous or foolhardy.

Athough Kate has been in contact with solicitors representing a couple of the other accused celebrities, we agree that she should refrain from contacting Starr's lawyer Dean Dunham. Looking him up on the web, I have seen that he refers to himself as a celebrity lawyer and is photographed in wig, gown and boxing gloves. We are glad that he is combative but do not wish to project this image ourselves.

Gary Farrow has sent me a heads-up to read Richard Littlejohn in the Mail Online. Yet again, Littlejohn has been both brave and accurate. Although the media are too fragmented in the modern era for him to have the same impact as Edward R. Murrow, he has played an analogous role in the Yewtree scandal. He has been early, he has been courageous, and he has been right. This time he draws a parallel between the experience of MP Peter Bone and the cases of Jim Davidson and Jimmy Tarbuck. I write to Farrow:

> Once again, he gets it all. He has led from the start. I'm sorry he never replied to my offer of a chat last autumn, but that's life. At least voices respected in a substantial part of the 'right-wing' press community, like his and Jane's, are being heard. No one on the 'left wing' has spoken up.
>
> It's so weird. The *Telegraph* has completely outdistanced *The Guardian* on this, *The Sun* has bested the *Mirror*, and the *Mail* has hit *The Observer* out of the park. So much for the lazy generalisation that it is the left that protects civil liberties.

To my Radio 4 producers Paul Bajoria and Sara Jane Hall, I offer the news of my latest rebail date, including my conclusion that for the first time I actually feel hope for the imminent dismissal of my case. I end,

> No matter how long they dither, they won't be able to turn shit into steak. I have to keep reminding myself that, no matter how difficult they make my life, there is still, and will always be, no case. When I remember this, I begin to think that sanity will prevail … I just don't know if it will be before or after a trial!

I receive a shocking phone call. A gentleman with whom I have communicated concerning my own case opens our conversation by saying, 'I may be joining your group.' He has received an invitation to attend Fulham Police Station within the next fortnight for interview relating to an offence. He may bring a solicitor if he wishes. Upon phoning the station, he has discovered that the incident is of a historical nature, dating to the late 1970s. I detect anxiety in a voice I have known for over forty years to be normally full of confidence. We arrange lunch for 11 April.

I go to the Barbican Theatre to see the great Italian actor Toni Servillo in *Inner Voices*. Servillo has recently starred in *The Great Beauty*, the Academy Award Best Foreign Language Film winner that had me so transfixed I sat through to the end of the credits as the cameraman slowly cruised down the Tiber. Malcolm Jeffries and I are astonished that the theatre is literally crowded to overflowing, with numerous standees.

'Have they cleared this with Health and Safety?' Jeffries asks.

Malcolm makes a passing remark that stuns me. He mentions that Nigel Evans has already been found not guilty of one charge. Huh? How can this be?

Son of a gun, my friend is right. When I check later, I see the BBC Lancashire News website reports that 'the judge Mr Justice King told the jury at Preston Crown Court to clear him of one sexual assault charge.

'He said jurors should consider a charge of attempted sexual assault instead.'

The *Inner Voices* audience, which clearly includes many countrymen, has come to adore Servillo and the Italian-speaking cast. Subtitles are provided for those in the audience who do not know Italian, but this part of the crowd must be confused. The audience is laughing in reaction to the lines as they are spoken by the actors, not as they are posted above the stage seconds out of synchronisation. To a non-Italian speaker, it seems that decidedly unfunny lines are getting huge laughs.

I briefly reflect on what my life would have been like had I paid more attention to the Italian half of my lineage. Would I have moved to Italy? Would I have eaten the Mediterranean diet all my life and weigh a stone less? I decide it would have been more likely that despite the beauty, culture and food of the land of my forefathers, its corruption, homophobia and religiosity would have made me want to imitate my grandfather and emigrate.

---

30 MARCH 2014

Full credit to Christopher! In our final bowling encounter of the quarter, requiring a lead of thirty-six pins to overtake me for the season, he takes me by forty-six. He achieves this in the final frame of the final game. A strike in the ninth and a spare in the tenth take him over the top. He beats me for the winter by an average of 0.9 pins per game. I can't begrudge him the title. I had a decent average day; he had two excellent games. He earned it.

Malcolm is regaled by the news. 'I wouldn't want it any other way,' he says. 'He is so competitive he can't bear to have you win even in the quarter of your greatest troubles. He knows you would recognise if he wasn't trying his best, so he goes all out.'

---

31 MARCH 2014

I receive a phone call from my old friend Steve Forbert. My association with this talented man goes back to 1978, when I introduced Britain to his music on Radio 1. We remain pals. Now he is touring Europe and is calling from Heathrow, where he is about to board a plane to Gothenburg. He wants to hear the full story of my dilemma. Summarising five months of horror in a ten-minute phone conversation is difficult, so I abbreviate paragraphs into phrases like 'they took away anything with a plug' – an admitted exaggeration, but one Steve likes. He repeats it: 'They took away anything with a plug.' I then add, 'And my iPhone.'

Finishing the conversation as his flight boards, Forbert vows his complete support and says, for the first time in thirty-six years of friendship, 'I love you.' It is a beautiful sentiment that touches my heart.

———————— I APRIL 2014 ————————

It is April Fool's Day, which many people associate with spaghetti trees and Noel Edmonds supposedly doing his Radio 1 breakfast show from a plane flying over Britain. For me it has been a birthday, first of Annie Nightingale and then my 1980s lodger Nick Fletcher. This year it takes on a special significance. This will be the first month since my arrest when I will theoretically have nothing whatsoever to do with the Metropolitan Police. They have handed my file over to the Crown Prosecution Service, whose next contact is due in the first week of May. This month is therefore an interval in the opera my life has become.

It is up to me to be as sane as I can. When the case began, it was on my mind about 98 per cent of the time. That is now down to 40 per cent. The majority of my life, though not a massive majority, is now lived without Yewtree on my mind. I could watch Tony Palmer's film about Maria Callas at the National Film Theatre last night with only occasional thoughts about myself.

I receive a few pieces of post, assuming most of them are birthday cards for my sixty-fifth tomorrow. The last one I open is not a birthday card. It is the hard copy of my Police Bail Variation, informing me that I do not need to appear at Charing Cross Station on 26 March and am now to report on 7 May.

I had received an email version of this yesterday from Kate. It is a little late. If this were how I first heard the rebail news, I would have turned up on the 26th for nothing. For a moment I am floored that the police, so punctual when they want to be, are in this case so lax. And then, once again, I dare to hope. Maybe they're not lax. Maybe they just couldn't care less. Maybe, to them, my case is already history and I just don't know it yet.

---

2 APRIL 2014

Today is my sixty-fifth birthday. None of the previous sixty-four started like this.

At 5.23 a.m. I awake from an odd dream. I am talking about music with Frank Sinatra. He says his favourite song is 'I Get a Kick Out of You' and his top singer is Shirley Bassey. I tell him that's strange, because David Frost has told me that both Bassey and Joseph Stalin have told him that song is their favourite, too.

None of these 'facts' are true. How on earth did I have such a dream? Shortly before going to bed I had read the *New Yorker* profile on Stalin's daughter Svetlana, so that explains part of it. And I had thought about Bassey yesterday because I had been reminded of being at a Buckingham Palace reception where Shirley talked warmly with Eric Clapton. I hear at least one Sinatra song every day. It's Frostie I'm going to have to think about.

Under ordinary circumstances, I would have a big party. When I lived in Islington I had an annual soirée with dozens of guests. This year, that would be inappropriate. The big party will wait until I am cleared. Today we must go in the opposite direction. At 1 p.m. we will convene the hardcore of Team Gambo: Chris, Jennifer, Malcolm and Christopher Simpson. Darren Cheek would be welcome, but he and his girlfriend Kleo are in Dubai on holiday. I am sorry that Malcolm's partner Coralie is unable to attend because of work, but she has still provided the chocolate birthday cake, using a Nigella Lawson recipe.

I had long known of a few famous people born on 2 April. Alec Guinness, Marvin Gaye and baseball pitcher Billy Pierce were the ones who most appealed to me as a child. The longer list of birthdate mates really rides the range, extending from Charlemagne to Hans Christian Andersen to Max Ernst, from Lou Monte to Leon Russell to Emmylou Harris. And, radio fans, don't forget that the novelty DJ Dr Demento was born in 1941!

Brian Glover's birth year was 1934. The former wrestler became noted as an actor in *Kes* and starred as The Supreme Being in the National Theatre's award-winning production of *The Mysteries*. During the interval of a play at the Royal Court, two teenage girls sought my autograph. I pointed at Brian, who was standing nearby.

'Why ask for my signature when you can get the autograph of God?' I replied, bringing looks of complete confusion to their faces but delight to Brian's.

Given my current situation, a couple of 2 April highlights on Wikipedia leap out at me. Giacomo Casanova was born on this date in 1725 and Serge Gainsbourg in 1928. I wonder how these renowned lovers would fare under Operation Yewtree. Émile Zola was born on this day in 1840. 'J'accuse', anyone?

Chris takes me to a celebration dinner at a Michelin-starred restaurant, Ametsa, which is based in the Halkin Hotel. It is superb. At his insistence, we have the tasting menu, which besides providing a prolonged period of culinary bliss, gives us an opportunity to reflect on the past half-year. For the first time, Chris reveals that during the media siege following my arrest he wondered if he was going to have to give up his new career plans for 2014.

> I thought I might have to stay with you all the time – I didn't know
> if you could be alone – and I thought, why is this happening to me?
> I'm just Chris Sherwood from Ashby-de-la-Zouch. Can I handle this?

> I remembered my wedding vows, recognised it was far worse for you,
> and knew I could deal with it.

It is a remarkable declaration of love and support from my husband, which reinforces my faith in him and my disdain for the authorities for putting him through this completely unnecessary ordeal.

---

3 APRIL 2014

I have two musical dreams before being awakened by the alarm at 6.40 a.m. In the first I am back at university and have to request a room change. Jimi Hendrix lives next door and practises until 3 a.m., drawing large crowds that block access to my room and keep me awake. It sounds contradictory, but in a dream I am being kept awake!

In the other dream I am a front-seat passenger in a car being driven by Mariah Carey. Her assistant is in the back seat. The radio plays her latest single, a song called 'I Will Always Love You' that bears no resemblance to the Dolly Parton/Whitney Houston classic of the same name. I have drawn up the running order for my Saturday-night show and know that it is number one in the new US chart. I let her in on the 'secret'. She and her assistant get excited. After all – and this is true – Mariah and Elvis Presley are tied in the list of artists who have had the most American number ones. They need but two more to match the Beatles, who are ahead with twenty. 'I Will Always Love You' will break her tie with Elvis and bring her to within one of the Beatles.

'I'm going to have to listen to the show!' she exclaims excitedly. 'Cyndi told me she listened when she was number one. She sat there going, "Oh my Gawd, I'm number one!"'

The account is worth mentioning because it demonstrates that I am having more frequent dreams about music and my radio career than about policemen. My subconscious is re-setting to life without Yewtree, even though there remains the threat that any day my solicitor may receive a call from the Crown Prosecution Service informing her that I have been charged.

At dinner last night I mentioned something that has occurred to me. I haven't heard of anyone being interviewed who might have corroborated my accusers' story. The trail must have gone ice-cold some time ago. Chris feels the police have given up and we just don't know it yet.

Deep down inside I know I feel the same thing, but I can't admit it. It's too risky to get complacent. I am jolted back to reality whenever I remember that I still face the possibility of a trial. Chris can tell whenever this happens by my body language. This morning on the Tube, realising that I am still under suspicion, I had one of my rage attacks, which he ended by placing his hand on my shoulder.

———————————— 4 APRIL 2014 ————————————

When Jennifer arrives in the morning, I request that we finalise my passport and visa arrangements for the trip to New York that Christopher and I will be making at Easter. I am currently renewing my American passport, a process that used to take minutes during a personal visit to the US embassy in Grosvenor Square but now takes four to six weeks, requiring a courier service costing $110. I am astonished at how the United States has made life much more difficult for citizens living abroad under the presidencies of George W. Bush and Barack Obama. We knew at the time of its passage that the Bush administration's Patriot Act would be a paperwork and security nightmare for ordinary law-abiding citizens, but we thought when we elected Barack Obama that life abroad would become easier. Instead, it has become more difficult.

I go to Le Pain to meet Janie Orr and David Hughes of the EMI Music Sound Foundation. Orr, chief executive officer, received an MBE in 2013. I have known Hughes since the early 1970s. I always remember him coming up to me at the end of a James Brown concert at the Rainbow Theatre, relating to me in shock that the Godfather of Soul would not see me for a *Rolling Stone* interview as planned because, as he put it, 'I made it without *Billboard* and *Cashbox* and *Rolling Stone.*' True enough. *Rolling Stone* did not exist until 1967.

Two hours fly by in the company of Janie and David. They are incredibly diligent at running the charity, which has improved the lives of countless youngsters by enabling them to purchase musical instruments. Today we are not talking music, however. I am giving them Yewtree's Greatest Hits, the by now time-tested series of horror stories that always reduces audiences to quivering jelly. The monitoring of Christopher's email and the internet-posted tariff of compensation for alleged injuries shocks them the most. When I tell them that the relationship between the police and the press has survived Leveson, they are not surprised. Hughes, who worked in local journalism in the 1960s, theorises that it is a legacy of Freemasonry. He relates how he was always receiving unusual handshakes in his early years in the business and suspects that ties between police and press were forged in the days when connections between Freemasons were professionally important. It is now hard to break these bonds, even if the Masons are no longer the social force they were. I have never thought of this, but then I have only ever known one person who told me he was a Mason.

I return home to paperwork hell. Jennifer has printed out my ESTA, a document required for UK passport holders to enter the US. I have applied for one because my American passport is being renewed and I have been warned that it might not be ready for my next trip to New York. I gulp when I notice she has answered 'NO' to the ESTA question,

> Have you ever been arrested or convicted for an offence or crime involving moral turpitude or a violation related to a controlled substance; or have been arrested or convicted for two of more offences for which the aggregate sentence to confinement was five years or more; or have been

a controlled substance trafficker; or are you seeking entry to engage in
criminal or immoral activities?'

I point out that I have been arrested. She blushes from embarrassment.
She thought 'moral turpitude' referred to drug use. After all, almost all
the other questions did. We therefore have to change the answer to this
question to 'YES'. Of course, to the ESTA computer, this could mean that
I have 'been arrested' ... or that I am 'seeking entry to engage in criminal or immoral activities'. 'YES' to one possibility is yes to all. This is a
reminder of what Jane Moore wrote about in *The Sun* after the release of
Jimmy Tarbuck ... that the falsely accused carry a taint of suspicion with
them for the rest of their lives.

We will have to re-submit to get the ESTA. For those of us who have
been arrested it requires 'a national police certificate (aka ACRO report)
that confirms and lists your complete criminal history'. We must include
a photograph which is certified by 'a manager' or similar professional. The
manager of the Whitehouse Apartments has gone home for the day. Jude
Kelly of the Southbank Centre is in Lanzarote on a windsurfing holiday.
I suggest Jennifer go downstairs to the manager of the building's estate
agency. He rises to the occasion and certifies that my photo is, indeed,
a picture of me. I write a cheque for £89 to the Police and Crime Commission and Jennifer races to make it to the post office in time for the
last pick-up.

---

5 APRIL 2014

There is a further reason for my strange recent optimism. It occurred to
me just before falling asleep last night that although I am forbidden to
contact my co-accused and do not know the accusations against him, he
must have been active in his own defence. He would have given the police
a statement and named people to interview in his support. He and his

solicitor, if he has one, will have constructed a case. Even though he and our accusers may be known to each other, I believe it almost certain that he did not have long-term relationships with Secondary and Primary of the kind I am alleged to have had. Someone in the building would have noticed the same strange male teenagers walking the corridors for years on end. No one mentioned it then or has mentioned it to me now. It is therefore likely, not just possible, that Sixteen has pointed out inconsistencies in our accusers' stories that cannot help but benefit me.

---

7 APRIL 2014

I have received a shocking phone call. Dr Charles Farthing, whom I have known for thirty years, has suffered a massive heart attack in the back seat of a taxi in Hong Kong. He has died in hospital.

This is an inconceivable death. It is unthinkable not just because Christopher and I have seen Farthing in fine form twice in the past year when he has been in London, once celebrating a landmark birthday with a *This Is Your Life*-type gathering, and again at a more intimate dinner party. This does not compute because Charles was at the top of his profession, making important contributions to the study of infectious diseases while working for Merck in Hong Kong.

Born in New Zealand, Charles found himself in London during the outbreak of HIV/Aids, and was one of the three physicians who became a public face of the disease. It was to build a dedicated wing of Farthing's hospital that John Reid hosted one of Elizabeth Taylor's dinner parties, where rich individuals paid $10,000 each to eat with her. Charles and I were the only guests at this dinner who did not have to pay the $10,000! I got a pass because of my media work concerning HIV/Aids.

The fight against Aids before the introduction of combination therapy was dark and desperate. Those of us who were in the trenches together feel like veterans of a war, and this is not to slight any survivor of actual combat. Charles and I had many deep conversations about the fight. These shared hours inevitably came to include personal confidences.

I have to send a message of sympathy, but to whom? I do not have his partner Dougie's email address, so I write to Charles's Merck account:

> To whomever is reading this,
>
> Be you Doug, brother, co-worker or even someone else, please let me extend to you my greatest sympathies on the passing of one of the great men of my life. I have profound memories of Charles's intelligence and courage during the 1980s in London. In one of my mental Polaroids, we are on breakfast television together, explaining the New Disease to the nation. At a time which required a combination of knowledge, calm and compassion, Charles communicated all these qualities.
>
> On a more personal level, I recall Charles taking me on his rounds one evening in the late 1980s.
>
> 'We are now going to see a young man from Turkey who is going to die in two days,' he told me. 'His family are coming to see him tomorrow.'
>
> When we entered the room, doctor and patient engaged in friendly chat. The Turk then asked, 'Do I have to see my family?'
>
> 'Yes,' Charles replied.
>
> 'We can never stop fighting, can we?' the dying man asked.
>
> 'We can never stop fighting,' Charles answered.
>
> I have never forgotten these words. 'We can never stop fighting' inspired me throughout the health crisis and inspires me today in different circumstances. The example of the brilliant and brave Charles Farthing will light darkness for the rest of my life.
>
> The young Turk did die in two days, as Dr Farthing predicted. Now they are both gone. Ultimately, we are all taken. We can only hope we leave behind persons whose lives are better for our having lived. Charles leaves many such people.

My love to all in the memory of Charles,
Paul Gambaccini

And Charles, I will be true to you up to 7 May and beyond. We can never stop fighting.

8 APRIL 2014

The day begins horribly. Christopher shows me something he has found on the web. Seeking details on the death of Charles Farthing, he has come upon a shocking YouTube clip from a source named Apple Daily.

According to Wikipedia, Apple Daily is 'a Hong Kong-based tabloid-style newspaper'. No joke: outside of war footage, neither Chris nor I have ever seen such graphic content of a man's death. Farthing is seen, prostrate and shirtless on a gurney, perhaps already deceased, receiving vigorous attempts at cardio-pulmonary resuscitation in a Hong Kong hospital. We cannot understand the Chinese-language narration, so are unprepared for the camera jump to the sight of Charles in a black body bag being placed into a vehicle. This intimate view of a friend's death will haunt me all day and for many days to come.

Sadly, it is not the only piece of fatal news. The newspapers are full of the death of Peaches Geldof at the age of twenty-five. Almost all reprint the last photo she tweeted, one of her as a child with her mother Paula.

Although it has been years since I was close to the family, I find this unbearably sad. I had known Bob Geldof and Paula Yates when they were courting. 'Courting' is, of course, a very polite word for the uncontainable passion they felt for each other in the early years of their relationship. I recall once taking them to a country music show at Hammersmith Odeon – was it Dolly Parton or Kenny Rogers? – in which their eyes were only on the stage about 60 per cent of the time. They were as loving a couple as I have ever known. I knew them from the days that they and the Boomtown Rats were sharing a house in Chessington after coming to England from

Ireland. It was in part because I had known nearly the full time period of their story that Bob asked me to give the eulogy at Paula's funeral. Their eldest daughter, Fifi, asked me for a copy of my script. Having endured so many news reports depicting her mother as a rock 'n' roll wild child, Fifi had found solace in hearing from someone who had known her, and treated her, as a serious human being. I would reprint the eulogy here, but it is on one of my computers the police took away and have not returned.

Paula died fourteen years ago. Now her daughter has passed away. It is too much for even people who are not in the family to bear, yet Bob has reached inside himself to write one of the most eloquent tributes I've ever read, saying of Peaches:

> She was the wildest, funniest, cleverest, wittiest and the most bonkers of all of us.
>
> Writing 'was' destroys me afresh. What a beautiful child. How is this possible that we will not see her again? How is that bearable?
>
> We loved her and will cherish her forever. How sad that sentence is. Tom and her sons Astala and Phaedra will always belong in our family, fractured so often, but never broken.

The literary Irishman in Bob always comes out when he is called. For all his reputation as a gruff, no-nonsense action man, Geldof was always a deeply feeling man.

I wish I could send Bob a letter of condolence today, but the police still have all my address books.

Can this day bring even more bad news? Yes. Just before going to bed, Christopher and I are told that Cliff Richard has been arrested.

---

9 APRIL 2014

Poor Cliff. His impending arrest has been the most trailed in the entire campaign. I know this because I Google the words 'cliff richard arrested' and find no news reports but an endless series of infantile tweets, some with doctored photographs and almost all with smirky comments. There are crude puns on titles of his hit songs. There are plays on the name 'Cliff'.

When the morning comes, after I have managed four hours of sleep, I call a contact at BBC News, who confirms that Cliff has been arrested. He adds an unusual point. The reason no print or broadcast news outlet has identified Sir Cliff is that none wishes to incur a public backlash if it turns out that he is never charged. The papers, perhaps more than the police, realise that there is an enormous reservoir of love for Cliff Richard among the British public, particularly among those persons over forty. To accuse him of being a sleaze for what eventually turns out to be no reason is to risk a Hillsborough-like backlash. This surprising exercise of discretion is proof, not that it was ever needed, that Cliff is more of a national institution than any of us. We all spent long periods having been arrested without charge, but the papers did not fear a backlash in naming us.

During a shower after an early-evening gym session, I cheer myself up by calculating the odds of having to go to prison. I figure that the prospect of being charged by the Crown Prosecution is about two in five. I can't help but honestly feel that I have a slightly better chance, three in five, of being dismissed. This is because I know that I am innocent, which is bound to affect my view of the case.

If I were to go to court, my advisors think that I have a two-in-three chance of acquittal. It should be three in three, but we always have to leave open the possibility of a miscarriage of justice. Were I then to be found guilty of something, the chance of a custodial sentence might be about one in two. Using mathematical formulae I learned in high school, this all adds up to a roughly 7 per cent chance of being sent to jail. This is actually not that bad, especially considering how dark things looked at the start.

10 APRIL 2014

The morning post brings a stomach-turning document. It is my Association of Chief Police Officers 'Police Certificate for Immigration Purposes'. I thought before I received my renewed American passport that I might need this for an ESTA visa to cover next week's Easter trip to New York. Now that I have my US passport I won't need to travel on my British documents, so no immigration officer need ever see this certificate, but this is upsetting anyway. I knew it would be a complete arrest record, but I did not expect the wording it uses. There are two items in the 'Summary of Convictions and Reprimands/Warnings/Cautions', which is in all capital letters:

> DATE OF OFFENCE 01/01/1978
> OFFENCE: INDECENT ASSAULT ON MALE UNDER 16
> POLICE FORCE: METROPOLITAN POLICE
> STATUS: IMPENDING PROSECUTION

and

> DATE OF OFFENCE 01/01/1978
> OFFENCE: BUGGERY (WITH BOY UNDER 16)
> POLICE FORCE: METROPOLITAN POLICE
> STATUS: IMPENDING PROSECUTION

Two things jump out at me. One is the 'STATUS' phraseology. 'IMPENDING PROSECUTION' is disturbing. The other is that there are, officially, two alleged offences. Is this just a recognition that we have not gone to court yet, or is it a revelation that the CPS has decided to charge me and there will be these two counts? Is this the unexpected way I have learned of the CPS decision?

At least the 'DATE OF OFFENCE' is reassuring. 1 January 1978 is several years before I 'performed' my first act of anal sex with anyone. Hopefully the witnesses who would appear on my behalf will be able to communicate how the accusations are out of the timeline of historic reality.

Of course, I don't know if the Association of Chief Police Officers have been in contact with the CPS on my case, but this reads as if there is the terrible possibility that they have unintentionally let the cat out of the bag, and I should alter the last paragraph to substitute the word 'accusations' with 'charges'.

I prepare to call Kate Goold for her reaction to the 'IMPENDING PROSECUTION' phrase by Googling the Max Clifford and Nigel Evans trials to see if there is any breaking development that I should know about before talking to her.

Before I can dial Kate, a friend calls. He tells me that Nigel Evans has been found not guilty on all charges. How can he know this? I ask him what his source is. I keep asking him what his source is as he goes on about it. Finally he tells me he saw it on BBC News and it will soon be everywhere. I looked at the BBC website less than a minute ago and it wasn't there! I go back to the site as my friend begins to ramble. He says that all of our cases, and the popularity of Justin Bieber and Miley Cyrus, are just smokescreens for what is really going on, and he has learned that the richest eighty-five people in the world now have as much money as the bottom 3.5 billion, who are enslaved to the elite, and the Rothschilds…

Here it is. The BBC front page has been refreshed. 'MP Nigel Evans cleared of sexual assaults'. I thank my wandering friend and phone Evans.

I know Nigel will not be answering his phone at this tumultuous moment, but I feel I must leave a message of congratulations.

'Nigel, this is Paul Gambaccini,' I say, 'happy to take my place in the queue of messages. Seeing as we last saw each other at the opera, I should say "Bravo!" Thank you, well done, and talk soon!'

ITV weighs in quickly with a piece that has obviously been written in advance. It includes this key passage:

He denied all of the accusations and now a jury has accepted that denial. But throughout a long trial there were hints that the MP was unhappy about the way police gathered evidence against him.

He claimed in interview that the 'victims' had not, in fact, volunteered their complaints but had only spoken of them when contacted by detectives.

In fact, even as they have [*sic*] evidence for the prosecution it became clear that more than one of them did not regard themselves as 'victims' at all.

And the *Telegraph* comes through again! Under the headline 'Nigel Evans: should "weak case" have been brought?' and the subhead 'Three of the alleged victims in the case against Nigel Evans told the court they did not believe any crime had been committed', Martin Evans, crime correspondent, writes:

The acquittal of Nigel Evans on sex charges will lead to inevitable questions as to why the case against him was brought.

It represents another failure for the Crown Prosecution Service North West, which recently brought the unsuccessful case against *Coronation Street* star William Roache leading to claims the case should never have been brought.

The evidence against Nigel Evans began to look weak when three of the alleged victims told the court they did not believe any crime had taken place.

All three were allegedly assaulted by the Ribble Valley MP between 2002 and 2009, but each told police they did not want to press charges against the politician.

Despite their insistence that they did not consider themselves to be victims of a crime, Lancashire Police and the Crown Prosecution Service pressed ahead with the prosecution, telling the victims it was not for them to decide whether there was a case to answer.

Nigel takes time out from his busy afternoon to ring. He tells me he will call upon his return to London to arrange dinner. He will be praying for good news for me before my rebail date of 7 May. His friends are giving interviews, openly discussing the actions of the police and Crown Prosecution Service. He hopes that his innocent verdicts will stop the unchecked progress of insubstantial allegations through to trial.

'Several people have told me that everyone passes the hot potato along, thinking it will be settled in a jury trial. No one wants to be the one to stop it. Maybe having so many innocent verdicts will make everyone re-evaluate this attitude.'

The Crown Prosecution Service releases a statement:

> The complainants in this case provided clear accounts of the alleged offending and it was right that all of the evidence was put before a jury. That evidence could only be fully explored during a trial and the jury has decided, after hearing all of the evidence, that the prosecution has not proved its case beyond reasonable doubt. We respect this decision.

I don't respect yours. The idea that senseless cases have to be presented to a jury, which will have the good sense to reject them, is a mockery of justice. It wastes millions in public funds and subjects innocent men to months of inconceivable stress, loss of employment and irretrievable expense. The Mail Online agrees, carrying the headline 'CPS in the dock after ANOTHER high-profile sex attack prosecution ends in acquittal: Ex-Commons deputy speaker Nigel Evans breaks down in tears as he is found NOT GUILTY of assaulting seven young men.'

Just before we go to bed, Christopher points out a surprising story on the *Mirror* website concerning the person arrested a couple of days ago for historic sexual offences: 'The *Mirror* can reveal that the man is a former BBC employee who is not believed to be a household name.'

If this is so, it is not Cliff Richard, and my BBC informant was wrong.

So were all those publications who assumed and hinted in the nudge-nudge-wink-wink tradition that the next arrestee was going to be Cliff. The news is non-news: Cliff Richard has not been arrested.

Another paragraph in the *Mirror* story is of more personal relevance. 'The *Mirror* can reveal that lawyers have been handed a full file of evidence in relation to [Paul] Gambaccini and [Freddie] Starr. The Crown Prosecution Service said they are now considering whether the men should be charged.'

―――――――――― II APRIL 2014 ――――――――――

The *Telegraph* has placed on its website an important blog by Dan Hodges. It is headlined 'The police and CPS have to stop dragging innocent people through the dirt'. Hodges speaks truth to power.

'It's difficult to imagine a more blatant and disgraceful abuse of the British legal system that the one Nigel Evans has just been subject to.' Don't hold back, Dan.

'For some reason, when it came to the Nigel Evans case, the police and Crown Prosecution Service decided to take these basic principles of justice, rip them up, and scatter them to the winds.'

Some of his observations have been made by others, but they are worth repeating because his summary is so precise and to the point.

> As the case unfolded, it became clear that there were problems with the prosecution's case. Quite a fundamental problem, actually. Three of the alleged 'victims' said they weren't victims at all.
>
> The first described the supposed crime against him as 'a big joke'. When asked by Nigel Evans's barrister if he'd believed the incident might end up in court, he replied, 'Never in a million years.' When the second 'victim' was interviewed by the police, he said: 'I do not wish Mr Evans to be charged as a result of what happened to me. I have absolutely no intention of making a complaint to the police and

I am making this statement as a witness and not as a victim seeking justice.' The third 'victim' told the police, 'I do not wish to pursue any kind of complaint against Nigel because I do not believe he has committed any offences.'

Given the insistence by the 'victims' that they weren't actually victims, the police then proceeded to do what any sensible investigative body would do in these circumstances. They tried to find witnesses who could convince a jury that those 'victims' were wrong.

Hodges has the police and CPS by the teeth and is not letting go.

Victim after victim stood up and said they weren't a victim. Witness after witness stood up and said they hadn't witnessed anything. Almost all of them attested to Nigel Evans's good character. This farce reached its nadir when the judge was forced to step in and explain to the prosecution that one charge they had filed was not actually an offence in law, given the evidence they had presented.

The *Telegraph* blogger quotes Nigel's solicitor, Daniel Berke, who explains,

I have dealt with cases involving allegations of rape and sexual assault before. Normally there would be a couple of detective constables investigating it and perhaps a middle-ranking barrister prosecuting. In this case there was a large police team. It came out in evidence that the police had gone out of their way to find complaints – two of which dated back ten years and both of whom said in evidence that they were somewhat surprised to find themselves in court. They also instructed senior Treasury counsel – a QC – which, again, would not be typical in a case like this.

Hodges has done his homework. Not only does he take exception to the police's post-match statement, he also follows through:

No one in this case had been subjected to sexual abuse. There were no victims. That had just been conclusively proved in a court of law. By the time Lancashire Constabulary's formal statement appeared on the force's website, the word 'victim' had been changed to 'complainants'. Even though, as we've seen, almost all of the 'complainants' weren't complainants at all.

This correction is a minor victory. For months I have been objecting to the use of the word 'victims' to describe anyone who accuses a public personality, whether they be actual victims, liars or fantasists. Finally, the word 'complainant', which covers all three possibilities, has been used.

Dan Hodges sums up with both gloves off.

> How much longer are we going to tolerate the current situation where the police and Crown Prosecution Service are able to persecute innocent men? Time and time and time again, high-profile prosecutions are brought. And time and time and time again, they are thrown out.
>
> There is a misconception that a miscarriage of justice only occurs when an innocent person is jailed, then subsequently found to have been not guilty of the crime. But the truth is a miscarriage occurs every time an innocent man like Nigel Evans finds himself in the dock, publicly accused of the most heinous crimes.
>
> It's no good everyone patting themselves on the back and saying 'Oh well, the system worked.' The system isn't working. The police and the CPS are dragging the names of decent, honest, innocent people through the dirt on a weekly basis. And it has to stop.

This is the best column I have read on the subject of the show trials yet, better even than those of Richard Littlejohn and Jane Moore. I look to see if there is an email address to which I can, against all advice, send congratulations and thanks. There is no such address, only a Twitter account, and I am certainly not going to tweet at this time.

At least there is one case that will not be going to trial. I lunch with my terrified caller of a fortnight ago, the one who was called into Fulham Police Station to face an accusation of a historic sexual offence. He is relieved that the allegation is inconceivably ridiculous.

A man has reported to police that he has seen a documentary about Jimmy Savile. In the programme he has noticed that Savile possessed a piece of cane furniture identical to one owned by the accused which he saw when he woke up in the latter's house in 1978 with a bleeding anus. He can't recall having sex with the man, but surely he must have been raped.

To me, this complainant falls into the category of 'distressed individuals'. I don't go so far as to say these people are 'liars', even though what they allege seems false. It's just that their mental state is such that they may not be able to distinguish fact from fantasy. I have no idea why they have lost perspective, so that's why I call them 'distressed individuals'. My accusers tell falsehoods, but I don't call them 'liars' in case they are 'distressed individuals'.

The general public will never realise the full extent of the reign of terror that the witch-hunt has generated. It only knows the cases that have led to arrests. Other men have been subjected to weeks or months of psychological torture for accusations that never reached the arrest stage. This period in British history is darker than the British people know.

Rarely does an article give reason for both elation and a groan, but *The Guardian* manages it just before bedtime with a story by Rowena Mason and Owen Bowcott headlined 'Attorney General demands answers from CPS over failed sex offence cases'. Dominic Grieve is due to meet Alison Saunders to 'discuss the unsuccessful prosecutions'. Will he be my cavalry, arriving to save the stagecoach at the last minute? I don't know if the CPS has made its decision whether to charge me or dismiss my case, although I suspect it has, but the timing of this meeting may be too late to rescue me: Grieve and Saunders are due to meet after Easter, not before, and my decision must be announced by 7 May.

My heart rises a couple of centimetres in my chest.

─────────────── 12 APRIL 2014 ───────────────

It should come as no surprise that the acquittal of Nigel Evans has generated more comment in quality newspapers and from politicians than the cases of William Roache and Dave Lee Travis. Nigel is himself a politician, and parliamentarians now realise that they are in the same position as show-business veterans, liable to be wrongly accused of sex crimes. I can hear their squeals here in London SE1, about one mile from the Palace of Westminster.

The *Financial Times*, which has studiously avoided most of the previous courtroom shocks, today has a large feature on its third page headlined 'Prosecutor under fire on sex case acquittals'. No Page Three beauties here. The photos are of Nigel Evans, Bill Roache, Michael Le Vell, Dave Lee Travis and Titus Bramble. Titus Bramble? 'A jury took just over an hour to find the former Sunderland player not guilty of charges of indecent assault in 2012.'

Martin Evans of the *Daily Telegraph* reports on one of the great injustices of the show trials staged by the British police and Crown Prosecution Service.

> Mr Evans, 56, was forced to pay more than £100,000 in legal bills to defend himself against a string of sex assault allegations and despite the not guilty verdicts will be unable to reclaim any of the money.
>
> His solicitor, Daniel Berke, said the CPS's decision to instruct Senior Treasury Counsel, Mark Heywood QC, was above and beyond what would happen in normal cases where the defendant was not in the public eye … Mr Berke suggested the decision had been based on Mr Evans's profile rather than the requirements of the case.

Berke is quoted as saying,

In my view the prosecution had put enormous resources into this case, seemingly over and beyond what would have been spent had the defendant not been somebody firmly in the public eye.

While the facts of the case were unusual, it was not a particularly complex case, so we were surprised by the decision of the CPS to instruct senior Treasury Counsel for a matter which would have normally involved the instruction of junior counsel.

Mr Evans has had to bear significant financial costs and while he was unanimously acquitted by the jury he is unable to recover any of those costs.

Had he chosen to be defended on a legal aid basis he would have still had to bear significant costs and would not have had the sort of representation needed to fight the prosecution case on an equal footing.

If, in a year's time, the Crown Prosecution Service and police wonder why some of us will have written books recording their infamy for eternity, it will be in part because they caused us such grievous financial loss we have had to do something to earn money. I am already more than £100,000 poorer in combined expenses and lost income, and I am not finished yet.

A survey of the editorial pages post-Evans finds that once again, shockingly, the left-wing newspapers continue to support injustice. The *Daily Mirror* opines 'It is too easy to criticise the Crown Prosecution Service ... Would it be better if the CPS acted as judge and jury and dismissed those making the complaints? No it would not. The proper course of action was to let a court of law decide.'

No, it was not. As Nigel has pointed out, too many people are letting ridiculous charges get into the courtroom because nobody wants to drop the hot potato. To force innocent people like Jimmy Tarbuck, Nigel and myself to undergo months of psychological torture just to allow baseless allegations to get an airing in court is manifestly unjust.

Once again, *The Guardian* is on the wrong side. It warns against setting the bar for prosecution 'specially high for celebrity defendants ... That would be a shocking outcome, especially when memories of the Jimmy Savile cases are so vivid and raw.' But this is far from the problem at the moment. The bar for 'celebrity defendants' is being set especially low. Is *The Guardian* really so ignorant it does not know where the injustice in this matter really lies?

I was looking forward to a quiet Saturday. I was going to walk along the Thames to Borough Market to have grilled cheese on Poilane bread. The *New York Times* has judged this 'The World's Greatest Sandwich'. I would follow with ice cream from 3Bis, a company from my grandfather's home town of Rimini. This weekly trek has become the least expensive bit of bliss I know. I would then have a nap and go into Chinatown for my weekly back rub. In the evening, Chris and I would venture to Camden Town for a fringe production by the theatre company that has accepted him as a member. Today, in short, was going to be case-free.

Fat chance, given the continued fallout of the Nigel Evans case. And fat chance, given the exposure by the *Daily Mail* of the late Liberal politician Cyril Smith. The newspaper is serialising and presenting highlights of a book called *Smile for the Camera: The Double Life of Cyril Smith* by Simon Danczuk.

The mere mention of Cyril Smith gives me the shivers. Although I saw him a couple of times at public functions, I encountered him only once. He terrified me.

Even though I have appeared on over a thousand live TV broadcasts, I have only known sheer fear twice. Once was during Live Aid, when the satellite to Philadelphia went down during the performance by Bryan Adams and I had to talk off the top of my head to a global audience until the connection was restored.

The other time was when I was about to do my weekly film review on TV-am. I had taken my customary place on the wing of the presenters' sofa. As the show went from Wincey Willis's weather forecast into a commercial break, the floor manager ran over to me urgently.

'You have to get off the couch!' he insisted. 'Cyril Smith is coming on!'

They were, indeed, positioning the MP for an interview after my film review. But he was too enormous to sit next to anybody on the wing of the couch. He actually occupied the entire wing. Anybody else had to get off, and I was 'anybody else'.

I was shepherded to an armchair in a part of the studio that was not customarily in shot. I was seated and left to address a single camera. There would be no jump cuts here.

The chair was inappropriate for broadcast purposes. It was a soft chair of the sort that swallows whoever sits in it. I felt myself sinking backwards, yet I customarily broadcast my film review leaning forward. I glanced over at the sofa and saw the man-mountain had taken his seat. I had never seen anyone so enormous in my entire life. He was the size of between two and three normal persons.

How was I going to cope? The commercial break was ending, I was on the edge of panic, and there was no way I could feel secure while constantly slipping back into the comfy chair.

And then Wincey walked by on her way out of the studio.

'Wincey!' I begged. 'I'm freaking out. Could you please stand behind the camera so I can have someone to focus on?'

Willis was a professional and instantly understood my predicament. When any of us are accustomed to doing a certain task in a certain place and our routine is altered with only seconds of warning, we are threatened. We need to focus on content, not props. By standing behind the camera Wincey gave me a familiar face to make me feel this was a regular broadcast, not the change of routine it was. After about twenty seconds my terror left me and I was able to concentrate on my work.

I've never forgotten this episode. Whenever I read a curious reference in a performer's memoirs to an episode of stage fright, I shudder from familiarity. Fright is … scary. In my case, fear has a face, and its face is that of Cyril Smith.

Bless Wincey Willis. Oh, Wincey Willis. Thank you.

---

13 APRIL 2014

Welcome to a special Sunday edition of What the Papers Say. What don't they? The air is full of stories related to Nigel Evans.

My jaw drops reading a leader in *The Observer*: 'Nigel Evans case: the CPS needs everyone else to keep a cool head too', it reads. 'The collapse of the Nigel Evans case must not stop the Crown Prosecution Service taking action against the rich and famous.'

Huh? Huh? And again: huh? Is this class war? Is this financial war? Is this carte blanche for any lunatic in the land to denounce the famous person of their choice?

Yes.

The Observer's concluding paragraph states of the CPS:

> Even before the recession, it was overstretched and understaffed. Yet still it maintains an extraordinary 85 per cent conviction rate, including highly complex cases; almost 690,000 convictions in 2012–13. Every organisation can improve and the CPS is certainly no exception but criticism of the kind now prevailing raises the danger that it will encourage only the easier cases to be investigated and prosecuted. The result could be that the rich and famous, along with the less affluent and unknown, gain unwarranted immunity. Now that would be unjust.

The Observer does not realise how many men have been falsely accused in this witch-hunt, nor does it appear to be interested in learning. I find myself restating that the quest for justice is not an either/or proposition. Large numbers of people were abused for years in this country without being taken seriously. That does not mean that the CPS should pass through to the courts flimsy or scientifically impossible accusations made in the context of a witch-hunt against famous people. To see a courtroom forced to consider a case that requires a suspect to have three hands, one which alleges abuse in a motor vehicle that had not yet been invented, and others in which prosecution witnesses deny having accused the defendant, is to debase the justice system.

The Labour Party continues to irritate. Deputy Labour leader Harriet Harman claims on Sky News that 'there should not be anonymity for those accused of sexual offences' and then says of the CPS that it acted 'independently'.

'People say they should never have taken this case in the first place. Our system is that the jury decides.'

On what planet has Harriet been residing recently? Yes, juries decide, but they should never have their time wasted with these travesties of justice in the first place.

14 APRIL 2014

I fell asleep earlier than Christopher last night. He retreated to his office and read an article on the *Guardian* website that upset him. He tells me about it first thing this morning. It upsets me.

The last time we had dinner with Anna Ford, she told me I should meet an exciting new liberal journalist named Owen Jones. He went to my alma mater, University College, Oxford, and is also an out gay man. So far, so good. Even without meeting him or knowing his work, I was proud of him.

It is unfortunate that today's piece is the first Owen Jones article I have read.

'Despite the Nigel Evans trial, the wrongly accused are not the main victims in rape cases', the headline reads. The subhead declares, 'Yes the innocent MP suffered, but we must not go back to the Jimmy Savile era and ignore those who've been sexually abused'.

After giving a rundown of how 'the acquitted are seen as the new victims',

Jones prattles on about how 'rather than false accusations, what should really chill us is this: in most cases in Britain in 2014, to rape is to get away with it'.

Excuse me. Can't both matters chill us? Since when did this become an either/or proposition? Owen, if you need me to say it, I'll say it: just because I have been fitted up, it does not mean that I want people to be raped and their attackers to run around unpunished. We all agree it is appalling that many persons have been abused and then ignored by a deaf society.

But this is not a new complaint. What is new is that the police and Crown Prosecution Service of this country are conducting a witch-hunt against public personalities, all to demonstrate that they are serious about paying attention to a kind of crime they previously ignored.

So ends my life as a liberal. For the past half-century I have given as much time and energy as I can to social causes that I thought deserved and needed them. I will continue to do so. But in the past I associated reform with liberalism because the right always seemed to be on the wrong side: Conservative Southern Democrats oppressed Negro Americans; Margaret Thatcher resisted Nelson Mandela and legislated against homosexuality; the Republican Party enshrined anti-gay discrimination in its party platform, ad infinitum.

But past results are no guarantee of future performance. The Labour Party and *The Guardian* are tone-deaf to life as it is lived in 2014. They are not only on the wrong side of justice and the wrong side of history; they are on the wrong side of reality.

15 APRIL 2014

The Ides of April is known across America as Income Tax Day. The Internal Revenue Service requires that returns be filed by this date. This will be no problem for me this year, as I have had no employment since I was arrested!

Even though I have torn up my Labour Party membership card and informed various partisans I am no longer interested in their communications, I receive a mass mailing this morning. It begins:

> Dear Mr Gambaccini,
> We can do better than this…

No joke. That goes straight in the bin.

Christopher and I prepare to fly to New York for the Easter weekend. On the remote chance that there is important news concerning my case over the holiday, Jennifer will leave a new message on the answerphone giving our emergency number in America.

Speculation about police attitudes is actually irrelevant at this stage. They sent my file to the CPS last month, so they can't revise it as a result of the impending Max Clifford verdict.

I now hope against hope that I will have no thoughts at all about the police for five days. It's Easter! Happy chocolate eggs to all our readers!

—————— 23 APRIL 2014 ——————

Because winter was long and cruel in New York, spring here arrived much later than usual. Blossom is everywhere. Every tree and plant in Central Park decides to explode in colour at the same moment. I walk about six miles a day, frequently contemplating the beauties of creation.

Yet this holiday did not start well. We took a late-afternoon flight into JFK, thinking this might avoid the usual incredibly long immigration lines. Until he gets his American passport, Chris might as well take a picnic and a folding chair for all the time he has to spend in the arrivals hall.

This time he was not the only one of us kept waiting. I put my new American passport into an electronic reader and withdrew a piece of paper with a big 'X' superimposed on my details. I was led into a side room where I was seated with what seemed like a measurable percentage of the population of Haiti, a flight having just arrived from that beleaguered country. Both my US and UK passports were taken by an unidentified officer.

I twice asked if I could get word out to Christopher that I was being detained. I was told this would not be possible but that I should not worry, everything would be cleared up soon.

Finally, a young officer explained my problem. I had applied for an ESTA which had been turned down, so the JFK computer assumed I was a British citizen trying to enter the US without a visa. The fact that I was an American citizen returning to the city of my birth cut no ice with modern technology. The computer evidently had not been programmed for the possibility of my being a dual citizen. The officer made a manual correction and the United States now recognised that I was an American.

Of course, I had not been turned down for an ESTA. I had cancelled the one I had been granted. Try teaching a government computer nuance. My own country thought I was a citizen of a different nation.

Re-entering the United Kingdom was easier than getting into the United States. In less than five minutes we reached an immigration officer. He took one look at me and beamed with happiness.

'Thank you for the great memories,' he said. 'And they are great. Rosko's Roundtable! I loved it. The '70s were great days, weren't they?' And then – no joke – he started singing 'Those Were the Days'.

'Those were the days, my friend / We thought they'd never end…' he crooned, in the middle of the immigration hall, without embarrassment.

The Mary Hopkin classic was actually a number one in 1968, but in the middle of a lovefest, who's quibbling?

Jonathan Clyde emails a copy of the *Times* comment on the Nigel Evans case by 'Notebook' columnist Daniel Finkelstein. I had been unable to access this because of the newspaper's paywall, but the wait was worth it.

Headlined 'Victimless crime? No, a victimless non-crime', the author cites examples of police and CPS references to 'victims' even after the Evans acquittal.

> Yet the entire point at issue in the Evans case was whether there were any victims. The jury had just determined that there weren't any…
>
> In order to defend themselves against public criticism, the police and the CPS were implying that crimes had taken place, despite the jury's judgment that they had not. They were putting their own need to defend themselves in the media above the decision of the court and the interests of Nigel Evans.
>
> As they both consider the things that they got wrong in this case, could they add this to the list?

I add Daniel Finkelstein to the list of journalists I will offer a drink when this is all over.

––––––––––––––––––– 24 APRIL 2014 –––––––––––––––––––

This morning I host the Ivor Novello Awards nominations announcement at the Ivy Club. It is my first public appearance in half a year … a strange phrase, I realise, since I walk around London every day, so in that sense make a 'public appearance' every few hours. Nonetheless, this feels different. I am not standing in a room as Paul Gambaccini. I am standing in the Ivy Club as PAUL GAMBACCINI, the famous guy, the broadcaster, the sex suspect. HIM.

The funny thing, is no one seems to care about the case. I had discussed with Chris what I should say if any reporter asks about it. But these are music journalists, and today they are only interested in songwriting awards. There is sanity in the world, if only on the top floor of the Ivy Club.

I have a good conversation with Dominic Major, the first member of London Grammar to arrive. Every year, one of the nominees attends the ceremony to be interviewed by the press. This time it is Major and his bandmates/co-writers Hannah Reid and Daniel Rothman. London Grammar find themselves in the category 'Best Song Musically and Lyrically' with 'Strong'. This contender is up against 'Best of Friends' by Will Doyle, Sam Fryer, Chilli Jesson and Pete Mayhew, better known as Palma Violets, and Steve Booker and John Newman for 'Love Me Again'.

Dominic relates that on his group's recent North American tour they decided to travel from Vancouver to Minnesota via bus. They went through many states most Americans only fly over. One night, they found themselves in a town with only three people on the streets. They experienced the full range of reactions from being adored to being ignored and loved the experience. They look forward to returning to the States.

While waiting for Hannah to turn up, I browse an issue of *The Spectator* in the Ivy Club's magazine rack. Rod Liddle has written a piece with the headline 'The Nigel Evans case proves that juries are smarter than our liberal elite' with the subhead 'Ordinary people still put common sense and fairness ahead of crusading zeal – thank God'.

> The former deputy speaker Nigel Evans, a charming, witty and good-natured man, was finally cleared last week of nine counts of sexual abuse of young men, including one charge of rape. Fighting the patently absurd case against him has cost him his job (with its extra salary), his entire life savings in legal fees (which will not be repaid, despite his total innocence) and eleven months of sheer, unmitigated torture. He is understandably bitter, furious that his case was prosecuted by the police with a 'zeal', as he put it; a zeal occasioned by a politically driven obsession, I would reckon. On the evening after he was cleared of all charges, the liberal elite's favourite media conduit, *Newsnight*, interviewed one of Evans's supposed victims, repeating all the charges. I hope Evans sues them.

Where was I? Oh yes, the Ivy Club. It is time to re-enter the Ivor Novello

nominations. I recite the list, with historical commentary on which nominees have been in contention before and who has won what, and then
get a couple of pictures taken with London Grammar. They all agree that
they don't like photo sessions, and I tell them that is not likely to change.

'I've been having my photo taken for forty-one years and I've never felt
comfortable with it. You're not going to start liking it in year eleven, and
you're not going to start liking it in year twenty-one.'

Daniel, Dominic and Heather seem to take some comfort from this, as
it validates their own aversion to posing.

'We're proud that we don't like it,' Daniel whispers.

I leave London Grammar to their interviews and go about my Soho
business.

I return home and turn on the computer to look for web coverage of
the Ivors launch. The *Express & Star*'s website reports: 'Gambaccini to host
music awards'. This in itself is hardly news, since I have previously hosted
dozens of award ceremonies. Wait, here's the subhead: 'DJ Paul Gambaccini is to host a high-profile music awards this year, more than six months
after his arrest as part of Operation Yewtree'. Then the text:

> The broadcaster was arrested by the Metropolitan Police in October as
> part of the force's investigation into historic sexual offences. Gambac-
> cini, who denied the allegations after his arrest and remains on police
> bail, will present the Ivor Novello Awards next month. He stepped down
> from his weekly BBC Radio 2 show after the arrest.

And another. *The Independent* reports that

> [Mike] Rosenberg is leading a 'new generation of songwriters' recog-
> nised at the Novellos, claimed Paul Gambaccini, who will present the
> Grosvenor House event.
>
>   It marks the broadcaster's first high-profile appearance since his arrest

as part of Operation Yewtree last year. Gambaccini was arrested by the Metropolitan Police in October as part of the force's investigation into historic sexual offences and denies all allegations.

Here's Mail Online:

> DJ Paul Gambaccini will host the ceremony – more than six months after his arrest as part of Operation Yewtree. The broadcaster was detained by the Metropolitan Police in October as part of the force's investigation into historic sexual offences. Gambaccini, who denied the allegations after his arrest and remains on police bail, stepped down from his weekly BBC Radio 2 show after the arrest.

Hmmm … that's the use of the word 'arrest' twice in one sentence. Sub-editor, please!

Sorry to steal a couple of claps of your thunder, London Grammar … and James Blake, Sam Smith and the rest. It is my sincere hope that this will fade into insignificance by the time the actual ceremonies take place on 22 May, at which point you can have all the headlines you deserve.

--------------------- 25 APRIL 2014 ---------------------

The trial of Rolf Harris has been slightly delayed and will now begin on Tuesday 6 May. Christopher has sent Kate Goold an email pointing out that 6 May is the Freddie Starr rebail date and the 7th is mine. The opening couple of days of the sex trials are the ones that gather the most news coverage, when the papers and broadcast media are full of the lurid accusations being presented. Could it be Yewtree might be attempting to find 'a good day to bury bad news', dismissing Freddie and/or me while the greater attention is focused on Rolf?

Kate has replied, 'Yes that is interesting, it may be significant – but I would like to know the reasons why the court have moved it before I read too much into it.'

——————————— 26 APRIL 2014 ———————————

You never know how people are going to react to seeing you.

Checking into Neal's Yard Dairy after having my weekly grilled cheese sandwich in Borough Market, I request a quarter-pound of Montgomery Cheddar. The seller says without hesitation, 'My father thanks you for saving his mind,' which is one of life's great opening lines. It turns out that in the 1980s, the cheese vendor's dad lived in Germany and listened to me on the British Forces Broadcasting Service (although his son identifies it as the BBC World Service, an occasional error among non-broadcasters). I was his link to English-language music and apparently rescued him from schlagers, the peculiarly German form of pop balladry. It's touching that he bothered to inform his son of my sanity-saving and that Junior has been generous enough to tell me.

A few hours later, I am walking down Charing Cross Road, having nabbed one of the day's last cheese croissants from Maison Bertaux for consumption at tomorrow's breakfast. I pass two elderly tramps sitting on the sidewalk near a gay pub.

'What do you know about gay?' an incredibly rosy-cheeked inebriate says to his companion, pointing at me. 'Paul Gambaccini's gay. What a load of bollocks!'

I get home before I experience any more of the West End's Saturday evening entertainment.

——————————— 27 APRIL 2014 ———————————

Until last week, I had been proceeding on a very unofficial calculation that the announcement on the 7th was 3/5 likely to be dismissal, 2/5 charge. As I approach the decision date, a stress-inducing experience I recommend to no one, the circumstances seem familiar. I've been here before, promised a decision on 26 March, and the result then was a further rebail. What makes me think that won't happen again? So I revise my chances to 45 per cent chance dismissal, 35 per cent charge, 20 per cent rebail.

28 APRIL 2014

I wake up and sit bolt upright just before 1 a.m. Was 'Yewtree 16', my co-accused former neighbour, rebailed when I was in late March? It suddenly occurs to me that I haven't the remotest idea. If he were not rebailed, it would have implications for my case … although, as is usual in the fog of this war, I can't be certain what those implications are.

I email Kate Goold first thing in the morning. She replies quickly. Yes, Sixteen was rebailed. So much for that breakthrough!

When I get home, the news is dominated by Max Clifford, who has been found guilty on eight counts of indecent assault. I can imagine that my case officer, who is also Clifford's, is feeling pretty good at this moment, but I can't stretch that assumption to think this must be a bad omen for me. The two cases are utterly different. Max faced seven accusers; I have two. His charges concerned one-off or infrequently repeated events; my allegations claim long-term relationships. And, most important difference of all, he has been found guilty, whereas I know I am not.

What strikes me is the outpouring of bitterness towards Clifford that flows after his conviction. What really makes an impression is the bizarre video, suppressed until now, of Max approaching and standing behind a *Sky News* reporter who is doing a piece to camera outside Southwark Crown Court, imitating the journalist's motions. If you've never seen it, stop now, go to YouTube and type in 'Max Clifford Creeps Up', which is a pretty sad title for a clip. If you are of a certain age, this will then have you looking up Margaret Thatcher coming up behind John Sergeant, which I had the thrill of watching when it went out live.

While watching news clips, check out David Mellor on Max Clifford. I knew Mellor when we worked together on Classic FM, which still employs him. He has let loose about Clifford on both Sky News and the BBC, telling the former, 'I'm not actually unkind about many people and I don't bear many grudges, but for him I make an exception, I hope he rots in hell.' Speaking with a sense of history, he adds, 'He built his whole career on what he did to me and it was so cynical.'

'What he did' was, apparently, invent the story that the minister made love to Clifford's client Antonia de Sancha, with whom he was having an affair, wearing a Chelsea football uniform. This caught the imagination of *The Sun* and football fans around the nation. Mellor subsequently resigned from the Cabinet, though not because of the Chelsea shirt. I am impressed that David kept his cool for twenty-two years. Googling stories on this subject, I find a 2013 interview with the *Daily Mail* in which de Sancha said, 'It was all rubbish made up by Max … It was definitely Max who came up with that football strip idea and it has, of course, haunted me and David Mellor ever since.'

---

29 APRIL 2014

I wake up to a new morning, the Day of the Anthill. I open the shades in my bedroom, which looks out onto Waterloo Station, and am momentarily shocked. Human beings are streaming through the arch and down the steps like so many ants descending the sides of an anthill. The roundabout around the IMAX cinema is jammed with cars proceeding at a snail's pace onto Waterloo Bridge. Then I remember. It is a Tube strike morning. All these commuters have been spooked and are walking to work.

Today is the half-year anniversary of my arrest!

It must be significant that I have not been obsessing about this. In fact, as my rebail date gets closer, I am becoming calmer. Why is this? One might have thought that, as the possibility of my being sent to trial (and spending hundreds of thousands of pounds!) nears, I might start getting some form of anxiety attacks. Why is the week before rebail turning out to be easier to take than I had imagined?

I can think of two reasons. First, I have been promised a decision by the CPS before and been denied one. Who is to say they won't think of another reason to rebail me this time, particularly considering that Freddie Starr is due his news the day before me? I would love to get excited about the prospect of being cleared, but I would feel like an absolute chump if I were to be optimistic and then get my hopes dashed again. And if I dare not get too optimistic, I must also not get too pessimistic, because that would be to unrealistically dwell on the negative possibilities.

There is a more subtle reason that I can neither enthuse nor panic at this time. I have adjusted to the life into which the police forced me. It has been so long since there has been a development in my case that it has become less a linear sequence of events than a state of being. I am unemployable, I am disgraced, I am losing money – and I've gotten used to it. I have been in this state of affairs for so long it is difficult to imagine a sudden jerk into yet another reality, whether being charged or cleared.

Here is a reminder of reality. My former neighbour Bob Hoskins has died. I once interviewed Bob about the film *Twenty Four Seven*, after which he wanted to discuss classical music. That was non-image, I thought. There was always more to Bob Hoskins than met any eye.

--- **I MAY 2014** ---

Al Feldstein, the creative genius behind most of the EC comics, including *Weird Science* and *Tales from the Crypt*, and, after Harvey Kurtzman's departure, *Mad* magazine, has passed away. Feldstein was the true triple threat: an artist, writer and editor. I go around our flat pointing out to Christopher and Jennifer watercolours by Marie Severin over stats of EC covers drawn by Feldstein. His science-fiction covers are among my all-time favourites in the genre. *Mad* was, of course, his commercial peak, selling 2 million copies a month in the 1960s. Alfred E. Neuman was not only the cover boy of the magazine but of the culture.

It was during this period of insane success that I visited their offices. As a young teenager in the early days of comics fandom, I was able to go into New York from Westport and meet the great comic editors. They had not yet been besieged by acolytes and considered occasional pilgrims welcome oddities. I had a great visit to *Mad*, during which I met the latest hire, *Spy vs. Spy* creator Antonio Prohias, who had just fled Cuba. He had to, because Fidel Castro considered him a personal enemy. Prohias could not speak English, and I had not yet started high-school Spanish, but we managed to communicate through our mutual love of cartooning. I interviewed Feldstein over lunch and was taken by him to meet publisher Bill Gaines, who was sitting in front of a bunch of bound volumes. I asked him what they were and he told me they were copies of every EC comic he had published. I was in fan-boy heaven. Feldstein was eighty-eight when he died, so his passing is no surprise, but it is a nail in one's own coffin when a favourite of childhood departs.

---

2 MAY 2014

R-5 (five days before rebail date), and we're still holding it together here on the South Bank.

I can tell I subconsciously believe I will be returning to work before too long because I had another music-related dream last night, one in which I attended a major U2 event with a new Radio 2 producer. I thought the hiring standards must have been relaxed since I was last at the BBC, because this producer was rather unkempt, to put it kindly.

We walked in and three of the four members of the group approached me. I noted that The Edge had chosen to stay backstage. I say 'three of the four', although I never actually saw the head of Larry Mullen. He was always just out of frame, with his arm or leg occasionally poking into sight.

Bono came over to me and said, 'I can only give you ten minutes,' which I guessed referred to an interview I did not know was going to occur. I assumed the man was Bono, but I couldn't vouch for it. He had a paper bag over his head.

I had been thinking about U2 in reference to my opening remarks at the Ivor Novello Awards on 22 May. Every year I summarise the past year's achievements by members of the British Academy of Songwriters, Composers and Authors (BASCA). During the last twelve months U2 were nominated for an Academy Award for their song 'Ordinary Love' from *Mandela: Long Walk to Freedom*.

Larry Mullen just being out of shot was a reference to my permanent amusement that the best-looking member of this quartet is the one who, being the drummer, is hardest to see and, not being a lead vocalist, is kept to the fringes of seating on television shows. As for Bono eschewing publicity by wearing a bag over his head, which would certainly amuse Adam Clayton and the other members of the group, this is an allusion to one of my favourite music business launches. When I was in college in the 1960s, *Billboard* magazine had a full-page ad for a singer with a balaclava over his head. He was called 'The Covered Man'. I found this so hilarious I've remembered it to this day. The 'man in the mask' appeared on *The Merv Griffin Show*, later explaining, 'My name is David Soul, and I want to be known for my music.' He did not wish to be known as the latest music industry pretty boy.

A few years passed, and he had wild success as the latest music industry pretty man. Actually, 'Silver Lady' is a pretty underestimated record.

In the late morning, I travel to 53/54 Doughty Street. These are the headquarters of Doughty Street Chambers, founded by Geoffrey Robertson in 1990. The firm has been a remarkable success, having expanded four-fold in a quarter-century. Geoffrey has become one of the nation's most prominent human rights lawyers.

We exchange experiences and catch-up details on the lives of mutual friends. My old University College, Oxford classmate predicts that, even if a false charge is brought concerning my two accusers, no jury would convict me of participating in consensual sex with someone aged sixteen or seventeen thirty-five years ago, since this is not a crime today. He feels that the CPS will not press charges against me, but that I will not be dismissed on my rebail date next week. There is the glaring case of Freddie Starr to deal with first.

After lunch, I prepare to take my afternoon siesta. I get as far as lying down when the phone rings. It is Kate Goold, sounding distressed. I have been rebailed yet again, this time until 7 July.

The Crown Prosecution Service has asked the Met for information from 'third parties' mentioned in the original round of interviews but not contacted by police. The officer phoning Kate will not tell her whether these 'third parties' are people or institutions such as the National Health Service or an educational organisation. It's difficult to speculate who the CPS wants to hear from if you don't know whether they are human beings or not.

Hearing me speak to my solicitor, Chris comes into the room. We put Kate on speakerphone as I mouth the word 'rebail'. Chris pounds the bed with his fist as Goold talks.

We gasp at the extent of the perfidy of the Crown Prosecution Service. Twice they have promised a decision as to whether to charge or dismiss. Twice they have wormed their way out of it with cryptic excuses.

I tell her that, as in the case of the 26 March rebail, the worst time for me was about three weeks before the date. Then the spectre of the sword of Damocles was over my head. As the appointment neared both then and now, I felt that the most likely outcome was another rebail. I had known it was Jimmy Tarbuck's turn to be released, and they were not going to let two people go in the same week. Now the case of Freddie Starr looms large. He is in his nineteenth month of arrest without charge, and his utterly outrageous case cries out for attention. They have to either charge or dismiss him on Tuesday. The fact that I am rebailed again suggests he will be dismissed, because they will not let two of us go in the same week. The Crown Prosecution Service and Metropolitan Police hold all the cards when it comes to the timing of the announcement of their decisions, and they always play them to their best political advantage. Ours is not to reason why, ours is only to be rebailed.

3 MAY 2014

In between and around going to Borough Market for The World's Greatest Sandwich and having my weekly back rub in Chinatown, I spend the day writing emails and making phone calls informing friends and supporters that I have been rebailed yet again. Even though I lump most of the emails into groups, such as New York friends, people I knew from Hyde Park Square, and so forth, it takes ages.

Checking to see if there is further fallout from yesterday's sentencing of Max Clifford, I notice that Sky News reports:

> Judge Leonard said that due to the age of the offences, that [sic] occurred between 1977 and 1984, Clifford was charged under an act from 1956, which set the maximum term for each charge at two years.
>
> Under later legislation passed in 2003, the maximum term would have been ten years, and for the worst instances would have been charged as rape, which attract a maximum life term.

This is oddly comforting. My police record, as prepared for my ultimately unnecessary ESTA application, said I faced 'impending prosecution' on two counts. If everything were to go wrong and the jury went off its meds, I could face a prison term of four years, which would be reduced to two for good behaviour. I remember these were exactly the numbers cited off the top of his head by one of my prospective barristers on 22 January. I may not have gone with him, but he is good.

On his way home from an Ashby reunion, Chris sends me a link to a column by Mick Hume, editor-at-large of sp!ked, 'Britain's first online-only current-affairs magazine'. It is called 'Clifford is a Creep, but what does that have to do with Savile?', and it is an excellent analysis of the Metropolitan Police and Crown Prosecution Service.

Hume writes, 'Yewtree is a huge publicity-driven fishing operation, actively seeking out claimants who are invited to accuse high-profile people of past sexual offences without the need for any forensic or other collaborative evidence. Indeed, it celebrates the possibility of evidence-lite convictions.'

Then he hits the bull's-eye. 'These trials seem to mark a shift away from an objective idea of justice based on evidence, towards a more subjective brand of justice based on feelings and attitudes.'

That's it! Part of the oddness I have felt about this historic storm is the departure from the traditional requirements of British justice. Evidence is no longer required. If enough people don't like a person, he can be charged. A claimed 'pattern of behaviour' is sufficient to convict.

The weekend of phone calls and emails continues as I try to let all of my friends know that I have been rebailed yet again. After all, if this is like last time, and I hope it is, they won't hear about it unless I tell them. There is still no sight of it when I Google 'Gambaccini rebail'.

I get through to Liza Tarbuck on first try and release a silent cheer. She is a busy woman. Indeed, she is with guests as we speak, but they can amuse themselves for a few minutes. It's always good talking to someone who has been through this, or is going through it contemporaneously, because it makes the first twenty questions unnecessary.

Liza says her parents are in Portugal. They had to go. Jimmy spent a great deal of time after his dismissal writing thank-you notes, and it was draining work. The case is still with you even when it's over.

The Tarbucks came to think of Jimmy's case as being like a lift ride up the Shard. You know when you get into the elevator. It is a big deal. You start to ascend. The ride is longer than any you have ever experienced, and commands your attention. You continue to climb. You go up some more. Soon the *ascenseur* itself becomes your world. You know you are between two fixed points, but the distance is so long you have no idea when it will conclude. Eventually, the new environment, the confined space of the lift, becomes your new normal.

And then it happens! You reach the end of the journey! You get off! One problem remains: you must now descend, in the same chamber, the same distance it took to get there. The Crown Prosecution Service washes its hands of you the day it dismisses you, but you have to negotiate your own trip back down to the world you left behind so many floors before.

Chris and I attend a dinner party at Ian McKellen's place in Lime-house. It has been years since I've been to Ian's home, during which time he bought the house next door and combined the two. The location is extraordinary: the north side of the Thames at a point where the river bends, allowing anyone sitting on the terrace to look in two separate watery directions. 'Sitting' in this case is definitely better than 'strolling around', since there is no restraining wall to keep wanderers from falling into the river. I tell Ian that I remember when he and David Owen were pioneers in moving into this desperately abandoned neighbourhood more than thirty years ago. He quickly corrects me and gives Owen full credit. The co-founder of the Social Democratic Party was the first to notice the potential of the derelict spot and bought three properties for a combined total of less than £5,000. While Foreign Secretary, Owen would have ministers from around the world pilgrimage to his beautiful home in an abandoned neighbourhood. Now McKellen and MEP

Michael Cashman are his neighbours and share what has become a glamorous part of London.

This is one of those rare dinners when I know all the guests. It is a joy. I can speak openly and expansively about Yewtree, knowing that everyone is genuinely interested.

Much hilarity ensues when I name the first of my two accusers. I am so accustomed to getting no response when I mention the names of the duo that I am startled when one of the dinner guests gasps in recognition. Everyone's attention focuses on the actor who has made the guttural noise. Alas, he has no knowledge of the person. It is just that, when he started his career and could not use his own name, he chose this name as an alias.

I enjoy the McKellen dinner so much that I do something I never do: I stay beyond the last Tube. Chris and I get a cab from Wapping to Waterloo. At least I now know how much one costs, in case Chris Evans ever plays 'Person or Personality?' with me.

---

5 MAY 2014

Today is a bank holiday, but there will be no rest for rebailed suspects today. I make and take numerous phone calls.

Brian Paddick relaxes me by telling me that it is not as rare as I might think that the Crown Prosecution Service goes back to the police after a recommendation. To me, it seems that the CPS has marked the Met's homework 'Not good enough, must try harder', but Paddick tells me the higher body sometimes asserts its authority, if only to justify its existence. When I opine that if the CPS thought it had a case they would already have charged me, he says this is so, because the law requires that they charge someone they believe has probably committed a crime 'forthwith'. The passage of months is not 'forthwith'. He points out that if the CPS does dismiss my case, they will want to be able to say that they explored every avenue that might have led to a conviction. No matter how trivial or puzzling the organisation's activities of the past two months may seem to me, they want to be able to protect themselves from possible accusations that my case was not investigated thoroughly.

I then have a long talk with my 1980–83 Hyde Park Square flatmate. It is the first verbal contact we have had since my arrest, and it is a source of joy. We are back in touch. He is absolutely livid about what is happening to me and asks, 'When are you going to sue them?' every twenty minutes.

He finds it darkly amusing that the police interviewed me once and him twice. They also went to Jersey to speak to a woman, a frequent visitor to our home during the period. This throws me. I had no idea that the police had been to Jersey when they hadn't gone to see Brad in Paris. From my perspective, Brad would be a far more useful source of information, since he knew my co-accused as well as me and actually lodged in my flat for a time. Then I have to consider that all points of view are not my own. The police would have chosen her for a reason. Were they checking out my flatmate's credibility? Did they want a woman's perspective on the lifestyles in the building? Unless I take a trip to Jersey myself, it is likely that this is one of the many aspects of this case that will never be explained to me.

I am treated to lunch at the Delaunay by Ivan Massow. He speaks of a recent dinner party hosted by his long-time friend Joan Collins. Although the *Dynasty* star may not remember me, we've been in the same room on numerous occasions, my favourite being a moment at Ken Follett's house when I saw her engaged in serious conversation with Salman Rushdie. This was during Rushdie's period living under a fatwa, which dates it as being around 1989, when Rushdie was being shepherded from place to place by security officers. In another fond memory from this period, I see Salman grooving shoeless at Douglas Adams's house during a performance by Dave Gilmour, Gary Brooker and friends. Only the other day, Geoffrey Robertson told me his most unforgettable story of the time. At a dinner with Salman, the author excused himself to go to the toilet. He never returned. The toilet was not in the restaurant, it was in his next safe house!

I never thought I would replace my Google search 'Greek philosopher 495–435 BC' with 'Freddie Starr', but I was working on an acrostic puzzle when Wes Butters emailed me the news that my fellow Yewtree suspect has been liberated by the Crown Prosecution Service.

A Crown Prosecution Service lawyer has said, 'We have concluded the available evidence does not offer a realistic prospect of conviction on thirteen of the allegations.' Perplexingly, she adds that it is 'not in the public interest' to prosecute on one allegation for which there is sufficient evidence.

Chris and I wait with trepidation for the inevitable reaction from Starr's lawyer, Dean Dunham. Although it is predictable that the 'lawyer to the stars' will have an attention-getting response to the news, I do not anticipate what comes next. The attorney and the comedian speak to reporters outside Freddie's home. Actually, the lawyer does most of the talking. Starr himself appears to be post-death. Jennifer exclaims that he seems to be 'chewing his own face'.

I honestly can't believe that either solicitor or client would choose to present such an image of deterioration. Starr is shaking, his mouth muscles moving involuntarily.

It is unbearable to watch this.

Watching the car-crash television that was the Freddie Starr news conference, I was convinced anew that I must keep my mouth meshed shut when I am ultimately released and the press ask me to condemn the police. Doing so may offer a few seconds of gratification, but it achieves nothing. Furthermore, at least in my case, the press were part of the problem, not part of the solution. They still show no signs of realising that they have become recruiting agents for the police, publicising every celebrity arrest and thus encouraging people either actually abused or not to add their two cents to the witch-hunt. After what newspapers both tabloid and broad-sheet put me through, I have no desire to help their circulations.

I also have no desire to insult the Metropolitan Police gratuitously. I have got to get past myself and respond in a way that will help the cause of civil rights. It's a long shot, but maybe, just maybe, as a result of my ordeal I will be able to make a constructive contribution to the country in which, long ago, I chose to live.

---

8 MAY 2014

The post brings an envelope that looks official. It is, but it is not an offer of a knighthood. It is the notification of my latest 'Police Bail Variation'. Just like the last time, it arrives after the day I was originally meant to report, so it is intended for the record rather than for advance notification.

The day of the latest rebail is indeed 7 July, but the time is 11 a.m. The last two appointments were scheduled for 5.30 p.m., to allow my officers time to return from trials in progress at Southwark Crown Court. This may mean that Operation Yewtree does not expect to have a trial running on this date.

An even more intriguing change is in the box 'Officer in Case'. It has previously read Two, the gentleman who did most of the talking during my interrogation. Now it reads Three. Have they switched because they've given up on the case … or because One and Two are simply too busy with other inquiries? We are not meant to know, we are only meant to ulcerate.

---

9 MAY 2014

Philip S. Smith, a criminal lawyer with Tuckers Solicitors, has penned an article for the Huffington Post called 'Freddie Starr Case Proves "Justice Delayed Is Justice Denied" – The Law Must Change'. He holds nothing back.

'Justice delayed is Justice denied – it is a vital and long-held tenet of the British legal system,' he writes.

> The announcement this week by the Crown Prosecution Service that they are to bring no charges against Freddie Starr after nineteen months of him being under arrest and kept on bail sadly shows yet again how that vital concept is being increasingly ignored by the state.
>
> It brings into focus once again the plight of individuals in every walk of life being arrested and kept on police bail for prolonged periods of time without charge often to facilitate what are little more than fishing expeditions by the police.

I'm putting on high-octane rock music as I read Smith's words. He has my juices flowing.

The lawyer takes the time to explain that the police can hold a person in custody for twenty-four hours, with an extension of 'a further twelve hours upon the authorisation of a superintendent', but

> the police can and, as a matter of routine, do interview individuals after arrest for only a few hours at a time then bail them to return to the police station to a specified date which is, invariably, months away. Thereafter, and it must be stressed that it is the norm rather than the exception, the initial return date will often be put back yet again without explanation to some date in the future whilst enquiries continue apparently endlessly – this will frequently, but not always, be done administratively and without the individual even being required to attend the Police Station.

Philip S. Smith is relating the story of my life. I have been rebailed three times so far without making planned visits to Charing Cross. And then he tells it like it is:

All the time, throughout this process, the individual concerned is dangled on the end of a piece of string. Their life is in limbo, they cannot make professional or personal plans with confidence since they are unaware as to how the investigation will proceed and with what end result. Their careers will invariably be rudely interrupted. The potential domestic impact is obvious.

The Tuckers solicitor offers his own possible modifications to the law and then concludes,

> The power of arrest has potentially heinous consequences for the suspect on the receiving end – it should be exercised more sparingly, with more consideration and with more scrutiny.
>
> The introduction of judicial oversight over prolonged periods of police bail should perhaps now be introduced. In an age of ever more sophisticated investigation techniques, many of them time consuming, it is the right juncture to act.
>
> That principle of 'Justice delayed is justice denied' is too important to be abandoned.

Yesterday I wrote a letter of appreciation to my old acquaintance Fiona Shaw for her marvellous performance at the Barbican Theatre in *The Testament of Mary*. It looks like another message of thanks is on the way, this time to Philip S. Smith.

---

10 MAY 2014

'Bridge over Troubled Water' by Simon and Garfunkel comes up on my iTunes. I sigh. I think back to when this record came in at WDCR, the Dartmouth College radio station. I listened to it in the record library and played it on my show that day. Years later, my brother Peter reminded me that I introduced it as 'the best record ever made'. Thank God it went to number one or I would have looked like an idiot.

The song now sounds like high art. People don't express themselves like this any more, musically or lyrically. 'Bridge over Troubled Water', or, as Simon and Garfunkel's engineer filed it during the recording sessions, 'Like a Pitcher of Water', dates from the pre-post-ironic period in popular music.

I can tell I have not been in the mood for sensitivity and beauty during the past seven months. Checking in on my ten top pop tunes for the first time since March, with the positions from that month in brackets, I note that 'Street Fighting Man' by the Rolling Stones has been the big mover. Coming up on the outside is an angry song that I recently downloaded again after my last iTunes was taken by police: 'Signs' by the Five Man Electrical Band.

(1) 1)   Brown Sugar / Rolling Stones

(3) 2)   Street Fighting Man / Rolling Stones

(2) 3)   Put a Little Love in Your Heart / Jackie DeShannon

(4) 4)   I'm Doing Fine Now / New York City

(5) 5)   Where Did Our Love Go / Supremes

(8) 6)   Band of Gold / Freda Payne

(6) 7)   #9 Dream / John Lennon

(–) 8)   Hey Jude / Beatles

(10) 9)   Palisades Park / Freddy Cannon

(–) 10)   Whatever Gets You thru the Night / John Lennon

This list is completely counterintuitive. I have always thought of myself as being more of a Beatles person than a Rolling Stones man. Paul McCartney was always my favourite Beatle. Yet there they are, the Stones and John Lennon, each with two in my Top 10 of the last seven months, obviously because those particular selections have suited my mood better.

On the classical side, there is even less change in the list. Beethoven, Schubert and Mendelssohn continue to, er, rock my world.

12 MAY 2014

Twice this weekend something happened that disturbed me. It had not occurred in the more than six months since my arrest.

I got depressed.

I finished a conversation with someone in which I mentioned how understanding my radio producers continue to be, and how they have reassured me that I will be back on air in the second half of July if I am freed on my next rebail date of 7/7. Then the thought hit me.

Why am I so foolish as to believe the Crown Prosecution Service yet again? They promised me a decision, charge or dismiss, on 26 March. They did not deliver. They then promised a decision on 7 May. They did not deliver. Now they promise a decision on 7 July. Why on earth should I believe them this time?

Freddie Starr was on bail for nineteen months. What makes me think that I will get off after 'only' nine?

The main source of hope, other than the fact that I am totally innocent, is that, after the liberation of Jimmy Tarbuck and Starr, I am 'senior' in the 'arrested without charge' category. I have been saying this to friends since my rebail. Why shouldn't I believe that? Ever since the sequence of show trial acquittals began, the press have acted as if the 'arrested without charge' trio were Starr, Tarbuck and Gambaccini.

But late in the day I have a sickening thought. We weren't a trio. I am not 'senior' in 'arrested without charge' after all. There's somebody else. Gary Glitter is Yewtree 1. He was arrested four days before Freddie Starr. He is still on bail. If Starr required approximately nineteen months, and Glitter is still uncharged after that same time plus four days, who am I to think I am going to romp home after what will be nine months, even if my case is simpler and groundless? If I were to remain under suspicion for as long as Starr, I would be rebailed constantly until 2015.

This is why, this weekend, I got depressed twice.

I am treated to dinner at the home of Caroline and Robert Lee. I have known them both for over forty years. Caroline, who cooks a very tasty salmon teriyaki, was Elton John's press officer between Penny Valentine and Laura Croker before becoming a long-time journalist at *The Observer*'s 'Food Monthly'. Robert is an attorney immortalised, to his own bemusement, in the very first verse of the very first Roxy Music single, 'Virginia Plain':

'Make me a deal and make it straight / All signed and sealed, I'll take it / To Robert Lee I'll show it / I hope and pray he don't blow it'.

Robert didn't blow it. Both he and Roxy Music did pretty well.

My gosh, I've just noticed that the internet site AZLyrics.com transcribes the words as 'To Robert E. Lee I'll show it'. How did the American Civil War get into this?

Nancy Lewis Jones is my fellow dinner guest. Her husband Simon is busy performing in the West End smash hit *Blithe Spirit*, in which Angela Lansbury is defying age, critics and gravity. When we share our updates on my case and on Yewtree in general, conversation inevitably turns to Freddie Starr. Nancy mentions that he has walked off breakfast television.

I Google the episode and find it easily. I am horrified. Susanna Reid is in the Starr house, interviewing Freddie for *Good Morning Britain*. Having introduced the segment with the juicy tidbit that the comedian had, while under suspicion, considered taking his own life, Reid asks, 'You've been in show business over fifty years. Do you think, over that time, you have done anything that could have been misinterpreted in terms of your relationships?'

Starr responds, 'Are you being serious?'

Reid replies, 'Well, I'm putting the question?'

'No, are you being serious?'

'Yeah…'

'Well, I want to end this interview now.'

'… but I have to put the question because…'

Freddie, after wrestling with his microphone, walks out of shot, though presumably not out of his own house.

I was part of the original *Good Morning Britain* team in 1983. Its found-ers had lofty aspirations to improve the nature and content of national debate. Over the years, the programme has devolved to what it is today. This must be the lowest form of tabloid television ever, with the possible exception of *My Man Boobs and Me*.

---
13 MAY 2014

I get the most frightening spam I have ever received. My computer screen is occupied by a message from the 'Serious Organised Crime Agency' of the 'Metropolitan British Police'. The logo includes the photograph of a police officer, two other officers apprehending a suspect, and Her Majesty the Queen.

The message is chilling, to say the least.

'ATTENTION!' it screams in red capital letters.

'Your browser has been locked up for safety reasons listed below.

'All the actions performed on this PC are fixed.

'All your files are encrypted.'

What now? They've already taken two of my computers, what's wrong with this one…

> You are accused of viewing/storage and/or dissemination of banned por-nography (child pornography/zoophilia/rape etc.). You have violated World Declaration on non-proliferation of child pornography. You are accused of committing the crime envisaged by Article 161 of the King-dom of Great Britain criminal law.
>
> Article 161 of the Kingdom of Great Britain criminal law provides for the punishment of deprivation of liberty for terms from five to eleven years.

What? Are they once again threatening me with prison for something I haven't done?

Wait a minute. Calm down. Although there were a couple of grammatical and typographical errors in my original bail document, there was nothing stated as oddly as what I have just read. 'You have violated World Declaration' would not cut it in English class. And since when has a British code been referred to as 'Kingdom of Great Britain criminal law'?

I read on. The road is long, with many a winding curve and several an ungrammatical threat. It all boils down to: 'Amount of fine is £100. You can pay a fine Ukash or PaySafeCard vouchers.' Instructions on how to obtain Ukash or PaySafeCard vouchers are given, and a link enables payment. If the fine is not paid within twenty-four hours, 'criminal case will be opened against you'. The further errors in phrasing confirm: this is spam, malicious spam, and probably spam to which quite a few people have fallen. It is the cleverest e-hoax since the Nigerian inheritance scam. Christopher and Jennifer confirm my impression that this is a vicious fraud, but one that has had special terrifying meaning for me. The only recipients who could have been equally horrified are actual, shall we say, zoophiles.

---

14 MAY 2014

Christopher sends me a link to a Guardian Media story about the Radio Academy Awards. This is because he has received a Google Alert that I have been mentioned in the story. It seems that Chris Evans is checking out of the presenter's role after six years. This means that my ten-year run is still the longest in the history books.

This is not why the ceremony has rated a piece in the newspaper. Monkey writes:

> Chris Evans enjoyed some early fun at guest presenter Susanna Reid's
> expense. As the face of ITV's *Good Morning Britain* took to the stage,
> the Radio 2 breakfast jock introduced her as 'the former breakfast queen
> of British television'. Ouch. 'The race is long. I'd check your contract,'

Evans told Reid, whose ratings fell to little over 300,000 last week. 'I'm mostly glad I came,' responded Reid.

What stuns me most about reading this is nothing about anyone's remarks. It's that the event took place and I wasn't even aware of it. I hosted the thing for ten years, when it was known as the Sony Awards, and now no one even tells me it's happening. I am reminded of the Paul Simon lyric from 'Fakin' It', 'When she goes, she's gone'. It looks like I am really gone.

At least Radio 2 won UK Station of the Year. I almost certainly was not on the highlights reel, but it's good to know that one of my two radio homes, the other being Radio 4, has taken the top prize.

───────────── 16 MAY 2014 ─────────────

I go into Soho to have lunch with my former PA Will Gresford, now the manager of Nick Mulvey. They had worked together when Mulvey was in the Portico Quartet, and now they find themselves in the bizarre but welcome position where Nick is a Radio 1 favourite with an album that is number nine in the midweeks. We keep our fingers crossed for a Top 10 placing in the Sunday chart.

'It would be so annoying to be number eleven,' says Will. Yes, but a year ago they would not have dared hope of having a number eleven!

───────────── 17 MAY 2014 ─────────────

I am having more radio dreams.

Yesterday afternoon I napped and awoke after a dream about an imagined *Kaleidoscope* item. We were in a basement studio of Broadcasting House as it was in the 1990s, talking about the career of comic-book artist and editor Dick Giordano with artists who had worked with him, Steve Ditko and Alex Toth. Although I had met Ditko at the 1964 Comic-Con, the co-creator of Spider-Man had become reclusive ever since, and in this dream I could hear his voice but not actually see him. He was always just out of the frame. Toth, on the other hand, was bent over in conversation with the engineer, energetically discussing his art collaboration with Giordano on the early 1970s series *Hot Wheels*.

This morning I woke up at 6.45 after a dream in which Lewis Carnie, head of programmes at Radio 2, assigned me an interim job during this extended period of being off air. I was to participate in a nocturnal spying mission for Great Britain, flying in helicopters over India and being dropped off at undisclosed sites. All I knew about the details was that I was provided with a gas mask.

'Don't worry, this happens all the time,' Carnie told me, producing a map that indicated locations where Radio 2 presenters had participated in nighttime operations inside India and, even more alarmingly, the United States. I politely declined the work, saying that I had a fear of flying in helicopters.

Elements of these dreams were taken from my waking hours. Yesterday was the day the landslide electoral victory of Narendra Modi was announced in India, and I recently contemplated which of my four pieces of original Alex Toth art to sell in the next Heritage auction. That these episodes were incorporated into dreams about radio demonstrates the continued presence of my old line of work in my mind. I have no idea if it foretells an actual return.

18 MAY 2014

Will Gresford can breathe easier. Nick Mulvey's album charts at number ten!

19 MAY 2014

The working week begins with a visit from the documentarian Charlie Russell. He wants to do a programme for Channel 4 about Operation Yewtree.

I agree to receive him because he appears from his internet presence to be a serious individual and because I once interviewed his grandmother, the novelist Dame Beryl Bainbridge.

Charlie and I sit on the terrace for nearly two hours on this baking-hot morning. Finally he has to retreat indoors. I am secretly delighted. We have had a morning in London when the sun has been too strong!

Russell is impressively dedicated to doing the right thing with his proposed documentary. I tell him, as I did the *Panorama* team, that I am delighted to speak to him about all aspects of my case, but cannot appear on camera or in voice track at this time. He leaves horrified by what he has learned in our session, and admits that he needs to read up in detail on aspects of law with which he has not been familiar. The police's ability to rebail a suspect in perpetuity has particularly thrown him. Charlie asks if I can put him in touch with other people who have been involved in the witch-hunt. I tell him I will let the ones I speak to know he is interested, and he agrees that this is the best course.

If only he had stuck around a little longer! I receive a phone call from Nigel Evans. I am glad that he has not forgotten me. He reaffirms his view that the CPS will not charge me and would have by now if they thought they had a case.

Evans draws my attention to an article he has written in *The Spectator* headlined 'Rape suspects need anonymity'. He has been motivated by seeing a newspaper headline 'Oxford Union president, 21, arrested on suspicion of rape and attempted rape'. Nigel writes:

> A photo of the beaming Oxford Union president, Ben Sullivan, dominated the front page in his swanky dinner jacket. He looked as if he had the world before him – until, that is, the police knocked on his door, warrant in hand. 'Are you Ben Sullivan?' they would have asked. The long, lonely journey to the police station would have followed, leading him in the opposite direction to his ambitions.

This could be a novel, except it's true.

'I could guess exactly what Ben was feeling,' Nigel says. 'He was released without charge on police bail – but even if this goes no further, his name is now indelibly linked to rape. Anyone who searches online for him will find these lurid accusations immediately – but struggle to find out that he was released without charge.'

Of course, I know absolutely nothing about this case. But the *Spectator* piece is simultaneously fascinating and inspiring. Having won his freedom, Nigel Evans is not retiring to a desert island. He is using his experience to try to help others.

Contemplating the plight of the recently liberated Freddie Starr, the former Deputy Speaker of the House of Commons muses, 'He was, in theory, free. But the whole affair had kept him in a virtual prison, the same one to which I was confined in the last year. He may have been given back his freedom, but the ordeal has cost him his health – as it cost me my career.'

Evans concludes, 'The solution is obvious: anonymity for those accused of rape, not just the accusers.' He talks this through cogently and coherently in an article everyone should read.

Along the way, he unintentionally does something none of us has done before. For the first time, a suspect in the show trials publicly reveals that some of us, though not all, talk to each other:

'I spoke to the comedian Jim Davidson during my days under this hateful suspicion, and he told me, "I know where you are. Every time you are not doing something else you are thinking of this," and he was right.'

The British police and Crown Prosecution Service have done something no demonstrating band of left-wing radicals could do. They have united large numbers of celebrities and politicians in demanding substantial legal reform. It will be a cause for which many of us will fight for the rest of our lives.

Although Nigel's article reveals considerable writing talent, he tells me in our telephone conversation that he will not be publishing a book after all. He may write it for reference purposes, but he cannot publish.

'A book has to be specific. I would burn too many bridges,' he acknowledges.

On one hand, I am disappointed. I would have loved to have read every twist and turn in his sordid saga. On the other, I am energised. I now have the field to myself. Unless someone else has been keeping a secret diary, I have the immense responsibility of making this the only accurate account of what it is like to have captured the undeserved attention of the sex police.

───────────────── 20 MAY 2014 ─────────────────

I am destabilised by a phone call from an old friend.

Peter Straker, whom I have known since the 1970s, calls to tell me that the police have requested an interview. They want to talk to him about me.

Straker? With all due respect to this talented theatre and cabaret artist – Peter Straker? How about the Man in the Moon? How about someone who knows more about this case than Peter Straker, like Lady Gaga? (Actually, though she doesn't realise it, Lady Gaga does know more about this case than Peter Straker, although that isn't much.)

It turns out that Peter has returned from tour to deal with a request from late March for the police to come to his flat to interview him about me. Naturally, he is not looking forward to having the boys in blue in his home. He has had the courtesy to tell me that he is going to call them, since once his interview process has begun the Met will not allow him to contact me until he has signed a statement.

Peter, like myself, has no idea what he could possibly add of value to what the police already know. He was never a visitor to my flat, nor I to his. They might as well have picked a name at random out of a phone book.

Which is what we agree they might have done. The phone book would have been mine, one of the thirty-eight diaries the police seized the day they arrested me and have not yet returned.

Of course, I have no idea if this is what they have done. When they do everything behind your back and give you literally no information about their investigation, you try to connect the dots, and you might erroneously draw a line between Dot 3 and Dot 15.

After thanking Peter for his call, I ring Kate Goold. She is in court all day. I send her an email.

'Notice this is after you were told my file had been closed,' I write.

> I have no idea what this could be about, as Peter and I were never personally involved, nor did we ever share a residence. This is a fishing expedition. It reminds me of Liz Kershaw receiving a phone call asking if she would like to make an accusation against Dave Lee Travis, and Nigel Evans having non-accusers forced to accuse him.

I have to talk to someone who knows Straker, so I send an email to my old Hyde Park Square flatmate. He responds wittily, 'He has not come to mind since 1985! ... No doubt if he has moved to the Caribbean they would want to interview him!'

---

21 MAY 2014

Good grief, as Charlie Brown used to say. Good grief.

My attention is drawn to an article in the *New Statesman* by Anoosh Chakelian: 'Oxford Union speakers urged to withdraw after rape allegations against president'. Apparently Ben Sullivan has returned to his position making the statement, 'As you may be aware no charges have been brought against me and I have the utmost faith in the police and Crown Prosecution Service and the British legal system as a whole. I know that sooner or later the truth will prevail and justice will be served.' This has not mollified two people, who 'are asking high-profile speakers to withdraw from Union debates'.

The *New Statesman* continues that the leader of the campaign calls it a 'push for equality in the Union'.

Nonsense. It is an attempt to pre-judge an accused man before he is even charged, let alone tried. That's it.

I have an amusing email exchange with my old friend Steve Forbert. The great singer/songwriter has just finished a tour and has asked for an update on my legal situation. I provide him with the hard facts and then say, 'To avoid going out of my head – which reminds me, I never interviewed Little Anthony! – I have had to accept this perpetual limbo as the new normal.'

'Going Out of My Head' by Little Anthony and the Imperials was an American Top 10 hit in 1964, but I know the pop connoisseur Forbert will know it. He certainly does, as he wittily quotes its lyric in his response:

'Totally freakin' ridiculous, Paul … all of it.

'I hope you can avoid going out of your head

'Day and night, night and day … and night.'

My gosh, now I want to get back on radio, if only to interview Little Anthony before it's too late! After all, no less a sage than Bob Dylan reportedly said, 'Rock and roll died with Little Anthony and the Imperials.'

I am not the only person in the house checking internet correspondence. Christopher, who has been monitoring the Twittersphere for me, brings an intriguing exchange to my attention. A Twitter user named Martin Walkerdine has directed a question to Mark Williams-Thomas, presenter of the ITV documentary exposing Jimmy Savile: 'Can you provide the status of Chris Denning, Paul Gambaccini and 73-year-old (Yewtree 17) arrested by Op Yewtree'. Williams-Thomas, an indefatigable tweeter and insider in this subject area, replies, 'All on bail – decisions soon on all bar the most recent arrest of the BBC interpreter'. Does he know something about me that I don't?

I now declare a 24-hour Yewtree holiday to concentrate on presenting tomorrow's Ivor Novello Awards.

---

22 MAY 2014

Before these feelings turn to memories, I should record my thoughts about today's Ivor Novello Awards. I am grateful that I was allowed to present for my twenty-seventh year and delighted that the ceremony yielded so many first-time winners. I am pleased that I managed to refrain from either freaking out or making any direct comment on my legal situation. As always, I am deeply touched that songwriters of different generations have met and shared love of their craft and respect for each other. Introducing Tom Odell to Jimmy Page and discovering that they were mutual admirers was a particular thrill.

One member of the BASCA board confided that at its first meeting after my arrest the question of who should present the 2014 Ivors was raised. The vote to retain me as host was unanimous. I was thrilled to hear this – not a single vote of dissent! I visualised a giant inflatable middle finger pointed in the direction of New Scotland Yard.

I never doubted that I should accept the invitation. An innocent man feels no guilt. But there was the nagging wonder if thoughts about my persecution would interfere with my concentration during performance. I worked on the assumption that, just as in previous moments of stress, the job at hand would take over my mind completely and enable me to focus on the responsibilities of the moment. This had certainly been true when I had been informed of the miscarriage of my son, and then my grandfather's death, on mornings of programme days.

I can't believe I just wrote the words 'the miscarriage of my son'. He would now be over thirty years old. I won't cheapen his spirit by hypothesising about what he might now be doing. I do know that the Metropolitan Police insult his memory by alleging that, instead of conceiving him, I was next door shagging teenage boys.

I managed to get through the Ivors yesterday without referring to Yewtree. I had anticipated I might be drawn into a comment by the opening remarks of Academy chairman Simon Darlow, but he avoided any reference and instead brought me on with the words, 'rock-and-roll Rolodex'. None of the presenters or winners mentioned my circumstances in their remarks, although I thought Ivors Inspiration Award winner Jerry Dammers might be going that way when I heard him say 'guilt'. No, he didn't – he said 'gilt', referring to the coating of the Ivor statuette.

Having steered a clear way through the ceremonies, I came to the menu of credits at the end, the obligatory recitation of the People without Whom This Would Not Have Been Possible. Every year I close by saying, 'I'll see you next year. Thank you.' I realised that if I didn't say it this time it would be of greater importance to regulars than if I did. So I finished with, 'I say this every year, and this year I mean it more than ever: I'll see you next year. Thank you.'

No one mentioned it at the ceremony, but many newspapers do this morning. The Press Association has picked up the remark and it has been carried by numerous publications. The *Express* website headline is 'Paul Gambaccini hosts Ivor Novello awards six months after arrest under Operation Yewtree' and the sub reads, in case anyone has an attention span of one second: 'DJ Paul Gambaccini wowed this year's Ivor Novello Awards six months after his arrest as part of Operation Yewtree'.

This episode still retains the ability to shock me out of my wits.

Today, I Googled myself. I never used to do this before my arrest because I had no interest in seeing how I was being misrepresented – as in the Wikipedia claim that I was the first person to hear the original remix of R. Kelly's 'Ignition'. But ever since my original rebail was reported in the press before I was told about it, I have periodically checked myself on the web to see if there is any news.

I search for 'Paul Gambaccini' and get one of the frights of my life. Usually when you Google yourself, your Wikipedia entry pops up with a large picture and several smaller ones. This time up comes the name 'Paul Gambaccini' and a photograph of Jimmy Savile.

This is ridiculous. Forget about personal behaviour and focus a moment on physical appearance. I've never smoked a cigar and I hope my hair has never looked as ridiculous as his. And yet Jim gets my main photo and, to its immediate right, a secondary picture, in this case displaying one of his establishment Honours. It is a gold star, which without benefit of caption could either be a royal emblem, a papal knighthood, or the deputy's badge from *Blazing Saddles*. Whatever it is, it's something I have never won.

For about five seconds I despair that I am forever associated with sexual abuse. Then I realise: these photos are not here because I have been arrested by Operation Yewtree. They are here because the most Googled articles about 'Paul Gambaccini' concern my broadcast remarks about Jimmy Savile. Number one on the 'hit' parade is 'Paul Gambaccini shocks 5 Live listeners with Savile necrophiliac claim'. This is an article with the classic quote from a Stoke Mandeville Hospital spokesman, who says, 'We are not launching an investigation into claims that Savile was a necrophiliac. We have never received any complaints as to that nature.' The second most popular posting, 'Paul Gambaccini: Jimmy Savile's work for charity hid his sex abuse', comes from the 1 October 2012 *Metro* website.

Having met John Lennon in life, I was always struck by how misrepresented even the most documented of human beings can be. Jesus Christ, having been born and died before the invention of recording devices, had no chance of being known in historically accurate terms. This is why his believers have to have 'faith'. What chance has someone like myself, considerably less significant than either of these two people? I am now recorded as looking like someone else and my police record alleges sexual behaviour with people I didn't even know. I can only conclude that if you ever read anything about anyone, don't believe it unless you have personal or documentary proof. Otherwise you will believe that Santa Claus exists but is, in fact, the Easter bunny.

26 MAY 2014

It is a bank holiday Monday. Christopher and I go bowling. We both are sub-par, but I beat him by two pins on aggregate, which is enough to send him into sporting frustration. The key to my win was a conversion of the 6–7–10 split, which I have not previously managed in over half a century of bowling. What was odd about it was that it looked so smooth and simple, like a snooker champion potting endless balls in succession, that it didn't even appear to be difficult.

Chris, competitive as he is, credited my victory not to this extraordinary spare, which he did compliment, but to a freebie mark I enjoyed when my gutter ball bounced back onto the alley to take out a lone ten pin. Oh well, earn one, get a second one free!

We walk into Covent Garden piazza and hear a busker performing 'Folsom Prison Blues' by Johnny Cash to a large audience. It turns out the crowd is not listening to him voluntarily but is queued to enter the London Transport Museum. No matter, he has a voice that, although lacking the special character of the Man in Black, is mellifluous and pleasing.

Then he interrupts the text.

'Hello, Mr Gambaccini,' he says on mic, somewhere between 'I shot a man in Reno' and 'just to watch him die'. After the next line, he adds, 'The Ambassador of Music. I love you.'

I am overcome. The police have failed to destroy my reputation. The relationship I have with my listeners survives.

Shortly after my arrest, it became apparent to me that I was going to have some unanticipated free time, enough to write a book … enough, perhaps, even to read Proust.

Last week I called Jack and Kathryn Zoeller to offer my latest case update. Kathryn answered.

'Oh, hi,' she said casually. 'I've just been reading Proust.'

That was it. Kathryn might as well have slapped my cheek with a glove. This was a challenge. I could wait no longer. I went to Foyles in Waterloo Station – it brings joy to mention the opening rather the closing of a bookstore – and purchased the one book of Proust they had, the new Penguin edition of Volume 1. For reasons that are explained in the introductory material, this volume is called *The Way by Swann's* rather than *Swann's Way* and the larger work *In Search of Lost Time* instead of *Remembrance of Things Past*.

It was either this or Thomas Piketty's *Capital in the Twenty-First Century*, which has become one of those books so well discussed that you feel you've read it even if you haven't. Piketty's volume is so popular it is bound to be in Foyles after an indefinite passage of time, perhaps even after I've finished Proust. I will get around to it, if only to spite the *Financial Times*, which in a colossal fit of pique has attacked the book for its interpretation of data.

If they doubt Piketty's conclusions, the FT should spend a few minutes in my building. When I moved in fourteen years ago, almost every penthouse was owned by people who actually lived in them. Nowadays it is rare to see more than three flats illuminated on a single evening. I am reminded of the words of a former friend who once said, 'Over half the most desirable residences in the world are unoccupied on any given night because their owners are in other of the most desirable residences in the world.'

Today, I experienced as preposterous a way to start a day as I can remember.

Beginning at 6 a.m., an obnoxious fast-talking voice boomed its way into the Whitehouse Apartments from somewhere outside. I could not believe the lack of consideration. I thought it might be someone on a flat-bed truck making an ill-timed political rant about European elections. No, it was something more obvious but less likely than that. It was a red-carpet event at the IMAX cinema; a red-carpet event at six in the morning.

Warner Brothers and Village Roadshow probably do not realise that the acoustics and architecture of the Waterloo roundabout guarantee that any loud sound, particularly one with bass tones, is magnified and thrown at the residents of the Whitehouse Apartments. I cannot have been the only person to be awakened by the premiere of the new Tom Cruise film, *Edge of Tomorrow*.

Edge of Tomorrow. Six a.m. Get it? Get it, and then shoot the publicist.

I find myself in Waterloo Station at 6.15 a.m. buying a mozzarella and tomato croissant for breakfast. I stagger home through the drizzle and open my emails.

Kevin Howlett has sent good wishes and a mention of an article by Libby Purves in Monday's *Times*: 'This cruelty to those in legal limbo must stop.' I immediately Google the piece and get as far as the second paragraph before the paywall kicks in and blocks the remainder of the text.

'So much for innocent until proven guilty,' Purves has written.

> The Oxford Union president is being damned even without being charged.
>
> Imagine living in a country where anybody could denounce you to the authorities for something both heinous and difficult to disprove. Imagine that the immediate result, without formal charge, was to stop you working for several years, maybe make you move out of your home and force you to report to police stations as if on probation. Imagine that your accuser is mistaken and that in any case the supposed misdemeanour would attract a prison stay of barely half this time. Imagine

that no apology or compensation was offered for your years of shame,
inactivity and waning confidence and that

'And that' what? I will probably never find out, as I will not fork over for any Rupert Murdoch paywall, but I am delighted that Libby is protesting.

Today is the completion of my first seven months on police bail without charge. Notice I say 'my first seven months'. I've learned enough about the duplicity of the Metropolitan Police and Crown Prosecution Service to know better than to believe that any particular rebail date will be effective. Will I have six weeks of 'arrest without charge' left – or will these 'first seven months' just have been the half of it?

Libby, keep writing!

And then it turns out she did! I am sent (not by her) a jpeg of her piece, photographed against what appears to be an attractive doily-like tablecloth. After the words 'and that', Purves concludes the paragraph with 'a defence costs your savings'.

'You do live in such a country, so do I.'

Purves quotes Magna Carta to demonstrate how the Britain of 2014 denies some of its citizens the rights granted to all 800 years ago: 'No Freeman shall be … disscised of his Freehold, or Liberties … or be outlawed, or exiled, or any other wise destroyed … We will not deny or defer to any man … justice.' Referring to the convention that once accused of a sexual crime, one will 'step aside' until cleared, she writes,

> Such suspension of life would be reasonable if it were for weeks or a couple of months: but not years. Note the words of the great charter 'or any other wise destroyed' and reflect how delay can destroy you. Yet teachers, medical professionals, broadcasters, entertainers, public functionaries, even, lately, one government adviser, are casually thrown into suspended animation, even if no charges are ever brought.

Thank you, Libby. You are a voice of sanity.

<hr />

29 MAY 2014

Yesterday evening I received a phone call from John Reid, who met yesterday afternoon with Jeremy King. Together they have hatched a scheme that may be a financial game changer in my sorry saga of endless rebailing.

In their three and a half decades as the London restaurant community's ultimate dynamic duo, Jeremy and Chris Corbin have accumulated hundreds of dedicated followers, who will try out one of their new restaurants as a matter of course. I will myself tomorrow, when Christopher and I volunteer for a trial meal at their new Marylebone eatery, Fischer's. Now Jeremy has offered to organise a whip-round for my legal expenses, to be conducted through his monthly customer newsletter.

I am treated to dinner at RSJ by Laura Croker, who has recently retired as the mistress of Elton John's website. I came to know Laura when she joined Rocket Records to work with Caroline Boucher, Elton's press officer, in 1976. I recall assembling a two-hour tape of 'Blue' songs for Caroline and Laura to play at the launch party of the *Blue Moves* double album.

She was not Laura Croker then. David Croker was running the label and she was the young woman with whom he fell in love. They married and had two daughters. One is a medical doctor and the other is about to become a PhD. Doctor doctor, indeed!

David was one of Elton's oldest friends, a fellow music buff from the days when he was still Reg Dwight. He was still as enthusiastic about music when in the record business as he had been on the outside. One day he told me that I had to come by the Wardour Street office to hear the worst demo he had ever received. It was from a man who caterwauled in accompaniment to Elvis Presley records.

Croker was still in middle age when he died suddenly from a heart attack. I was asked to give the eulogy at his funeral. Within a period of a few years, I performed a similar service at the funerals of John Peel and Gus Dudgeon. I found that it was natural for me to address the coffins of my friends, which in all cases were positioned mere feet from me. I could not ignore the fact that their bodies were lying directly in front of me. I spoke to where the head of the person would be, as I had in life.

But in the case of David Croker, I did not know which end of the coffin contained his head and which end bore his feet. I briefly panicked that I might speak to the part of the box that someone like Laura knew was the wrong end. I solved this problem by addressing the middle of the coffin.

Now, years after his death, David has done his old friend a last service. Laura tells me that Elton has taken a renewed interest in vinyl LPs and has set up a deck in the gallery of his home in Old Windsor. As a Christmas present, she gave him David's collection of vinyl discs by Elton's hero Leon Russell. He was deeply touched. But EJ didn't know the end of it. His office had been able to supply him with a couple of his own original vinyl albums. He thought that they had come from the Rocket files. In fact, they were from David Croker's collection. Elton now has his old pal's copies of his original releases.

---

31 MAY 2014

Christopher is still sleepy when I wake him up this morning, even though he has a Chris Sherwood Personal Training client at 9 a.m. and has to be bright and breezy. My beloved husband reveals something he has not told me.

For the past week he has been having an evolving series of dreams. The Metropolitan Police have been trying to taint me by smearing him, distributing flyers to the general public inviting them to accuse him of serious crimes. It will only take two people to denounce him for the police to be able to arrest him. In these dreams, Chris has not told me of the police campaign against him because he has not wanted to disturb me.

Now, in waking life, he must. He can no longer keep the nightmares a secret because they have affected his sleep.

Every person who has loved another human being will understand the increased anger I feel against the Metropolitan Police. Even though I thought that I had involuntarily pressed myself to the limits of rage, I resent them even more than ever. They have not only tortured me for seven months, they have tortured my husband.

---

2 JUNE 2014

My favourite ghoulish television commercial was for a 1940s compilation album I saw in the United States in June 1973. I can date it precisely because Vaughn Monroe, a major American hit maker of the 1940s best known for 'Riders in the Sky' and 'Let It Snow, Let It Snow, Let It Snow', had just died.

'Hi! Remember me?' the host of the ad asked. 'I'm Vaughn Monroe!'

Well ... er ... *was* Vaughn Monroe...

There were people in the '70s who still remembered the '40s, and there are obviously people today who recall the '70s.

Today, the 1970s return in an even more bizarre way. The BBC news website reports that 'The jury at the trial of Rolf Harris has seen video footage that prosecutors say contradicts his claim he could not have visited the location of one of his alleged assaults.

'The footage, from ITV game show *Star Games*, was filmed in Cambridge in 1978.'

The article gives some background: 'Rolf Harris was the captain of the "theatre" team, whose members included Robin Askwith and Rula Lenska. His opponents included Davy Jones, of the Monkees, and singers Patti Boulaye and Dave Dee.'

Even though *Star Games* was thirty-six years ago, I have talked about it with Chris. I even referred to it when I did obituaries for Davy Jones last year. This was the televised celebrity sports series at which, while playing in goal, I deflected a sharp shot from Jones with my forehead. It was one of the most painful moments in my life. I was congratulated on a great save while wondering if I was about to keel over unconscious.

I have three memories of that competition. The Davy Jones shot on goal was the most physically painful experience. The most emotionally painful was my blown tee shot in a golf competition with Dave Lee Travis. There I was, filmed for television, rolling my drive into a bunker. I would happily have covered myself with sand, or mud, or any available form of dirt, anything to avoid being seen at that moment.

And then there is a mental Polaroid. It's one of the most vivid recollections I have of an expression on someone's face that spoke otherwise silent words. The young pop star John Cougar, who had not yet reverted to his real name John Mellencamp, found himself in the last stage of a relay race dashing for the tape against Tony Blackburn. As he rounded the turn on the last lap, his face seemed to be crying out 'How did I get here? How did I, a boy from Seymour, Indiana, wind up on a television show in Cambridge, England, with a false name and a ridiculous costume, not making music, but running against a disc jockey I don't even know?'

I find it curious that whoever vetted the *Star Games* series for the Rolf Harris trial didn't take the opportunity to throw my golf scene with Dave Lee Travis in as a bonus. What titillation that would have provided! I'm reminded of those scenes in films in which army officers tell their men that only a few of them will be coming back. Imagine if, when Michael Aspel had gathered us for our opening pep talk at the start of *Star Games*, he had said, 'I should warn you that thirty-five years from now three of you will be arrested as perverts.' That would have got eyes shifting around the dressing room! My morbid fantasy is slightly ruined by an inexact memory as to whether Harris was in the same episode as Travis and I, and as to whether my duffing made it to screen or was relegated to the cutting-room floor. But then, as lawyers tell me, all memory is faulty after three and a half decades.

3 JUNE 2014

Jennifer has spoken to a shopkeeper on Lower Marsh whose son is a London policeman. The officer has said that his station house has been resisting the efforts of the Met to arrest a local man on suspicion of historic sexual offences, saying they cannot act without evidence. I find this fascinating. During the last eight months I have been focused on celebrities who have been arrested, but it has only been recently that I have had cause to consider the wider disruption to society caused by the witch-hunt. Certainly my friends who have nothing remotely to do with my case have been terrified by being approached by the police to make statements. My friend who was interviewed concerning the possible rape in 1978 of a man who claimed he had recognised a piece of Jimmy Savile's furniture as having been in his home a quarter of a century earlier is a prime example of a person terrorised by a flimsy allegation. And now there is another category of human beings negatively affected: other policemen and policewomen, responsible and diligent public servants who happen to believe that evidence is more important than rumour, 'old school' law keepers who feel that the old objective justice system is still superior to the new subjective, accusation-based system.

How many lives have been negatively affected? A barrister friend says that what he wants most of all at this stage is for a Freedom of Information request to learn about all the ridiculous accusations that have not led to arrests. How much police time are we wasting here? How many lives are being blighted by this hysteria? What is the cost to the taxpayer?

Coming back from dinner with Dartmouth classmate Larry Killgallon, I run into radio producer John Sugar at the South Bank entrance to Waterloo Tube Station. He voices support and asks relevant questions about my ordeal. His female companion then says, 'A lot of people are waiting for your book.'

Gulp! How did this get around? Now I have a further responsibility to finish this book … not just to myself, not just to the historical record, but to whoever is actually anticipating it.

4 JUNE 2014

Revision of this book is delayed by the receipt of an email from Kate Goold. In response to her written concern about my latest rebail, she has heard back from my case officer, who has started out with the usual evasions. The CPS has my file but he is not willing to tell us the date of receipt.

> I am also not able to provide you with the nature of the enquiries being conducted by police at this time but can assure you they are being conducted in an expeditious manner.
>
> There has been a change in reviewing lawyer at the CPS which has resulted in further enquiries being conducted.

He signs off gracefully, but my heart sinks, as I explain in a reply to Kate:

> This idea of a second CPS lawyer getting a shot at me is not very encouraging. Am I target practice? Do you think the change in 'reviewing lawyer' is a discouraging development, or might he or she have left the case for some everyday reason like maternity leave or job switch?
>
> Or is this another area in which speculation can only lead to madness?

Kate replies rapidly.

'I don't think the change has any significance at all,' she says. 'Lawyers move around a lot at the CPS and lots are leaving!'

The next email is from Larry Killgallon, last night's dinner host.

'Unfortunately, Victor Hugo was right,' he says: 'True or false, that which is said of men occupies as important a place in their lives, and above all in their destinies, as that which they do.'

Larry adds, 'I wish you the best in clearing your good name.'

―――――――――――― 5 JUNE 2014 ――――――――――――

My recent question 'Whatever happened to Gary Glitter?' has been answered by the BBC website. 'Gary Glitter charged with sex offences', it says.

With no disrespect meant to either Glitter or his accusers, I selfishly breathe a sigh of relief. I am now back in the position I thought I was two weeks ago, the longest-serving in the 'arrest without charge' category, before I remembered that he and Chris Denning were also waiting for action. Now they have been charged. I'm next at bat.

In the evening, Christopher and I attend the annual Terrence Higgins Trust Friends for Life dinner. This gala is always an opportunity for reflection on my life, if only because I still have one. Aids did not take me. I am of the generation that always thinks of lost loved ones at an Aids charity event.

During what I'll call the cocktail hour – can a charity fighting a fatal disease have a 'happy hour'? – I give host Stephen Fry an update on my situation. I have been told by a mischievous Labour insider that Fry is due to host a Labour Party gala next month. Because I cannot resist, I ask, 'Stephen, the Labour dinner?'

He says, 'Yes?'

I say, 'No.'

I tell Fry about the shun at last year's Thousand Club dinner, about Miliband speaking to Jude Kelly and not acting upon her words, about Harriet Harman's unfortunate interviews, about party plans to give former Director of Public Prosecutions Keir Starmer a prominent role.

I see a literal representation of the song title 'A Whiter Shade of Pale'. Stephen turns ashen and responds, 'I'll have to withdraw.'

Moments later, the Friends for Life dinner has an opportunity for contemplation while considering the recent heart attack death of Dr Charles Farthing. Stephen Fry pays tribute to him from the podium.

He also mentions my dilemma and asks the audience to give me its support. I receive a prolonged ovation. Christopher and I sit at our table, moved beyond measure. Nearly every organisation with which I have been associated has shunned me, but the THT has publicly embraced me.

The Globe production of *Twelfth Night* dominates this year's Tony Awards nominations, and Stephen must pack to fly to New York tomorrow morning. He leaves the event as soon as Elaine Paige has finished her cabaret performance. On the way out, he whispers, 'I'll write to Ed and withdraw. I can't support what they've done.' What a pal!

---

6 JUNE 2014

It is a hot, sunny day, so I tell Chris that this is the day I should go back and see Hyde Park Square. My old flat is only about a twenty-minute walk away from our lunch venue of Café Anglais. Today is perfect for such a saunter. Chris comes with me.

I point out all the local landmarks. Oh my gosh, there is the site of the restaurant where, forty-one years ago, the Rice brothers and I agreed to do *The Guinness Book of British Hit Singles* together! Here is the pub which, curiously, one of my accusers claims to have seen me in, although as a non-drinker I can't have been in it more than once a year when I was in the neighbourhood.

Then we are there, standing outside the Hyde Park Square apartment building. I haven't been here in years. The front door has changed from black to brown. I point out to Chris which windows were mine and which were part of my co-accused's apartment.

Chris looks up to my old flat and sums it up: 'So this is where nothing happened.'

---

8 JUNE 2014

Paul Bajoria, the producer of *Counterpoint*, has generously forwarded a column written by Paul Donovan and published in the 25 May edition of the *Sunday Times*.

Donovan's piece, what Bajoria calls 'a curious mixture of the supportive and snide', is right on in its important point. The author wants another series of *Counterpoint*. He has noticed that this year's series has been pushed back quarter after quarter as I have been endlessly rebailed. He then informs listeners of the complete radio silence that the BBC has imposed upon me. He informs me, too: I know that I have not transmitted any new programmes, but I did not know that 'even a repeat of one (on Britten's *War Requiem*, made in 2004) was withdrawn by Radio 4 Extra'.

Paul Donovan reports that 'after forty years of broadcasting on all BBC radio networks, and several commercial ones, including Classic FM and Capital, he has become a spectre at the feast. We are not able to hear him. Whether that's his or the BBC's decision is not known.'

Of course it isn't known. It was in March that I withdrew my stated desire not to be on air after my arrest, but no one has publicised this decision and no member of the press has asked me about it. The decision to keep me off air after the original period of uncertainty has been entirely the BBC's.

The *Sunday Times* critic speculates that 'Gambaccini may lose the chairmanship – which he once called "my dream assignment" – to someone else. Russell Davies, Matthew Sweet and Suzy Klein would all do it well'. So they would, and I am relieved to know that Donovan will approve of my suggested temporary replacement by Davies should it become necessary.

Then something happens that I have never seen in a newspaper. A radio critic attacks the justice system.

'Gambaccini has denied all the allegations,' Donovan notes. 'He was released on bail, pending further inquiries, until January; then rebailed until earlier this month; then rebailed again until a date in early July.' He missed another rebail in there, but I'm not criticising, since it was not publicised.

'If he were in custody, this would not be possible, and he would have to be either charged or freed; but he is not in custody, so it is.'

Then comes the dambuster conclusion: 'Like him or loathe him, this situation is unsatisfactory.'

Something constructive must emerge from this suffering. I hope that the increased attention being given to the endless rebailing process will lead to law reform that ends it. No one should ever again be put through what I have endured.

9 JUNE 2014

A highlight of my reading career has occurred. Proust has nibbled the madeleine.

10 JUNE 2014

The *Financial Times* reports Mike Tyson as having said: 'Everyone has a plan, until they get punched in the mouth.'

What we consider to be words of wisdom are often aphorisms, sometimes unintended, which have resonance at a particular moment in our lives. I don't consider Dean Martin to be a great philosopher, but when he told a reporter that he never worried about things beyond his control, I knew I had found a modern Seneca. When I was asked to attempt a classical music chart show on the new radio network Classic FM and wondered if a failure in this unprecedented format might hurt my career, I was encouraged by an observation by Shirley MacLaine, who said that no one should worry about their failures because other people are unaware of them, precisely because they were failures.

Now Del Bryant, son of Boudleaux and Felice Bryant, writers of Everly Brothers classics including 'Bye Bye Love', 'Wake Up Little Susie' and 'All I Have to Do Is Dream', is leaving his post as CEO of Broadcast Music,

Incorporated (BMI). He tells *Billboard*, 'I'm ready for a little of that question mark in life from which every opportunity springs.'

Del, join Dean and Shirley. This line is appropriate for my changed life. The police have imposed question marks upon my life. From these punctuation points come new possibilities.

John Reid calls to say that Peter Straker has rung him. The singer reports that he has replied to the police request to interview him but they have not phoned him back. He will not press the matter and may remain forever inquisitive about why he was ever dragged into this mess in the first place.

——————————— 12 JUNE 2014 ———————————

I had lunch yesterday with Keith Harris, whom I have known almost my entire professional life. He is a 'lifer', one of us who works in music because he loves it. Currently, he is director of performer affairs at PPL (Phonographic Performance Limited). He continues his relationship with Stevie Wonder, whom he started with as operations manager in 1978 and still represents in Britain.

Keith treated me to a meal at my favourite London Italian restaurant, Bocca di Lupo. As I enjoyed a sequence of small dishes, heavy on the vegetables and olive oil, I told Harris that my Italian grandmother, who did her own cooking, lived to be ninety-eight.

My host told me that not long ago he was seated next to Bill Wyman at a music business function. Keith asked Bill what he thought about Yewtree. Wyman told him that he had approached the police, asking if they wished to discuss his relationship with the teenager Mandy Smith, and was told they were not interested.

God bless Bill, another 'lifer' who has done a fantastic job with charity work and pursued his love of the blues long after his departure from the Rolling Stones. But he and Smith, who married when she was eighteen, were the ultimate tabloid couple, and their adventures, both real and imaginary, sacrificed acres of trees for newspapers to chronicle. If the police are more interested in the alleged sexploits of broadcasters like myself than '60s artists who actually talked about young love and were admired by groupies, we are truly in a topsy-turvy world. I told Keith Harris that I envisioned Donovan buying up all existing copies of 'Mellow Yellow' and urging Sony to delete it, but that extreme action does not seem to be necessary. If you are a huge rock star, Plod does not appear to want you.

This morning, I Google Bill Wyman to see if there was anything about this subject on him. Good God, there he is in the *Daily Mail* of 31 March 2013, relating precisely what Keith has told me. The headline is 'Police "not interested" in Wyman's affair with 13-year-old Mandy Smith, who claims she slept with him when she was 14'.

I have not been smoking too much 'electrical banana'. The article quotes Bill as saying, 'I went to the police and I went to the public prosecutor and said, "Do you want to talk to me? Do you want to meet up with me, or anything like that?" and I got a message back, "No".

'I was totally open about it.'

The *Mail* adds, 'The Metropolitan Police refused to comment on Wyman's claims.'

It does appear that there is one class of person who is sufficiently famous to arrest and then there are the international household names whom the police consider too popular to pursue. I note from a BBC report dated 2 May that Roy Harper

> has denied twelve charges of historical child sex offences. The 72-year-old entered not guilty pleas to all counts of sexual assault at Worcester Crown Court on Friday. A trial, expected to last twelve days, will take place on a date yet to be confirmed. West Mercia Police said the offences are alleged to have been committed in Herefordshire between 1975 and 1977 and relate to one victim.

Harper is beloved by fellow recording artists for his fine but relatively obscure work. John Peel adored 'When an Old Cricketer Leaves the Crease'. Harper is better known by the general public for singing lead vocals on Pink Floyd's 'Have a Cigar'. He was a great favourite of Jimmy Page and Robert Plant of Led Zeppelin, who named a track on their third album, 'Hats Off to (Roy) Harper', after him. By inconceivable coincidence, *Led Zeppelin III* is back in the Top 10 of the album chart this week as a reissue in both the UK and US. West Mercia Police may have thought that they have been pursuing an unknown pop performer, but here he is in this week's Top 10.

---

13 JUNE 2014

Kate Goold has had a conversation with Jeremy King concerning the restauranteur's desire to start a fighting fund to cover my legal fees. Kate is struck by his goodness.

'What a lovely man,' Goold writes. 'I am so pleased that you have so many good and strong people behind you who want to do everything they can to help.'

Jeremy tells my solicitor of the two paths he can take. The first is the email approach, where he requests funds from the 700 or so recipients of his monthly newsletter. The second is a personal appeal to friends with a bit of spare cash.

Goold discourages the newsletter approach. Its recipients include the editors of two newspapers and their publications might wish to mention the drive in their pages. She is not afraid of the two particular papers, but is worried that a 'horrible tabloid' might sensationalise the story and return me to newsprint, attracting one or two unhinged persons to 'come forward'. I feel that there is a less than 50 per cent chance of this happening, but have to agree that even 10 per cent is too high.

Fortunately, King intuitively understands the dilemma. He is willing to take the time to make personal contact with potential donors. What a hero!

In the early evening I receive a copy of an email that Stephen Fry has sent to Ed Miliband, withdrawing as the host of the Labour Party gala dinner on 9 July and also indefinitely withdrawing his support from the party.

I take Christopher to see *The Magnificent Ambersons* at the National Film Theatre. I asked him if he would see the film with me because I want to share with him the origins of part of my broadcasting style. Welles's narration of portions of *Ambersons* taught me how to speak professionally. It doesn't mean that I have his vocal quality. It does mean that I emulated him all my life. His diction, his pauses, his rises and falls … they make me sigh every time I hear them and, in the case of this particular film, I have heard them many times. Just the opening words of some of his speeches – 'The magnificence of the Ambersons', 'And now Major Amberson', 'Something had happened' – send me into an elevated state of ecstasy. The credits are the greatest of any film, and the last twenty seconds are the best ending to any motion picture ever. 'My name is Orson Welles. This is a Mercury production.' The boom microphone swings into the distance and Bernard Herrmann's music swells dramatically. If we all had to be subjected to a twenty-second tape loop of our choice, this would be mine.

16 JUNE 2014

Yesterday I was walking down Charing Cross Road when a young black man eating a sandwich opposite the Garrick Theatre gestured to me. I went over to hear his thoughts.

'You said the same thing as David Icke and they took you in for it. It's unfair, man.'

I didn't quiz him on what it was that David and I agreed on, but thanked him for his support.

I did not expect anything further to come of Stephen Fry's email to Ed Miliband and had no intention of showing it to anyone else, but someone obviously has. Alastair Campbell has written to Stephen offering to intervene to clear up the matter which, he said, was probably due to some misunderstanding at a lower level of officials. I assured Stephen that the only Labour Party representative who spoke to me was Iain McNicol and the one who spoke to Jude Kelly was Ed Miliband. If Alastair wants to refer to Ed Miliband and Iain McNicol as low-level officials, his head is probably still in the Tony Blair clouds.

Walking through the West End, I encounter Lynda Bellingham dining with two friends on the terrace outside J. Sheekey, the fine seafood restaurant in St Martin's Court. Lynda and I have occasionally run into each other for nearly forty years. During the heyday of quiz shows, we would sometimes find ourselves on the same television programme.

Now she is a national hero. Lynda has been open about her terminal cancer, making reference three times during our half-hour together that she has been given 'months, not years' to live. She has shown her whitened hair openly on TV, making no attempt to conceal her ordeal. Ironically, she says, one of the effects of her chemotherapy is that her skin has been cooked from the inside, making it appear that she has been on holiday. Naive well-wishers have congratulated her on her tan.

Bellingham listens attentively and with horror to my 'greatest hits' selection of the past eight months. Having been a beautiful woman regularly seen on television, she is only too aware of how many fantasists mistakenly believe they have had relationships with celebrities, a phenomenon of which the police and Crown Prosecution Service appear to be blissfully unaware. She regales the table with true stories of the 1970s, when behaviour that is now considered unacceptable was commonplace. She tells of the celebrity who placed his erect penis in her hand during a rehearsal with an entire studio orchestra watching. This was considered a prank, not an assault, by everyone present. No one would dare do it now.

I embrace Lynda warmly. Because of the unpredictability of both the timing of her illness and the next time we run into each other, we can't say farewell, but I am glad our lives have often intersected.

I have dinner with Nigel Evans at his flat in Westminster. The veteran Tory politico Rob Hayward, who has been a constant source of support, is also there. He tells me that a newspaper is keen to run the Stephen Fry/Ed Miliband story and I urge him to call the reporter off. I remind Rob that my solicitor has advised against my receiving any publicity until I am cleared. Whether this Labour Party flap can be kept out of the papers indefinitely is out of my power, as emails are probably being copied around Westminster as I write.

Evans finds himself juggling two roles, his long-time position as a Member of Parliament and his new part as a crusader for law reform. He assures me that Home Secretary Theresa May is aware of my personal circumstances. He has continued to speak out against unequal anonymity of accuser and accused and of the British phenomenon of 'arrest without charge' with endless rebailing. Nigel has deliberately and considerately avoided using my example in this context and has concentrated on the case of the president of the Oxford Union Ben Sullivan.

17 JUNE 2014

Chris and I play the nine-hole golf course at Northwick Park. This intriguing facility recreates nine of the world's most famous golf holes. Fortunately, most of the best-known holes are short! The one occasion on which I dare use my driver, I blast the thing to kingdom come. Unfortunately, I blast it at a 135-degree angle, so my ball winds up on the tee two holes over, having gone over a clump of trees. It doesn't even occur to me to yell 'Fore!' Who in the woods is going to complain? A deer? When I emerge from the forest to search for my ball, a shaken golfer on the distant tee points it out to me. From here on in, it's irons only.

The beautiful dry June continues. The fine weather has been important to me. My coping strategy requires that I do not focus on any particular rebail date as my potential deliverance. I have learned that the CPS do not keep their promises about decision days and will rebail you as they wish. Although I would be delighted if my case were to be dropped on or before the given date of 7/7, I try not to think about it and concentrate instead on making the most of the summer. Enjoying the late evenings out of doors is deeply pleasurable. So is golfing with Chris without having to take an umbrella.

───────────────── 18 JUNE 2014 ─────────────────

I note the *Daily Telegraph* headline 'Oxford Union boycott campaign leader denounced by keynote speaker as "intimidating"'. The subhead is 'Jennifer Perry, CEO of the Digital Trust, has accused the boycott campaign leaders of putting women's safety at risk by attempting to derail her talk', the reference being to a campaign to have guests cancel their appearances unless president Ben Sullivan steps down. Sullivan was arrested on 7 May on suspicion of rape and attempted rape.

I am delighted to see that A. C. Grayling, Master of New College of the Humanities, has pointed out that Sullivan is 'innocent until proven guilty' and must not be a victim of 'the kangaroo court of opinion'. I have no idea what New College of the Humanities is, unless the venerable New College Oxford has changed its name, and will now Google it.

I am horrified to note that David Mepham, the UK director of Human Rights Watch, has gone along with the campaign, as have Interpol Secretary General Ronald Noble and *Dragons' Den* judge Julie Meyer. Human Rights Watch now joins Amnesty International in my charity bin.

I find myself in the unusual position of being 100 per cent opposed to someone I don't even know. The prose of the boycott leader is stomach-churning. She had publicly made the nonsensical claim that Sullivan remaining in office 'continues to offer prestige and power to someone who is being investigated for rape. This undermines the severe nature of allegations of sexual offences.' Now she and her student associate have been lobbying scheduled Oxford Union guest speakers to drop out as a sign of support for 'those of us currently pushing for a culture of equality'. Equality of what? Fact and fiction?

That was quick! Yesterday I wrote about the Ben Sullivan case. Today I walk into the kitchen and Jennifer is listening to the Jeremy Vine show. Nigel Evans appears to discuss the Oxford affair. Police have told Sullivan, via his lawyer, that no action will be taken against him. In the words we have come to expect from the Crown Prosecution Service, 'We have decided that there is insufficient evidence to prosecute a 21-year-old man from Oxford who was arrested following a complaint of rape and a complaint of attempted rape made by two women. We will be writing to the complainants to explain our decision in more detail.' Evans puts it in the honest and straightforward words that witch-hunters hate: 'Ben Sullivan is innocent, Jeremy. Ben Sullivan is innocent.' Another commentator appears on the show, but I catch only a fragment of the broadcast, enough for Nigel to make another appeal for anonymity until charge. I know that when he speaks like this he is speaking for me and for others in my position who have had to endure months of what Sullivan has lived through.

'In the clear after six weeks of agony', a Mail Online headline reads, 'Oxford Union president accused of rape is told by police they are taking no further action'. It is agony, and my heart goes out to Ben Sullivan.

It is terribly awkward to admit, but once again the right-wing newspapers, traditionally my *bêtes noires*, are on the right side of the Ben Sullivan story. I am astonished to discover an *Express* column by Virginia Blackburn. She is right on it:

Ben has been through a nightmare and he is just the latest in a long line of men whose lives have been trashed on the back of some kind of collective guilt over not apprehending the disgusting Jimmy Savile when he was alive.

Jim Davidson, Freddie Starr, Jimmy Tarbuck – all these men were arrested on suspicion of sex offences in the full glare of publicity only to be told that actually there wasn't a case against them.

But that didn't stop at least one of them, Jim Davidson, losing work on the back of it, while Starr recently looked as if he was practically on his last legs. Heaven knows what the toll has been on his health.

This has got to stop. Men's lives are being ruined by allegations that are not strong enough to stand up in court.

The *coup de grâce* comes near the end of the piece:

'The arrests of Ben, Tarby, Nick-Nick Davidson and Starr should never have been made public.

'It has benefited no one, involved a great deal of suffering on the part of people who are innocent and carries more than a whiff of malevolence.'

The leader of the unsuccessful movement to get Ben Sullivan to step down from the presidency of the Oxford Union gets more exposure in the *Daily Telegraph*, which quotes her as saying that even after Sullivan has been cleared, persons accused of rape should not be granted anonymity before charge.

If someone is able to be named, that's going to encourage other people to come forward. If you look at the Jimmy Savile case, scores of people would not have come forward unless he had been named in the press.

Being able to name people is something that helps police investigations go much smoother and will encourage more people to come forward.

I cannot believe this woman. She has learned nothing, even from crushing defeat. It does not occur to her that 'being able to name people' encourages not only genuine victims but also liars, fantasists and hysterics.

Even the Huffington Post gets in on the Ben Sullivan act. The line that gets my attention is 'a petition to make Sullivan step down as president was signed by high-profile journalists including Laurie Penny and Owen Jones...'

Not him again! It truly saddens me that someone whom I might have been close to in another life takes positions antipodal to mine in this one.

And then today's press gets personal. Christopher has shown me a Google Alert informing me that Andy McSmith of *The Independent* has run a diary item with the headline 'No Fry in that night as comic pulls out of Labour event':

> Stephen Fry has pulled out of a big Labour Party fundraising event because he doesn't like the way the party treated one of his friends.
>
> Paul Gambaccini was one of the celebrities swept up in Operation Yewtree. He was arrested in October, released on bail but has not been charged. The 65-year-old DJ is a longstanding Labour sympathiser who was expecting to be invited to a previous party fundraiser. But when the invitation arrived, after the avalanche of publicity that surrounded his arrest, it was for his partner Christopher Sherwood only.
>
> Gambaccini, I am told, angrily compares Labour's rejection of him with the way the Conservatives stood by the MP Nigel Evans through his highly publicised trial. Stephen Fry sympathises. Labour's hopes of getting the comic and national treasure to their 9 July event are fading, though Alastair Campbell is trying to mend fences.

Although this story could have been leaked by any of several people – by now there must be many within the Labour Party who know the situation with Stephen – it takes two seconds for Chris and me to make an educated guess as to McSmith's source. The key is in the praise of the Conservative Party. We suspect that the tip has come not from a Labour Party member but from a Tory friend familiar with the support Nigel received during his ordeal. I have never made the partisan comparison in conversations with friends. It must be someone who enjoys making the Conservatives look good. Of course, in this case, the Conservatives do look good.

21 JUNE 2014

The *Daily Telegraph* has run the Stephen Fry story, and in an unexpected context. No national newspaper likes to print an unmodified report that a competitor has beat them to the day before, so political editor James Kirkup must have a new angle to take the story further. He does.

'Miliband aide quits and Stephen Fry may be next' is the headline. Kirkup has cleverly melded the Fry anecdote with another angle in his lead sentence: 'Ed Miliband has suffered fresh political setbacks with the defection of a former aide and the potential loss of Stephen Fry as a backer.' Sentence two kicks like a mule as well: 'The Labour Party is also beset by rumours and suspicions about an alleged plot to undermine Mr Miliband that has been linked to Ed Balls, the shadow Chancellor.'

Kate Goold is out of the country due to a bereavement in her family. The circumstances are sad, but I am glad she is not in Britain to see me in a couple of newspapers. She would tear out somebody's hair, if not her own.

'Mr Fry is said to be unhappy about the way the Labour Party has treated his friend Paul Gambaccini, a broadcaster,' the *Telegraph* reports. The details are the same as in yesterday's *Independent*, but caged in caution:

> Mr Fry is said to be unhappy about the decision and to be considering pulling out of next month's event as a result.
>
> Mr Fry declined to comment publicly, but the Labour Party confirmed that his support is now in question. 'We are grateful for all the support Stephen has given us in the past and are hopeful he will support us again in the future,' a spokesman said.

This story has greater force than if it were merely about the gala dinner. The defection of former Labour advisor Phil Taylor, who has quit the party and joined the Liberal Democrats, the suggestion of former minister Tom Watson that some Millband advisors have made 'schoolboy errors' and should be sacked, and the float that shadow Chancellor Ed Balls is behind fratricidal criticisms of the leader are internally more damaging.

After a few days of thinking through the ramifications of Stephen's withdrawal from his hosting role, it occurred to me late yesterday that he would have to be replaced. Who would the party ask? I have no idea, but Jo Brand, long-time Labour supporter, has previously hosted some events. Jo, who is as fine a person as she is witty a comedian, had asked me at Sandi Toksvig's reaffirmation of vows if what she had heard about the party and me was true. I said it probably was. Yesterday was a good time to fill her in on the details.

This morning I receive an email from Jo, saying:

> I am so sorry to hear of the way you have been treated. A Labour Party that behaves like that is not really one that I recognise.
>
> I have written to Iain McNicol expressing my disgust at your treatment.
>
> I have withdrawn my subscription and intend not to support them again unless you tell me that this has somehow been satisfactorily resolved.
>
> My very best wishes to you,
>
> Jo.

What a woman! Go, Jo!

---

22 JUNE 2014

I do something foolish today. I get even angrier than normal.

Getting mad is a daily occurrence during this ordeal. I have rages against the police and CPS about four times a day. But this time I get mad externally, not internally. This is not in character. It looks and feels odd.

Especially with someone like Neil Kinnock. I have known Neil for over a quarter of a century and proudly campaigned for him to become Prime Minister. This may sound strange to any tabloid journalist who has earned a few meals disparaging Kinnock because he is Welsh, has red hair and is not a male model. But I felt, and still feel, that Neil Kinnock has done more for democracy than anyone else in Britain during the forty-four years I have lived here. It was he who made the Labour Party electable again after it had become a fringe organisation with no hope of being voted into power. Britain had effectively become a one-party state, and praise be to the man who made it a viable democracy again.

Sunday morning is the time of the week when I have always been at my most fragile. It is to the week what Christmas is to the year: that part of the calendar when our normal supports have been removed and we are on our own. Christopher sleeps in this morning, so I am at the mercy of unfiltered emotions when I happen to read that Neil Kinnock has defended Ed Miliband.

I lose it and fire off a furious email to the former Labour leader. I tell him that Labour is now on the wrong side of justice, supporting the show trials and offering a political role to Keir Starmer. I explain to Neil that he was personally still in the highest echelons of my respect and affection, but that I cannot read his praise of Ed Miliband without taking exception.

I copy Christopher in on this tirade, since he cannot vet it before I send it. Whoops. Maybe I should have waited. Chris is upset, feeling that I have made a mistake. He thinks that so far I have played my game correctly, keeping all my darkest emotions to myself and only expressing myself to key individuals at useful moments. Now I have gone wide. There is a chance that the email will circulate among the Labour leadership and that it might attempt to strike back at me. After we complete our Sunday bowling, with one game in which we both perform above our averages and a disastrous second game in which we both set low scores for the quarter, Chris suggests I send a second email to Neil, an apology. I should express regret that I have lost my cool and make it clear that my email is not part of a wider campaign to badmouth Miliband. After all, for all Kinnock knows, I might be sending negative posts to numerous people.

My husband is right. I send a follow-up email. With Stephen Fry, Jo Brand, Jude Kelly and heaven knows who else expressing their disappointment at my treatment by the party, the current leadership might well think I am attempting some sort of revenge. It has no way of knowing that the present sequence of events was initiated by a mischievous member of the Labour inner circle and that I have been amazed to watch it take flight on its own power. As I say to Neil in my second correspondence, 'I am now one of those rare celebrities, one who does not want any publicity at all.'

---

23 JUNE 2014

Today is our second anniversary. It was on 23 June 2012 that Christopher and I successfully bucked that year's rainy season and had our civil partnership at Le Manoir aux Quat'Saisons on what turned out to be a dry and warm day. We return to Great Milton today for an anniversary lunch. This time, the weather is perfect.

Chris is taken by a sculpture of a stag and a deer and has us pose by it while his camera snaps a shot on a timer. On return to London, he posts it on his Facebook page with the line from our wedding vows taken from the song 'All the Way': 'Through the good or lean years, and for all the in-between years, come what may'. He gets twenty 'likes' in the first twenty-one minutes. For somebody who is not Beyoncé, this is pretty good.

The Manoir team are on form. The meal is delicious. It is more than delicious. It is a visual and gustatory triumph. At one point Chris sighs and says, 'These are delicious comics.' For this is how I am paying for this anniversary treat: not with funds from my rapidly shrinking British accounts, but with my American debit card, which draws from the New York account into which I have been putting the receipts from sales of vintage comic books and art. (Readers who work for Inland Revenue should not get excited at this point: these sales are carefully recorded in my tax returns.)

We return home permanently happy and temporarily fat. Among the emails awaiting me is one from Lord Kinnock, who has digested my two letters of the previous day. His balanced reply is a model of taste and temper that manages to defend both me and Ed Miliband. Neil understands that politics is not my main interest at the moment and that I am not engaged in a campaign to discredit the current leader. He wishes me well and looks forward to the day when I am beyond suspicion and working for the party again.

Stephen Fry calls. The poor man is obviously suffering stress on my behalf. He is experiencing what basketball buffs would call a 'full-court press' from the Labour Party, seeking to have him reconsider his decision to step down from hosting the gala dinner on 9 July. It has been mentioned to him that Charlie Falconer offered me the hands of understanding and possible legal advice late last year. Tessa Jowell has now drawn the assignment of whispering sweet nothings into Stephen's ear, although what dear Tessa, with whom I have no quarrel, has to do with the matter is beyond me. Stephen and I talk frankly, and I assure him that I am removed from politics at this time and don't really care what decision he makes, as long as it is informed – which it now is. I point out that, if he did wish to host the dinner, he could use it as the occasion to make relevant remarks. He seems to think this is a possible solution. Fry floats the idea that perhaps he can get 'face time' with Harriet Harman. At the least, we finish the conversation with Stephen knowing he has my blessing to do whatever he feels is right.

24 JUNE 2014

Rarely do I have cause to praise an editorial page piece in *The Sun*, but I do now. Yesterday evening I clicked on a link sent by *Counterpoint* producer

Paul Bajoria. It directs me to a Guardian Media piece about a column in *The Sun*. It amuses me that Paul knows about what is going on in *The Sun* only because he reads *The Guardian*.

As Roy Greenslade headlines, 'The Sun's Trevor Kavanagh rails against the iniquitous use of "police bail"'. In a piece that takes up two-thirds of the editorial page, Kavanagh, managing editor of *The Sun*, writes, 'It is not justice to wait years for trial.' A cartoon depicts Lady Justice, customarily standing on top of the Old Bailey, seated, her blindfold removed, having a sandwich and a cup of tea and saying, 'Be right with you…'

Claiming in italics that 'today, in modern Britain, an estimated 57,000 people are languishing on police bail for up to three and a half years without trial', Kavanagh inveighs against the uniquely British practice of endless bail. He points out, again in italics, that 'the question here is whether justice is being served or abused by the indefensible gap between arrest and trial. Or whether there should be a time limit. It is an eternal truth that justice deferred is justice denied.'

The man is hotting up. He leads to a powerful conclusion:

This is a growing crisis and needs to be solved with a statute of limitations, a fixed limit of three months between arrest and charge.

We must clear out the overly political and grotesquely inefficient Crown Prosecution Service, which has become a law unto itself, and speed up the administration of justice.

As Roy Greenslade points out, part of what Trevor Kavanagh is saying is raised for institutionally convenient reasons. 'He has in mind several colleagues and ex-colleagues who are among the worst cases because they have spent more than six months – and some up to thirty months – on bail without being charged.' These are journalists caught up in what the public refers to as 'the phone-hacking scandal'. But the *Guardian* columnist supports the *Sun* managing editor – you're unlikely to see that statement again – and says, 'I am also sympathetic to their plight.' He then points out something that I have previously mentioned:

> The UK system of arrests without charge baffles Americans. The system of 'police bail' is also extraordinary when measured against custom and practice in many other jurisdictions.
>
> It may be said that this has long been the situation and that journalists didn't worry about it until they experienced this unjust procedure. Now it has become something of a cause célèbre.
>
> Well, there may be something to that. But so what? The substantive point is that it is manifestly unfair for people to live for months on end with an axe swinging over them.

Around midday there is closure on at least one long-running phone-hacking case. Andy Coulson has been found guilty and Rebekah Brooks acquitted.

A bizarre interview with Prime Minister David Cameron has appeared on the BBC website which is almost the mirror image of Jeremy Paxman asking Michael Howard the same question twelve times in the vain hope of getting an acceptable answer. This time Cameron gives basically the same answer three times: 'I am extremely sorry I employed him. It was the wrong decision and I am clear about that.' All the while he never addresses the real issue, which is the extent of the influence of Rupert Murdoch in his government. What is more scandalous is that the reporter does not raise this obvious subject.

I suddenly realise that the resolution of this case might be a positive sign for me. I was arrested within hours of the beginning of the Brooks trial. Now that she is a free woman, might I be cleared within, if not hours, days?

25 JUNE 2014

At the end of the day I catch up with Matthew Engel's *Financial Times* commentary on the *News of the World* verdicts. He notes that the influence of Rupert Murdoch over national life 'is reaching a natural conclusion as he gets older and his empire more like a normal corporation', then asks, 'But will anything else change?' He answers his own question:

'Forget it. Politicians will cultivate potentates of the press as long as they perceive them to be powerful. Police and journalists will meet in bars and have deep discussions because it makes sense for them to do so … Will anyone care? Hardly. We are all guilty.'

In the evening I receive an email from my devoted friend Andrew Fallaize giving me a heads up that Radio 4 is going to devote the night's edition of *The Moral Maze* to the issue of anonymity for rape suspects. He realises that it might not be the kind of programme I want to hear at this time, but that I would at least want to know it was being transmitted.

Andrew is right on both counts. I tune in. Michael Buerk gives his customary even-handed solemn introduction and four panellists present introductory views. Nigel Evans gives a very calm, first-person account of what it is like to live as a publicly accused, ultimately acquitted suspect. A victim of a terrible rape then gives her testimony.

It is here that I have to stop listening. In the midst of her harrowing story, the brave woman states that very few accusations of sexual offences are false. This statement goes unchallenged by the others on the programme. If you are discussing the advisability of anonymity for sex abuse suspects you should mention that there is a chance they are being wrongly accused. Is no one in this society interested in slander any more? Can we all just accuse each other of the vilest crimes with impunity?

---

26 JUNE 2014

Today's news is dominated by one subject: Jimmy Savile. Three years after his death, he is still topic A.

'Jimmy Savile NHS abuse victims aged five to seventy-five', the BBC headline reports. The review into his conduct in twenty-eight National Health Service hospitals reveals what the Department of Health calls 'depraved activities' that make 'shocking reading'. The most detailed sections are devoted to Leeds General Infirmary and Broadmoor.

The BBC begins its summary of the Leeds investigation with the line 'Savile had a well-known fixation with the dead and the report contains allegations he posed for photographs and performed sex acts on corpses in the hospital mortuary.'

Wes Butters, who presents the mid-morning show on BBC Leeds, phones me and begins his conversation with the words 'You were right!' He is referring to my appearance on *The Nicky Campbell Show* on 5 Live in October 2012, in which I mentioned a tabloid journalist's boast that everybody working for his newspaper knew the Jimmy Savile necrophilia story. Nicky replied: 'That particularly lurid accusation that you have just brought to people's attention is one that has not been in the public domain.' Today I send Nicky an email with the simple words, 'It's in the public domain now!'

--- 27 JUNE 2014 ---

Brian Paddick, Baron of Brixton, wants me to know that he has made a speech in the House of Lords calling into question the practice of interminable bail without charge. He also tells me that this is in the Liberal Democrats' 'pre-manifesto' and may or may not make it to the final document. I am as grateful as ever to Brian for his concern. He has invited me to lunch at the Lords on Tuesday.

'Let's stir them up,' he says.

--- 28 JUNE 2014 ---

I don't want to say I'm missed at Obit Central, but…

I wake up this morning to read the sad but anticipated news of the death of the musical giant Bobby Womack, who wrote the Rolling Stones's first number one, 'It's All Over Now', and made numerous classic R&B recordings including 'That's the Way I Feel About Cha', 'Lookin' for a Love' and 'If You Think You're Lonely Now'. Bobby wrote the Wilson Pickett hit 'I'm in Love', to which Christopher and I walked down the aisle. Sigh. Chris and I hug. We have lost a member of the wedding.

I click on the BBC television tribute and learn that, late in his career, Bobby Womack teamed up with one of his brothers to form Womack and Womack. What? After gender reassignment surgery? Brother Cecil's partner in Womack and Womack was his wife Linda! It really is time to promote a next generation of go-to eulogisers. In this case, Trevor Nelson or a hybrid of Pete Tong and Zane Lowe could have offered valuable insights.

The BBC website asks, 'Have you met Bobby Womack or did you know him?'

Well, yes. I still have the tape of our Womack segment of *The Other Side of the Tracks*, recorded at his home in Los Angeles … but the BBC wouldn't want to know about that right now.

Today marks the completion of eight months on bail.

What have I learned?

I have learned what really matters in life. The first is life itself. When it is light, get up. When it is dark, sleep. When it is sunny, go outside.

Love your partner. REALLY love your partner. This is the person who truly loves you and makes great sacrifices for you. Without him or her, you will go crazy.

Discover the things that sustain you. As intellectually respectable as reading Proust and playing classical piano or as disreputable as working on acrostic puzzles and listening to 'Street Fighting Man' every day, not to mention walking three miles every Friday for a grilled cheese sandwich and reading Mike Mignola comic books – whatever gets you through the day … will.

Go to the gym, or take equivalent exercise. It's amazing how wonderful los-ing half a pound will make you feel when the world around you is out of shape.

Surround yourself with friends. They will keep you sane. It's amazing how wonderful maintaining sanity will make you feel when the world around you has gone stark raving mad.

Every day now my thoughts come back to the Bauhaus artist I inter-viewed when I was a teenager.

'I was in a concentration camp. My wife died there.'

If he could prevail, I, who am less provoked, can, too.

---

30 JUNE 2015

Nigel Evans has called. I return the message and learn that the *Telegraph* has reported that Ben Sullivan's accuser admitted she spoke falsely.

Jennifer goes out and returns with a physical copy of the newspaper. I am treated to Facebook exchanges between Sullivan and a female student 'who cannot be named for legal reasons'. Having had consensual sex with the Oxford Union president, she says, among other self-incriminating things, 'I was drunk, crying and half dressed, no one knew that I'd just got back together with my boyfriend – that's how people got the wrong idea.

'My boyfriend didn't find out until someone told him. He then broke up with me. I still feel so, so guilty about cheating on him.'

The *Telegraph* continues:

> When asked whether she believed the rumours were true, she added:
> 'I know it must be absolutely awful for you but it's not something I
> wanted people to find out – being known as a cheat is no fun. And no,
> of course they're not. I was far too drunk, that's it.'

This adds fuel to Nigel's fire for not naming sex suspects until they are charged and granting equal anonymity to accuser and accused.

Rolf Harris has been found guilty on all counts. Inevitably, and self-ishly, I take great interest in noting that his day for sentencing is Friday. This is the working date before my rebail day.

I email Kate Goold, pointing out this coincidence, and note it was consistent with Christopher's observation of 25 April that a conviction in the Rolf trial would allow the Metropolitan Police to drop my case the next working day. I tell her that I am under the impression that Yewtree success in the Harris case cannot at this late moment lead to an emboldened determination to prosecute in mine. Is this correct? She replies that the CPS has to rule on what it has.

Now I have to do something, anything, to avoid obsessing on the anticipated decision. I prepare to go to the gym.

I put my shorts on, but my visit to the gym is delayed. Shortly after the Rolf Harris verdict, I am informed that I have been rebailed yet again, this time to 15 September. This in itself is not surprising. Rebailing is what the Met and CPS do. What disgusts me is the reason given. The CPS has directed the Met to re-interview my original accuser, 'the victim Primary'.

It is now obvious that they do not have a case against me. If they believed they did, they would have been legally required to charge me by now. So my accuser gets a second bite of the cherry? I am flabbergasted at this new low in the British legal system. He didn't play his part in the play properly and now gets a second performance? I realise more than ever that this witch-hunt is results-driven, not based on the merits of cases. Somebody wants to convict me and will do anything they can to achieve that end, despite the injustice required. Like Dolly Parton's Jolene, they are being cruel just because they can.

I phone back Nigel Evans, who must be surprised to see my name pop up on his caller ID so shortly after we have spoken. He is enraged by an aspect of this rebail I had not considered. How long does it take to interview one person? They could still do it now and get it finished by the original bail date of 7 July. They don't need an extension to perform their stated task. Even the longest interview in history will not take two and a half months. As Evans eloquently points out, that's two and a half months' more of loss of earnings, severe stress, and damage to reputation. After all, some people will believe that if the inquiry is taking this long there must be something to it.

I reluctantly instruct Jennifer to start de-framing some of my comic art for shipment to America. If I'm not earning from employment, I have to get funds somehow. This time it's goodbye to two Chester Gould *Dick Tracy* originals, a Marjorie Buell *Little Lulu*, a romance splash page by Alex Toth, a *Superman* panel by Wayne Boring, a *Sandman* page by Colleen Doran, a *Smokey Stover* Sunday by Bill Holman, a couple of EC cover watercolours by Marie Severin, Murphy Anderson's re-creation of the cover to the first issue of *The Shadow*, the Christmas Eve 1922 *Wee Winnie Winkle* page by Martin Branner, and a Second World War *Congo Bill* splash by Fred Ray. Perhaps this can be advertised as the Crown Prosecution Service pedigree collection.

---

2 JULY 2014

Jude Kelly calls at 8.15. She had held a meeting on next year's Women of the World Festival at the Southbank Centre. Harriet Harman had been at this non-partisan event. After the meeting, Jude mentioned a couple of the issues concerning me to Harriet. A female assistant of Ed Miliband joined in to say that Tessa Jowell has already called me.

Huh? Thirteen years ago, yes, but now?

These Labour Party misstatements have become more and more surreal. Miliband tells Stephen Fry that someone is going to call me. A party official tells Jo Brand that somebody has called me. An apparatchik tells Jude Kelly that Tessa Jowell has called me. None of these statements have any relation to reality. Why are they even talking about me? I couldn't care less. It is clear that they are only interested in retaining the patronage of Stephen, Jo and Jude.

A good deal of today is spent replying to emails of support coming in after I notified my friends of the latest rebail. As this process goes on, I accumulate more and more friends taking regular active interest in my plight. This is 95 per cent of the time beautiful and buoying. The other 5 per cent, however, is draining, because I have to keep them all informed of the latest developments. Last night I sent email explanations of my re-re-re-rebail to a few individuals and groups like 'my friends from Hyde Park Square', 'my American friends' and so forth.

---

3 JULY 2014

I have been off the scene with *America's Greatest Hits* for eight months, but I haven't missed much. *Billboard* reports that in the first half of this year, the soundtrack to *Frozen* was the only album to sell over a million copies, moving a healthy 2.7 million. This is the third year in a row in which only one album has exceeded the million mark in the first six months. 'Happy' by Pharrell Williams is the bestselling single of the year to date, selling 5.6 million. Twelve songs have shifted over 2 million copies this year, compared to thirteen last year. Digital album sales are down 15 per cent on last year and singles are down 13 per cent. Revenues from music sales continue to decline as consumers turn to streaming. People in the trade don't seem to want to face another obvious major factor, which is that there is currently no transcendent star who excites everyone at the same time in the traditions of Sinatra, Elvis, the Beatles and Michael Jackson.

Brian Paddick is first on the email list today, clocking in at 8.08. He has managed to speak to a senior Liberal Democrat staffer in Parliament. Sadly, the former schoolmate of Secondary cannot recollect my accuser. So deflates another balloon.

By utter coincidence, Jude Kelly, having been told about Tessa Jowell's alleged conversation with me, has now run into Tessa herself. The former Cabinet minister, with whom I was always on good speaking terms, says she is willing to talk to me now, but she did not want to call direct in case I did not wish to speak to her. Jude says it should be Ed Miliband who talks to me. Jowell excuses herself for a moment and confers with an aide of Miliband, who says, 'That will not be possible.'

---

4 JULY 2014

I finish *The Way by Swann's*, Volume 1 of *In Search of Lost Time*. I have loved this book. I have never read anything like it. I have marvelled at the change of perspective from first person to third and back again, gasped at the audacity of sentences so long they could almost come from the last chapter of *Ulysses*, and admired how sensory sensations are evoked by prose. I have grimaced noticing how Proust, a closet case of his time, sometimes uses heterosexual characters to have experiences or express sentiments that almost certainly were drawn from same-sex relationships, even though the author also dares to incorporate gay and lesbian characters in the novel.

Most of all, I am in awe of his success in communicating the power of beautiful music. His readers will know that by inventing Vinteuil, as Alex Ross states, 'Proust ventured into an esoteric subcategory of fiction – stories about composers who exist only in the pages of books.' Swann is captivated, indeed, transported, by 'a little phrase' in Vinteuil's sonata, and in a sublime four pages Proust is able to sum up better than any music critic I have ever read the profound effect music can have on a human being. I am such a human being; music has affected me in this way; Proust has described the experience.

Stephen Fry and I exchange emails concerning l'affaire du Labour. I conclude an update on my legal situation with, 'Remember that I really don't mind if you host the Labour dinner, as long as you make some sort of appropriate remark on policy to someone.'

Fry replies, 'Be assured I shall make that remark, Paul. I will say that if the Labour Party doesn't stand for justice, social AND individual, then it stands for nothing.'

It has been five days since I learned of my latest rebail, and I keep remembering more names of people whom I should tell the news. One is Peter Straker. Since I have been told that the police have not followed through on their request to interview him after he called them back, I figure it is safe to phone him. Whoops! He was called three days ago by Officer Four, still desiring an interview. No one is any the wiser as to why puzzled Peter has been chosen. When he expressed his disbelief at being included in the process, Four would only say, 'We just want to eliminate you', which seems like an extraordinary verb to use in any context. Peter indicated he did not wish to be interviewed in his home, and an alternate venue has not yet been selected.

Maybe the alternate venue for Peter Straker could be a motor-racing track! Over the weekend, I received the startling news that Brad Spurgeon has finally, after all these months, been interviewed. He was spoken to while in this country covering the Formula 1 British Grand Prix for the *New York Times*. Keeping things kosher, he gives me no indication of either what was asked or what he said in reply.

Thinking of Brad can't help but make me think of some choice oldies, such as 'Go Your Own Way' by Fleetwood Mac. He was my lodger in Hyde Park Square so long ago that, when he visited Iran, the Shah was still in power. He has been as startled as anyone at the eccentric accusations made against me so many years later. Though he signs his statement on the day he has given it, he has yet to agree to appear if the case goes to court. I can't blame him. Not only is the whole thing too fantastic for the average person to take in, Brad is in the unusual position of knowing both my co-accused and I, and may not wish to be dragged into what is bound to be a lurid spectacle.

8 JULY 2014

I should say little today, because everyone else says so much. Today we get the long-awaited explosion of the Westminster paedophilia scandal. We could tell it was coming when Leon Brittan was recently named by newspapers in connection with two separate events. That was the build-up to the big one. The long-festering 1980s story is now a public matter.

It is a relief to me that there is finally a sex scandal about which I am clueless. I don't know any of the principal politicians, unless one counts having to get off the TV-am sofa to make room for Cyril Smith as 'knowing'.

In the afternoon, I pay a visit to Tim Rice, who is across the street in a dressing room at the Royal Festival Hall awaiting rehearsal of a show paying tribute to his lyrics. He has enjoyed a comment made on *Newsnight* by a speaker responding to a woman who claimed that the entire nation was gripped by the trials of celebrities.

'No, it isn't,' Tim relates the reply. 'You are, and the media are, but the general public are not.'

I mention the parliamentary scandal, knowing his London home is in Barnes, site of the Elm Guest House at the centre of the scandal.

'I am willing to testify you have been wearing a chastity belt for the last forty years,' I tell him in jest.

'You won't have to. I didn't move to Barnes until the mid-'90s.'

I return home, leaving Tim to his apotheosis. I am staggered to meet in the lobby the grandson of the outstanding lyricist Don Black, like Tim an occasional collaborator with Andrew Lloyd Webber. I know Don's sons but have never met one of his grandchildren, let alone one with a beard.

Within an hour, I bizarrely 'complete the set' when I receive a phone call from Lloyd Webber himself. He has had lunch with Lewis Carnie of Radio 2 and has been horrified at the executive's tales of my torment. In our conversation, Andrew is sincerely and repeatedly repentant that he has not called to offer his support earlier. He invites me to lunch at the Delaunay, which these days is just about the best form of support I can think of.

I awake to find an email from Neil Gaiman, who is briefly back in his home country. Neil and I once thought it amusing that he had been born in Britain and moved to America, while I took the opposite route. It was as if we had been parts of a trade between sports teams. Now I don't think it's so funny. I'd love to go back to the States with him. The *New York Times* bestselling writer has met with Stephen Fry and, having been informed of my case, has sent his support.

Gaiman has written, 'You were kind and supportive to me over the years, and I am appreciative and have not forgotten.' This is a good guy. What he says is true: I presented the first Radio 4 dramatisation of one of his scripts when we 'staged' a brief section of *Sandman* on *Kaleidoscope* back in the 1990s. Nearly twenty years later, he rated a full six-part adaptation of *Neverwhere* on the network with James McAvoy, Natalie Dormer, Benedict Cumberbatch and Christopher Lee. *Neverwhere* had the names and the airtime, but at least *Kaleidoscope* got there first.

Cycling in the gym later, I recall that the Labour gala dinner is being held at this very moment. I shrug and keep pedalling. To misquote Lesley Gore, it's not my party, and I can't cry if I want to. Instead I have my own gala dinner of smoked salmon with mozzarella and avocado, followed by cherries and vanilla ice cream. I then watch Argentina defeat the Netherlands in a penalty shoot-out. I've probably had the better evening.

Just before I go to bed, I receive an email from Stephen. He tells me that during the course of his remarks, generally supportive of Labour, he has made pointed comments about the current state of British justice. This was an incredibly brave thing to do, seeing as Keir Starmer was in the room.

'When I reclaimed my seat next to Ed he was furious with me,' Fry writes. 'Neil Kinnock came up and hugged me for saying what I said. So I left early without reciting the closing speech I was booked to do.'

What a hero! I write back to Stephen:

'Thank you, Stephen, for fighting the good fight.

'Thanks, too, for mentioning my situation to Neil Gaiman. I received two emails from him today. This is the first time in my life I have ever received an email from an author on a day that I have bought one of his books. This never happened with Proust.'

─────────────── 10 JULY 2014 ───────────────

I get up and am still performing the Trilogy of Cleanliness when I have to leave the bathroom. The phone is ringing. It is Jude Kelly. Her partner Andrew, boating off Greece, has read about the Labour dinner.

This is the Information Age in a nutshell. When I was in Greece years ago, you couldn't read a newspaper unless it was a hard copy, you had to be on land to buy it, and it took a day or two for it to get there. Now Andrew is reading today's *Guardian* online while afloat. The conclusion of Ben Quinn's article reports that 'Jay Stoll, public affairs director at the Jewish Leadership Council, tweeted: "It's all gone bizarre as Stephen Fry launches into speech on Operation Yewtree. Talks about necessary belief in legal system."'

Christopher has received an email from someone who was present at the gala, confirming that Stephen made barbed comments relevant to my case. The guest reports that he did not name me, but 'everyone' knew he was talking about me. Of course, 'everyone' may be the kind of exaggeration that an elite makes about its own membership, and there may have been scores of people present who hadn't a clue what Stephen was talking about, but it's nice to know that the people who should know knew.

I receive another email from Fry, responding to my message about Neil Gaiman. In his, he refers to the other Neil, the one we have known even longer than Gaiman, Baron Kinnock:

'The hug of appreciation and understanding from Neil made up for it all. But it made me miss the old days and standards so much.'

I look forward to lunch with Andrew Lloyd Webber at the Delaunay. I have an insane attachment to the restaurant's chicken schnitzel with a side of pickled cucumber, and the prospect of the combination has me salivating. Andrew phones to move our appointment back by half an hour, as he is attending his daughter's school sports day, at which she is receiving an award. I am heartened by this emphasis on family, even by the man who is now officially called … pardon me while I Google this … either Baron Lloyd-Webber or the Right Honourable the Lord Lloyd-Webber Kt. How interesting is this? 'Lloyd-Webber' is hyphenated when Andrew is referred to by title, but in real life 'Lloyd Webber' never carries a hyphen. I offer to be Paul Gam-Baccini, but it's probably a little late for that now.

Andrew is clearly sincere when he apologises for not having gotten in touch sooner. It is genuinely odd that we have not talked since my arrest, since we have known each other for forty-one years and run into each other every few months. Before he can make a couple of helpful suggestions, he excuses himself to visit the gentlemen's room. He returns rather quickly via the front desk, where he whispers something to the maitre d' before coming back to the table. It turns out there has been an incident. Someone is seriously ill. Going back there a quarter-hour later, Lloyd Webber admires the way that Chris Corbin and team have dealt with the situation efficiently without disturbing diners, but is slightly shaken that he has witnessed a genuine medical emergency. The Baron of Sydmonton resolves his personal needs by using the disabled facilities.

During the course of the afternoon, Kate Goold writes to inform me that she has received a response to her protest at the length of time until my next rebail. Officer One has written that 'the interview is in the process of being arranged and I will let you know as and when it is arranged.

'I have spoken to the reviewing lawyer at the CPS and she does not consent to her details being passed at this time.'

In other words, I am not allowed to know who is in charge of my case at this time. Every time I detect a glimmer of hope, communication from the Metropolitan Police makes creation itself go dark.

─────────── 11 JULY 2014 ───────────

I was taken to lunch today by Lewis Carnie and Radio 2 weekend editor Mike Hanson. Because I have been speaking to Lewis after every rebail, he has followed my case closely. I find myself telling Hanson things Carnie already knows, as if Mike has come in during Act IV of *Hamlet*. Both are completely understanding and supportive.

In the evening, I mull over the aspect of this latest rebail that has everyone befuddled: why should it take two and a half months to interview one person? I recall my case officer's choice of words in saying that the police had to 'arrange' the interview. Could it be that Primary does not live in London?

─────────── 12 JULY 2014 ───────────

Today, Christopher is going to Scotland for the T in the Park festival. He will return to London in three days. His boyhood friend Adam, a leading music promoter in New Zealand, is in the UK for a holiday and has obtained 'access all areas' passes. Chris is ecstatic at the prospect of seeing Ben Howard tonight and the Arctic Monkeys tomorrow.

I support the trip, but I can't help but be slightly apprehensive about it. The three days will be the longest period I have been on my own at home since my arrest. I never wish to be a baby, but I don't know how I will respond to being alone with the anxieties recently imposed upon me. I have filled my dance card with social engagements to keep me diverted, but Christopher is the glue that has been holding me together, and I don't yet know what it will be like to be without his company for three days. We will find out together.

─────────── 13 JULY 2014 ───────────

I make an unsought appearance in the *Mail on Sunday*.

'Fry stuns Labour gala as he hits out at sex abuse investigation', the page-nine headline screams. In smaller print, the subhead yells, 'Miliband rebukes TV star after he attacks former DPP', which is a concise way of saying that three people have been involved in an exchange of words. And what words! Even though Stephen had told me via email that he had made relevant remarks that upset the Labour leader, I had no idea what they were. Now I read that, after reminding the audience that the 799-year-old Magna Carta is the basis of constitutional rights, he has 'complained that less than 50 per cent of those people held under Yewtree have been found guilty and that those who make false accusations should be prosecuted'. Fry has pointed out that Keir Starmer was in the room, and then, according to the newspaper's informant, spoke 'about how the law should be toughened up to deter people from inventing claims about sex abuse'. The unnamed guest added, 'Ed looked as if he'd swallowed a wasp.'

Stephen has been both considerate and skilful in avoiding mentioning me by name. However, the *Mail on Sunday* knows full well whose case has inspired the speech. Fortunately, although the publication mentions me by name twice, it does so absolutely accurately, stating that after my arrest I was 'released on bail' and have 'never been charged with any offence'. It adds, 'Fry, 56, is understood to be infuriated that the failure to charge Mr Gambaccini has received significantly less publicity than his arrest, leaving an unfair stain on his character.'

The newspaper uses the opportunity to mention the famous people involved in Yewtree, acknowledging that 'cases were dropped against comedians Freddie Starr, Jim Davidson and Jimmy Tarbuck after months of destructive publicity'. It also throws in the criticism that Scotland Yard has faced over the phone-hacking scandal, with the key line, 'At least thirty journalists remain on bail, some of whom have been in that position – unable to resume their careers – for more than two years.'

Of course, Starmer and Miliband are asked for their responses to Fry's attack. The *Mail on Sunday* quotes 'a source close to Mr Starmer', which is often newspaper language for Mr Starmer himself. It is no surprise that the Labour Party darling and his close friends offer a rebuttal. What is significant is that 'a spokesman for Ed Miliband' goes on the record as saying, 'Ed Miliband fully supports the work of Operation Yewtree and has made clear all along that our thoughts should be with the victims.'

That's it, in as clear a statement of policy one could ever make. Ed Miliband supports the witch-hunt. He knows of and supports my unjustified arrest and my nearly one year of psychological torture by the Metropolitan Police and Crown Prosecution Service. Ed Miliband supports arrests without any incriminating evidence. He supports allegations by people who do not even know the person they are accusing. Ed Miliband and his Labour Party officially support the recent mutation of the British justice system from the centuries-old, internationally respected, objective, evidence-based system to the subjective rumour-and-accusation-based system.

Having seen that *The Independent* picked up on a *Mail on Sunday* story without giving credit, a typical rewrite ploy used by almost all British newspapers, I wonder if any other publication has printed a variation of this one. I Google 'Stephen Fry Labour gala' and am confronted with something I had not expected. The *Daily Mail* has already posted its Monday rejoinder to its Sunday sister's article.

'YOU ARE WRONG, MR FRY!' screams its headline. 'Comedian condemned by campaigners after his "rant" attacking sex abuse inquiry', says the subhead.

The *Mail*, which has famously hostile relations with my old friend, leads the story with the sentence 'Stephen Fry faced a furious backlash last night…', teasing the reader with the prospect of full-scale bitchiness at 100 paces. In fact, the 'furious backlash' comes not from 'campaigners' but from a single complainant, a gentleman of whom I have not previously heard and thus have no impression. This is typical British newspaper practice: finding one person who will speak a publication's opinions or, if the paper has no views on a subject, stir for the sake of a good, circulation-increasing story.

I do not recognise the name of the children's charity that the speaker represents. This is not to disparage the organisation or its cause. After all, I have always supported the NSPCC and been happy to do my small bit for Children in Need. This gentleman's views, however, are extreme.

'Alison Saunders and other prosecutors deserve a medal to "dare" to prosecute people who are rich and famous,' he is said to have said. 'If it is a witch hunt to go after people who rape and abuse our children, whenever it may have happened, then I'm all for it.'

Under ordinary circumstances, I would roll my eyes heavenward and move on. Actually, under ordinary circumstances, I would be reading the *Comic Book Price Guide* or some other more edifying publication. But I can't help but notice these words. They are printed only one column away from a picture of me.

I've never thought of myself in terms of 'people who rape and abuse our children', and I certainly don't want other people to. It is a completely irrelevant subject for me to be in the same room as. I might as well be one column away from a discussion of the virtues of Marmite. I have absolutely nothing to do with it. How did this lunacy ever happen? I never talk about Marmite and I have never had anything to do with the subject my photo now adorns.

It's 1 a.m. The virus passes through my system. This story, I convince myself, is not going to bring forth hysterical bandwagoners. I can relax my guard and fall asleep. The next thing I know, it's 7 a.m.

---

14 JULY 2014

I have a delightful dinner with Kid and Gudrun Jensen. We discuss the bittersweet possibility, perhaps now a probability, that it will never be safe for me to live in Great Britain. I may well move back to New York.

'But that wouldn't be such a tragedy,' I smile to Gudrun, pointing at Kid. 'The original reason we came here is over. The Beatles broke up!'

Kid smiles in agreement. 'That's right!'

───────────────── 15 JULY 2014 ─────────────────

Christopher has returned and we have been joyfully reunited. I have given myself brownie points for having lived three days on my own with the sinister soundtrack of Yewtree playing in the background all weekend. It is hard to ignore for more than a few minutes at a time. Having it in my mind is like listening to *Metal Machine Music* for a year.

I tell Chris of my half-hour conversation with Kate Goold yesterday. She continues to be deeply distressed about the latest two-and-a-half-month rebail period. She has considered the wisdom of a judicial review. I have as well and have concluded it would not be worth trying to arrange at this time. My objection is not financial, since I have friends who will help me with large legal fees, but the time period. By the time we achieve a judicial review, the rebail period will be over. If we knew that in September I would be rebailed yet again to late autumn, it would be worth undertaking, but it would be £20,000 down the Swanee if we scheduled a judicial review for October that then proved unnecessary.

I have told Kate my conclusion that the Metropolitan Police probably advised against charging me when they handed the CPS my file in February and that it is probably the CPS who have been faffing around ever since. She agrees. My theory is based on the fact that it is the CPS who keep telling the Met to do this and that and this and that and are prolonging the ordeal. Her reasoning is that her communications with Officer One give her the impression that he is distancing himself from what he has to tell her. I say that the reason I have been rebailed two and a half months this time is that the CPS are probably taking their summer holidays.

The pause on the line is pregnant.

'I agree,' she says.

17 JULY 2014

Yesterday Christopher and I journeyed to the Norfolk village of Aylsham, where his parents live. It is a joy to be in the country during a heat wave. Thirty degrees Celsius is not much to write home about in New York, but in England it always gets welcome attention.

Today we spend an afternoon at the beach front in Cromer. I haven't seen a beach this long since Chris went surfing in Biarritz.

Our trip to Cromer has a sweet interlude. As we walk on the pier, numerous people ask me to pose for photos with them and sign autographs to them. News of my disgrace has not reached them. If it has, they do not believe it. Whenever I contemplate a future outside of Britain, I am reminded that there is a reservoir of affection here that I cannot and do not see on a daily basis. Obviously people who do not recognise me or do not like my work do not approach me and do not care about my future, but I feel some sort of responsibility to the audience that would like me to resume my work when and if it becomes possible.

Back in Aylsham, Chris and I take advantage of the warm weather to enjoy a long walk through the village and its surrounds. We note the beautiful natural location of the water mill, and feel disappointed that, although roughly half the structure has been converted into flats, the other has fallen into disrepair, with overgrown grounds. We walk down a long path that, due to a large number of stinging nettles, is treacherous for men wearing shorts. And, suddenly and to our great surprise, we find ourselves at the house of Stephen Fry's parents.

I can't believe, bearing in mind all the recent press mentioning Stephen and I in the same mouse click, that we find ourselves, on foot as if in pilgrimage, at the home of his elders. Of all the parents' houses in all the towns in all the world, we walk into theirs, or at least into their driveway. Chris and I debate whether we should ring the doorbell, but decide against it. It would be nice to tell them we were grateful that they had given birth to such a wonderful son, but what if they didn't know us from

Adam and thought we were Mormons or groupies or Jehovah's Witnesses or snooping journalists … there are too many possibilities, so we resolve to wait until our next visit. It will surely come, and we can ask Stephen to warn his family in advance.

<hr>

20 JULY 2014

I try not to write on Sundays. On the seventh day, even God rested from obsessing about Operation Yewtree. But sometimes events take over.

Today, after bowling, I emerge from Waterloo Tube Station and am tempted to check out the *Mail on Sunday* at WHSmith.

Under the subhead 'Finally, Fry gets it right', Peter Hitchens writes on his blog: 'I can't stand Stephen Fry – smug, vain, tedious Leftist that he is.' An incident at his late brother Christopher's memorial service has left bad feelings.

Hitchens proceeds:

> So it gives me no pleasure to praise him for saying at a New Labour gathering that accused persons are innocent until proven guilty. This is never more so than when the accusation is child abuse, a charge so horrible it makes people forget their duty to be just.
>
> Shame on those who have since attacked him. The presumption of innocence is never more vital than when only a few people will stand up for it. On this, we're shoulder to shoulder.

With that, I breathe deeply and return to my Sunday, preparing for house guest Darren Cheek. Shortly after he arrives, we have an unanticipated emotional moment.

I am continuing to downsize in preparation for a possible move back to New York City. Not only do I offer Darren six comic character statues to be divided between his girlfriend's children, I present him with two of my three remaining Cow Parade figures. As I hand over Elvis Cow and Supercow, we both choke up. Cow Parade is part of our shared history. When we were in New York during the summer of 2000, we visited as many of the novelty cow statues scattered around the city as we could. We particularly loved Cowabunga, the surfing cow, and the Street Cow Named Desire.

We pilgrimaged to the World Trade Center to see the Twin Cowers, one of which had television transmitting antennae on its head. We took the opportunity to take the lift to the top of one of the towers. Noting an airplane flying up and down the Hudson River many floors beneath us, I commented to Darren, 'I wonder if the police know about this plane.' The following year, they didn't.

For me to be willing to part with two of my three Cow Parade cows proves that deep down I really feel I might have to emigrate. Darren senses this, I sense this, and so, from the quivering of the lei around his neck, does the Elvis Cow.

21 JULY 2014

I journey to my GP to check out my heart. That sounds much worse than it is. It's just that I am absolutely determined that Yewtree will not cause me an ulcer, stroke or heart attack. I want to make sure that the slight chest pains I have occasionally had in the past couple of months are not symptomatic of failing health.

My doctor gives me an ECG, compares the result to my ECG from last year's health screen, and pronounces it 'perfect'. He also declares my blood pressure to be 'perfect'. He explains away the occasional chest pains with flashes of feeling in the fleshy part of my palm as being 'chest wall pain' that is a natural by-product of unnatural stress.

This is precisely the good news I had hoped to hear. What I am told next could not have been anticipated. My doctor has been remarkably controlled as I have told him my horror stories about the police, and now I know why. He tells me that there is an organisation in the medical profession that also pulls people out of circulation for months at a time. A doctor accused of misbehaviour can be put on ice for up to a year waiting for his case to be discussed. By the time the council has ruled, the accused will have lost many of his patients, who cannot time their illnesses to suit the availability of their doctor. My physician tells me that he knows of colleagues who have grown depressed, taken their own lives or emigrated after falling foul of this process. I leave my doctor's office feeling less alone.

22 JULY 2014

I walked past Broadcasting House yesterday en route to my doctor's. In the words of the song from *A Chorus Line*, 'I felt nothing'. It had been so long since I had been in that part of Regent Street that my main reaction was utter surprise that a Middle Eastern restaurant has been replaced by a Byron. I looked at Broadcasting House and thought not of my last appearances there, but of my original Radio 1 mentors, all now deceased, executives John Walters and Teddy Warrick, John Peel, and my other two favourite period DJs, the equally dead Kenny Everett and Alan Freeman. It is they who gave the organisation the professionalism and excitement that made me proud to be on board.

Oddly enough, in stark contrast, all my original Radio 4 mentors, Rosemary Hart, John Boundy and Paul Vaughan, are still alive, at least as of today. Was the Radio 4 lifestyle healthier? (Vaughan is hanging in at eighty-eight, which reminds me of Arthur Ferrante. Ferrante and Teicher of 'Exodus' fame were my boyhood piano-playing idols, the first people I ever asked for autographs. Arthur always claimed he wanted to live to be eighty-eight, the number of keys on a piano. He aptly made his personal exodus twelve days after he achieved that goal.)

23 JULY 2014

Chris and I will be going to his hometown of Ashby-de-la-Zouch tomorrow for two days. He is going to be an usher at the wedding of his boyhood friend Ben Pollard, who attended our own civil partnership party in 2012. It is unlikely I will have the time and opportunity to write during the next couple of days.

I will be intrigued to meet another of Christopher's schoolmates. He is now a police officer. This man has been supportive and useful to us during our ordeal, providing an insider's perspective on what Metmen might be thinking and what may be behind their superficially hostile behaviour. For example, he has pointed out that the re-interview of my accuser might not be an invitation to improve his flimsy story. It could be a challenge to tell the truth now they realise he has not been telling it.

28 JULY 2014

French and Saunders played a season at the Shaftesbury Theatre in 1990. On opening night, I went backstage to congratulate them, arriving at the same time as Lenny Henry and just before John Cleese. When Cleese walked in, he took one look at Dawn's husband, who had been on television a great deal recently, and bellowed, 'Lenny! You should work less!'

Henry looked at me out of the corner of his eye. It was great to be greeted by name by the legendary Python, but what on earth did he mean by 'You should work less'?

Cleese explained.

'When people don't see you on TV, they don't think you're not working. They just assume they've missed the show. You don't have to work as hard as you do.'

Those words came back to me in the last few days as Christopher and I attended the wedding of his friend Ben in Leicestershire. Quite a few people approached me over the two days with affectionate and appreciative greetings, speaking warmly about their years hearing and watching my programmes. One man walking his dog by the A42 interchange at Ashby-de-la-Zouch stopped, gaped, and said, 'You're the most famous person I've ever met! What are you doing here?' After we explained we were attending a friend's marriage, he said in disbelief, 'Who's next? Shergar?'

This gentleman, and the other people who came up to me during our two-day trip, couldn't care less that I hadn't been on radio or TV recently. John Cleese was right. You don't have to be working this week for people to remember you. Maybe we should all work less.

Alison Saunders has appeared on the Andrew Marr programme.

I check the BBC website, which reports:

> Asked if celebrities involved in recent alleged historical sexual abuse cases had been pursued because of their stature, she replied, 'That's not what we are doing – I'm very clear about this.
>
> 'We are not pursuing particular types of people.
>
> 'What we are doing is reacting to people who have come forward with complaints.'

Those complaints would never have been made had the Metropolitan Police not set up a dedicated website and dedicated phone line and invited members of the public to denounce celebrities.

The website contains a clip in which Saunders uses the word 'victim' four times in thirty-seven seconds and never once uses the words 'accuser' or 'complainant'.

--- 29 JULY 2014 ---

Happy anniversary to me. It was nine months ago, at 4.38 a.m., that Christopher and I were awakened by police going around the house saying things like 'Buggery!' and 'Who are those boys?' Today I begin my tenth month on bail.

For a couple of hours in the early morning I feared I might be awake for the anniversary. I went to bed at 11.15, woke up at 12.19, and could not get back to sleep. An acrostic puzzle? Not enough to send me back to sleep. A midnight snack of a cheese straw with some Montgomery Cheddar? No postprandial doze. Some reading? No dreamland. The latest issues of *Abe Sapien, BPRD: Hell on Earth, Fables* and *Saga*? Still awake. I tried to sleep again at 2.05. No luck. At 2.19, I thought, 'I do not want to be awake for this anniversary.' I wondered if it was the pressure of the approaching hour that was keeping me up, or if I simply wasn't tired enough because I had taken a nap in the afternoon. Maybe the steam bath I had enjoyed in the early evening had somehow kept me zingy.

I wasn't having an anxiety attack – I did not feel the need to wake Christopher or call someone five hours behind in New York – I was just awake, annoyingly and persistently awake. Finally, I had a preposterous image of a friend doing something impossible and I thought, 'Ah! The beginning of the fade!' The next thing I knew it was 5.57, I listened to the Radio 4 headlines at six, and then it was 7.34.

By coincidence, this anniversary is marked by a trio of happy social occasions. I receive hospitality from three friends I have known for a total of over 100 years. After lunch at Fischer's with Charles Foster, I race home to change into shorts – it is, after all, 27 degrees today – for a visit to Kew Gardens with Anna Ford. I return home for a shower and a quick nap before reconverting to long trousers for dinner with Judy Craymer. I get home well after 11 p.m. after a first-class day of friendship and food. This time I sleep well and deeply, with no need for a midnight snack.

My visit to Kew, where Anna Ford has her new home, is delightful. The weather is perfect, and we have a long stroll in the gardens, by and around the lake, pagoda and hothouse. Although finally retired from high-powered service with various committees and charities, Anna is still sharp as a tack about current affairs and politics. She has been following all the show trials in detail. She had no idea before the campaign that suspects in Britain could be rebailed indefinitely, and considers this wicked. When I tell her that in exasperation I voted for the Green Party in the recent Euro elections, she exclaims, 'So did I!'

My hostess gives me a tour of her new home, one of a group of attractive and secluded terraced houses near the common. The house is, intentionally, much smaller than her former family home. Her two daughters are now settled in their own adult lives and there is no need for a large property. I am touched that there is no evidence on any of the walls of the artwork of her late husband Mark, a respected editorial cartoonist. I ask as politely as possible if this is because she does not wish to be constantly reminded of it. Anna explains that the art has all passed on to the children, and they are free to do with it what they wish.

An acrostic keeps me company on the Tube trip home. My turnaround is a success and I actually arrive at the Wolseley seven minutes before my dinner date with Judy Craymer. I am taken to our table, where, by incredible coincidence, I am seated next to Brian Paddick. He is dining with a respected elderly gentleman who expresses pleasure at our meeting. When Craymer arrives, I introduce her to the Baron of Brixton, who is friendly but cannot comment on my predicament while in company. The minute his guest visits the facilities, he leans over and explains to Judy his interest in my case.

The *Mamma Mia!* mogul is so sweet. She would do anything to be helpful in my case, but can't think of anything she can do. As we leave the Wolseley, she insists we have dinner again soon with Christopher, and she wishes me well for 15 September, or whatever date might prove decisive.

---

30 JULY 2014

I ask Jennifer to phone Google. Can a person even phone Google? We shall see.

I'm tired of Googling myself to see if there has been any news coverage of my endless rebailing and seeing a picture of a cigar-toting Jimmy Savile staring me in the face. It is still the case that if you Google Gambaccini, all the front-page photos are of Savile. Someone somewhere at Google must realise that I am not, never was and never will be Jimmy Savile.

The history major in me objects that a site taken seriously by researchers is reporting something so wildly inaccurate. The Gambaccini in me does not want my Italian relatives to think that I have taken up smoking.

<hr>

I AUGUST 2014

I check my email and there is a middle-of-the-night message from Darren. It is timed 03.11.

> Just sending an email as I just had a pretty vivid nightmare a little earlier
> which you featured in … struggling to sleep now so thought I would
> send love and say I'm thinking of you and the horrible stuff that's going
> on for you always (even in my sleep it would seem)
>   Much love as ever – d xx

As always in moments like this, I curse the Metropolitan Police for causing my friends to suffer.

Alastair MacGregor, my first friend in this country, has also emailed, confirming our lunch date for next Wednesday. I am startled to see that my modest pal has the words 'Biometrics Commissioner' in parentheses after his account name. What or who is a 'Biometrics Commissioner'? I Google the term and find to my astonishment on the gov.uk website that 'the Biometrics Commissioner is independent of government. His role is to keep under review the retention and use by the police of DNA samples, DNA profiles and fingerprints.'

Typical MacGregor. While his brother Neil has enjoyed highly publicised and justified fame, Ali has happily flown under the media radar for his entire career. He even became a QC without my knowing it!

I write back,

> Congratulations on this Biometrics Commissioner business. I had no
> idea. As a matter of fact, when I saw it in your email name, I thought
> it was some sort of internet joke I was not in on.
>
> Well, let's put this to good use. Do you have any DNA samples of me
> from 1978? If so, we can match it against the bloodstream of Primary.
> OK, OK, gross … but I'm reaching for anything here…
>
> Always, Paul

---

2 AUGUST 2014

Today is a Saturday. I have not performed my Radio 2 Saturday evening
show since last October. Indeed, after checking in to see the time slot was
in good hands, which it was with Johnnie Walker and Craig Charles, I
stopped listening. Having to be reminded that my career has been stolen
is hard. I can't bear it. I don't want to hear Radio 2 on a Saturday evening.

Which is probably why I didn't know that Johnnie Walker isn't doing it
any more. This week I received a check-in call from Kevin Howlett, who
casually mentioned that he had recorded a mini-series with Ana Matronic
from the Scissor Sisters. The programme was going out in the first hour
of my old time slot. It had already started!

I'm a fan of the Scissor Sisters and loved Ana Matronic's tribute to Siouxsie
Sioux at the 2012 Ivor Novello Awards. Nonetheless, to learn that she
was in my old time slot and I didn't even know it shows how distant I now
am from my radio career.

I know that most, if not all, of my Radio 2 and Radio 4 colleagues believe
that the accusations against me are false. But they don't do anything about
it. They are British. They were brought up to be submissive, subjects to a
monarch and underlings to an elite. It doesn't occur to them to challenge
the police. In America … or at least in my generation of Americans … we

would have had days of action, letting the public know we were refusing to perform in solidarity with our wronged colleague. We would challenge the police and the Crown Prosecution Service to put up or shut up.

Today is another beauty in this memorable summer. At midday I cannot resist walking to Borough Market for my second World's Greatest Sandwich of the week. While having my 3Bis ice cream, for I succumb anew to that great treat as well, I decide to check out the Baby Shard. I haven't seen it lately, and I want to see if it's finished. It is odd that the Shard looms large in our bedroom and dining room views, yet the Baby Shard, a large building when you are standing next to it, is not visible.

The edifice certainly looks finished. Whether the Murdoch publications have actually moved in yet or not, they all intend to. A poster in front of the Shard seeking corporate tenants announces companies that have chosen to locate in the two-building complex. This billboard is amusingly misleading, as over half of the organisations listed are Murdoch properties, including the *Wall Street Journal*. Someone who did not know who owned what newspaper would think that the Shard and Baby Shard were a mecca for media, rather than a cost-saving headquarters for News UK.

Finding myself at the Shard, I realise that Southwark Crown Court is across Tooley Street. Even though it is Saturday and it is conceivable that a reporter might see me at the venue of Yewtree trials, I have to satisfy my curiosity, and circumnavigate the large brown stone building. No one bats an eyelid.

I return home to find an email from former BBC deputy Director General Mark Byford.

'Very sad to hear about Mike Smith,' he opens.

How odd, I think for a second. I didn't know Mark liked the Dave Clark Five, for whom Mike Smith was the lead singer. Furthermore, the vocalist died six years ago. Mark is a little late in expressing condolences.

Oh, wait.

'Fond memories of him on Radio 1 in the '80s' is the second line.

It is no wonder I thought of the Dave Clark Five's Mike Smith. I never considered it possible that the DJ Mike Smith would go before 'us'. He was only fifty-nine. I call Tim Blackmore, one of Smith's mentors, to express my sympathies. I tell him they used to say you knew you were getting older when the police were younger. Now we knew we're getting older because our dying colleagues are younger.

I tell Blackmore my favourite Mike Smith story. What it says about Mike is, quite simply, how much he loved Sarah Greene, now his widow. It is one of the greatest demonstrations of love I have ever known.

Driving home from Radio 1 on the M4 flyover, Smith was listening to a colleague who infuriated all of us by telling false or negative things about us on air. This time he said, 'Did the *Pops* last night. Sarah Greene's dressing room was next door. Mike, she was not alone.'

Furious, Smith waited for the next motorway exit, got back on in the opposite direction and returned to central London. Arriving at Broadcasting House, he stormed into the studio, told the technical operator, 'Segue two records', and started strangling the DJ. Halting before he killed the man, he said, 'Next time I won't stop.'

That's love. Bless Mike Smith and Sarah Greene.

---

4 AUGUST 2014

Jennifer has not had a reply yet from Google concerning the photo error depicting Jimmy Savile as 'Paul Gambaccini'. However, I don't feel so bad when I research a comic strip artist named Charles Kahles. The creator of *Hairbreadth Harry* is listed as being 'age 136' in his Wikipedia entry. They have his correct birth and death dates; they just haven't noticed that being dead ends life.

---

5 AUGUST 2014

I have arranged with the University College office to donate more classical

CDs when Christopher and I spend time in Oxford on Friday the 15th. I will have given my entire collection of opera CDs to the Music Society, save for a handful of personal favourites. The librarian in me now yields to the pragmatist. I have accepted that Classic FM will never come calling again, not being remotely the same station it was when I worked in Academic House and then Oxford Circus, and unless Radio 3 indulges in some sort of twentieth anniversary sadomasochism I am unlikely to be invited back there.

Heritage Auctions in Dallas and, to a lesser extent, ComicConnect in New York are currently auctioning off books and original art from my comic collection. Justice is taking another holiday this August, and to psych myself up into thinking I am moving in some sort of right direction, I have arranged for material to be sold in auctions in five consecutive weeks.

---

6 AUGUST 2014

Chris attends a matinee of *The Crucible* at the Old Vic. The production is one of the most acclaimed shows of the year, but I can't face seeing it. I'm living it.

Instead, I lunch with the Biometrics Commissioner. He tells me that he has spoken to two leading academics expressing the wish that when the dust has died down someone will do a statistical study of how many accusations against celebrities during the Yewtree era have been false – not just charges on which defendants have been acquitted, but also complaints to police that never resulted in arrest. This may require use of the Freedom of Information Act, but Ali feels it must be done so we will know precisely what it is we have lived through.

When I return, I note that Christopher's copy of *The Week* is on the dining room table, open to a review of Dan Davies's book *In Plain Sight: The Life and Lies of Jimmy Savile*. It includes a quote from the dead man that he had 'a great way with sub-normals'. I feel vindicated after the fact.

In my interviews on breakfast television and *Panorama* in late 2012 concerning Savile, I had recalled the phrase that his programme assistants had used to describe his sexual preference was 'the now politically incorrect expression "underage sub-normals"'. I am relieved for accuracy's sake that I had recalled the right phrase, even if it is a cruel one.

7 AUGUST 2014

Today I put down Proust in favour of Jim Davidson. I never thought I would do or even imagine doing that.

Yesterday I read the translator's introduction to *In the Shadow of Young Girls in Flower*, the second volume in the latest Penguin translation of *In Search of Lost Time*. I anticipated that today I would begin reading the novel. Instead, I breakfast with Rob Hayward, who tells me that there is an article about Jim Davidson in the *Daily Telegraph*, which he has brought to Le Pain Quotidien. It is a review of the comedian's Edinburgh show and mentions his new book, *No Further Action*. I immediately recognise the phrase as shorthand for the kind of letter a dismissed suspect receives. Oh my God! Jim has beaten me to it! His is the first book by one of 'us'. This I must read, before Proust, before the next Michael Chabon novel, before the next Mike Mignola comic book. I dispatch Jennifer to track a copy down at Foyles, either in Waterloo Station or on the South Bank, or Waterstones in Notting Hill Gate, where she is going shopping. The mission is a failure: the book is not published until later today.

I Google Davidson. *The Guardian* pans the show and mentions the book in two separate pieces. The *Express* notice is a five-star rave, the kind Charles Foster Kane expected Jedediah Leland would give Susan Alexander. The *Edinburgh Reporter* also goes the whole five-star hog. The *Times* critic awards only two stars but does offer the informative tidbits 'no apology, no mention of his £500,000 legal bill'. It's always daring to attempt jokes about a comedian's act, but Bruce Dessau of the *Evening Standard* pulls it off in his middle-of-the-road three-star review by saying, 'There might be no Yewtree case to answer but, despite approving cheers from his fans, some jokes in this show are positively criminal.'

It turns out Edinburgh is a warm-up for a full-fledged national tour also called *No Further Action*. I also learn that the book has a subtitle, *The Darkest Year of My Life*. I can relate to that.

---

8 AUGUST 2014

I ask Jennifer to go to Foyles in Waterloo Station to see if *No Further Action* is available today. It is not and, according to the company computer, is not in any Foyles store. However, there is a copy – one copy! – at Waterstones in Trafalgar Square. This is depressing. Whatever the virtues of the account I am about to read, it deserves more attention than this. What if the book I am writing is also met with a national yawn?

Jen journeys to the shadow of Admiral Nelson in search of Jim Davidson. I have always associated Nelson's Column with a locker-room attendant in the Dartmouth College gym. During my final term there in the spring of 1970, I took saunas and dieted for two months to lose a twenty-pound spare tyre. One day, when the former sailor was handing me a towel, I told him I would be going to England in the autumn to attend Oxford University.

'When I was in the navy, I went to London to see the statue of Admiral Nelson,' he sniffed. 'And what did I find? Birdshit!'

On my first trip to London, I discovered what he meant. It was the height of the pigeon plague, and guano covered the hat of the national hero.

Now Trafalgar Square is pigeon-free, and Jennifer can shop without fear of getting a wet head. She returns with *No Further Action*.

I read the first page. I read the second page. I can't stop. I have to have all of this book inside me, now. I need to osmose it, to ingest it, inject it. In the words of Elvis Presley, 'I Want You, I Need You, I Love You'. With the exception of a lunch break, I read the whole 336 pages straight through.

My copy of this week's *Economist* is trashed. That is because it is the only publication at hand while I read *No Further Action*. In the white space surrounding the obituary of 'Sir Peter Hall, a champion of cities', I write my first note, 'page fifty-four top & bottom', and it is all marginalia from there on in. The smiling face of the late Sir Peter is surrounded by my scribbles. The previous page is the next to go. I make a record of every passage from which I gain information about Operation Yewtree and every section in which, unknown to Jim Davidson, he and I experienced something identical.

What really gets my goat is the revelation that Davidson was stalked by tabloid journalists and photographers before his arrest even when he did not know why they were hanging around outside his house. He learned from them why they were there.

'You know something is wrong when there are lurkers,' he writes at the beginning of his third chapter. I didn't get my 'lurkers' until the media cordon formed outside my home after my arrest, before I was named. Davidson had it before he was nicked! (Drat. I had promised myself to avoid the obvious pun on 'Nick-Nick' Davidson, and here I go falling into it unconsciously.)

Who is it in the Metropolitan Police who tips off the press? I repeat as I did several months ago that I am not accusing my case officers, or indeed anyone else working on Operation Yewtree. But it only takes a few bad apples to contaminate a barrel, and someone in the force does it.

As a Yewtree case begins, so does it end, with the tabs knowing first. On page 236 of his memoir, Jim receives a message from a friend who works at *The Sun*.

'Understand that you are likely to get NFA. Would love to give you some money for an interview.'

'Who was NFA?' Davidson thinks. 'I immediately thought my remortgage inquiries had come up trumps.'

Only then does he realise what 'NFA' must mean. He calls his friend at

The Sun and is informed that the tip 'didn't come from the police but from the man who started this entire Jimmy Savile thing off. The ex-detective that did the TV programme exposing Savile's behaviour.'

The author is perplexed. 'But how did he know? Was he in regular contact with Yewtree?'

I am staggered. There are three substantial scandals on one page. Why did the Metropolitan Police allow a civilian to know confidential details of Operation Yewtree? Why did they reach a decision of no further action and not inform the suspect until it suited their own public relations purposes? Why do the Metropolitan Police and *The Sun* retain intimate relations post-Leveson?

Davidson has produced a compelling volume. Respect, Jim.

11 AUGUST 2014

My brother Peter calls from New York. He wishes to relate a disturbing dream incorporating elements of my treatment by the Met and the currently controversial case of Eric Garner, a Staten Island man who died when placed in a chokehold by a New York policeman. In the nightmare, Peter was riding a Metro North train into the city in the same carriage as Aleksandr Solzhenitsyn, who once lived in exile in Vermont and could conceivably have been on such a train. A brigade of officers jumped the Russian novelist and put him in a chokehold. Peter, fleeing, turned around to see the dissident quite dead, his head hanging limply from his neck.

Only one year separates we two oldest Gambaccini brothers, and I am touched by how empathetically Peter is experiencing my ordeal. He is suffering on my behalf.

I receive a welcome phone call from Liza Tarbuck, and we try to identify the big questions. Discussing some of the themes from Jim Davidson's book, we agree that the continued symbiotic relationship between the police and press is unacceptable. Beyond that, we're stumped. The questions are too big for us to even guess the answers.

Liza and I believe that Davidson has raised one of the key questions in the witch-hunt, which no one seems to be asking. Exactly who thought this up and considered it a good idea? Upon the answer to this will follow other important questions. What has been the role of central government in ordering, or at the very least tolerating, the unscrupulous collection of celebrity scalps? What has been the role of the Murdoch empire in trying to paint the BBC as a hotbed of perverts? Have the foot soldiers of the Metropolitan Police been delighted or embarrassed to take as gospel truth the lies and rantings of chancers and fantasists? It is unlikely that police, press and politicians will voluntarily disclose this information, so if the public ever wants to know the full story of this miscarriage of justice it will have to demand it.

Kate Goold informs me that Officer One is on leave. I knew that my oppressors would be having summer holidays, but the confirmation that it is actually happening at this very moment does not uplift.

Personal factors also 'pile on' my dark mood. Today is the first day of Jennifer's trip to Switzerland and as such is a preview of next month, when she will be leaving my employment to return to education. I am relieved that this is her decision rather than mine, as I will no longer be able to afford a personal assistant and would feel cruel terminating her position, but her absence will introduce another empty space into my daily existence. In addition, Chris has confirmed he will be joining his university friends for three days of surfing in late September, timed between his performances at the Almeida. I cannot complain; you marry a surfer, he surfs. I will miss him nonetheless and will once again be required to build a social programme without him.

---

12 AUGUST 2014

I am jolted by a tweet from NBC that appears in the margins of a page of the online *New York Times*. It expresses sympathy at the loss of Robin

Williams. Huh? Is this a prank? Does this mean he has died? How can that be? Robin Williams is a life force. He can't be dead. Refreshing the front page of *The Times*, I learn that he is just that. In so doing, at one in the morning, I become one of the first people in Britain to learn that this greatest of comic actors, a man who managed to combine the genius of his idol Jonathan Winters with phenomenal public popularity, has indeed left the living.

As I lie in the darkness, I realise there are two other reasons I feel flat. The euphoria of having sold some vintage comics in a Dallas auction yesterday has worn off, and now I again have to think about raising funds via means other than employment. Secondly, what has been my equivalent of employment for the past year, writing this book, seems to be over. At this point, either it's got it or it doesn't, and I'm going to have to choose my next project.

At the start of this, I wondered if I could write enough for a book. Now I've written too much and will have to edit.

13 AUGUST 2014

Now Lauren Bacall has passed away. Commentators note that two film giants have gone on successive days. It often seems to be the case: Robert Mitchum preceded James Stewart in death by one day, for example. Directors Ingmar Bergman and Michelangelo Antonioni were even closer, managing their only collaboration on 30 July 2007.

But at least Bacall and Stewart could hold their own with their companions in morbidity. The celebrity double deaths I remember best are those in which one of the departed is completely and unfairly eclipsed by the other. Aldous Huxley was the author of one of the touchstone novels of my youth, *Brave New World*, but his passing on 22 November 1963 went unnoticed because of the assassination of President Kennedy. More recently, Farrah Fawcett-Majors, whose demise would ordinarily command untold column inches, barely got a look-in because she departed the same day as Michael Jackson.

A modern trend becomes apparent from the response to the deaths of Robin Williams and, to a lesser extent, Lauren Bacall. As Jimmy Durante famously said, 'Everybody wants ta get inta the act.' Now legions of social media users share their reactions, even if they are no more revealing than 'So sad' or 'Thank you for making us smile'. Minor celebrities validate their own existence by tweeting of their hours or days spent in the vicinity of the star and linking to photographs taken with him. Not long ago the public, upon hearing the news of the death of a beloved figure, looked to television or newspaper responses from designated mourners. Now that I think about it, I was one of those. But now society does not wait for the reactions of others. It expresses itself immediately and directly.

In that spirit, I will share my evening spent in the presence of Lauren Bacall. It was at the Wigmore Hall in June 1976. The legendary pianist Arthur Rubinstein was giving his final recital. My idol wrote of this event,

> The last concert of my career was the one I gave at Wigmore Hall in London for the benefit of the hall, which was in danger of being demolished. My concert was to give an example to other artists in order to save this old endearing place. As for myself, it was a symbolic gesture; it was in this hall that I had given my first recital in London, and playing there for the last time in my life made me think of my whole career in the form of a sonata. The first movement represented the struggles of my youth, the following andante for the beginning of a more serious aspect of my talent, a scherzo represented well the unexpected great success, and the finale turned out to be a wonderful moving end.

It was more moving than any of us had anticipated. When taking his curtain call, Rubinstein, who was losing his sight, hushed the crowd by saying, 'Please, no more. I cannot see the keys.'

At the interval, I had seen the cellist Jacqueline du Pré, stricken with multiple sclerosis, being pushed through the foyer in a wheelchair. Lauren Bacall came into view with a friend. The Hollywood great had recently become a stage star, winning a Tony Award for *Applause* and bringing the show to London. She obviously was now accustomed to speaking more loudly than necessary in close quarters.

'Oh look,' she pointed out to her friend. 'There's Jacqueline du Pré. How depressing!'

At the end of the show I found myself backstage, waiting for Rubinstein to descend a staircase to meet his admirers. Bacall was in the front of the crowd.

'Maestro!' she exclaimed.

Rubinstein responded without losing a beat.

'I am not so blind that I cannot see your beauty.'

Let me point out that in recalling this evening at the Wigmore, I do not claim special familiarity with Lauren Bacall. There were more than 32,000 nights in her life when I never met her at all.

---

14 AUGUST 2014

Chris comes onto the terrace and tells me he has received an email from a friend.

It reads simply, 'Well, finally, Cliff.'

So it begins. We read the news on the BBC website. A convoy of police have entered the Berkshire home of Sir Cliff Richard. (A precise count later reveals that 'eight plain-clothed police officers in five unmarked cars arrived to conduct the search which ended at about 15.30 BST'.) Detective Superintendent Matt Fenwick of South Yorkshire Police makes a statement confirming that his force is investigating 'an allegation of a sexual nature dating back to the 1980s ... The owner of the property is not present.'

The website report states: 'The BBC understands it relates to an alleged sexual assault at a 1985 event where US preacher Billy Graham appeared at Bramall Lane, Sheffield.' Good grief. I had a quarter-hour conversation with Billy Graham on that tour, in the green room at TV-am as we were preparing for our respective appearances with Michael Parkinson.

Nigel Evans sends a Facebook message to Chris asking if I have Cliff's number. He considers the way the story leaked to be extraordinary. I don't know what he's talking about, but I can't wait to find out. I watch on the website. Extraordinarily, a BBC newsman reports from outside the gates surrounding Cliff's home, but does not explain how his report happens to include footage of police cars arriving at the estate, nor aerial video taken from a helicopter.

I am so mad about this I email the reporter, a personal acquaintance from my BBC days. 'I hope this finds you happy and healthy,' I begin.

> Why do you acquiesce in totalitarianism?
> Why did you not mention in your Cliff Richard report that the media had been tipped off about the police raid of which you showed so much footage? Who supplied your aerial footage, God? Why do you not name the recognised intermediary through whom the police spread their malevolence? Are you proud to be part of the witch-hunt?
> Regards, Paul

(Talking about Cliff Richard in print is going to be one of those nightmare assignments like writing about Elton John. No one knows who you are talking about if you refer to 'John'. In the same way, nobody has the remotest idea who 'Richard' is.)

To my surprise, 'Richard' breaks his silence and speaks. 'For many months I have been aware of allegations against me of historic impropriety which have been circulating online,' a statement says.

> The allegations are completely false. Up until now I have chosen not to

dignify the false allegations with a response, as it would just give them more oxygen. However, the police attended my apartment in Berkshire today without notice, except it would appear to the press. I am not presently in the UK but it goes without saying that I will co-operate fully should the police wish to speak to me. Beyond stating that today's allegation is completely false it would not be appropriate to say anything further until the police investigation has concluded.

The *Mail* reports that 'police were seen taking a number of items from the property in the Sunningdale area of Berkshire for further investigation'. I certainly hope these pieces didn't include any medication, because Cliff will not be seeing these for many months to come. The Met still haven't returned a single item of their haul from my home ten months ago.

The time has come for the Great Revulsion, and it is past time to demand an answer to the biggest question of all: who is the master of the witchhunt? Who is the highly placed individual who demanded a campaign against ageing celebrities and insisted that all accusations, no matter how frivolous or insane, be treated as true? Who has corrupted the British justice system with his or her zealotry, lowered the tone of national life and made England a laughing stock among nations of the Western world? Who is the Witchfinder General?

The bulk of my afternoon is taken up with supportive phone calls from friends here and in America expressing their disgust at Cliff's arrest and the hope that I am OK. So much for the reading, writing and piano playing that I thought I would be doing today.

I reach a tipping point. I have not made an attempt since my arrest to contact BBC Director General Tony Hall, but today I can hold back no longer. I write to him, Helen Boaden and Lewis Carnie, copying in my producers, simply saying, 'Below please find an email I have sent to your reporter. I've had it. The BBC should be ashamed of itself.'

The issue is not whether the accusation against Cliff Richard has any validity. Time alone will tell that. The issue is that the BBC has voluntarily become an agent of the police.

I have turned a corner. A few paragraphs above I referred to 'a personal acquaintance from my BBC days'. I realised within seconds of writing that I had spoken of those forty years in the past tense. I do not have a relationship with the BBC at this time, although I may forge a new one at some point in the future. As Chris put it bluntly earlier this week, 'They sacked you and stopped paying you.'

It is the BBC that has destroyed my love for the BBC. No one else could have done it. For decades I would have walked a million miles for one of its smiles. Now I do not even care if it gets its charter renewed. I will always advocate financial support for the radio service, which is the best in the world, but the corporation as a body has lost the moral high ground.

Good Lord. Fifty-five minutes after my email of protest, the BBC website adds a sidebar to its Cliff coverage. Home affairs correspondent Danny Shaw takes note of Richard's complaint

> that the press appeared to have been given advance notice that his home in Berkshire was to be searched – whereas he hadn't been. He was referring to the reporters and camera crew from the BBC who were outside when police arrived. It used to be common practice for police to let reporters know they were about to raid a celebrity's house or make a high-profile arrest. It was part of the trade of information and favours between cops and hacks that has so recently fallen into disrepute.

After talking about the case of Harry Redknapp, Shaw notes that 'two years ago, the Leveson Inquiry concluded that police operations involving the media should be "controlled more tightly" to avoid the "perception of favouritism" and the "risk of violating the private rights of individuals"'.

Shaw then blunders by claiming that 'since then, tip-offs have dried to a trickle despite a series of high-profile arrests'. Has he never heard of Jim Davidson and Paul Gambaccini?

However, he accurately concludes that the Sir Cliff media meal 'appears to be a deliberate attempt by police to ensure maximum coverage. That's not illegal – but there are strict guidelines – and the force may have to justify its approach in the months to come.'

The summary of this terrible day comes from my brother Peter, who emails from New York: 'Jeezus, this is so horrifying, with so many treacherous characters. I wish there were more courageous figures in the media to call this what it is.'

---

15 AUGUST 2014

Chris and I go to Oxford for a trip that serves two purposes. First, I deliver the second half of my opera CD collection to the University College Music Society. Secondly, we visit the revamped Ashmolean Museum, one of the tasks on my bucket list of things to do before and if I move back to New York. Thank heaven Chris is in superb physical condition, as he lugs the extremely heavy suitcase full of CDs from the railway station all the way down the High Street to Univ.

On the train back to London, I nap between Didcot and Slough. Although intending to doze, Chris gets right into his emails. When I awake, he shows me a superb blog by Anna Raccoon, 'Cliff Hanger'. A spokesman for the South Yorkshire Police has stated that his force did not tip off the press on the raid on a property Cliff purchased, as Raccoon phrases it, 'twenty-three years after the alleged offence is supposed to have occurred 176 miles north'. The spokesman has said, 'The BBC had their own sources. The information was not released by South Yorkshire Police.' Anna states bluntly, 'There should be an investigation. Another investigation – to unmask the police officer who tipped off the media. Questions should be asked in the House of Commons.'

How about asking who tipped off the press about every one of us? One of Anna Raccoon's readers, 'Chris', writes, 'As the late Mike Smith bravely pointed out that day on Twitter, the area where DLT lived had been swarming with press for over an hour before the police arrived mob-handed to arrest one 67-year-old law-abiding citizen.'

I have had no response from the BBC hierarchy concerning my complaint about its Cliff coverage, apart from Helen Boaden's promise to make sure that the news department sees it. Paul Bajoria, my *Counterpoint* producer, does call, and we speak for thirty-eight minutes. At the end I tell him that after the blanket nationwide publicity sought and achieved by the police, poor Cliff must now await his bandwagoners. Bajoria knows this is true. Even people outside the witch-hunt now understand that the police publicise their suspects so that the media can serve as their recruiters. How disgusting that BBC television, which once presented Kenneth Clark, Jacob Bronowski and David Attenborough, should now be one of these agents.

---

16 AUGUST 2014

As George Harrison would say (and did, in *Yellow Submarine*), it's all too much. The papers are full of Cliff Richard stories, many commanding front pages. There seem to be two sorts: tabloids salivating at the prospect of bandwagoners making further accusations against Cliff, and more serious newspapers condemning the entire operation. The South Yorkshire Police and the BBC come in for particular abuse. Not only has Richard not been charged with any offence, he has not been arrested, and not only has he not been arrested, he has not even been interviewed, yet he has been treated like a major criminal.

One of my favourite pieces appears in *The Independent*. It is by Geoffrey Robertson. The headline states bluntly: 'The way the police have treated Cliff Richard is completely unacceptable'. Robertson's first line is: 'People believe that where there's smoke there's fire, but sometimes there is just a smoke machine.'

This is a variation, and I begrudgingly admit a superior one, to my approach to my own case: 'Not only is there no fire, there's not even a match.'

Geoffrey surprises me by mentioning me. 'What will happen now? If the outrageous treatment of Paul Gambuccini and Jimmy Tarbuck is my guide, Cliff Richard will remain in a cruel limbo for eighteen months or so until the police and the CPS decide whether to charge him.' I am grateful for the QC's support, even with a misspelling of my surname.

The BBC is on the receiving end of a shit storm. Its coverage of the Cliff raid is a brand catastrophe, which is likely to cause the corporation major and lasting damage. Today it is condemned not only by the usual suspects, who would like to see the BBC hindered and Rupert Murdoch helped, but by many supporters, nauseated by its collaboration with the police in the persecution of a national icon.

We know why the South Yorkshire Police have conducted this raid in as highly publicised a way as possible. In the absence of evidence, it needs a second accusation against Cliff to construct the 'pattern of behaviour' necessary to arrest him. Extraordinarily, it tells the public what to accuse him of by revealing the allegation against him. The BBC has acted as the recruiting agent of the police. It has reduced itself to the status of *Pravda* in the Soviet Union.

My sympathies are with Cliff for the barbaric way in which he has been treated. Yet I have to admit it is good for me. All the things I have wanted to say about Operation Yewtree and its related inquiries are now being said by other people, many being of power and influence. There was a time not many months ago when I was, to misuse the motto of my alma mater Dartmouth College, 'a voice crying in the wilderness'. Now every point I would like to make about my experience is being made by someone else. I can sit back, read and marvel at how the police have mismanaged the entire affair. My anticipation that this witch-hunt would rise and fall in parallel with the Salem trials is proving spookily prescient. To maintain the interest of the press and public, the police have to move ever higher up the food chain. Inevitably, they one day overreach and lose support. Is Cliff proving to be the Case Too Far?

I am also relieved because the name of Mark Williams-Thomas is now being reported widely as a key player in what I consider a witch-hunt and he considers a … whatever he considers it. I have been hesitant to discuss him in this book because I do not wish to accidentally say anything libellous. Also, unlike many bloggers, I do not want to say anything of which I am not certain. I do not know him. I therefore choose to err on the side of discretion and refrain from talking about him. Now, however, his role is being openly discussed, both by supporters and by detractors. Newspapers report that Cliff's accuser approached Williams-Thomas after his Jimmy Savile documentary. He referred the man to Yewtree, which sent him to South Yorkshire. Looking at Mark's Twitter account, he seems to send more tweets in a week than I have in my entire life.

The media explosion of the past two days has taken a great deal of pressure off me. Just for that I would knight Sir Cliff a second time.

---

17 AUGUST 2014

Charles Foster is at battle stations first thing in the morning and sends a piece from the *Sunday Times* by Rod Liddle. Foster observes, 'We truly live in mid-seventeenth-century England and the CPS, aided by plod, is the new Matthew Hopkins.' When Charles, as establishment a figure as they come, having run the British Forces Broadcasting Service and been a lifelong Conservative, is alienated, I know that the police and CPS have lost much of middle England.

The *Sunday Telegraph* itself amuses me greatly by repeating Geoffrey Robertson's choice comments from yesterday's *Independent*. This includes the misspelling of my surname as 'Gambuccini'. The Huffington Post also reports Geoffrey's remarks and duplicates the error. Maybe they are all talking about somebody else.

The ITV website reports. 'Sir Michael Parkinson has told ITV News the investigation into his friend Sir Cliff Richard and others "feels like some sort of witch-hunt".

'He said anyone who has not been charged with a crime should not be named by police or have their names reported in the press.'

Parkinson's comments appear within moments on many newspaper websites. I am grateful for his intervention, since I obviously fall under the purview of his remarks. They may be too late for me, but they are not too little.

I find myself wondering if Michael remembers the TV show on which we appeared with Billy Graham during the evangelist's 1985 visit to the UK. He has interviewed so many celebrities he can be forgiven for forgetting individual programmes, but you would think that some archivist would be searching the TV-am tapes for what would now be considered a conversation of interest.

18 AUGUST 2014

I have sent an email of thanks to Ric Nardin, my American friend from Oxford days who attended both our US wedding and our UK civil partnership ceremony. Nardin called from the States last week to say he had sent a topical present, hoping it would be sensitive and not hurtful. He was very concerned that I might misinterpret his intentions, and wanted to make sure I knew they were only supportive. Naturally, I was intrigued by what his gift might be.

When the FedEx parcel arrived a couple of days later, I understood his reservations. They were unnecessary. It's a great piece. Ric has sent me a framed montage with a variation of a Billie Holiday civil rights classic printed at the top: 'British Yews Bear a Strange Fruit / Lies at the Leaves / Truth at the Root'. Two British policemen sit on a yew tree with a genuine Nazi swastika button at the bottom. I hang the artwork on the staircase in a line of sight with the precise spot where Officer One announced I was under arrest. It will have to do for now, a blue plaque being out of the question.

Of all the comments about the Cliff case today and the expressions of concern I have recently received, my favourite is an email from Beth Gordon concerning her young son: 'Over breakfast this morning, Joseph, who I've told an abridged version of events to, suddenly said, "Mummy, you know your friend Paul? Why don't you tell the police they're wrong until they stop it?"'

---

20 AUGUST 2014

Ah, 1985, the year the percentage of *Billboard* Hot 100 hits by British artists peaked, eight consecutive number ones were by UK acts, Cliff Richard sang at a Billy Graham rally near Sheffield and … wait a minute! Cliff! 1985! Was that the year we had a dinner in Newcastle that I will never forget?

The reason the meal was unforgettable was that Cliff ordered a glass of wine and I asked for mineral water. When the waiter brought the drinks, he instinctively gave Richard the water and me the wine. We both collapsed with laughter. Cliff Richard couldn't have ordered a glass of wine, could he?

I was in Newcastle for my Channel 4 show *The Other Side of the Tracks*, covering the recording of an episode of *The Tube*, the year's popular music broadcasting phenomenon. Cliff and Killing Joke were the musical guests. The glass of wine was the real killing joke.

To check it was the same year as the now famous Billy Graham Sheffield rally, I go to Google. Can there be a reference to that episode of *The Tube*?

There certainly can. Not only is there a reference to the episode, there is the episode. Without naming me, Cliff tells the story of the two beverages to illustrate what it is like to live with The Cliff Richard Image. The *Tube* programme is dated 25 January 1985, which means that my dinner with Cliff was on the 24th. Mission accomplished! Thanks again, Tim Berners-Lee.

The morning is highlighted by long conversations with Joan Armatrading MBE and Sir Nick Partridge. They were both guests on my Radio 4 fortieth anniversary programmes, which now seem to have been made thousands of years ago. Joan and Nick have both been supportive throughout my period of false arrest, and today express their distaste for the treatment of Cliff Richard.

Last night I told Malcolm Jeffries that I have become accustomed to being constantly rebailed. Christopher and I actually think of this unlimited period as the new normal and can't imagine it will ever change, even though we know it one day must.

---

21 AUGUST 2014

I am staggered by a report in the Mail Online, which states that BBC News has claimed its handling of the Cliff Richard story was 'balanced and proportionate'.

'A lengthy statement posted on the corporation's complaints website explained that broadcasting the story was in the public interest in light of other allegations of "historic abuse by prominent people".'

This is not the story at all. The real story is that the BBC has collaborated with the witch-hunt. Why has the corporation I joined in 1973, full of belief and admiration, become compromised and craven?

I know that the treatment of Cliff will be a conversation topic at tonight's buffet dinner at the London flat of Nigel Evans. I arrive at 7.30. Chris, having had an eight-hour tech rehearsal at the Almeida, joins the informal party three hours later. 'It looks like a meeting of the Falsely Accused,' he says.

It is indeed a meeting of the Falsely Accused, because another of the guests is Ben Sulllivan, already the former president of the Oxford Union, now wondering what to do with his adulthood. This may be the first time that three of 'us' have been in the same room since the beginning of the witch-hunt.

I drink in Sullivan's account of his ordeal to the last drop. It is always amazing to discover how 'we' independently develop similar feelings about certain public officials and newspaper columnists. We discover that we share a particular antipathy for one journalist. A lawyer present at the party briefly lowers the tone by revealing that he has 'shagged' this individual. I am particularly impressed that, like myself, Ben has torn up his Labour Party membership card, feeling that Ed Miliband and company 'just don't get it' and play to what they perceive to be public opinion.

Ben Sullivan is a young man who could not have been more brazenly and falsely framed. He agrees that many commentators seize upon new sex cases to buttress their old opinions.

'Facts are things to be ignored,' he says of these writers. 'They already know what they feel and facts are annoying.'

At least Ben has had one benefit of youth. As he points out, he did not have to worry about bandwagoners making accusations against him dating from the 1970s or 1980s.

I thank Nigel for never mentioning my name when he refers to me in media interviews. This is deliberate and considerate on his part. I am particularly grateful for the mutual delicacy of Nigel and Jeremy Vine doing a pas de deux about my endless rebailing without once saying 'Gambaccini' or even 'Gambuccini'.

'This is when you know you're famous,' Rob Hayward observes. 'When people talk about someone and everyone knows who they're talking about without the person being named.' This is a kind of fame I can do without. Bring back the days when I was John Peel's junior!

At one point in the evening, I comment that I have gradually been able to devote more of my energies to subjects other than my case. I now only consciously think about my ordeal about 25 per cent of the time. Both

Nigel and Ben reveal that, even though they have been cleared, they still find themselves thinking about their cases 25 per cent of the time. Not much to look forward to there, then!

As I bid my goodbyes, Sullivan asks me to give his regards to Stephen Fry. He adored Stephen's denunciation of Yewtree at the Labour gala dinner.

'He's a god,' Ben effuses, speaking for much of his generation.

I get home just before midnight, leaving latecomer Christopher to enjoy more of the hospitality of Nigel and friends. I discover an email that Chris has sent a few hours before, warning me that Tony Hall has made a statement and I should not send an angry message to anyone until we talk. In one sense, the email is too late: I have already seen Hall's letter to Keith Vaz in defence of corporation coverage of the Cliff Richard raid. In another sense, the email was unnecessary: having had my say on the day, I don't wish to work myself into a lather every time someone at the BBC says something infuriating.

<hr>

22 AUGUST 2014

Having enjoyed the World's Greatest Sandwich at Borough Market, I am stopped outside the National Film Theatre. A man I recognise from years ago tells me that he has just bought my old episodic autobiography *Love Letters* off Amazon and is reading it.

I'm glad he is! If only the Metropolitan Police had believed what I wrote in that book, my case would not be happening and the British taxpayer would have been saved hundreds of thousands of pounds.

I'm always fascinated by the odd precision of Amazon prices, so I check for myself. New copies of *Love Letters* now start at $55.96. Someone is making a bit of cash – I'm not, the book being long deleted. However, a 'used' copy, which sounds in pretty poor shape, can be yours for $0.02, giving new meaning to the old phrase 'cheap at any price'.

Stephen Fry returns Ben Sullivan's greetings.

'I am very touched,' he writes from the closest Stephen will ever get to an email-free holiday,

> and how encouraging and comforting of you all to have each oth-
> er's experience for solace and strength. The whole business is turning
> sane. Maybe the Cliff debacle will be a turning point, who knows? But
> I know plenty of people now who are questioning the whole last few
> years of rabid insanity. Pass on my best to Ben Sullivan. I followed his
> case with horror.

I do send Ben best wishes from Stephen, and then wonder. Does Ben have a good singing voice? Five decades ago we never did launch our planned student government band, The Teeth. Any chance now for a group called The Falsely Accused?

<hr>

23 AUGUST 2014

The Spectator has printed a rave review of Jim Davidson's Edinburgh act in its edition dated today. After praising his playing to the house rather than delivering a generic set, it cuts to the chase.

'But the routines are a mere ornament to the legal centrepiece of the show,' the magazine reports, and then details his discussion of Operation Yewtree. The grenade in the room explodes.

'Over a tea break in the midst of his interrogation he asked the detectives to explain to him, off the record, what lay behind the witch hunt. The cops said they'd been ordered to treat all allegations as true "unless proved otherwise".'

The change in centuries of British legal tradition is confirmed. We are now guilty until proven innocent.

I have told Chris that we have to prepare for the next proclamation from on high, which is due by 15 September. There are three possibilities:

1) If I am rebailed for a fifth time I will seek judicial review. I will accept financial hospitality from friends who have offered it and will seek to have my case discredited and dismissed.

2) I cannot ready a response to being charged, since I don't know exactly what the specifics might be. In such a situation, invention would be the mother of necessity, but until my accusers and the police decide what their mendacious inventions will be, I cannot devise a response.

3) If the case is dismissed, I must have a statement ready to roll. This would not be a proclamation delivered in a public place. The nation has grown accustomed to seeing speakers orate from the steps of Southwark Crown Court, but since I have not been tried I will be nowhere near there if and when I get my NFA. I'm not going to inconvenience my neighbours by inviting the press back to our building for a driveway news conference. I will simply give my statement to Kate Goold and ask anyone who is interested to contact her. Mind you, at this distance from my arrest, there may be no interest, which would not be a bad thing.

There are two people that I have to clear my statement with before I make it public. The first is Chris. I write what I would like to say and show it to him. He laughs at the beginning and then approves. He appreciates my continuation of the theatrical theme I began in my response to my arrest, when I alluded to *The Scottsboro Boys*. I now have to email the proposal to Kate for her reaction. Since she has been against my ever making a statement I am not certain she will be happy about releasing one at the finish line, but I can but wait and see.

This is my prospective statement:

Shakespeare had words for everything. He had three titles that perfectly describe my experience of the last eleven months.

First, *Much Ado about Nothing*.

Second, *The Comedy of Errors*.

Third, *All's Well that Ends Well*.

There may be members of the press who will ask me to give interviews or make provocative statements. I will politely decline. To discuss horror is to trivialise it.

I will never trivialise the eleven months of psychological torture to which I have been unjustly subjected.

Besides, it will all be in the book.

I would like to thank the people of this country for their support during the past year. Wherever I have gone, I have been stopped in the street by members of the public offering encouragement. I am very grateful.

I'll be back at work by the end of the month.

Thank you.

---

25 AUGUST 2014

So much for thinking a bank holiday weekend might be a break from coping with my case. Having gone to bed at 11 p.m. on Saturday night, I was awakened after midnight by a terrible nightmare in which Chris and I were sleeping in a modernised version of my old Hyde Park Square flat when Officer One arrived with more accusations.

There has also been no respite from press attention to the case of Sir Cliff Richard, who has now been interviewed by South Yorkshire Police. A particularly good summary has been offered by *The Week*, which samples the Rod Liddle and Geoffrey Robertson QC pieces and adds an online article I have not seen. Frank Furedi on Spiked-online.com says that the investigation of Cliff, as with our other cases, has 'nothing to do with fighting or solving crime' and is in fact about 'impression management', giving the public the idea that the police are actually doing something useful about child protection. Furedi writes that 'a system of justice that is prepared to inflict collateral damage in the interests of a so-called greater good is really subverting the integrity of due process'. So say all of us.

I cannot escape the Metropolitan Police. Just as I settle in to enjoy the 25 August edition of my favourite magazine, the *New Yorker*, I encounter the ten-page article 'The Spy Who Loved Me', the story of 'an undercover surveillance operation that went too far'. It is an account of a Met man who, while infiltrating an animal rights group, conducted a long-running affair outside his marriage and fathered a child. He is not the only officer to have had sexual relationships with unsuspecting civilians. What is un-avoidable in reading this shocking piece is seeing the lengths to which the Metropolitan Police go in denying information not only to the victims of their operations but to respected international press. What chance do I have of finding out the story behind my persecution in the aftermath when even the *New Yorker* gets a reply like 'It would be inappropriate for us to comment in any further detail.'

Charlie Russell has been in touch requesting an hour-long chat in the flat as part of his proposed documentary. I send Charlie an email saying,

> It's OK for you to come over and do an hour, providing that I do have veto power over the show. Is this what you would call 'final cut'? Any-way, there is another condition … that we do not mention sex. You can mention Operation Yewtree and the Metropolitan Police, but I can-not discuss the specific accusations against me. The reason, of course, is that they are 100 per cent fictitious, and I do not wish to give them any oxygen. I think you understand that as long as I am in Britain I will be fighting for my life, my livelihood and my freedom. These are far more serious matters than any television programme, even one by you!

Within half an hour, Russell, who clearly has nothing better to do this rainy bank holiday, gets back to me. He generously agrees to my condi-tions. 'This is about what it's like to be in your position, hounded by the law, left in limbo,' his email reads. 'It's not really about the case itself at all.' We will set a filming date for later this week. Pardon me, *Panorama*. Forgive me, Kate.

---

26 AUGUST 2014

In a year in which the expression 'You couldn't make it up' has proved true on a daily basis, you really couldn't make this one up. The latest star to attack the police practice of naming (or leaking the name of) an accused celebrity before charge is … Daniel O'Donnell. The mere mention of his name may induce a chorus of 'so what' from the sophisticates in the audience, but the Irish singer is in fact the artist with the longest string of consecutive years with a new album in the UK chart. He has placed a new LP in the list for twenty-six straight years as of this writing.

O'Donnell has been quoted in the *Belfast Telegraph* as saying that it is 'absolutely unfair and unjust' that his friend Cliff Richard has been publicised at this early stage of his case. His remarks are judiciously tempered:

'I think the way it has all been conducted is definitely unfair and not in keeping with the law. It is like there is some kind of witch-hunt,' he is quoted. 'It's not the first time this has happened and an individual's name has been made public before being charged. In some of these cases, the person was later deemed not to have a case to answer. But, by then, the damage was done to the person's reputation.' Making it clear that opposing the 'witch-hunt' is in no way antagonistic to genuine victims, he adds, 'As well as everything else, this also diminishes the legitimate cases of people who have been abused.'

This morning I complete one of Thomas Middleton's acrostic puzzles. Only when I have finished it do I realise that it is a quotation from the book *Locked in the Cabinet* by Robert Reich. It was because of Bob that I applied to Oxford University in the first place. Seeking to escape Richard Nixon, I thought of going to University College because 'wherever Reich has gone, they will want more of where he came from'. I was right. This means that, indirectly, Bob Reich is responsible for my being in my current predicament. If he had never excelled at Dartmouth, I would never have applied to Univ. If I had never come to England, I would never have been arrested by the Metropolitan Police. Thanks a lot, Bob!

---

28 AUGUST 2014

Kate Goold has taken issue with the first portion of my prospective 'freedom statement' in the interests of protecting myself from possible bandwagoners and scurrilous publicity.

Mention of *Much Ado about Nothing* could incite a few distressed individuals who thought I was disrespecting my accusers to contact the police with more invented allegations. Citing *The Comedy of Errors* could lead a tabloid newspaper – Goold had one particular publication in mind – to report the specifics of my case, since a source in the police would be happy to provide them. Either course would lead to the kind of sensationalist publicity that we have been trying to avoid.

Although I really liked my Shakespeare statement, I have to yield to Kate's recommendation. There is no sense in running the course for eleven months and then tripping over the last hurdle.

A colleague of my solicitor at Bindmans had a further reservation. Noting recent hideous cases of beheading, hostage-taking and mass murder in the Middle East, she suggests I alter the word 'torture' in the phrase 'psychological torture' to 'trauma'. Acknowledging that even my fate has been nowhere near as horrible as those who have suffered recently in that part of the world, I agree to the alteration to 'psychological trauma'.

Now what? When in doubt, top and tail. I started this process with the Scottsboro Boys, so I will finish with them. My statement will now read:

Since I was falsely accused on 29 October last year, the Scottsboro Boys have received posthumous pardons and I have been completely cleared. These are results.

There may be members of the press who will ask me to give interviews or make provocative statements. I will politely decline. To discuss horror is to trivialise it.

I will never trivialise the eleven months of psychological trauma to which I have been unjustly subjected.

Besides, it will all be in the book.

I would like to thank the people of this country for their support during the past year. Wherever I have gone, I have been stopped in the street by members of the public offering encouragement. I am very grateful.

I'll be back at work by the end of the month.

Thank you.

Except, of course, I have no idea if I will be back at work by the end of September. Kate informs me that she has received a brief email from Officer One, telling her that my report date of the 15th will be 'effective'.

'Effective' has a different meaning in legal use than in everyday parlance. It means that I will actually be expected to report to Charing Cross Police Station, whereas previously I was rebailed several days in advance of the given date and was not required to physically turn up.

There were three possible outcomes on my previous report days: charge, dismissal or rebail. Now there are still three possible outcomes, but with one significant change. I could still be charged, my case could still be dismissed, or I could be re-interviewed at the order of the Crown Prosecution Service. This would presumably be in the wake of the purported re-interview of my original accuser, though we have not yet been told whether this has actually occurred. It would have the same delaying effect as a rebail, since the material would have to be sent back to the CPS, but we would at least have had some 'progress'.

No rebail means no judicial review, and just as well. Kate has come back with a description of the process that is at great variance with my expectations. I had to ask her once again to excuse my ignorance of the British legal system. I thought a judicial review meant that a judge reviewed the merits of the case in private. Apparently this is not what it means at all. The mere filing of a request for judicial review would be publicised, throwing all prospects of privacy out the window. The proceedings of the request process would be disclosed or leaked, meaning that sensitive details we have kept from the press would possibly be reported. This is all before a ruling was even made as to whether the request for judicial review would be granted or not.

---

29 AUGUST 2014

Kate has had a conversation with Officer One which makes her deeply pessimistic about 15 September. She advises that I prepare myself to be charged.

Goold feels that there is no prospect of being dismissed if I turn up at Charing Cross Police Station. She feels that there are only two possibilities: charge or re-interview. She is probably right. All of the Yewtree suspects I am aware of who were released without charge were let go via a communication to their lawyer or by a 'no further action' letter. They were not freed on site. This makes sense, in a perverse sort of way. Having decided not to proceed with a suspect, the police are not going to want to waste an additional calorie of work on him. That includes having what for them will be unproductive meetings.

Of the two remaining options, my solicitor feels a re-interview is unlikely. This is because she has been told, in response to her direct question, that my accuser was never re-interviewed after all. The *raison d'être* for the two-and-a-half-month rebail turned out to be bogus.

I am typing this sentence at the request of Charlie Russell, the filmmaker who is in the flat to shoot footage while I am still in my rebail period. He wants to capture what it is like to live in limbo. Part of this is to film me working on this book. Since it is likely that there will be some sort of decision within three weeks and I have not allowed any other cameraman into the house, Russell will probably have a dubious exclusive.

He is here on the precise day I begin my eleventh month on bail.

---

30 AUGUST 2014

I have emailed a few people concerning the prediction that I will be charged on 15 September. However, I can't help but have a sneaky feeling that dismissal could still be on the cards.

One reason for this odd optimism is a report from Gary Farrow OBE, who through both his work as a PR and his marriage to the *Sun* columnist Jane Moore came to know several of the journalists bound up in the branch of the phone-hacking scandal known as Operation Pinetree. What is this police obsession with trees?

Farrow reports that quite a few journalists got ready for their 'effective' police visits. Their lawyers assumed charges would be made. On the morning of the planned meetings, these solicitors received emails telling them that the cases were over. Using his typically straightforward phraseology, Gary says, 'They like to fuck with your mind.'

My friend Phillip raises an intriguing possibility. He suggests that the police may have not re-interviewed my accuser despite their stated intention to do so because he may have disappeared or changed his mind. I mustn't forget that I'm not the only person who finds ten months of tension difficult to take. If my accusers thought they were in for a quick hit, they were mistaken, and could have had second thoughts, particularly upon learning that any trial would take another eight months or so to occur. At first I think Phillip is being imaginative, but since this entire episode is fanciful, there is a slight possibility he could be right.

Christopher and my brother Peter independently point out a further source of hope. Since the police never re-interviewed my accuser, they have nothing now that they didn't have on 30 June, unless something has developed in the deep background. I have been told that the CPS are required by law to charge someone who they feel is a criminal. If they are going to charge me now they should have charged me then.

Alan Ayckbourn, the modern master of farce, has nothing on these guys.

——— 1 SEPTEMBER 2014 ———

Our three-day break to Copenhagen looms. We depart Sunday morning very early. I would say 'bright and early', but it's so early it won't be bright yet. I look seriously at the city map for the first time and discover that Christopher has booked an Airbnb apartment in the city centre, within walking distance of the most strategically located Metro station in the entire town. We can get there from the airport without changing trains. I am relieved. Now all I need to figure out is when to get my kroner, in advance or at Copenhagen Airport.

Joan Armatrading calls to report that she has received a letter purporting to be from Jeremy King. She wants to know if it is legitimate. Yes, I tell her. Our favourite restaurateur has indeed started his fundraising campaign. His letter moves me greatly. It is so kind that I will not quote it for fear of being accused of having written it myself.

Gwyneth Williams, controller of Radio 4, calls to check in. She is seeking a progress report. As we begin speaking, I know she is preparing to be polite and tell me that the recording of the new series of *Counterpoint* will have to proceed without me on Friday in the Broadcasting House radio theatre. She wraps the news in a cocoon of genuine concern. She says at least four different times that she will have her fingers crossed for 15 September and hopes that I can be back on air soon. As far as I'm concerned, Gwyneth is a keeper.

Bearing in mind that a charge now appears likely, I have emailed Dame Helena Kennedy requesting the contact she has for a private investigator.

Although the wording of her return message is merely meant to convey that she is on holiday, it stuns me.

'I am sorry,' she writes. 'We are now in Salem. I will get the number to you.'

Honey, we are all in Salem now.

I don't like the way I feel tonight. During a screening of the new Lasse Hallström film, *The Hundred-Foot Journey*, I get a feeling not distant from depression.

Part of this is directly attributable to a ridiculous eating experience last night, when I bit into a supposedly stoneless olive that hadn't been pitted after all. One of my teeth lost the battle. When I removed the mess from my mouth there were elements of black olive, brown stone and white tooth. It looked like an amateur test drawing for a new national flag.

My long-time dentist, Peter Lawrence, manages to fit me into his busy schedule today and shows me an X-ray of the now not-all-there tooth. Thank heaven the damage is nowhere near the nerve. He smoothes the surface and assures me I will not suffer pain before the 45-minute session he schedules for 11 September. I can travel to Copenhagen without fearing toothache.

This news is reassuring, but the fact remains that my tongue occasionally makes contact with my damaged tooth. We are ordinarily not consciously aware of our head. We know we have one, but we don't think about it. Tonight, sitting silently in the screening room, I became aware of it. My thoughts ... those not directed at Helen Mirren, Om Puri and co. ... are focused on my tooth, my mouth and my cranium, which is a ridiculous way to watch a movie. With my emphasis so strongly on the physical, all thoughts that do not have counterparts in the material world fade. My obsessive rage diminishes. I am left with a very flat feeling, that I was destined to spend the next two weeks in a limbo land as dark as the unlit cinema.

Unlike my arrest, which came without warning, my possible indictment approaches with plenty of advance notice. I become more real, not imaginative, about what is happening. Forget about the whys and wherefores of how this case came to be brought. At this point there is no reasoning, only experiencing, and I may be about to experience another profound injustice.

I attend the press show of *Little Revolution*, the new play by Alecky Blythe at the Almeida Theatre. It concerns the Hackney riots of 2011. Christopher is in the show and has taken great pleasure and pride in preparing for the premiere. Having had a nap before travelling to Islington, I am alert throughout the performance. I feel in the moment to such an extent that my own problems seem a vague and distant nightmare.

Until actors portraying Metropolitan Police come on stage. The minute I see them I feel angry and repulsed. I know so much more now than I did three years ago about how the Met treat people that my feelings about these disturbances have changed.

While reading today's thirty-page quota of Proust, I am struck by what may be the reason I have not feared a charge as much in the past eighteen hours as I recently have. We are dreading 15 September because Officer One told Kate Goold the date would be 'effective'. But he would never have told her this if she hadn't emailed and then phoned him, trying to get some sort of hint before she went on her two-week sabbatical. We would still be merrily cruising along towards the bail date as we have all previous ones, without a clue as to what might be about to happen. It could be that we've gotten excited about nothing. Of course, that last sentence will look naive if I am actually charged on the 15th, but today I am not as worried about it as I was yesterday at this time, which is a relief.

At lunchtime Christopher and I take Jennifer to her farewell lunch. She leaves my employ tomorrow. We go to Brasserie Zédel. Chris Corbin and Zédel manager Stephen Macintosh happen to be at the front door as I arrive. I don't know if Chris realises that today I have received my first cheque from his business partner Jeremy King's fundraising campaign. Joan Armatrading followed her request for my bank details with a direct funds transfer two days ago; today I have received a cheque from Ivan Massow. To have followed Ivan in his life arc from living in a squat to being in the financial position to help me out is extremely touching. I decide that since Corbin has not been directly involved in the campaign, I won't mention it. If he is keeping tabs, he will know about it, since Ivan's gift came via Jeremy.

I do tell Chris and Stephen that I am at Zédel for my PA's farewell lunch. They ask whom I am going to get to replace her. I have to talk around the subject, not wishing to let them know that I cannot afford to hire someone new. The pros that they are, they arrange that at the end of the meal, when Christopher and I are reeling from the richness of our chocolat liégeois, Jennifer is presented with three almond cakes on a presentation plate with the chocolate lettering 'Merci Beaucoup'. We have had a great lunch. At the end, Christopher asks his sister what the best and worst moments of her employment have been. The best, she says, was attending my Burt Bacharach *Friday Night Is Music Night*. The worst was having to tell me she was leaving.

Charlie Russell has viewed the footage that he shot in the apartment last week and is very pleased with it. After the compliment comes the next request: can he film me leaving home en route to the police station on the morning of the 15th? I congratulate him on being professional and ballsy enough to ask directly for what he wants. However, I have to inform him that I cannot guarantee that the 15th really will be effective, and that there will come a point, although I don't know what that is yet, where the moment will become genuinely private and for Christopher and me only. I propose that Russell ring back on the morning of Saturday the 13th, when we will have a sense of whether I really am going in on the 15th. Yewtree has a strict sense of weekends and holidays, so if I haven't heard by Friday the 12th I won't hear anything on the 13th or 14th.

---

6 SEPTEMBER 2014

While there are a couple of weeks left in astronomical summer, meteorological summer having given up the ghost at the end of August, Christopher and I are off for three days to Copenhagen. This is our 'summer holiday'. Of all years, I could have used a long break in 2014, but Christopher's acting performance and rehearsal schedule has kept us in London. If I wanted to flatter myself, I would say that I have been a supportive husband, but being honest I admit that during the crisis I rely on his support and choose to be close to him.

Just after I have finished choosing three days' worth of wardrobe, which is considerably more than three changes of clothes, I get an email from Ben Sullivan. Responding to the news that my solicitor fears a charge on my 'effective' bail date of the 15th, Ben informs me:

> I didn't hear that I had been NFAed until my bail date. My lawyer also said that the more the police give an indication of what will happen, the more likely it is to be good news … i.e., they are much more likely to tell you that the bail date is going to be effective if the reason is NFA rather than charge (they want to protect the element of surprise as much as possible). When I read that this bail date would be 'effective' I was filled with a sense of (very) cautious optimism.

'(Very) cautious optimism' is more than I have dared allow myself recently. This reading of the runes by Ben temporarily exhilarates me. For about ten seconds I have the feeling that it might be over. I have not had the weight of this experience lifted off my shoulders since last October. The usual anxieties kicked in at the eleventh second, but it was a great ten seconds while it lasted.

Rather than stew about this 24/7, let's go away for three days. Let's hope it is wonderful, wonderful Copenhagen.

---

11 SEPTEMBER 2014

Having just returned from Denmark, it is an odd but fitting surprise to encounter Sandi Toksvig, Britain's favourite Dane, outside our apartment building.

'My wife is trying to get out of the garage,' the Radio 4 presenter explains. Son of a gun, her wife really is trying to escape. We open two doors and Debbie exits. We stand on the concrete pavement swapping stories of Copenhagen, the comedian's hometown. Sandi lowers her head in reverence when we agree that the food is fantastic.

My former team captain on *Call My Bluff* gets the last word once again. I have not spoken to her about my case since she and Debbie renewed their vows in a ceremony at the Royal Festival Hall on 29 March. I explain that I first learned that the operation does not demand evidence, only people who agree, when Yewtree rang Liz Kershaw and asked if she wished to make an allegation against Dave Lee Travis. Sandi says, 'They phoned me and asked if I would like to complain about anyone.'

'Anyone?' I repeated, genuinely shocked.

'A-n-y-o-n-e,' she replied slowly.

The Times today carries on its editorial cartoon page a substantial article by Daniel Finkelstein. Called 'Why Jim Davidson's ordeal matters to us all', the article has a subhead: 'The arrest of celebrities is shining a light on a flaw in our legal system that leaves thousands of suspects in limbo'. Finkelstein offers a summary of Davidson's *No Further Action*. I utter a silent scream of delight. Someone from an upmarket newspaper has finally taken this essential book seriously. All the sections of the comedian's book I have wanted to shout about from the rooftops are here, including, remarkably courageously for a Murdoch newspaper, the fact that the comedian learned of his NFA from a friend from *The Sun*.

Towards the end of the piece, as Finkelstein is writing about the eternity of British bail, I make a cameo appearance.

> The police are allowed, effectively, to keep people on police bail for as long as they wish. Paul Gambaccini, for instance, was arrested in October 2013 and is still on bail. What on earth is going on? How can they possibly be investigating that case nearly a year later? It is a gross infringement of his civil liberties.

It looks as if I have a new best friend at *The Times*! I now officially exist as a wronged person. I am particularly tickled that Finkelstein mentions me without qualification. I am not 'broadcaster Paul Gambaccini' or 'journalist Paul Gambaccini', I am just Paul Gambaccini, and it is assumed people know who I am. That momentary giddiness ends when I realise that at the moment, of course, I literally am not 'broadcaster Paul Gambaccini' or 'journalist Paul Gambaccini'. I am unemployable and am civilian Paul Gambaccini.

Chris returns after midnight from a post-performance dinner with friends. My 'effective' bail date is now only three days away. However, the Dave Lee Travis retrial is overrunning. We agree that my most likely outcome on Monday is not a charge or NFA but yet another rebail. This is a sensational conclusion to reach, since legal advice tells us otherwise, but we can't see me being freed while DLT is still in the dock.

---

12 SEPTEMBER 2014

I have lunch with Christopher Simpson across the street at Canteen. As I leave the flat, Chris appears at the threshold of his office and says, 'Only a few hours left for a rebail. They won't do it over the weekend.'

Simpson and I sit in the glorious sunshine of our blessed extended summer. Halfway through my roast chicken and my companion's macaroni and cheese, my husband cycles up in helmet and protective glasses.

'I have news,' he says. He leans in and whispers so I hear it first. 'Rebail.'

In the few moments that I have been out of the house, Kate Goold's colleague Rhona has called.

As Chris recalls it, when he answered, 'Hello, Paul Gambaccini's office,' Rhona asked, 'Hi, is Paul there, please?' and words very much like these were exchanged:

> C: No, I'm afraid he's out at the moment. Can I take a message?
>
> R: OK, can you just let him know that Rhona from Bindmans called?
>
> C: Oh, hi, Rhona, it's Chris. How are you?
>
> R: I'm good, thanks. I'm just calling with news, but not really bad news.
>
> C: He's been rebailed?
>
> R: I'm afraid so. I'm really sorry.
>
> C: Oh, don't worry. It's exactly what we expected given that the Dave Lee Travis trial was delayed.
>
> R: Yes. Well, sometimes the CPS move in mysterious ways and other times they move in pretty obvious ways.
>
> C: And this is a pretty obvious way.
>
> R: Yes, and it's so wrong that Paul's case, which is very different from all the other cases, gets mixed up with them.
>
> C: I know. Did they give a reason?
>
> R: Well, I spoke to the police officer, who said that the CPS are still deliberating and haven't reached a decision.

C: That makes it pretty obvious what's going on.

R: Yes, and I'm sorry you're going to have to tell Paul.

C: Don't worry, it's what we were expecting, so it won't be any great shock.

The tentative, but not precise, date is 6 October.

The look on Christopher Simpson's face is priceless. He has once again witnessed one of the most private moments of my Yewtree year. Not just witnessed, been part of.

Now it begins: emailing all my friends in the UK and US who are awaiting news of my Monday court date. Since the police have jumped the gun by three days, I at least have some time to complete the task and don't have to do it all in one marathon session.

---

13 SEPTEMBER 2014

My attention is drawn to an item in Janet Street-Porter's column in today's *Independent*. It is called 'The Kafkaesque plight of Paul Gambaccini', which I will quote – how can I not quote something so supportive?

After introductory material, Janet writes:

> His life has been turned upside down. How can the police need a year to decide whether to charge someone? Why should bail be indefinite? In 2013, 57,000 people were on bail in the UK – more than 3,000 had been held for over six months. The Law Society has proposed a 28-day limit on bail, and Liberty, the rights organisation, is campaigning for a six-month limit. There are dozens of people who have been held for more than two years. This is a shocking state of affairs, and the treatment of Paul Gambaccini is a disgrace.

I've known Janet since the mid-1970s. I have followed this smart, talented and unafraid woman through the frequent ups and occasional downs of her career, including her unintended casting as Minister of Youth or whatever they called it at BBC Television. But I haven't spoken to her since my arrest, which means that some well-wisher has filled her in on my case.

If I were a betting man, I would wager that the matter Street-Porter has addressed will be the most likely subject for legal reform when all this is over. The other two are a statute of limitations on sex crime allegations and equal anonymity for accuser and accused. An end to endless rebailing seems to be the topic that is gaining traction in the newspapers and the House of Lords.

It is only in the afternoon that I learn that Dr Michael Salmon was charged yesterday. He is Yewtree 17; I am 15. I have been leapfrogged in the charging process. This partly explains why I was rebailed yesterday instead of the planned date of Monday. Throughout my experience, every rebail has been carefully timed to occur with a more sensational Yewtree development. Last time, I was rebailed the day Rolf Harris was convicted. Before that, it was the day Max Clifford was sentenced. The effect has always been to bury news of my rebail. This works to my benefit, since it keeps me out of the press, so I am not complaining, but I know that this technique is not used to be considerate to me.

When I mention the coincidences of the last paragraph to a lawyer, she laughs. She cannot believe that the CPS are organised enough to co-ordinate so sophisticated a calendar.

---

14 SEPTEMBER 2014

Radio 2 holds its annual Festival in a Day at Hyde Park. I am grateful to be invited and still considered part of the team. Indeed, even if it is only for economic reasons, my Saturday evening programme is now scheduled for a midweek late-night repeat, although whenever that will occur is up to the Crown Prosecution Service.

Christopher and I attend and are warmly greeted by old friends. Everyone we speak to is horrified by my Yewtree anecdotes. I've known Tony Black-burn for forty-three years and he has never been so tactile. As a matter of fact, he has never been particularly tactile at all, but he embraces me a couple of times yesterday in a show of support.

I keep having to preface my stories with 'Chris has heard this dozens of times'. I admire his stoic smile. One of the anecdotes that knocks eve-ryone sideways is the Sandi Toksvig 'A-n-y-o-n-e' phone call.

The first encounter we have is perhaps the best. We meet Tom Watson MP, whom we have both admired for a long time. Tom immediately tells me how he had been following my shun by the Labour Party.

'You were with us when nobody wanted to know,' he recalls. 'In all the dark years when nobody wanted to know, you were there. You stood by Gordon. You were the last one left!' When we fill him in on the precise details, he is even more horrified, but shrugs and says the current leader-ship operates differently from its predecessors.

15 SEPTEMBER 2014

The day begins with a phone call to Kate Goold, who has returned from her sabbatical. The latest rebail means that she is no longer as pessimis-tic about a charge as she was the last time. The 'effective' date proved not to be effective.

Wait a minute, the move to 6 October isn't the latest rebail. Kate calls me back to tell me that my next date has just been moved back to 13 Octo-ber. 'The Custody Suite is booked on the 6th.'

Jokingly, Christopher says that is too bad. A lover of custard, he was looking forward to my going to the Custardy Sweet.

16 SEPTEMBER 2014

I am touched by the avalanche of email love that I am receiving from friends after the latest rebail. What distinguishes this tsunami of support from the previous ones is the total contempt they have for the police and CPS.

In response to my subject heading 'Rerererererebailed', one of my Monty Python friends goes one better and writes 'Fuckemfuckemfuckemfuckem-fuckemfuckemfuckemfuckem!!' A knight of the realm opines, 'The police and the CPS should be sent to Syria!' A journalist from *The Observer* simply says, 'Jesus fucking wept Xxxx'. 'Oh for fucks sake' is the simple message from a former television presenter. 'B*****DS!' is the one-word thought of a leading figure in the Labour Party.

Two composers with whom I have worked express their disappointment with humour. 'Very sorry to hear that,' writes Oliver Davis of London. 'Did you ask them which year?' Alastair King in New York says, 'They can't milk this much longer. Poor cow must be dry already!'

'The Custody Suite sounds lovely,' replies Paul Bajoria. 'I hope you have sent them plenty of riders.'

Lest the reader get the impression that all my friends are either foul-mouthed or comedians, or both, there are also solemn responses.

'Our support for you is unconditional and unwavering,' write a loving couple from Vermont. 'Hopefully in a few weeks it will no longer be needed.'

A music producer in Birmingham quotes Psalm 109:29: 'Let my accusers be clothed in disgrace, enveloped in a cloak of shame.' I admire his deep knowledge and note that I should probably remember this one for a conversation-stopping comment at parties.

'You know,' I can tell anyone who gets fresh, 'It's like Psalm 109:29. Let my accusers be clothed in disgrace, enveloped in a cloak of shame.' That'll either stop them in mid-sentence or cause them to turn around and walk away.

A friend from Hyde Park Square days who was interviewed on my behalf gets down to the real nitty-gritty: 'I hope you can sue the Met and CPS for a few million on the grounds of mental cruelty and loss of earnings.'

As a trend watcher, I am fascinated by the unanimity of hostility now felt in the arts and entertainment world towards the police and CPS. They should not be expecting many complimentary tickets in the foreseeable future.

At least there is some good news today. When I Google myself I once again see photos of myself rather than Jimmy Savile.

---

17 SEPTEMBER 2014

Mathew Bose phones during a break in his commercial voiceover work. He has come down from Leeds for the day and wants to check in on my case.

The actor is best known to the general public for his role as Paul Lambert in *Emmerdale*. I take the opportunity to ask him about another person who has graced the cast of the soap opera, David Easter. Not long ago I had Googled 'accused *Emmerdale* actor' trying to find news about my old friend Cy Chadwick and was startled to find the Mail Online headline '"I am relieved this ordeal is now over": *Emmerdale* star speaks of his joy after being cleared of rape allegations'. The photo was not of Chadwick but rather of David Easter.

What is going on here? Not being a fan of soaps – not even as a boy, when they were finding their footing in afternoon American television – I've never heard of the apparently estimable Mr Easter. Wait a minute, I do recognise him ... he was in the 1979 movie *The Music Machine*, which was directed by my friend Ian Sharp, and I saw him at the Palladium as Pharaoh in the Jason Donovan take on *Joseph and the Amazing Technicolor Dreamcoat*.

(My memories of this show by Tim and Andrew always begin with my great pal from college, David James Carroll, who originated the role in America at the Brooklyn Academy of Music. Taking the subway back into Manhattan after a performance, he revealed that cavorting on stage in a loincloth was no fun. 'I have to wear this audio backpack up my ass.' David went on to earn two Tony nominations before his untimely death.)

Fast-forward to 2014, and the Mail Online subheads on the David Easter story, complete with asterisks, tell the story:

> The actor, 54, was accused of historic assault seventeen years ago on woman in her forties * Alleged victim made claims after seeing him play Gil Keane in *Emmerdale* * Questioned by police but it has now been dropped due to a lack of evidence * Mr Easter spoke of his relief and says the 'allegations were unfounded' * Lawyers claim alleged victim used the Jimmy Savile scandal to try to 'cash in'

Several points about this puzzle me, but Mathew cannot help me. His time on the show did not overlap Mr Easter's. As a matter of fact, nor did it overlap Cy Chadwick's. I am as clueless as I was before he called.

One thing that does leap out at me is the desire of David Easter and his lawyer to go public on a case that presumably could have stayed private. This is not the kind of issue a person wants to be associated with, as Freddie Starr learned when he aired his grievances in public and was hit with more accusations. There must be a reason Easter went wide on this. Perhaps I will learn in another thirty-five years.

And why haven't I heard anything new about the Cy Chadwick case? Maybe I haven't been looking in the right places. I Google him, and up comes an article from the 30 June *Daily Mirror*. 'Former *Emmerdale* actor Cy Chadwick wept yesterday after he was cleared of indecently assaulting a young boy almost thirty years ago. A jury took less than two hours to unanimously acquit Chadwick, 45, who played bad boy Nick Bates for ten years on the ITV soap.'

In the words of the film *Little Big Man*, 'My heart soars like a hawk.'

---

18 SEPTEMBER 2014

Charlie Russell is due at 10 a.m. for an update on his film project. Being only seven pages away from finishing the second volume of Proust, I sit down at 8.30 and polish it off.

I give myself a few brownie points for now having read the first two books of *In Search of Lost Time*. This one, *In the Shadow of Young Girls in Flower*, was even more impressionistic than the first. Plot is not Proust's strong point. The most dramatic thing that happens in the entire 531 pages is that, at a crucial moment, the hero does not get kissed. But even more than in the first and more famous volume, Proust takes pages to convey a feeling, describe a sensation, universalise specifics. A typical and important one comes near the end of the book.

'One way of solving the problem of existence, after all,' he takes a deep breath and continues,

> is to become so closely acquainted with things and individuals we once saw from further away as being full of beauty and mystery, that we realise they are devoid of both: therein lies one of the modes of mental hygiene available to us, which though it may not be the most recommendable, can certainly afford us a measure of equanimity for getting through life, and – since it enables us to have no regrets, by assuring us we have had the best of things, and that the best of things was not up to much – in resigning us to death.

Charlie arrives. He interviews me on the latest developments in my case, particularly the rebail until October and the Custardy Sweet delay. As usual, I have to do a little verbal juggling to avoid saying more than I believe is wise, although he is a formidable interlocutor and asks what interests him. I trust him, and Chris does, too. My husband is happy to make cameo appearances as he walks around the house.

We discuss how Chris can tell from my body language when I am having a rage attack. As we discuss these periods, which by now are thankfully down to one or two a day, I casually mention that when I get furious at

Ed Miliband, I play the Timi Yuro hit 'What's a Matter Baby', imagining the Labour leader has gone down to a crushing electoral defeat. To demonstrate, I sit at my desk, play the song on iTunes, and narrate the lyrics to camera. This turns out to be the best footage of today's session. Even as I am doing it, I realise that, in televisual terms, it is 'working'. When the song is over, Charlie tells Chris it is the funniest thing he has ever filmed.

The lyrics are, courtesy of Eden Music, Inc.:

> *I know the reason you've been crying, oh yes*
> *I heard she won't be needing you*
> *How does it feel being the one left behind?*
> *What's a matter baby? Is it hurtin' you?*
> *I know you found out she's been cheating*
> *And I heard she even told you she was untrue*
> *How does it feel being on the outside lookin' in?*
> *What's a matter baby? Is it hurtin' you?*
> *Remember, remember when I needed you so bad?*
> *Remember, remember what you had to say?*
> *You told me to go find another shoulder to cry on*
> *And you laughed, you laughed and you walked away*
> *I know that you've been askin' 'bout me. Ha ha!*
> *Well I'm sorry, but I've got somebody new*
> *And my hurtin' is just about over*
> *But baby, it's just startin' for you.*

I tell director Russell I realise that, far from suffering 'crushing electoral defeat', Ed Miliband is likely to be the next Prime Minister, but that will be then, and this is now, and this year I take comfort when and how I can get it.

At various points during the day I check to see if the jury has reached a verdict in the Dave Lee Travis case. The first site I am directed to, Mirror (what – no 'the'?), suggests I am looking at a report on a Greek trial: 'Updates as Dave Lee Travos jury consider verdict'. Unfortunately, the jurors have retired for the day. There is neither verdict nor ouzo.

---

20 SEPTEMBER 2014

'You are going to make British legal history,' Andrew Lloyd Webber predicts in a phone call. His powers of prognostication are exercised over the length of time I have spent on bail. He has returned from a stay in New York to find that my case continues long past what he thought possible. Reading the Daniel Finkelstein piece in *The Times*, he has been shocked.

Andrew feels that enough people of influence have been similarly horri-fied to ensure a change in the law in the near future. Apparently Geoffrey Robertson is going to use his appearance at the Cheltenham Literature Fes-tival on 4 October to call for some sort of reform. Geoffrey and Andrew bonded over the subject of the mistreated Stephen Ward, about whom Robertson wrote a book and Lloyd Webber a musical. The composer may attend the QC's talk. 'It's on the night *Phantom* is due to open in Moscow, which due to current events I am less inclined to attend,' my old friendly acquaintance says. 'I can't believe this is happening in my country.'

I am grateful again to Janet Street-Porter, who writes about my case once more in today's *Independent*. 'There should be a time limit on police bail' is her headline.

'Now the Lib Dems are considering whether to put a time limit on pre-charge bail in their 2015 election manifesto,' she reveals. This is the first time that the clause Lord Paddick has been telling me about has been publicised.

'Another week has passed since I wrote about the fact that BBC pre-senter Paul Gambaccini was arrested by Operation Yewtree in November 2013, and still hasn't been charged with anything,' Janet continues, using for her timing not the date I was arrested but the day my identity was publicised. 'Are the police really making active inquiries, or are they just inept? I think we know the answer.'

In the evening, I tell Christopher about Andrew's phone call. Once again, he offers a cool and incisive perspective.

'If there is law reform because of this, it would have been worthwhile.'

He's right. I've been stretching the elastic bands of my brain trying to think of an outcome that could make the past year anything more than a close brush with totalitarianism. If hundreds or thousands of people could be spared what I have experienced partly as the result of what I have undergone, the ordeal would indeed have been worthwhile. As a Royal Shakespeare Company veteran turned franchise icon might say, make it so.

---

22 SEPTEMBER 2014

Darren Cheek has come to stay as a houseguest for two nights, a welcome and convenient visit while Chris is spending three days surfing in Portugal.

At dinner we manage to speak about the Scottish referendum and other topics before inevitably getting around to the latest in my case. As I think of the Labour Party's support for false arrest and psychological torment, I marvel that Ed Miliband would tie his party's fortunes to such a lame horse. Why were the police confident they could get a conviction on a dumb accusation that would have required time travel? And then I have a 'Eureka' moment. If Archimedes could have a revelation in the bath, I can have one in the Delaunay.

Maybe they weren't. Maybe the Met were not sure they could get me on that particular allegation. All that mattered was that it was an allegation. By publicising it they could get bandwagoners with more credible accusations and create the illusion of a 'pattern of behaviour'. They were frustrated not because they backed a nag in the first place but because they didn't get any better runners after publicising my arrest. And why shouldn't they have expected others to 'come forward'? They had in almost every other case. They ran the race for four months and, after all opportunities for foreign travel had been exhausted, gave up expanding the case and submitted it to the Crown Prosecution Service. The CPS, having been handed a horse-poo bag, have kept it smelling up their office for what is now over half a year, unable to turn shit into Shinola but reluctant to lose face too quickly by admitting that the case is complete crap.

When, at bedtime, I phone Chris in Iberia, he instantly agrees with my theory.

'Of course,' he says. 'They arrested you on a Tuesday but named you on a Friday, in order to get maximum press coverage over the weekend, assuming they would get bandwagoners.'

Whether he is right, whether I am correct, the extension of this case beyond all reasonable extent is making us both conspiracy theorists, juggling the behaviours of the police, the popular press and politicians. The campaign is so insidious that some conspiracy theory must be correct. We just don't know which one it is!

23 SEPTEMBER 2014

Even though I have been checking every few hours for a verdict on the Dave Lee Travis case, I always knew there would be a good chance that I would hear it in an unexpected fashion. So it is when I return home from lunch with Aaron Cezar of the Delfina Foundation to find an email in my inbox from Nancy Jones with the subject heading 'DLT "Guilt"'.

I go straight to the BBC website and learn of the irony. (This is irony, isn't it, or is it just coincidence?) Having been cleared of twelve charges the first time around with two hung counts, DLT was sent back to trial by the Crown Prosecution Service on the two unresolved matters. He was then hit with a new accusation. It was the new one on which he has been convicted.

This falls right into place with my thought about my own case last night

– that the police may not have been certain of a conviction on my allegations, but that didn't matter because they were confident publicity would bring forward numerous bandwagoners, at least one of whom could nail me. They probably never dreamed that no one would join Primary and Secondary.

———————— 25 SEPTEMBER 2014 ————————

Tim Rice arranges and pays for … pays for! … a pair of tickets to his Broadway smash *Aladdin* for when Chris and I are in New York in October. I label it 'his' show when there are actually four writers, but he did pen the words for the show's big song, 'A Whole New World', so you would think he would get the occasional freebie. We talk for more than half an hour about developments in the witch-hunt.

I receive one of the most unexpected phone calls of my life. Jim Davidson calls for a long conversation in which he offers complete support and 'much love'. We talk for nearly twenty minutes, during which time he tells me several things that were not in his book. I am extremely grateful for this strength from 'the other side', someone who has already been through what I am still enduring. There are only a few of us who know what it is like to be us, and Davidson knows. He offers words of wisdom for the aftermath: 'Our job is not to get revenge. Our job is to survive.'

———————— 26 SEPTEMBER 2014 ————————

I get up. I turn on the computer. I go to the *New York Times* website. I cry.

'Jeter's Fitting Farewell at Yankee Stadium' is the front-page headline. 'With the eyes of a sport upon him, Derek Jeter smacked the winning hit in the final at-bat of his final home game.'

Even though I am from the Bronx, I was never a fan of the 'Bronx Bombers', the New York Yankees, because I adored Willie Mays of the

New York Giants, who played nearby. But no one who loves baseball can have been unaware of the remarkable Derek Jeter. Even someone who does not know or like the sport can appreciate his contribution, not only to playing excellence but to personal standards.

In an era when star athletes go from team to team for ever-increasing salaries, Derek Jeter stayed with the New York Yankees for twenty years. This type of loyalty is unheard of today. Furthermore, he maintained the highest personal standards. A colleague of Christopher's from his advertising days worked with several of the world's leading sportsmen. She recalls that they all slept around and were rogues, except for Jeter, who was a model gentleman.

Last night was the final home game that he played at Yankee Stadium. It was not expected that the Yankees would come to bat in the ninth inning because they were leading 5–2 at the end of the eighth. Everyone assumed the Orioles would roll over and that would be the end. But the Baltimore Birds managed to tie the score in the top of the ninth, forcing the Yankees to come to the plate one more time. A player named Antoan Richardson reached second base, bringing Derek Jeter to bat for an unexpected additional appearance.

I watch the ensuing eight-and-a-half-minute 'Derek Jeter's Last At Bat at Yankee Stadium (full)' on YouTube. On the first pitch, Jeter hits safely into right field to score Richardson with the winning run. The capacity crowd goes bananas. Teammates swarm onto the field to embrace him. One by one, he greets them and, as he does, you notice several things. Even though the game is over, the fans do not leave. They stay standing in continuous ovation. The Yankee victory song, Frank Sinatra's 'New York, New York', plays over the loudspeaker system. Outside of Derek's field of vision, a group of former teammates and his original manager Joe Torre line up for their chance to salute him. These all-time greats stand silent and unmoving in tribute. Jeter finally sees them and greets them all warmly. He runs over to the stands and visits his parents.

And then, when there is nothing left to do, he does something perfect. He walks out onto the now-empty field, goes to his position of shortstop for one last time, and bends down in the infielder's crouch of readiness. The moment only lasts for a few seconds. It can last no more. The greatest shortstop in the history of the New York Yankees leaves the field.

By now I have completely lost it. Somewhere around the second minute I tear up. By minute three, water is rolling down my cheeks. I have loved baseball like I have loved oxygen, loved it since I was five years old, when I worshipped the Say Hey Kid and thought Giants pitching ace Johnny Antonelli was my cousin (he wasn't). More time in my life has been spent playing and watching baseball and softball than all other sports put together. I have experienced and observed moments that were thrilling, exhilarating, or simply deeply satisfying. This single moment combines all these elements and more. This is sport as art.

I am reminded that there is goodness in the world, there is beauty and there is truth. Not only will I experience these things again, I can experience them now, appreciating moments like Derek Jeter's farewell.

I go downstairs, where Christopher is having breakfast, and announce to him before he can see me that something beautiful has made me cry. I don't want him to think I am weeping over some tawdry development in Operation Yewtree. Chris has seen Derek Jeter in action at Yankee Stadium and knows of his legacy. As devoted to sport as any man I have ever known, my husband 'gets' the moment. Watching me cry for the first time this year, he starts to cry, too.

'I can't believe that after all you've been through, I see you cry for the first time, and it's because of baseball,' Chris says. 'And you made me cry.'

---

27 SEPTEMBER 2014

I have received a letter from Ed Miliband. Of course, he doesn't know it.

It's a mass mailing electronically signed by King Klutz. It tells me I can renew my Labour Party membership 'and help fight for a fairer society'.

Here is an organisation with huge debts, 'still deep in the red', as the *Financial Times* put it on 29 July, wasting money, even if it is second-class postage, sending begging letters to a man – *moi*, to be precise – who has less chance of donating to it than David Cameron. I've previously asked them to take my name off the mailing list, but no such luck. Will the Labour Party not exercise the 'right to be forgotten'?

It is a bit more melancholy that I have received a solicitation from the National Theatre to renew my patronage. Had I not been tapped on the shoulder by Big Brother last October, I would happily be continuing my contributions. I was for years on the rota of National Theatre Platforms interviewers, hosting events, some memorable, in all three theatres. Recently I hosted two fundraisers in the Olivier for free, out of sheer enthusiasm for the NT. Yet when I was arrested no one from the organisation got in touch to ask what my case was all about. All communication, except for asking for money, ceased.

18 SEPTEMBER 2014

I host an evening honouring Quincy Jones at the Royal College of Music. Quincy has asked for me personally, which is quite an ego boost when you are otherwise unemployed. I perform my basic roles of traffic cop, getting contributors on and off stage, interviewing Quincy alone and, later, with songwriter Rod Temperton, and conducting an audience Q&A.

Jones, a true citizen of the world, has done just about everything worth doing and visited everywhere worth visiting during his eighty-one years, short of appearing in the Major League Baseball All-Star Game. It is always a pleasure to talk at his leisure. This time I am particularly ... here comes the word ... thrilled to have Temperton join him on stage. Rod, whom I have always found a gentleman, has a reputation as a recluse, but in show business this merely means that he does not seek publicity.

I have to ask what was for me, but apparently nobody else, an obvious question: why Vincent Price for the rap on *Thriller*? We now know that he was spectacularly right for the job, but what gave Temperton, who wrote the words, the feeling that Price would be the man?

'I was thinking of Elvira,' Rod answers, referring to the Los Angeles television horror hostess. Like John Zacherle in New York years earlier, the voluptuous Mistress of the Dark linked low-budget creature features and fright fests to provide continuity.

Quincy had a better suggestion.

'My wife, Peggy Lipton, knew Vincent Price. I told Rod I'd have her ask him.'

'I thought he was dead!' Rod exclaims, cracking up the audience.

These two dear old friends are a great double act, bouncing back and forth.

> So Quincy tells me Vincent Price is coming into the studio at two in the afternoon the next day. I have a meeting in the morning that goes from breakfast to lunch and forget all about it. At noon Quincy calls me and says, 'Do you have anything yet?' I tell him it will be alright and start writing words down. I'm writing in the cab to the studio. I get there and I see Vincent Price getting out of a limousine. He is delayed by fans seeking autographs. I tell the driver to go to the back door and rush in, telling a secretary to type up the words. By the time Vincent got into the studio, the words were on his music stand. He had never been in a recording studio and spoken to a rhythm track, but he got it in two takes.

Two takes for one of the best-known spoken-word passages in history!

'Quincy remembers what happened next,' Temperton says, passing the ball back to his teammate.

'He asked me if it was OK,' Q picks up. 'I told him yes.

'"Back in the closet," he said, and walked out through the double doors.'

Today I begin my twelfth month on bail. What have I learned?

Nothing about my case, that's for sure. I have not spoken to any police officer since the day I was arrested and have been forbidden by my bail conditions to attempt to get in touch with my accusers. I still know nothing about the two complainants except that they took horse-riding lessons in Hyde Park and that one of them was a pupil at a famous public school, that one of them claimed to have met me in Waitrose in Finchley Road where I allegedly told him to 'fuck off', while the other claimed that a person who had never lived in my apartment had once answered my doorbell and told him to 'fuck off'. Outside of their common two-word vocabulary and shared penchant for four-legged friends, I know nothing about them. Perhaps when this is all over they will ride off into the sunset together chanting obscenities.

Today I receive an email which is heartening to get on the eleven-month anniversary of my arrest. Daniel Finkelstein of *The Times* tells me:

> I am now taking the police bail issue up in a focused way. I raised this with Chris Grayling about an hour ago and (between us strictly for the moment) he agrees that something needs to be done.
>
> It is, however, a Home Office issue so Richard Harrington (MP for Watford) and I are going to seek a meeting with Theresa.

For those who need a glossary, Chris Grayling is the Lord Chancellor and Secretary of State for Justice. Richard Harrington was once assistant to the managing director of Waitrose, so he knows more about Waitrose in Finchley Road than I do. Theresa is presumably Theresa May, although there is a medium in Long Island named Theresa Caputo appearing on the Dr Mehmet Oz television show today. She might have more of a clue about this case than any of us. After all, her latest book is called *You Can't Make This Stuff Up*.

Finkelstein wrote a good piece in *The Times* on Saturday called 'The dubious policy at the roots of Yewtree', telling the Liz Kershaw story. I have told this so many times that I now recite it like a jukebox selection. At least this time there is an embellishment. Finkelstein reported that Liz, having heard Yewtree were calling around for her, rang them.

'"Hi Liz," said the officer who answered. "We've been trying to get in touch with you but we realised we've been talking to the wrong Liz Kershaw."'

Then Finkelstein quoted the officer giving the best précis of Yewtree strategy I have yet encountered.

'"If it was just one girl obviously the Crown Prosecution Service would probably throw it out. But if more than one girl came forward, well…"'

'The clearest statement I have ever seen of the dubious policy of using legally weak individual allegations to support each other.'

---

30 SEPTEMBER 2014

Here we go again. Gary Farrow emails me with a link to BBC breaking news: 'Radio DJ Neil "Dr" Fox arrested in London by police investigating claims of historical sex offences'. By the time I get there, the story, which is only three sentences long, is number one on the most popular stories chart. This will be cold comfort for Neil, who for years had the nation's highest-rated chart show. It isn't the kind of number one that DJs dream of.

This is not a Yewtree. The police officers have come from Westminster. They arrested Fox after he came off today's breakfast show at 10 a.m.

Daniel Finkelstein is obviously having an interesting Tory Party conference. Yesterday he emailed of his meeting with Chris Grayling. Today he informs me, 'I have now spoken also to the Home Secretary. Talked about the politics of it with her and she was very open to the thought that she should act. Will arrange to see her to talk further. Will let you know as we go along.'

I am struck yet again how all the issues that now matter most to me — an end to indefinite rebail, equal anonymity for accused and accusers, and a statute of limitations on sex accusations — seem to be discussed exclusively by Conservatives. Labour still shows no interest in justice.

Stephen Fry hosts the launch of his book *More Fool Me* at a function house in Portland Place. The kick-off for a volume of Fry autobiography does qualify as an 'event'. Sales in six figures are expected. The book has even attracted a first-of-its-kind notoriety with the first two pages of the chapter 'Moral or Medical?' being a simple list of all the places in which Stephen consumed cocaine years ago. The first sentence on the third page reads:

'I take this opportunity to apologise unreservedly to the owners, managers or representatives of the noble and ignoble premises above and to the hundreds of private homes, offices, car dashboards, tables, mantelpieces and other available polished surfaces that could so easily have been added to this list of shame.'

From my perspective as a non-user who has never known cocaine, I marvel at two things. First of all, Stephen was in his heyday a sniffer about town, snorting his way around London and even taking the powders in Fortnum and Mason. Cocaine for him, chocolates and candied chestnuts for me: this has been the substance abuse story of my life.

The second aspect of this that impresses me is that he has gotten away with beginning a chapter with a two-page list. This is as revolutionary a literary technique as I can recall, as equal in its bravado to Nora Ephron dropping recipes into the text of *Heartburn*.

Hugh Laurie is at the launch. He is in fine form, greeting old friends with genuine affection. Hugh enthuses to one pal how great it is to be back home from Los Angeles.

'London has been beautiful,' he purrs, 'beautiful.'

Then he remembers that I am there.

'I know it looks different right now from your perspective, but it is.'

1 OCTOBER 2014

To my astonishment, Neil Fox is reportedly talking to the press outside his London home. To each his own.

'I'll work hard to clear my name,' he is quoted as saying. 'Obviously I had a very stressful day.' Bearing in mind he was reportedly questioned for seven hours, this falls into the category of Understatements of All Time. He is also not exaggerating when he says, 'It was a complete surprise.'

Kate Goold (remember her? My case has gone so quiet it's hard to believe she's still my solicitor) responds to the Fox case from her lawyerly perspective.

'Soon, all police resources are going to be diverted into investigations into alleged sexual assaults from the '70s and '80s,' she only half-jokingly predicts. 'That's when Theresa May will start listening to a possible statute of limitations.'

2 OCTOBER 2014

Andrew Shaw calls from Manchester relaying a friend's cynicism about the latest celebrity arrest. He has asked if Neil Fox has been accused of impersonating a doctor.

It seems that last night, while Christopher and I were enjoying the hospitality of Nigel Evans, Stephen Fry was appearing on *Newsnight*. I watch his exchange with Evan Davis on the BBC website. Stephen has taken a bit of guff for discussing his historical drug use. While I'll leave the subject of cocaine to people who have actually used it, I can't help but note that Davis steers the conversation to historical sex abuse.

Once again, I get the feeling that I am being discussed without being present. The BBC report reads:

> Fry also said it was wrong to use the term 'victims' for alleged victims

'before the case has even come to court, before certain figures have even been charged'.

He said: 'If they're guilty then quite clearly there should be evidence, but they shouldn't be hung out like flypaper to try to attract other 'oh yeah, I think he touched me too when I was that age'.

I sense that Stephen has made a contribution to the English language when I attend a dinner with luminaries including Tim Rice, interior designer Vanessa Brady OBE and Lewis Carnie. One of the guests mentions that Fry has been on *Newsnight* and attacked the practice of putting suspects into play like 'human flypaper'.

All is not fun and games, though. I am informed during this dinner that yet another of my former Radio 1 colleagues has been accused and had his computers taken by police. In his case, the allegation has not led to an arrest. At what point does it become an official travesty that the disc jockey profession has been singled out for accusations of historic sexual abuse, as if all perverts were DJs and all DJs perverts, as if no women ever inappropriately touched men, as if sportsmen and businessmen never offended?

--- 3 OCTOBER 2014 ---

Today would have been my mother's ninety-fourth birthday. She passed away at the age of ninety-one, so she has missed Yewtree. I'm glad she was spared my case. She knew I loved this country, and would have found it bewildering that it had assumed several characteristics of the world's most repressive regimes.

I get excited hearing 'Street Fighting Man' by the Rolling Stones broadcast on Absolute Sixties. No matter how good a song sounds when you play it at home, it takes on immediacy and full force when it is heard on the radio. Then it is not just an oldie, it is music in the moment, and it is, at least for three minutes and eighteen seconds, alive. I know it is 3.18 because I am looking right now, in a frame next to this, at the list of my iTunes selections in order of plays. 'Street Fighting Man' has emerged to become the runaway number one since my arrest, with 105 listens. The opening hostilities between Keith Richards and Charlie Watts are as good a capture of anger in cyberspace as I have heard. 'My name is called Disturbance,' Mick Jagger has just sung.

The record is ironic, of course, which has escaped most people. The whole point is that 'In sleepy London town / There's just no place for a street fighting man', hence the often-quoted line 'Then what can a poor boy do / Except to sing for a rock 'n' roll band'. There is no chance of my becoming violent, but every chance of me expressing my anger through music.

And if I don't immediately credit the copyright holders, ABKCO Music, they might become angry.

---

4 OCTOBER 2014

Today, Andrew Lloyd Webber makes a dramatic statement on my behalf at the Cheltenham Literature Festival, where he appears with Geoffrey Robertson QC in the discussion of the case of Stephen Ward. Drawing a link with the wronged man in the Profumo scandal trial, Andrew states that 'I am going to get into deep water here, but there seems to be an abuse of the system going on at the moment which is intolerable'. The *Gloucestershire Echo* quotes him as saying, 'They seem to arrest someone and wait to see if someone else comes out. In the case of Paul Gambaccini he is left in limbo unable to work ... which seems wrong.' There is hardly anyone more establishment than Baron Lloyd-Webber, so the Cheltenham event is a useful sign of support that could eventually lead to law reform.

This could be the last chapter of this book until my next date with the Metropolitan Police, an appointment Christopher senses will be decisive. We fly to New York tomorrow for eight days of sanity and return the morning of my rendezvous with 'The Custody Suite'. Either this book ends very soon, or we're in for a second volume.

The day dawns beautifully in my hometown. It is, as Christopher's Spart-acan friends say, a bird, a bluey, a bluebird in full.

Chris and I have been fortunate. The weather on our New York holiday has been gorgeous. We have had a four-day extension of summer. Since my host Deborah's apartment is on the East Side, and most of our personal and entertainment destinations are on the West Side, we have been cross-ing Central Park numerous times, enjoying different variations of paths and roads. We have roamed in the Ramble, passed by the Plaza and shuf-fled past Sheep Meadow. The park is a paradise. Unsafe to enter in my young adulthood, it is now a mecca for families, athletes and pedestrians. If we lived here, I could spend time in a different part of the park every day for a fortnight and never repeat myself. It is an attractive possibility.

Today we view three apartments, as arranged by my old realtor Carol Gat, thankfully still in the game. The first two are in a building on 57th Street that was considered state of the art when it was erected in the 1990s. It enjoyed commanding views of Central Park. Recently it suffered the most modern of architectural fates, being dwarfed by a new neighbour across the street. The tower known as One57 is as close to a pie in the face as a building can be, destroying the outlook. The apartments we are shown are still advertised as having 'Central Park views', but this is only true if you consider catching a glimpse of the park around the corner of the structure facing you as a 'view'. To make things worse, as we enter the master bedroom of the second of the two flats, Carol, who has a sublime sense of the details of her trade, cuts to the chase and, in the presence of the vendor, says, 'I hear a motor.' She is right, as she always is. A whirring motor is visible on the roof of a nearby building.

'It hasn't bothered the owners,' the sales representative cheerfully says, but I imagine sleepless nights with a buzzing inside my head. We quickly move on to the third viewing.

It is a high-floor apartment in Lincoln Center. It is a revelation. We walk in and Chris and I independently have the same thought: 'I could live here.' It has the most simple of floor plans, a living room and two bedrooms side by side, but all have wall-width picture windows with commanding views of the Hudson River and New Jersey. We are a measurable part of a mile up in the sky, and the horizon is so far away, it is hard to tell there is one. I hear the Pet Shop Boys singing 'Go West'. Granted, the clear blue sky helps today's view, but I can't help but imagine endless beautiful sunsets.

The current owners have shown a keen sense of the New Yorker's fetish for closet space, and my CDs and books would probably fit. This building has the only private pedestrian access to the cultural buildings of Lincoln Center, where I would probably spend as much time as I do now in the Southbank Centre. Many of my favourite food shops and restaurants are within walking distance. My brother lives only a few minutes away.

'Buy me! Buy me!' the apartment shrieks at us. We cannot yet succumb to its siren call, but knowing this kind of option is open to us if we have to leave Britain is tremendously reassuring.

---

10 OCTOBER 2014

I arise at 6.30 in a still-dark New York City. I check my emails to see if there is any news from Kate Goold. Chris and I have concluded that today is the last day on which I might receive another rebail. Come Monday, I will either be released before my scheduled late-afternoon visit to the police or charged at the station house.

There is a message from Kate, but it contains no news. She asks what she should do if she receives any word today. Do I want to hear it, or would I rather wait until I am back in London on Monday morning?

I reply that if it's bad news, I don't want to hear it. It would be gruesome knowing that I was leaving a country of freedom to face trial in a police state. It could wait until Monday morning. Ignorance may not be bliss, but it is at least bearable. Good news, on the other hand, is welcome any time.

After sending the email, I begin shaving. As I apply the shaving cream I get a slight feeling of dizziness.

Oh no, I pray, don't let it happen. Nonononono. Don't let this happen again.

Fourteen years ago, when I was living in County Hall North, I had a severe dizzy spell as part of an anxiety attack. That time I had to crawl out of the bathroom into my bed, where only by lying in a single position could I avoid the sensation that the universe, or at least my immediate surroundings, were revolving around me at breathtaking speed. My assistant Christopher Beecham arrived shortly thereafter to find me in that situation and sat with me for two hours until I recovered.

Now I hasten to finish shaving before an attack can set in. I do, and it does. This time I don't have to crawl, but do manage to stagger down the hallway to the room in which Christopher is still sleeping. It is now 7.45. He is due to awake at 8. I know he won't mind being deprived of fifteen minutes of sleep if it means he can nurse me during sudden illness, but I have to wake him gently and talk him through the situation calmly. I hold a towel in case I have to vomit. Although I rarely lose my lunch, and don't this time, it feels like I might any second.

This time, lying on the bed is of no use in allaying my symptoms of dizziness. I have to sit in a particular position. Even while I am still, the room swirls around me at a nauseating pace. And I am sweating. I am really sweating. Chris marvels that my hair is wet, as if I had taken a shower. My clothes are soaked through. This is an ideal way to lose weight: sweat it off without moving a muscle.

Chris gets a phone call and leaves the room to take it. I am left on the bed in my precarious sitting position. I can't lean left. I can't lean right. If I do either, the room swirls like the Hadron particle collider.

Chris returns to the room. He gets on the bed and bestrides me so I don't fall either way from the impact of what he is about to tell me. There are tears in his eyes.

'I have good news,' he says. 'No further action.'

The phone call was from Kate. When Chris had seen she was ringing, he had left the room in case the content of the call was distressing. Now he has returned with joyful news.

This was never the condition in which I expected I might receive it. For the entire fifty weeks of my Yewtree experience, I have managed to avoid illness. I haven't even had a cold. Now I learn that my case is dismissed while in the middle of an anxiety attack.

I call Kate back. She has few other details and does not even know yet if my co-accused has also been NFAed. I point out she has my release statement on file if anyone should ask for a response, although she must make sure it is updated and 'eleven months' is modified to 'twelve'. Chris suggests a vital addition of three words, which I accept, and recommends I delete reference to this book, which I do.

I don't want this statement forced upon a waiting world, but merely available if anyone expresses interest. Goold is not certain it will be needed today anyway. She is going to call the police back and see if they can delay releasing the news until Monday, the day of my return.

Having your case dropped by the Metropolitan Police and Crown Prosecution Service is the best therapy I can recommend for curing an anxiety attack. I can suddenly move without fearing I'm going to fall over. I no longer think I'm going to be sick and I've stopped sweating. I go to the computer in the living room and open my emails.

So much for Kate thinking the police might follow her proposed timetable and keep the story quiet over the weekend. To my astonishment, the lead email in my inbox is from Mike Hanson, the weekend editor of Radio 2. He wants to know if the good news is true. Scores of emails flood in before my eyes. I Google various news websites, beginning with the BBC, and the story is on all of them. There has been a coordinated release of the information within about an hour of my hearing it.

Nigel Evans was really prepared. Within two hours the *Telegraph* carries his bylined article 'Paul Gambaccini ordeal reinforces need to protect identities before charge'. When I saw Nigel earlier in the month he had told me that he expected me to be NFAed. He obviously meant it. He was ready, and his article eloquently expresses the case for what he calls 'anonymity until charge'. He concludes, 'Justice Secretary Chris Grayling should wait no longer and protect the identity of those under investigation but not charged.'

I'm preparing to read the rest of my press when Chris tells me that he has had a missed call from a Los Angeles number. We Google it and it turns up an equity firm. He phones and asks if anyone has rung him. The operator is at a loss to guess who it might be. I get an inspiration. Does Moscow Paul work there? Yes, he does. Within minutes, he calls back.

I sigh. The press, which I want to read so badly, is going to have to wait. A chat with Paul is always of a minimum half-hour's duration.

Any lack of enthusiasm I have for talking at this moment flies out the window the minute we start. What my former lodger has to tell me is explosive. One of the Metropolitan Police officers who flew to LA to interview him has called to tell him that the case has been dropped. In so doing, he happens to mention that the Met thought the chances of a successful prosecution were 3 to 5 per cent, when the current climate requires 70 to 80 per cent.

Three to five per cent? I spent a year on bail for a 3 to 5 per cent chance? I ask Paul to repeat the figures. He does. Still in disbelief, I say, 'Not thirty to fifty?' He replies again: 'Three to five.'

Paul has further important information. Sixteen has also been NFAed and wants to speak to me. He has given Paul his number so I may ring. As it is already evening in London, I will wait until the morning.

Besides, the press awaits. I grit my teeth and start to read. I have always anticipated that the Crown Prosecution Service, rather than saying I was 'not guilty' or 'innocent', would use the weasel words 'insufficient evidence to convict'. But even I am staggered by its final statement. The CPS soils me with its own excrement.

The CPS spokeswoman says, 'Having carefully reviewed this case, we have decided that there is insufficient evidence to prosecute in relation to allegations of sexual offences made by two males believed to be aged between fourteen and fifteen at the time of the alleged offending.' It is noteworthy that not only is there 'insufficient evidence to convict' me, there is 'insufficient evidence to prosecute'. In other words, there is none. There is no, and never was a, case against me.

The statement, though gratifying in that sense, is horrifying in another. This is the first time the specific allegations against me have been made public. Mentioning them is completely unnecessary. Going down for the third time, the CPS is trying to drag me down with it.

This smear on my character will stay with me to the grave and beyond. Newspapers will report this accusation and it will be part of their cuttings files for all time. Obituaries will mention it. This type of gratuitous character assassination is unacceptable in a just society.

The Crown Prosecution Service disseminates lies. It's time to stop respecting it just because it has the word 'Crown' in its name. So does Royal Crown Cola, and most people drink Coke or Pepsi.

Alright, Clown Persecution Service, let's do it. You want it, you got it. Let's go mano a mano. You've thrown down the gauntlet. I take it up. Now that my bail restrictions have been removed, I am going to investigate your precious 'victims'. I will discredit them.

II OCTOBER 2014

Well, that wasn't hard. Within a few hours I learn more about my case than I did in twelve months.

I call Sixteen as he requested yesterday. It is the first time we have spoken in years. He tells me that Primary and Secondary both lived in our neighbourhood in the late 1970s, on feeder streets leading into Hyde Park Square. I did not know them, but being teenagers at the time they probably knew the building that their local Radio 1 DJ lived in.

Late last year, Christopher and I tried for days to discover information concerning Secondary. Nothing came up on Google that was helpful. What we didn't know was that all we needed to do was to add the phrase 'hacked to death' and the name of a certain Third World country.

'Hacked to death'? Third World?

Up comes an article from a national newspaper published more than twenty years ago. A horrible headline tells the grisly story. I read on in disbelief.

Secondary returned from work to find his wife hacked and battered to death by a gang of robbers.

I can't help but think of a prayer I was taught as a child: Hail, holy queen, mother of mercy, our life, our sweetness and our hope…

The thieves then attacked Secondary with knives, seriously wounding him.

… To thee do we cry, poor banished children of Eve: to thee do we send up our sighs, mourning and weeping in this valley of tears…

They beat him until he told them where the money was. When he feigned death, they left.

… Turn then, most gracious advocate, thine eyes of mercy towards us…

He hit the panic button to alert security. The killers were captured. Chris and I know this because we read the proceedings of the resulting court case.

… And after this, our exile, show unto us the blessed fruit of thy womb…

Searching for clues in my own case, I have opened a door I should not have. Inside is only horror. Enough. This is terrible. Although I cannot be certain the reports are accurate, I have to believe they may well be.

Why would a man who has endured unimaginable wrongdoing inflict injury upon other innocents? How could anyone who has survived the rigours of an unbearable court case wish to go back to the witness box?

I already know that Secondary did not go to the police. The police went to him. Primary had accused us, and when the police asked if anyone could corroborate his claims, he gave them the name of Secondary. This does not necessarily mean that Secondary wished me ill.

It would certainly fit what Secondary has supposedly told an intermediary. In Sixteen's account, Secondary told a mutual acquaintance that he never accused me and had said to the police that he would not testify against me in court. Secondary also says that he never liked Primary, whom he considered unreliable. 'Primary was expelled from Catholic boarding school at the age of fifteen for making a false sexual allegation against a priest.'

Excuse me?

'Primary was expelled from Catholic boarding school at the age of fifteen for making a false sexual allegation against a priest.'

Oh my God.

He has form.

If Sixteen is correct, when Yewtree opened up and the government offered money, Primary did it again. This time his target wasn't a priest. It was a man who made a conscious decision not to become a priest. Me.

There will be plenty to think about as we fly back to London from New York on Sunday night. The main thought is that it appears I have endured a year of psychological torture because the police bought the act of one man who had done this before, many years ago, and who did it again, seemingly because the Metropolitan Police invited the public to accuse celebrities and told them, 'You will be believed.' They sowed falsehood, and they reaped lies.

---

13 OCTOBER 2014

This was going to be my bail date. The case being dropped, I do not have to appear at Charing Cross Police Station at 5.30 p.m. as previously arranged. It's just as well. I'm exhausted. I arrived home this morning after an overnight flight to find 300 emails and an overflowing answer machine waiting. Flowers sent by Margaret McDonagh, Tom Robinson and Sue Brearley have already been placed in vases by Darren Cheek, who stayed in the house last night.

Among the messages of support awaiting me are good words from Radio 2 colleagues Tony Blackburn, Bob Harris, Annie Nightingale, Dermot O'Leary, Suzi Quatro, Liza Tarbuck and Johnnie Walker. How sweet it is to be loved by them.

The front-of-house staff inform me that several reporters had made personal appearances in the hours after my clearance. Shaun Wooller of *The Sun* left a handwritten note on a piece of torn-out notebook paper requesting that I call him 'or come out to speak to me briefly'. He, and others, obviously thought I was holed up inside, as I had been in the days after my arrest. It really was useful that we were in New York at the time.

With all good wishes to Wooller, who is a reporter doing his job, it mystifies me where *The Sun* gets its endless supply of chutzpah. This is a newspaper that has printed false or misleading material about me for decades. When I was arrested, it made a meal of it for days. Now it dares send somebody to my home pretending to be a friend? It is a peculiarly British habit to be beastly to someone and then pretend the next day that there are no consequences for beastliness, that the offended person will be only too happy to suit up and get back in the 'game' that passes for tabloid journalism. I did not grow up in Britain, and do not play the game.

The day is devoted to making a dent in my messages while taking two blissful ninety-minute naps. The magnitude of the job is daunting. I understand why Jimmy Tarbuck, having begun the task of writing thank-you letters, found it overwhelming and went to Portugal.

---

14 OCTOBER 2014

I am struck by how many of my sympathetic messages come from members of the House of Lords. It is hard matching the impression of stuck-up lords and ladies I had when I was a newcomer to the UK with the cross-party bunch of hard-working achievers I know in the current House.

15 OCTOBER 2014

I awake in the middle of the night to see that Christopher has sent an email with a link – *The Independent* has run a story about a speech that Home Secretary Theresa May is expected to make today to a College of Policing conference under the headline 'Journalists' phones to be off-limits to police'. Buried as the last line in the story, at least the last line that survived the edit, is 'She will also say that the college is to investigate whether a statutory time limit is needed on pre-charge bail to "prevent people from spending months or even years on bail only for no charges to be brought".' This is great news that makes going back to sleep easy.

By the time I get up in the morning, almost all the other papers have picked up on the story, and they have inverted the *Independent* priorities. They are focusing on bail reform. I am the poster boy in the coverage, with all the stories save one using me as an example of someone kept on bail unreasonably long. Even *The Sun*, which had sensationalised my arrest, runs the story on page two with the first sentence 'Home Secretary Theresa May will today blast police for keeping celebrities and journalists on bail for years.' This clearly includes a veiled reference to the phone-hacking suspects who have been kept on edge for over a year, but I don't mind their company when we're talking social change.

'It comes just days after DJ Paul Gambaccini described the "trauma" of being on bail for a year on sexual abuse allegations. The Crown Prosecution Service dropped the case last week.' *The Sun* goes so far as to use the word 'torture' to describe the experiences of the 'journalists and other suspects'.

What a difference a year makes. After I was arrested, I felt like I was waving from a parallel universe, desperately trying to attract the attention of someone, anyone, who might wish to bring to light the injustice I was experiencing. Today, nearly every paper is noticing, and I seem to have been the tipping point in the case for bail reform. I could not feel more relieved. Perhaps my determination to make a contribution to civil rights after my case ended will actually bear fruit.

Kate Goold relays a request from BBC News for my reaction to the Home Secretary's statement. I am still accustomed to being ignored by the media, and it does not occur to me that anyone might quote me. I state what Chris and I have already concluded: 'If my ordeal can help prevent other persons from suffering a similar fate, it will have been worthwhile. That is why I respond to Theresa May's initiative with enthusiasm. I hope it leads to change that will prevent future injustices.' Having given Kate this statement, I think nothing more of it.

The day runs away with itself. Christopher and I prepare to spend the afternoon and night at the new Beaumont Hotel as the guest of co-proprietor Jeremy King. We are in on the ground floor of a new venture, even if our room is on the first floor. There is another reason for us to be excited. This is the first night in nearly a year that the police haven't known where we are. We go to the spa, we enjoy a complimentary dinner in the Colony Grill restaurant, and I gape at the team photo of the 1929 Chicago Cubs.

This shrine, seen daily by unsuspecting visitors to the gentleman's room off the foyer, contains three individuals of enormous importance. Rogers Hornsby is the all-time National League batting champion. William Wrigley is the founder of Wrigley gum, a packet of which was, in 1974, the first product ever scanned with a bar code. Club president William Veeck is the father of Bill Veeck, the baseball impresario who staged the sport's greatest stunt in 1951 when he hired a three-foot-seven variety artist to bat for the St Louis Browns, ordering him to bend over to reduce his strike zone to 1.5 inches. The pitcher could not deliver to such a small area, and the small man drew a free pass to first base. He was replaced by a pinch runner, concluding his career.

Hornsby and Veeck were memorably connected the following year, 1952. The former player was now managing the Browns. Seven midgets attended spring training hoping to make the roster, but Hornsby sent them all away.

The hotel is great. The team photo is the ultimate.

—————————— 16 OCTOBER 2014 ——————————

We have asked the Beaumont to deliver *The Times* as our morning newspaper, realising that this is the cheap way to beat its paywall. I do a double take when I see the page-seven headline: 'Paul Gambaccini hails Theresa May's move to reform police bail'.

Who would have guessed? We have been incommunicado in a hotel with only Kate Goold knowing our whereabouts, yet this morning I awake to find myself the belle of the reform ball. The quick statement I gave Kate Goold has achieved wide circulation.

The *Mail* headlines 'Paul Gambaccini welcomes Home Office plans to limit length of time suspects can be on police bail after his ordeal lasted twelve months'. But the real stop-the-press paper is the *Telegraph*, which has three pieces about me. The first, by '*Daily Telegraph* reporter', is headlined 'May backs bail limit after 5,400 in limbo for more than six months'. In addition to being grouped with Jim Davidson and Freddie Starr as long-term bailees, I am the subject of a quote from John Harding of Kingsley Napley solicitors: 'The Paul Gambaccini case shows only too clearly that lives are put on hold and reputations damaged by investigations that go on and on, sometimes with no eventual charges.'

The second *Telegraph* piece concerning me is an extended item in Allison Pearson's column. Allison, a fine writer of years-ago acquaintance, opines, 'At last, sanity prevails for gentle Gambaccini.' I include her final paragraph not to compliment myself but to demonstrate her generosity of spirit:

> Paul Gambaccini is a gentleman, with the emphasis on gentle, and among
> the most knowledgeable people ever on popular music. It is shocking
> that he has been put through this ordeal in a free country. Let us hope
> that he can resume his life where he left off. Strike up the band!

But the most important Gambaccini-related item in the *Telegraph* today is the leading article, titled '"Parking" suspects on indefinite bail is unjust'.

I am delighted to be associated with this call for change. This is the first *Telegraph* editorial to mention me since the paper celebrated my Radio 3 programme being dropped. At least this one is more generous.

Not everything of interest and quality in today's press concerns Theresa May and me. *Billboard* makes one of this year's most entertaining typographical errors. Discussing Thom Yorke's new album release through peer-to-peer file-sharing company BitTorrent, the music business bible reports that 'the album bundle has surpassed 3.5 downloads already'. I bet Thom is waiting for the next .5.

<hr>

17 OCTOBER 2014

I have a second phone conversation with Sixteen. He cancels our Sunday dinner with great regret. His radiotherapy has left him 'skeletal' and too weak to attend a restaurant.

I am terribly sympathetic with his health dilemma. There but for fortune, et cetera. But I am also itching to meet him to learn more about Primary and Secondary. Today I learn that the latter now lives near Regent's Park. The temptation is almost too great to resist! I know his name, even his middle name, I know his profession and I know he lives near Regent's Park. Should I attempt to approach him?

<hr>

18 OCTOBER 2014

The day is unexpectedly spent with extended family business. My teenaged godson calls in tears and asks if he can come over. He has been living with his grandparents, but his granddad died earlier this year and now his grandmother is undergoing concentrated care. To make things even more unbearable at home, one of his aunts has accused him of being the death of her father and the cause of her mother's decline.

I was asked to be the boy's godfather while he was still a foetus. His parents were excited about his forthcoming birth, but I knew there was likely to be trouble. They were teenagers with no income and no prospects. His father, my next-door neighbour in Islington, was a sweet child to me but a terror to almost everyone else. He was likely to get into trouble, and he did.

Dad could not deal with early parenthood and one day said, 'I can't cope', exiting eastward to Essex. Mom was in no state to take the boy on, having walked in front of a mammoth McDonald's lorry on the Holloway Road at four in the morning and taken years to recover. The grandparents came to the rescue, but, at least for today, I do. My godson is a good kid, so I'm glad to play my part, but I can't believe the irony. Ten days ago I was forbidden by bail conditions from unsupervised association with children under sixteen. Today I'm responsible for one.

---

20 OCTOBER 2014

Christopher and I have a pleasant dinner with Sandi and Deborah Toksvig, who are staying in our building while their London base is being organised. After a few moments, it is evident that they don't know I've been cleared. They haven't read British newspapers for years.

'Either there's something unpleasant about a friend of mine or something about me,' Sandi explains. 'It's too upsetting.'

We break the good news and the general exultation can be heard as far as … well … the next table.

---

21 OCTOBER 2014

I have my first meeting with Kate Goold since my clearance.

For the first time, Kate expresses the opinion that she was certain I would never be convicted. Nonetheless, she was afraid that if I did go to trial I would be a changed man, never able to believe in Britain again and certainly never able to trust the police. I would have emigrated upon acquittal. I ask her if she ever feared I would jump out of a window, and she quickly replies, 'No.'

From Kate's office at Bindmans I go to the first meeting of the Ivor Novello committee in this year's awards cycle. There are a few new members. One of them, Gary Barlow, mentions in passing that he hasn't read an English newspaper since 1999, reminding me of Sandi Toksvig's comment of the previous night. Chairman Gary Osborne criticises the Crown Prosecution Service for revealing the details of the accusations against me after deciding they were not worth pursuing. He asks, 'Why reveal the ages of the people you didn't have sex with?'

I awake from a nap to be told by Chris, 'You were just on the news.' What is it this time? It's the 4 p.m. newscast on the Steve Wright show, and the announcement has just been made that I am to return to Radio 2 on 15 November. I check my emails and Chris has forwarded one from a friend who works at the Royal Bank of Canada. He attaches a report from the Press Association titled 'Cleared Gambaccini Returns to Radio'. It begins, 'Presenter Paul Gambaccini is to return to the airwaves next month following a year away from broadcasting following his arrest for historic sex crimes' and concludes, 'Paul will return to his usual BBC Radio 2 show – presenting *America's Greatest Hits* – from Saturday 15 November and his role presenting *Counterpoint* on BBC Radio 4, covering the semi-finals and the final of this year's competition, to be broadcast from Monday 24 November.'

This is how we learn about ourselves.

22 OCTOBER 2014

'Bang bang,' Cher and then Nancy Sinatra famously sang, 'my baby shot me down.' Kate has received a letter from Sixteen's solicitor that will make our quest to learn about the origins of my case more difficult. Sixteen has indicated that 'he would rather not be involved' in my investigation. It is a polite letter conveying completely understandable sentiments. My co-accused is now literally fighting for his life in his battle against cancer and has more personal things to worry about than my reputation. His is, after all, undiminished, as only a few people know he was ever arrested.

To add an element of surrealism to the letter, it is signed by the solicitor David Rowntree, known to the general public as the drummer of Blur. During the past year, the bizarre has been commonplace. Hardly a day has passed without something unpredictable occurring. Still, this is like getting a letter of legal advice from Noel Gallagher.

Kate understands my disappointment at this reply. We are going to have to do more of the work than we had thought.

In the evening, Christopher Simpson delivers the papers before we go to the Wigmore Hall to see Simon Keenlyside and Emanuel Ax perform Schubert's *Winterreise*. Chris did me the favour of collecting all the newspapers published the day after I had been released, when I had been in New York.

The papers can wait. Schubert can't.

---

23 OCTOBER 2014

I am approached by a Labour Party insider to see if I would be willing to co-host a fundraising Christmas party for the Terrence Higgins Trust. Of course I would. I will be eternally grateful that, unlike other charities I supported for decades, the THT refused to shun me during the past year. The politico asks if I would mind if sympathetic members of the Labour Party attended. Of course I would not. The more money for the THT, the better. I am told there is a potential subtext here, with some Labourites below leadership level wishing to extend an olive branch to me. Apparently internal party polls show Labour under Miliband losing next year's election, and these people are looking to the future already. Three members of the

shadow Cabinet – Andy Burnham, Yvette Cooper and Chuka Umunna
– are supposedly being mooted as the next leader, although only one of
these is considering a challenge before the general election.

I find this X-ray of the Labour Party mildly interesting, but hardly of
urgency. Our parting last autumn was complete. As long as Ed Miliband
is leader, I won't even think about party politics.

It is too long since I have visited the home of Tom Robinson and Sue
Brearley. They live just a bit too far south on the Northern Line to be on
my regular routes of travel. But theirs is a house of love, and any visit is
a joy, particularly this evening, when sympathetic dinner guests include
old friend Chris Smith and when we are treated to a drop-in visit by Tom
and Sue's daughter. I am staggered that this person I last saw as a child is
now a beautiful and accomplished young woman.

I tell the gathered guests that Brian Paddick intends to raise the bail
issue in the Lords. Chris, now Baron Smith of Finsbury PC (which presumably does not stand for Politically Correct), expresses his support, and
adds that he will be interested in asking a question about how much my
case cost the taxpayer. I take a sudden renewed interest in a Radio 4 programme that is not my own. *Today in Parliament*.

---

24 OCTOBER 2014

Only today, two weeks after the dropping of my case and with Christopher in the house in case I have a temper tantrum and need calming, do I
look at the papers published the day after my release. It's a good thing I've
delayed, because I would have had a rage attack looking at some of them.

The coverage of the case is utterly predictable. Those newspapers that
have had a good Yewtree are best. Those that supported the witch-hunt
are worst. It's that simple. What's fascinating is that each of the papers that
covers the story in depth takes its own particular angle.

The *Telegraph* is best, running more than half a page of both fresh and background material under the headline 'Gambaccini in clear after twelve months of torment'. Crime correspondent Martin Evans has expertly blended my statement, Nigel Evans's considered reaction, Andrew Lloyd Webber's supportive comments at the Cheltenham Literature Festival and other material, including, for the first time in the Yewtree chronicles, a photo of Carla Bruni presenting me with the Sony Gold Award for lifetime achievement. This piece makes a clear case for equality of anonymity.

The *Daily Mail*, which has won Silver on this issue during the past year, runs a quarter-page story, 'Gambaccini in clear after sex assault inquiry', with the subhead 'But CPS smear him over "attacks on boys"'. Reporter Neil Sears observantly notes that the specific allegations had never been made public before. The main barb of his piece is that the CPS are very bad losers who can't let me go without gratuitous insults.

The Times, which has taken Bronze on Yewtree, gains ground on the outside with a page-two story, 'Broadcaster cleared of sex crimes after torment of one year on bail'. Sean O'Neill is the only reporter to cite the new and tantalising revelation that 'police sources conceded that the case against Mr Gambaccini had been "weak and should not have taken so long to resolve"'. He also takes the gloves off and throws what has become *The Times*'s right hook: 'The length of time it has taken to resolve his case will raise further concerns about the potential abuse of police bail and whether sufficient resources are being devoted to a soaring number of historical abuse cases.'

The Independent buries the story on page twenty-six with the topper 'No charges for Paul Gambaccini', but at least it leads the page. *The Guardian* puts its four-paragraph 'Gambaccini will not face claims over sex claims' at the bottom of page eighteen, underneath the more important story 'Search for owner of lost wallaby that closed road'. Reporter Josh Halliday, who undoubtedly meant well, was the victim of a typical *Guardian* misprint: 'He thanked his lawyers, friend and members of the public for support', as if I only had one friend. Well, at least he's a good one.

I resumed my broadcasting career after dark. The Radio 4 music quiz

Counterpoint always records in evening sessions before a live audience. The variation is in the venue. The show floats from Maida Vale to Salford to last night's location, the radio theatre in Broadcasting House. There is another alteration in tonight's routine. Russell Davies, who has been sitting in for me doing the heats of the competition, is to host the last of them. After an interval, producer Paul Bajoria will welcome me back and I will host the first of the semi-finals.

Filmmaker Charlie Russell wants to capture the event for his mooted documentary. He makes one of his occasional visits to film me leaving home, travelling to Broadcasting House and returning to the air. He has assumed I would go to the BBC by car. No, I tell him, I always take the Tube. Living in central London, I don't have an automobile, and I have learned never to depend on pre-arranged taxis. Too many of them never show up or don't appear on time, leaving me in a state of anxiety as to whether I should rush out to get a different cab or simply wait in hope. You do not want to work yourself up if you are about to make a broadcast. The Bakerloo Line is perfect. The York Road entrance is only yards from my door. Four stops later – three during this period when Embankment Station is out of use – I'm in Oxford Circus, a short walk from Broadcasting House.

And so we have the bizarre spectacle of Charlie Russell filming me in a Tube carriage as I read an article about Billy Joel in this week's *New Yorker*. Heaven knows what the other passengers think. Perhaps as a sign of Londoners' acceptance of their loss of privacy, no one complains or even acknowledges the camera.

The more important misassumption that Charlie has is the natural belief that returning to the air will be a significant and stressful moment for me. A couple of times he asks me, 'How does this feel?' and I can only answer, 'Normal.' It is normal for me to be doing a radio programme. What has been abnormal is life on bail. I tell him that the difficult part of daily existence is making the transition between them, three-quarters of my time readjusting to reality and a quarter of my life, as Nigel Evans and Ben Sullivan predicted, still spent in the world of insanity, writing my book, trying to learn more about Primary and Secondary, and doing all the wrapping up with Kate Goold concerning the Met and the CPS.

I arrive at Broadcasting House and am met by Paul Bajoria, who ushers me in because I no longer have an effective pass. I immediately go into the control room of the radio theatre, where Russell Davies and the staff are hard at work.

Then we rehearse, which merely consists of sitting at the presenter's table flanked by the production assistant Steve Garner and adjudicator David Kenrick, checking levels and running the contestants through a practice quick-fire round to make sure their buzzers are working.

Russell does his show. After an interval, Paul Bajoria introduces me. My return to work is greeted by the warmest reception of my career.

The one element of the show that slightly unnerves me is the new part, the acknowledgement of the work of Russell Davies.

'Our thanks to Russell Davies for hosting this year's heats,' I say. 'Russell meets all the requirements of a *Counterpoint* presenter: veteran broadcaster, good mind, bad jokes. I hope to keep up that standard.' Davies approves it, Bajoria goes with it, and the audience like it. Good. The only hard part is over within ten seconds. The rest is, as I said to Charlie Russell, what I do.

---

25 OCTOBER 2014

I encounter a man I have not seen in years outside Leicester Square Tube Station. He set up a fan website for me before most people were interested in websites, and I have not checked it since last decade. I have even forgotten its web address. To my astonishment, he reports that he has accumulated about a thousand emails for me, many of them sent since my case was dismissed. He proposes to vet them for spam and forward the others in instalments.

26 OCTOBER 2014

I receive the first batch of emails from my website host. It comprises twenty-three pages. There, on pages twelve to thirteen, is a supportive and grateful message from the first man with whom I ever had sexual intercourse. He had sent his email shortly after my arrest. Eleven months have passed. Will he still be on one of the two phone numbers he gave?

The first number is dead. The second one is working. He answers, and we speak for thirty-six minutes.

An entire adulthood is condensed and conveyed. We agree that on his next visit to London we will have to meet. It has been thirty-one years, since 1983. He confirms, with anecdotes that are consistent with the date, that this was the year in which we knew each other. The implication for my case is obvious. Primary accused me of having sex with him in 1978. The first man I ever had sex with dates our friendship to 1983. Primary was five years too early. The police don't know this for sure, however, because they never did contact this first lover. He would not have been difficult to find because he is an RAF veteran and the government must have his current address.

Christopher and I have Sunday lunch with two lawyers and someone who works in the Home Office. I bring them up to date on Sixteen, Primary and Secondary, and break the news that I have discovered Secondary's current address through social media. I tell them my hopes of hiring a private investigator to learn more about Primary and Secondary. At least I might get answers to the two big questions: why did Primary accuse me and did Secondary even accuse me?

Everyone listens carefully. Everyone says I am wrong.

They all think that engaging a PI would be both expensive and dangerous. Since we do not know the mental states of either of the two individuals, it would be possible that engagement of an outsider might trigger further accusations. It is also possible that a PI might unintentionally violate the civil rights of one of the two men, leading to a different kind of action against me.

After we talk the subject through comprehensively, I have to agree with them. It isn't hard to give up the idea. I already know enough to make me happy. Unless and until the police supply Kate Goold with transcripts of the original interviews, which might change my impressions, I am left with my current conclusions. I believe that Secondary would have been too traumatised by the trial of the men who killed his wife to ever seek to be in a courtroom again, and I do not believe that someone who has been the victim of horrific violence would ever wish to inflict harm on an inno-cent person. As for Primary, it is best I do not approach this live wire, and I am content with having heard from a reliable source that he was expelled from school for making a false sexual allegation. The real issue is not his integrity. It is how he managed to play the police. Don't they feel, shall we say, sheepish at having been duped, to the dimension of hundreds of thousands of pounds of taxpayer money?

I leave the lunch to attend a critics' screening of *The Imitation Game*, the Alan Turing biopic starring Benedict Cumberbatch. The hardened hacks give the movie an ovation. It, and Cumberbatch, deserve it. The film has a special piquancy for me. It reminds me of the historic homophobia of the British police, who drove to their deaths both Oscar Wilde and Alan Turing. Without those two men we would have fewer great plays, and the ones we did have would be performed in German. The movie's end cred-its carry the statistic that British police arrested tens of thousands of men in the twentieth century on bogus sexual indecency charges. Thousands of those arrests were obtained through the use of agents provocateurs. I go into a rage typical of the past year.

And then I catch myself. I don't have Christopher to recognise my body language, put his hand on my shoulder and stop me, but I have internalised his intervention. After a year, I know that anger only corrodes the body and mind of the person who feels it. It never touches its subjects. If the emotion I feel about the police is going to be expressed effectively, it can only be through working for law reform. Tormenting myself, being bitter and twisted in public and alienating decent police officers who might, in their own time, improve the service, is not effective policy. I must leave the great majority of honest police to reform their own force, with appropriate nudges from government.

Goodbye, Metropolitan Police. Our Dance of Death is over.

---

28 OCTOBER 2014

Today concludes one year since my arrest. Today I end this book.

Great Britain persecuted me from 29 October 2013 to 10 October 2014. Its agents entered my home in the middle of the night, took away sackloads of my possessions, arrested me on trumped-up allegations, disgraced me in the national media, deprived me of employment and kept me on bail for twelve months even though they knew that they had no case against me. These are the actions of a totalitarian state.

The most amazing thing about this is that no one who participated in the campaign against me thinks that he or she lives in a totalitarian state, nor wishes to. They are oblivious to the roles they played in my persecution. This includes police officers, tabloid journalists, lawyers in the Crown Prosecution Service and all the 'good Germans' who were part of organisations and political parties that shunned me for fear of taint. None of them originated the witch-hunt that victimised me, but all of them went along with it because to resist it demanded more courage than any of them could summon.

The people of Great Britain have always been wonderful to me. They gave me a home when I moved from America. They gave me a quality education and a career beyond the dreams of any dreamer. They were personally kind whenever and wherever I met them for four decades.

They deserve better. I hope they fight for it. I hope they get it.

They said it couldn't happen here. It did. It happened to me. Unless there is reform, it will happen again. It could happen to you.

What are you going to do about it?
Love,
Paul Gambaccini

Epilogue

The Baseball Hall of Fame catcher Yogi Berra, the inspiration for the cartoon character Yogi Bear, was known for Yogiisms such as 'It's deja vu all over again' and 'When you come to a fork in the road, take it'. Sadly, he was wrong when he said, 'It ain't over till it's over.' In the months following the dismissal of my case, I learned many things about it that had previously been withheld from me.

Kate Goold managed to acquire two troves of information before the Metropolitan Police closed down any further disclosure. Together they constituted treasure. One was a chronology of the case. It listed twenty-one dates, beginning with these seven:

04/04/2013	Allegation recorded enquiries commence
16/04/2013	Victim 1 interviewed using ABE [Achieving Best Evidence]
26/04/2013	Extensive enquiries to identify venue and 2nd suspect
02/08/2013	Venue of offences identified

19/09/2013	Further enquiries
26/09/2013	Victim 2 identified
29/10/2013	Subjects arrested (x2)

The other document obtained by my solicitor was a partial case log. It showed numerous different officers signing in and out before the first week of September 2013, making me realise that the officer who told me on the day of my arrest that 'we have twenty people working on this case' was not kidding.

The most important discovery hidden in the second document, however, was the revelation that on 5 September, my case was dropped for 'insufficient evidence'. The case was over before I even knew it existed.

I was staggered. The police had spent over half a year on my case before I was arrested. No one had told me. I also had no idea that 'Victim 2' had not appeared until Month Six. Surely if Primary had thought that Secondary was a key part of his complaint he would have mentioned him in the first half-year? Why did Primary wait until the case was dropped for 'insufficient evidence' before blurting out the name of Secondary?

The timeline reveals when Primary was identified and then when he was interviewed. With Secondary, however, it states only that he was identified but never that he was actually interviewed. If indeed he was interviewed, we were never told where. Therefore, he may never have made a formal or admissible allegation. This may help to explain why the police refused to offer any transcript or video confirmation that Secondary had indeed accused me.

Furthermore, why did the police refer to Secondary as '1st Victim' in the sheet of accusations given to me the day I was arrested, when in fact he did not come into the case until Month Six? In my lengthy interview at Charing Cross Police Station, Officer Two told me that the Met were listing Secondary first because they gave more credence to his claim than that of Primary. Their given reason was that since Primary approached the police with his complaint, he had an interest in the case that Secondary did not. Secondary made his supposed complaint only when approached by the police, so they believed that he was more reliable. I do not know at what point in their investigation the police learned about Primary's past form of making a supposedly false sexual allegation at school, but that may help to explain why they listed him last.

I did not question this logic until after my case was dropped. Not only did I then see that Secondary was apparently never formally interviewed, but I was also approached by an acquaintance of Secondary who claimed that he had never accused me and said he would never testify in court against me. I am left wondering – was my year on bail really based on an allegation from an unreliable witness who offered insufficient evidence and had form in making a false accusation, coupled with a tenuous allegation from a man only introduced after the case was initially dropped? Did the police know that these 'allegations' alone were insufficient to obtain a conviction, but press ahead anyway under the assumption that, as in many prior Yewtree cases, more allegations would arise after press coverage of the arrest? Only the officers involved and Secondary himself will ever know the truth.

*   *   *

Fourteen months after sackloads of my possessions were seized by the Metropolitan Police, and two months after my release without charge, I learned that my possessions were to be returned by two of my case officers. I told them that they could leave the items in the foyer and I would retrieve them.

No, I was told, the policemen would like to come up to my apartment.

I did not want Metmen to return to my home. They could leave the bags downstairs and I would come get them. No, they would like to talk to me.

I got it. They wanted to say they were sorry.

And so, in only slightly guarded terms, they did.

'I genuinely hope you're going to be OK and you're just going to carry on,' one of them said.

The foot soldiers knew the generals had sent them on a bad case.

'An allegation from one lady or two ladies against [name of convicted Yewtree suspect] and then more people decided to come forward,' one of the officers said. 'With yourself, when your name was in the press, no one else did come forward.'

'With [name of same convicted suspect] phone call, phone call, phone call,' said the other officer.

'Did you know about "hacked to death"?' I asked one officer.

'We know about that,' he replied.

I raised the issue of Primary's expulsion from boarding school for making a false sexual allegation.

'I know all about him,' the officer said. 'We know everything about both of them.'

'We were intrusive in finding out about them,' he added. 'In-tru-sive.'

'I suppose I will never know his state of mind in doing what he did,' I said.

'We'll never know,' the officer replied. 'I have my own opinions. I have opinions about everything, opinions about every job we do in my career, but I'll never know.'

He concluded on this subject, 'It's impossible to find out what's in somebody's head.'

This was as remarkable an experience as any in a year of inconceivable events. Two police officers had pilgrimaged to my home to confirm that I had been wronged.

Their behaviour was in stark contrast to that of the Commissioner of Police of the Metropolis, Sir Bernard Hogan-Howe. He appeared on the Radio 4 *Today* programme and was interviewed by John Humphrys.

Mentioning me by name, Humphrys asked the Commissioner point blank if he would like to comment on my case. This was the lawman's golden opportunity to use words the Met had yet to employ such as 'We apologise', 'We're sorry', 'We got it wrong', 'Paul is innocent' or 'Paul is not guilty'. Hogan-Howe chose not to use any of these words. Instead he said … nothing. He went into a defence of interminable police bail.

My first reaction to Hogan-Howe's refusal to apologise to me was 'The Commissioner is not a gentleman,' or words to that effect. I then realised I did not know whether the Commissioner was a gentleman or not. I did not know him. What this exchange really demonstrated was that he was lawyered up to his nostrils. The rank-and-file of the Metropolitan Police were telling me I had been wronged, but the Commissioner dared not even mention my name for fear of lawsuit.

On the day of my dismissal, when Sixteen also received his No Further Action, his lawyer was told by an officer of the Met that 'we expect trouble from Gambaccini'. They persecuted me for a year, and their first concern was that they would get trouble from me? But this quickly became a theme. Four people told me that the police feared I was going to sue them.

This said two things. First, the police know I have reason to sue them. Secondly, they are afraid of lawsuits, period.

And so they stonewall. They refuse to admit any error. They refuse to supply all but the most elementary disclosure to the Falsely Accused. To this day, I know nothing about Primary except that he took horse-riding lessons in Hyde Park and had supposedly been expelled from boarding school for making a false sexual allegation.

The refusal to supply basic information took its most ludicrous form when Kate Goold wrote to the police on 16 December 2014 asking for answers to five very basic yes/no questions. One was whether 'Suspect Two' in my police log was in fact Yewtree 16. Another was whether Secondary had in fact accused me.

'[Secondary] was identified on 26 September 2013,' she wrote. 'Please confirm whether [Secondary] actually provided a statement or made any specific allegations against my client. There is no mention of him being interviewed using ABE in the chronology.'

In early February 2014, Goold received a letter of reply from the solicitor representing the Metropolitan Police claiming that 'Questions 1–4 specifically relate to the detail of the investigation and as such, we will not address these points.' The legal letter from the Met solicitor concluded, 'No further disclosure will be provided in the absence of a proper legal basis for doing so.'

In other words, sue us and we'll see you in court.

If Secondary is reading this book, would he like to tell me whether he did accuse me or if the police misrepresented him? If my case officers can visit me, so can he.

* * *

It had infuriated me that in making its dismissal of my case in October 2014, the Crown Prosecution Service had stated, 'Having carefully reviewed this case, we have decided that there is insufficient evidence to prosecute in relation to allegations of sexual offences made by two males believed to be aged between fourteen and fifteen at the time of the alleged offending.' There was no excuse for putting into the public record in the second half of a sentence accusations that had already been discredited in the first half.

Kate Goold made this point on my behalf in a letter to the CPS dated 17 October 2014. She received a response on 18 December:

> It is entirely appropriate for the CPS to make a public statement of the kind in question. The operation in question has attracted considerable publicity. It is in the public domain that your client was arrested in connection with that operation and indeed your client's arrest – including whether he (and others similarly arrested) should be named, and

why it was that your client and others arrested as part of the operation were on police bail for prolonged periods. Moreover, there is in general a clear and compelling public interest in explaining CPS decisions not to prosecute in cases like this.

I disagree. It is never in the public interest to disseminate lies.

*   *   *

For four months after the dismissal of my case, I resisted all requests for interviews. My wounds were so raw that I was in danger of turning any discussion into a rant. I also knew I didn't have to say anything, as the media was speaking for me. Every point I would want to make was made for me by some individual or another in every serious newspaper except *The Guardian*.

Then, in February 2015, I received an unexpected invitation to testify before the House of Commons Home Affairs Select Committee on the issue of police bail. To me, this was not an invitation. It was a summons. This was an opportunity to speak before the nation's leading lawmakers.

I was told I would be asked questions on the issue of bail and my opinions of Operation Yewtree. I was also asked to submit a document that would let the MPs know my opinions on these subjects.

So began one of the most unpleasant weeks of my life. I wrote an article which could have been subtitled Fifty Shades of Rage. I showed it to Kate Goold and Christopher. They freaked.

My solicitor wrote back immediately saying that I could not possibly submit the screed I had penned. Chris simply said, 'No.' I got back in touch with the Select Committee liaison, who informed me that I was no longer expected to write about Yewtree and should concentrate on my thoughts about bail reform. I wrote a new and temperate article, which won the approval of both my solicitor and my husband.

At this point, Chris had a stroke of inspiration. Sensing that the legislators might not have the time to read my entire piece, he suggested I supply a simple timeline of my case, the dozen dates that provided the details of my arrest and numerous rebails. This proved to be the single most important contribution I have made to the cause. The MPs were in disbelief over the number of times I was rebailed and over how many of these announcements coincided with what I called 'Yewtree win days', on which my postponement would not be noticed by media wishing to concentrate on legal spectaculars.

The document I submitted to the House of Commons Home Affairs Select Committee follows.

Appendix: Submission to the House of Commons Home Affairs Select Committee

I have always supported victims of sexual abuse. My credentials on this score are impeccable, since I was the first celebrity to criticise Jimmy Savile on television, days before the famous documentary was aired. I believe that victims of abuse and persons who are falsely accused are natural partners in the fight for justice. It is not an 'either/or' proposition.

I was arrested by the Metropolitan Police on 29 October 2013. They arrived in force at my home at 4.38 a.m., took away sackloads of personal belongings which were not returned for fourteen months, and presented me with risible allegations. I was given a report date of 8 January 2014.

On 13 December, my husband said he had seen on social media that I had been rebailed until the end of March. I knew nothing about this. I called my solicitor, who also knew nothing about it. My personal assistant then told me that news of my rebail was on the BBC and ITV websites. I had not realised a person could be rebailed without knowing it. The police justified this news break by saying, 'We have not broken any of our rules.' Emailing my solicitor at her office, even without knowing if she was there, was considered sufficient notice.

The Metropolitan Police passed papers to the CPS on 10 February 2014. My solicitor was told the CPS would offer a definitive decision on my case on 26 March. However, on 20 March, they jumped the gun and rebailed me until 7 May. I was never told what information they were seeking, only that it was not mine to provide.

On 2 May, the CPS jumped my rebail date by five days and moved me to 7 July. The reason given was that they needed to obtain 'information from third parties'. They would not reveal whether these 'third parties' were human beings. They could be institutions. It was obvious to me that, since there was no possible evidence to collect against me in this fictitious case, the CPS had not collected anything damaging and were just twiddling their thumbs, hoping someone else might accuse me while I was on prolonged bail. This is a particularly sinister aspect of unlimited bail. The authorities hope that if someone is held out in public long enough, a new person will eventually accuse him.

On 30 June the CPS made an early announcement again. I was rebailed until 15 September. The reason given was that the police needed to re-interview my accuser.

When I told a friend of this latest rebail, his reaction was: 'It does not take two and a half months to interview one person.' He was right. As a matter of fact, they could still interview him the next day, or the day after that, and still make the original bail date of 7 July. 15 September was ridiculous.

However, it was also the day after the Dave Lee Travis retrial was due to end. It was scheduled to run the first two weeks of September. I believed that the Crown Prosecution Service was sitting on me until the end of the Travis trial, that it did not want the DLT jury to know that a former Radio 1 DJ could be innocent.

This was consistent with what I had come to feel: that the CPS appears to use individual cases as pawns in a broader chess game it conducts for its own public relations purposes. The suspects who had been held on bail without charge for many months, such as Jim Davidson, Freddie Starr and Jimmy Tarbuck, were dribbled out one by one. For example, I was certain I would not be released on 26 March because that was also Jimmy Tarbuck's latest date. At that point he had been on bail longer than I. It was his turn to be released.

My solicitor Kate Goold pointed out to police that it does not take two and a half months to interview one person. She was told, 'The interview is being arranged and we will tell you when it has been arranged.' This was not an accurate statement. At the end of August, she learned my accuser had never been re-interviewed after all. I had been rebailed for two and a half months for nothing ... except, I believe, to influence the Travis trial.

It was obvious from the outset of his trial that it would go beyond 15 September. I therefore believed I would be rebailed again. On 12 September, I was, this time until 6 October, a date that was later extended until 13 October because 'the custody suite is booked'.

On 13 September, reading of the charges lodged the previous day against Dr Michael Salmon, I realised what had been happening. I was always rebailed on Yewtree 'win days'. I was rebailed on the day Max Clifford was sentenced. I was then rebailed on the day Rolf Harris was convicted. I was next rebailed on the day Michael Salmon was charged. On each of these days, if a media outlet wanted to run a story on Yewtree, it would not be about me. The Crown Prosecution Service was seemingly sitting on me indefinitely and did not want the public to know. Was that the case? It was only when I became the longest-serving uncharged Yewtree suspect that courageous people in the press like Daniel Finkelstein, Jane Moore and Janet Street-Porter started writing about my dilemma and the necessity for bail reform. Finkelstein spoke to Theresa May, and she delivered her call for change.

Dave Lee Travis was sentenced on 26 September. I learned of my No Further Action while in New York on 10 October. I was told that day that a Metropolitan Police officer, standing down one of my potential character witnesses, told him that the force believed the chances of a successful prosecution were between 3 and 5 per cent. I had spent twelve months on bail, eight of those with the case in the hands of the Crown Prosecution Service, for a 3 to 5 per cent chance.

Many people, in expressing their sympathy for what I had to undergo, have emphasised the element of loss. They have asked how much money I lost. Considering both cancelled income and legal expenses, the total is over £200,000. BBC Radio stopped paying me the moment I was named in the press. I did not realise it could unilaterally break my annual contract, but there was a legal technicality by which it could. ITV and BBC Television edited me out of programmes which had already been recorded and for which I had already been paid. I became instantly unemployable, and received no new offers. In my case, the topic of 'anonymity before charge', or at least 'equal anonymity of accuser and accused', is relevant, although it is not the subject of today's hearing, because had I not been publicised before a charge that never came, I would not have become unemployable. I had no income at precisely the time I had to pay tens of thousands of pounds in legal expenses, none of which I can ever reclaim under English law.

I was determined not to fall ill, as so many wrongly accused suspects had in the course of the Metropolitan Police and Crown Prosecution Service campaign. The general public will never know of their suffering. I resolved to survive, and through increased attention to diet and exercise managed to lose a stone, but I did experience one particularly unpleasant reaction. Every day I would suffer six or more rage attacks. Since my case was a complete invention, I had no cause for remorse. I did have cause for fury, and I had to take great care not to suffer physical deterioration because of anger. Although I never acted out my anger, I felt it in my body. The one change in behaviour this caused was a fear of walking across bridges, which for someone who lives on the South Bank like myself is relevant. I did not wish to find myself suspended over the Thames halfway across a bridge while in the midst of a rage attack.

There was another health issue. Because I was constantly being rebailed, my emotional state began to resemble a seismograph print-out, up and down with sudden extreme twists and turns. I would dare to hope and then be disappointed again. After this happened several times, I took a completely cynical view of the CPS and just accepted that my situation of endless rebailing was the New Normal.

The interminable sequence of bail dates was also a great inconvenience to the radio executives and producers with whom I work. They were all waiting for my return and had to make new programming plans every time my case was postponed yet again.

I was distressed that for a year my bail conditions dictated that I was not allowed to have unsupervised access to children. After all, I have nieces, nephews and godchildren whom I love.

Most of my long-term relationships with organisations were lost. Charities I had helped to found or fund ignored me. The political party I had publicly supported, for which I raised funds for over a quarter of a century, shunned me. Only five organisations stood by me. I will support them for the rest of my life.

Anyone who is part of the Information Age can imagine the disruption to my life caused by the seizure and retention of my computers for over a year. I had to replace the old ones and, for example, rebuild my iTunes library, a waste of time, effort and money that continues to harass me every day as I eliminate duplication from the merger of old and new systems.

Despite all these negatives, there is a greater loss. I have lost my faith in the British justice system.

No one loves a country more than someone who has chosen to live there. I was not born here. I chose to live here. I came here when I was twenty-one years old. I had won scholarships to what I felt was the world's greatest university, Oxford. I believed Britain had the world's greatest culture, both high and popular. I was sure Parliament was the greatest legislature in the English-speaking world.

The British people did not disappoint me. They gave me a first-class education and provided me with a quality health service when I needed it. I was able to enjoy a career that was impossible until I lived it.

Imagine how much I loved this country. Imagine my disappointment when it betrayed, psychologically tortured and abandoned me. My unqualified love for Great Britain has been qualified.

I will always love the people of this country. They deserve better than they have. I hope they get it.

The men and women of this committee can give it to them. It is in your power to move forward the great cause of bail reform. No one must ever suffer what I underwent — an indefinite period of arrest without charge.

It is in your power to ensure that thousands of persons will never have to experience what I did. Please help them. And please help me. Help me to love this country like I once did.

<hr>

PAUL GAMBACCINI CASE TIMELINE

4 April 2013   Allegation recorded enquiries commence

16 April 2013   Victim 1 interviewed

5 September 2013   Case dropped for 'insufficient evidence'

26 September 2013   Victim 2 identified

[Paul Gambaccini knows nothing of the above until after his case is dismissed.]

29 October 2013   Paul Gambaccini (Yewtree 15) & Yewtree 16
                    arrested, bailed to 8 January 2014

13 December 2013   Gambaccini learns from media he has been rebailed
                    to 26 March

20 March 2014   CPS rebails PG to 7 May

2 May 2014   CPS, seeking 'information from third parties',
                    rebails PG to 7 July

[This is Max Clifford sentencing date.]

30 June 2014   CPS, asking Met to 're-interview the victim', rebails
                    PG to 15 September

[This is Rolf Harris conviction date.]

12 September 2014   CPS, 'conducting inquiries', rebails PG to 6 October

[This is Dr Michael Salmon charge date.]

15 September 2014   Rebail date moved to 13 October; 'Custody suite is
                    booked' on 6th

10 October 2014   No Further Action

*   *   *

O n 3 March I gave forty-five minutes of testimony to the Home
Affairs Committee of the House of Commons. I was followed by
Chris Eyre, Chief Constable of Nottinghamshire Police and ACPO Lead
for Criminal Justice, a very civilised man, who gave his views on bail. The
bill was topped by the Director of Public Prosecutions, Alison Saunders.
The Commissioner of the Metropolitan Police, Sir Bernard Hogan-Howe,
gave testimony on another day.

I received an email on 19 March that made me do a double take. Was
this an early April Fool? It was an embargoed copy of the Home Affairs
Committee report on police bail, due to be released the next day. It advo-
cated significant reforms, affirmed my innocence, and instructed the CPS
to 'write and apologise to Mr Gambaccini, explaining why the case took
so long when the original police investigation was dropped for insufficient
evidence a month before he was even arrested'. The email also contained
this short-form press release:

> *Stop shaming suspects and holding them in indefinite limbo, say MPs*
> The Home Affairs Committee of the House of Commons has today
> published its report on police bail. The committee's main findings are:
>
> *Anonymity before charge*
> - Suspects should have the same right to anonymity as the
>   complainant in sexual offences, until the time that they are
>   charged.
> - If the police wish to release information on a suspect, for policing
>   reasons, then they should do so in a formal way.
> - There needs to be zero tolerance on the police leaking information
>   on a suspect in an unattributed way. It is in the interests of
>   the police, post-Leveson, to demonstrate that they understand
>   the level of public distrust that has built up over the informal
>   relationship between the police and the media.

Introducing a time limit on bail

- We recommend that an initial time limit on bail of 28 days should be introduced. A decision to rebail at 28 days could be taken by the police, but subject to challenge by a senior police officer independent of the investigation.

- Decisions to rebail should be reviewed at three-month intervals by the courts.

- The onus at each review should be on the police to justify the reason for rebail and introduce certainty to a process that at present keeps suspects in limbo for an unspecified period and with poor information as to why. It should encourage the police to use bail less, to investigate more thoroughly before arrest, and to finish investigations more quickly.

- The police can apply to the courts for exemptions from the review process if they can justify that the nature of the case means the investigation will be complex, such as where evidence needs to be retrieved from overseas. The proportion of such cases should be small.

No further action

- The committee considered the case of Mr Paul Gambaccini. Where a person has been on bail for longer than six months, and where the final decision is to take no further action, the CPS should write to the individual explaining the decision. The CPS said that they write to the complainant to give an explanation when a case is not proceeded with. It is unfair to write to the complainant and not to the person who had been complained against.

Rt Hon. Keith Vaz MP, Chairman of the Committee, said:
'A reform of police bail is long overdue. The police only need to have

reasonable suspicion that an offence has taken place to arrest someone. It is unacceptable that, even with little evidence, people can be
kept on bail for months on end and then suddenly be told that no
further action will be taken against them without providing any information as to why.

'Paul Gambaccini was left in limbo for what he described as "twelve
months of trauma", his life was put on hold, his employer stopped his
contract and his costs from lost earnings and legal fees totalled £200,000.
The CPS should write and apologise to Mr Gambaccini, explaining
why the case took so long when the original police investigation was
dropped for insufficient evidence a month before he was even arrested.
They must do so in other similar cases.

'Suspects deserve to remain anonymous until charge. Police use of the
"flypaper" practice of arresting someone, leaking the details, then endlessly rebailing them in the vague hope that other people come forward
is unacceptable and must come to an immediate end. It is inexcusable
that information about suspects is released to the media in an informal,
unattributed way. We have seen how destructive this can be to a person's livelihood, causing irreparable reputational damage and enormous
financial burden. The police must advocate zero tolerance on leaking
names of suspects to the press before charge.'

Further Information:

Committee inquiries: Police Bail Committee Membership is as follows:
Rt Hon. Keith Vaz (Chair) (Lab) (Leicester East); Ian Austin (Lab) (Dud-
ley North); Nicola Blackwood (Con) (Oxford West and Abingdon);
James Clappison (Con) (Hertsmere); Michael Ellis (Con) (Northamp-
ton North); Paul Flynn (Lab) (Newport West); Lorraine Fullbrook
(Con) (South Ribble); Dr Julian Huppert (Lib Dem) (Cambridge); Tim
Loughton (Con) (East Worthing and Shoreham); Yasmin Qureshi (Lab)
(Bolton South East); David Winnick (Lab) (Walsall North)

The Crown Prosecution Service responded to the Home Affairs Committee report with a press release in which it promised to write the proposed letter of explanation to me. As of 1 August 2015, I had not received such a letter.

Every day, some well intentioned acquaintance asks me how I am coping in The Aftermath. Have I been able to draw a line under the experience yet?

Only this week, the wife of someone who was given a very rough ride by the police asked me if Chris and I had mentally gone to very dark places. She and her spouse had, and still found the experience difficult to live with.

I know the truth of what I have endured. I acknowledge the horror. I move on. I dedicate the remainder of my life to my family, my friends and the cause of justice.

On 27 May 2015, Her Majesty Queen Elizabeth II delivered the Queen's Speech. From her mouth came the promise to limit police bail by legislation during the course of this parliament. Let it come to pass, and let it be the beginning of the reforms this country so desperately needs.

A first-class nation deserves first-class law enforcement. What happened to me must never happen to anyone else. It must never be déjà vu all over again.